PROFILES OF POPULAR CULTURE

A RAY AND PAT BROWNE BOOK

Series Editors
Ray B. Browne and Pat Browne

Profiles of
Popular Culture

A Reader

EDITED WITH INTRODUCTION AND
SUGGESTIONS FOR FURTHER STUDY BY
RAY B. BROWNE

THE UNIVERSITY OF WISCONSIN PRESS
POPULAR PRESS

The University of Wisconsin Press
1930 Monroe Street
Madison, Wisconsin 53711

www.wisc.edu/wisconsinpress/

3 Henrietta Street
London WC2E 8LU, England

1   3   5   4   2

Printed in the United States of America

Library of Congress Cataloging-in-Publication Data
Profiles of popular culture : a reader / edited with introduction and suggestions
for further study by Ray B. Browne.
        p.   cm.
"A Ray and Pat Browne book."
Includes bibliographical references.
ISBN 0-87972-872-8 (hardcover: alk. paper)
ISBN 0-87972-869-8 (pbk.: alk. paper)
1. Popular culture—United States.   2. United States—Civilization.
3. United States—Civilization—1970- .
4. United States—Social conditions—1980- .   I. Browne, Ray Broadus.
E169.12.P745   2005
306´.0973—dc22   2004028324

CONTENTS

Contents   vii

PREVIEW

Popular culture is the culture of the people collectively and singly. Sometimes it is well known and widespread, sometimes restricted to small groups, localities, even individuals. But the types are well known. Everybody recognizes some aspect of culture—"I know the type," "I've seen that kind of advertisement before," "I've read that kind of story," "I wish they wouldn't repeat that kind of TV show or movie so much."

In the collection of articles that are included in this book, therefore, some types are only identified and described with no examples given. It is assumed that the instructor and the student will know the type sufficiently well to be able to identify and describe it and find examples in the texts of the other kinds of popular culture included in this book. To a certain extent, therefore, this book is a seek and find, a kind of treasure hunt for the aspects of life in which and by which we live.

PROFILES OF POPULAR CULTURE

The Generalities of Cultures

RAY B. BROWNE AND PAT BROWNE

Though daily existence is made up of specific events and localities, all are tied together somehow in the flow of generalities. Events of one day are part of what happened yesterday and will continue to occur tomorrow in the same or a different location. But in order to make some kind of sense out of these recurrences we need to have generalities that connect them and tell us what they all mean. We constantly search for the keys of connections which fit us into the life cycle and answer the questions common to us all: Why are we here? Where are we headed? What does it all mean? To be sure we all begin on a common footing we need to be sure we understand what popular culture is.

Popular culture is the system of attitudes, behavior patterns, beliefs, customs, and tastes that define the people of any society. It is the entertainment, diversions, icons, rituals, and actions that shape a society's everyday world. It is what we do while we are awake, what we think about and how we approach the thought, and what we dream about while we are asleep. It is the way of life we inherit, practice, change, and then pass on to our descendants.

3

Popular culture is the current mature extension of folk culture, the culture of the people. With improved means of communication and electronic media in American culture, folk culture expanded into popular culture—the daily way of life as shaped by the popular majority of society. Especially in a democracy like the United States, popular culture has become both the voice of the people and the force that shapes that voice. In 1782, the French commentator J. Hector St. Jean de Crèvecoeur asked in his *Letters from an American Farmer,* "What is an American?" He answered that such a person is the creation of America and is in turn the creator of the country's culture. Indeed, notions of the American Dream have been long grounded in the dream of democracy—that is, government by the people, or the popular rule. Thus, popular culture is tied fundamentally to America and the dreams of its people.

Historically, culture analysts have tried to fine-tune culture into two categories: "elite"—the elements of culture (fine art, literature, classical music, gourmet food and wine, etc.) that supposedly define the best of society—and "popular"—the elements of culture (comic strips, best sellers, pop music, fast foods, etc.) that appeal to society's lowest common denominator. The "educated" person approved of elite culture and scoffed at popular culture. This schism first began to develop in western Europe in the fifteenth century when the privileged classes tried to discover and develop differences in societies based on class, money, privilege, and lifestyles. Like many aspects of European culture, the debate between elite and popular cultures came to the United States. The upper class in America, for example, supported museums and galleries that would exhibit the finer things in life that would "elevate" people. As the twenty-first century emerges, however, the distinctions between popular culture and elitist culture have blurred almost into invisibility. The blues songs (once denigrated as "race music") of Robert Johnson are now revered by musicologists; architectural students study buildings in Las Vegas, Nevada, as examples of what Robert Venturi called the "kitsch of high capitalism"; sportswriter Gay Talese and heavyweight boxing champ Floyd Patterson were co-panelists at a symposium on literature and sport at the State University of New York–New Paltz in 1992. Examples go on and on but the one commonality that emerges is the role of popular culture as a model for the American Dream, the dream to pursue happiness and a better, more interesting life.

Popular culture is one of the most changeable aspects of our way of life. Literally here today and gone tomorrow, popular culture is never static but always dynamic. Its origins and movements are everywhere. Because popular culture has had various meanings over the years, a clear and precise definition is necessary.

The nature of popular culture makes it particularly difficult to define. As used today, the term is relatively new though its subject matter is as old as human society. In addition, popular culture must overcome two barriers: prejudice and the various definitions associated with it. Together they can be summarized in the statement, "I know what it is and I don't like it."

Yet every academic field has had to cope with popular culture to one degree or another, especially lately. Such fields as anthropology, sociology, religion, communications, theater, and, to an increasing degree, history, literature, and psychology have had to work to some extent in the broad fields of the everyday culture of people. Each has developed its own definition. Generally the definition has been associated with entertainment and leisure time activities, and usually with a negative connotation.

With the explosion of democracy in education since World War II has come a firm insistence on the inclusion without prejudice of democratic aspects of life. This changing attitude has brought a new attitude toward this inclusion and new fields and new seriousness and dignity toward those fields.

At first the new attitude and the resulting new subjects were treated with derision and fear—fear that the old canon and its shibboleths would be destroyed and replaced, and derision as a weapon to fight for retention of the old. Linguistically, in the fight to keep popular culture out of academia, the terms of derision were *pop culture, mass culture,* and *cheap trash.* Some academics and the general public—speaking through the media—seized on the term *pop culture* because it was short, quotable, and convenient and because it set apart and cheapened the culture it named. This downputting continued for at least a decade.

But familiarity, though it breeds contempt, can also foster respect. So it was with the recognition of the place popular culture—read *everyday cultures* in the plural—has played in the emergence of the United States as one of the leading nations for democracy. Academia and the public at large—except for a conservative group who think in terms of yesteryear's clichés—have dignified the field by calling it popular culture and recognizing that in a democracy the proper studies are of democratic institutions. Democracy demands an understanding of its strengths and weaknesses if it is to survive. A case can be made that democratic life poses greater possible triumphs and more potential threats. Thrones and empires topple when ruled by people who forget or ignore the culture of their power bases. A case could be made that Rome fell because the emperors forgot the popular cultures which created and supported it for a thousand years. Crime novelist John Maddox Roberts, in *Saturnalia* (1999), writing of the Rome of Caesar, reveals a mountainous knowledge of details of daily life in Rome at that time but criticizes the aristocrats in power for having forgotten their folk roots. Perhaps their greater flaw was in despising and never trying to benefit from the cultures of their conquered people.

Other nations have likewise stumbled. Hitler's Third Reich, which was prophesied to last a thousand years, died early partially because its popular culture power base crumbled. And Communism's Berlin Wall toppled because the leaders did not appreciate the will and power of the masses they claimed to serve. Popular culture levels up and, as a hurricane gains strength from the warm waters at its base, generates irresistible power. Not to recognize this potential and to keep it struggling as an undesired, outside alien invites destruction. The fighting chant "power to the people" really means "power to the people's cultures." That power is becoming stronger and stronger—and needs to have its base and dynamics understood.

Along with the public's—and media's—recognition of the power and importance of everyday culture has come the realization in academia of the importance of everyday cultures of the present and the past in understanding the world around us. There has not yet been an enthusiastic open-armed embrace by all academics, but demands are marching around the walls of the ivory tower as though they enclosed the biblical Jericho. If the walls haven't yet come tumbling down, cracks are evident, and many people are coming out of the city to see what the action is, and even to join in the call for a more open academic awareness and approach to education and the things that are important in education and life.

What then is a proper and workable definition of popular culture? We have said that it is far more than entertainment and leisure time activities. It is the bone and flesh of a society from which the spirit emanates and soars—or falls.

Popular culture is the way in which and by which most people in any society live. In a democracy like the United States, it is the voice of the people—their practices, likes, and dislikes—the lifeblood of their daily existence, a way of life. The popular culture is the voice of democracy, speaking and acting, the seedbed in which democracy grows. Popular culture in all societies—from the most authoritarian to the most democratic—democratizes them and makes democracy truly democratic. It is the everyday world around us: the mass media, entertainments, diversions; it is our heroes, icons, rituals, everyday actions, psychology, and religion—our total life pictures. It is the way of life we inherit, practice, modify as we please, and then pass on to our descendants. It is what we do while we are awake; it is the dreams we dream while asleep, as well as where and how we sleep and how long.

Obviously then, since many manifestations of people's behavior are dictated by race, history, custom, gender, age, locality, and group size, popular culture actually consists of many overlapping and interworking cultures, like scales on a fish. The only way to talk of a singular popular culture is to realize that it is a mixture of many small and large cultures which are controlled by elements smaller than and different from the large national picture, the living fish.

The many ethnicities of people and their histories and cultures from around the world who have poured into the United States over the past two centuries have brought their many elements of cultures and added them to the dominant Protestant western European base. So the culture of the United States today is a broader stirring, both vertically and laterally, of all the people who make up our society. It would have been completely different if this continent had been discovered, colonized, and developed west to east instead of east to west, by Asians instead of Europeans, or south to north instead of north to south, by Catholics instead of predominantly Protestants. The same basic human needs would have been present, but their traditional and current development would have been entirely different in expression and degree. Culture developments are driven by and develop within the needs and constraints of a people. They extend in directions and to degrees allowed by the physical, mental, and emotional attitudes.

Popular culture has nothing to do with popularity in the sense of number of people engaged in it. That kind of popularity has to do only with how widely something is used. It also has nothing to do with quality, though at times we might wish it did. Popular culture is the lifestyle and lifeblood of groups—large or small—of people.

In 2004—popularly (if not mathematically) considered the beginning of a new millennium—an estimated 327 languages and dialects are spoken in the United States. The smallest ethnic and nationalist, cultish, religious, or political group using one of those languages or dialects lives in and by their everyday culture. That culture identifies the people and makes them cohere as a part of the larger culture of the United States. The dominant popular culture is like a patchwork quilt that covers the many smaller groups. In such societies, citizens must speak several cultural languages, those of their own—and similar—group, and that of the dominant culture. As the peoples of the earth necessarily become more and more mixed, any and all cultures will become more complex.

Popular culture has nothing to do with so-called quality, with the "good and beautiful" in life as distinguished from elements which are considered neither good nor beautiful. Some aspects of culture are positive, some negative, some beneficial, some detrimental. Popular culture, especially in a country like the United States, is the total of all ways and means of life, for better or worse, desired or undesired.

Popular culture in many instances is distributed by the mass media, but other, more old-fashioned, media-like habits, such as the "grapevine," gossip, imitation, observation, and indifference, are much more powerful controls. We control popular culture at the ballot box and, of course, on Wall Street and other sites of unrestrained democratic capitalism.

The complexity of popular culture can be illustrated in the following diagram. It is in this context of easy fluid movement and mixing of cultures, then, that we talk of the popular culture—singular—of the United States. The degree of comprehensiveness and complexity of this culture is demonstrated by the contents of this volume, which is about the popular culture of the United States.

In a capitalistic democracy, taxpayers and voters pay the piper and consequently call the tune. In the sea of culture, in President John F. Kennedy's words, the rising tide eventually floats all boats at the same level, though the rise may seem slow. In the present outbursts of democratic culture, you can hardly identify the cultural status of a boat owner by where he or she docks the craft. The demands of ethnopietistic, nationalistic, cultist, religious, political, economic, and gender groups display varied flags on their crafts and create many eddies of water movement. But all float on a common body of the United States— mixed with those from around the globe—popular culture.

The cultural historian Jacques Barzun once said that to know America one must understand baseball. That may have been correct when he called the play and might even be useful today, but it is not sufficient.

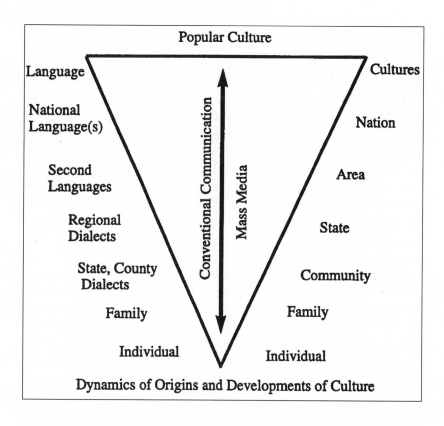

There are thousands of aspects of American life that all of us must comprehend in order to understand the United States and ourselves.

As the voice of the people, popular culture makes up another philosophical aspect of society, the humanities, and should properly be called the New Humanities. Historically, people who treasure the humanities have insisted that they teach us how to live life most fully. The humanities are those attitudes and actions that seem to make us different from other animals and superior to them in our love for and treatment of other animals and human beings in compassion and empathy. Often traditional humanists have treated the humanities as though they were to be denied to the ordinary taxpayer as being above his or her understanding and appreciation or not possibly a part of their nature. But the New Humanists believe that this traditional elitist point of view is tunnel visioned and short sighted and not acceptable in a democracy. In a democratic culture, one cannot assume that only a few elements, those historically accepted by a fraction of the population, make up the potential of the humanities and their enrichment of the human race. The humanities and human potential are much more complicated. Years ago, in his *Essays Ancient and Modern,* the very elitist poet T. S. Eliot recognized the heavy duty of popular culture in perpetuating culture when he cried out against popular books, in his time a major force in dispensing popular culture : "I incline to come to the alarming conclusion that it is just the literature [nowadays read entertainment] that we read for 'amusement' or 'purely for pleasure' that may have the greatest . . . least suspected . . . earliest . . . influence upon us." Though his bias was strained, Eliot was right. To paraphrase what someone has said in another context, "We have seen our popular culture and it is us." United States popular culture is ourselves and our country, and we, for better or worse, are our popular culture.

We must understand what popular culture is and we must know its value. For some, respecting it may not be easy. Most of us honor the concept of democracy while tending to avoid at least some of its practical applications. Indeed, we try to prove that some of us are more equal than others, and using our popular culture as the down side of that proof is sometimes convenient. It is easy to make a scapegoat of elements of our popular culture and the people who participate in it.

The main trouble in understanding popular culture is that the differences among the elements seem to be slight. But that sameness is only seeming. The very essence of humanity is based on the democratic assumption that all individuals may be nearly alike to the casual observer and have equality of opportunity, but in fact have differences that are profound. So, too, with popular culture. The differences between elements may seem to be negligible but are in fact deep. For example, anyone who says that all rock 'n' roll music is alike simply has an undistinguishing tin ear. Anyone who says that popular fiction is all alike does not understand popular fiction. And so on. In the final analysis, anyone who says that all fast food hamburgers are alike has a palate trained to detect and appreciate only major differences in food, which means that the gourmet tongue cannot differentiate between subtle differences.

As long as these deficiencies persist in observers of popular culture, we will be unable to understand fully and appreciate that popular culture. In many ways, one of our first tasks is to appreciate the subtleties of popular culture and through that appreciation come to understand it.

This collection of readings and introductory notes is an effort to make clear all elements of popular culture. Because of restrictions of space and availability some elements are slighted. But all are represented or touched on. The field of study is both enlightening and enjoyable.

Welcome to a great adventure of discovery, recognition, and enjoyment. . . . Dynamic societies are always open to change. In fact they thrive on it. From its beginning America has been driven by a people who looked beyond the western horizon to see what lay beyond the setting sun.

Studies of American cultures have generally aspired to follow this vision but until recently have failed to live up to the challenge, being content to study the fields that had been established as important and therefore in need of further investigation rather than being modified into new areas of investigation. This attitude was especially hobbling through the years in the development of American Studies programs in some academic institutions.

For years the standard approach to this field of study has been the so-called formula and myth and symbol approach. A formula was established for looking at things, thinking about them, and treating them. Good examples of the formula can be found in romance stories, talk shows on television, cop shows, and science fiction movies. The formula was usually developed by what is known as myth and symbol; that is, myths and symbols are the machinery or carriage on which a society loads and carries its way of looking at life.

In simple uncomplicated societies myths and symbols and formulas may be sufficient to maintain a people's way of life. But in complicated societies such as those in the world today they are not sufficient. Formulas must grow and myths and symbols must develop as times change. It is something like the computer world around us today. You can hardly drive down the street with your new computer beside you in the car without seeing the glaring billboard announcing a new sophistication which your computer does not have. In such a situation the solution to your problem is not to take your machine back but to add on as new developments come along.

Such also should be the study of American culture, which is rapidly developing into Popular Culture Studies. American—and world—societies are quickly being modified electronically. Students of culture increasingly realize that they must take into consideration all aspects—all drives, all expressions of energy—of culture if they are to understand the world around them. Fortunately also they are discovering that old formulas, myths and symbols, interpretations, and readings of facts must be reconsidered. They are no longer sufficient, and may not even be appropriate. Attitudes and understandings change. In 1979 Gene Wise published a liberating essay pointing out the weaknesses of the conventional approaches to the study of (all) cultures, especially American, and suggesting that scholars work in all the associated and nonassociated disciplines and cull from them the elements of culture that enrich mankind's life on earth (*American Quarterly* 21, no. 3, 292–337). His counsel was well given. Beginning with archaeologists, say, we must unearth the past yet again and reinterpret what we discover. All of life in one way or another touches on all other aspects.

The most fruitful way to study popular culture, therefore, is by standing on the methods used in the past and reaching out and up to new ideas about conventional subjects and working over them with well-informed but open minds.

Portions adapted from *The Guide to United States Popular Culture*, eds. Ray B. and Pat Browne (Bowling Green, OH: Popular Press, 2001). Used with permission of the authors.

SUGGESTIONS FOR FURTHER STUDY

1. In the present advanced stage of understanding the importance of studying popular culture, do you think the full arguments advanced in this introduction are necessary?
2. In view of your various academic backgrounds and futures, discuss how you think popular culture studies are going to be helpful to you in the future.
3. Choose a major or minor field of popular culture (such as music, fiction, TV) and use it to demonstrate how this introduction has modified or changed—or confirmed—your point of view.
4. Read Gene Wise's essay, mentioned above, and see if his arguments are persuasive in broadening cultural studies.

MYTHS

Myths apparently have always been a part of humankind. They are attempts to understand and get along with oneself, society, and the world. *Myth* has two meanings. The first is that of a false notion, as in the myth of "man the invincible." The other meaning of *myth* is far more important, and it is the one we will be concerned with in this chapter, as in the belief that material superiority automatically brings happiness.

The world has always been large and mysterious, and people's efforts to understand it have caused them to create an existence outside themselves. So we have had the myths of superior existences and worlds, the Garden of Eden and paradise, the actual—or spiritual—world from which we are taught we sprang, to which we might be able to return, and which we should always aspire to and try to imitate. These are myths of the past, and we have nourished them in the myths of history: life was different in the past—sometimes better, sometimes worse—and somehow peopled with creatures larger than ourselves—sometimes superior, sometimes inferior. Thus in America our past is filled with such semi-mythological people as Washington, Lincoln, Davy Crockett, and Franklin Delano Roosevelt. In addition to mythological people, we also entertain myths of things, of ideas and dreams. Thus we have the American myth of success (with hard work any American can succeed), the myth of American superiority (because we live in the "land of the free and the home of the brave") to the world's other people. Myths explain us to ourselves and tend to keep us standing tall and looking up at our greatness or could-be greatness.

Myths exist in at least three forms: supernatural, secular, and those that work between the two, trying to mix the supernatural with the worldly and making an effort to elevate the secular onto a higher plane. Just as some people will have nothing to do with the supernatural myth, many—including highly educated scientific people—cannot be persuaded that what they have believed and "verified with their own eyes" can be anything but true.

Throughout history the world has been peopled by creatures of unusual size. Genesis records a time when "there were giants in the earth." The hierarchy of such creatures has played an important role in human cultures. They can be outlined somewhat as follows: At the top is God(s) or some form of deity opposed by the Devil (Satan). Below the highest are the semi-sacred, such as saints and demigods. Next in descending order come the mythological giants and monsters, such as Homer's cyclops, the Bible's Goliath, and many others who try to destroy human beings. Below them come secular deities and animated icons, followed by heroes and heroines, then heroes and "superior" people, and then celebrities who sometimes are given some of the attributes of genuine heroes. Supporting the level of heroes and celebrities are the ordinary run of "equals" in society, and they in turn are supported by the "inferiors" who in a democratic society are difficult to find. In all societies these hierarchies below God and Satan are constantly conflicting and moving up and down. The importance of the role of hero and its function in human society is to provide the power in humanity's constant conflict with the force above that denies its rise to equality. The list follows in the role of the hero in his/her state of permanence, decreasing power and potential upward mobility.

> God(s) (Satan, devils)
> Saints, demigods
> Giants, monsters
> Personalized superior people
> Admired people, celebrities, well-known people
> Equals—democracies
> "Inferiors"

One of the most obvious and ever-present of the "superior" human beings is the hero. For decades the myth of Bigfoot, a giant apelike creature seen in mountainous districts throughout the world and called various names (Yeti, Abominable Snowman), has been believed, along with the Loch Ness Monster in Scotland and, some people would say, little people in big flying saucers from somewhere out there in space.

The mystery of the Loch Ness Monster was proved a hoax when its perpetrators explained it. Yet vast fortunes are spent—much of it federal money—each year to plumb the waters of Scotland's Loch Ness in the hope of finding some trace of the monster. P. T. Barnum once said that "there's a sucker born every minute." Might he have said, "There's a believer and self-deceiver born every minute"?

Some myths are so much larger than life that they are in fact what are called archetypes, that is, they are universal and multicultural. Often they have to do with the birth and growth of children, or at least those are the associations we make with them. We have Donald Duck, for example, Bugs Bunny, Barbie, Sherlock Holmes, and many others. The following article outlines the universal drifts and drives of myths and heroes/heroines.

Hero with 2000 Faces

RAY B. BROWNE

Heroes serve as models and leaders of people and nations because they reflect the projection of the consensus of the dreams, fantasies, self-evaluations, and needs of individuals and of society itself. Like a lens, heroes concentrate the power of people, of a nation, and serve as the muscle for the movement and development of a people, which they epitomize. In a simple society as that reflected in the Epic of Gilgamesh (3000 B.C.), the Greeks' Odysseus, or the biblical Goliath they are simple and straightforward, tending, in the words of Joseph Campbell, to be "monomyths," serving definite and clear purposes in society.

In more complicated societies, however, heroes wear many faces because of their many responses to the numerous needs of individuals, groups of people, and national purposes. As the needs get more complicated, so too do the heroes; as people get more sophisticated the heroes become less modeled on the conventional demigods of the past, less clear cut and obvious. In a volatile and swiftly moving society like the present, heroes undergo rapid transformation, frequently developing in ways and for purposes not immediately apparent. Twentieth-century American heroes, existing in a highly technological society and driven by the electronics of mass communication, change quickly. But they still develop along the lines of the conventional hero and they serve no less important purposes than their counterparts of old.

In our day the hero still has the conventional body and soul of his predecessors, still serves the mythological purpose of helping to explain ourselves to ourselves, and helps us maintain a stability and national purpose, but appears in different guises. The hero, as outlined by Northrup Frye, Freud, Jung, Lord Raglan, and dozens of others, has developed the thousand faces, as recorded by Joseph Campbell, into thousands of faces, and the number is growing. These are genuine heroes, as useful as those of old. They are not so stable, so formulaic, so stereotyped as those of conventional mythologic proportions of old, but they are essentially the old heroes tailored to suit different peoples. Gods can live only by filling the needs of the society they serve; otherwise they become relics, useful only in studies of origins and the past. They cannot serve living purposes for the living.

To a large extent, naturally, modern heroes are developments, though not inventions, of the technological media simply because the media are our present-day means of communication. To many observers the media create celebrities not heroes. Daniel Boorstin, an elitist negative evaluator of the media, feels the hero was a being who achieved something, the celebrity merely a name. As he cleverly phrases it in *The Image: A Guide to Pseudo-Events in America:* "The hero was a big man; the celebrity is a big name." Elaborating on the celebrity, Boorstin says: "The celebrity is a person who is known for his well-knownness." The tense in Boorstin's verb is significant. Apparently he feels that, as the Bible says, there were giants on the earth in the old days but there can be none in our time.

There is, of course, some validity in the observation, but it has its limitations. The hero-celebrity schism is more the tool of the phrase-maker than of actuality. It is something like the unfortunate term "fake-lore" that folklorist Richard M. Dorson coined early in his career to try to distinguish between what he thought was genuine and "specious" folklore (folklore being of the people, "fakelore" a commercialization of the genuine article) and remained trapped by the term for most of his academic life, though in his later years he admitted that difference, insofar as there is one, is not similar to his distinction and far more subtle. The difference between the hero and the celebrity is largely artificial except in definition. Both exist on a continuum, and there is much of both in each. True, most heroes have done something, something perhaps even "heroic" in the old sense of the word. But not all. Contrary to Boorstin's assertion, not all heroes have done something, or even exist. Paul Bunyan, for instance, patron saint of loggers and especially of people who are not loggers, has been for over a century the hero of woodsmen. Giant in size, boisterous, independent, generally indifferent to the niceties of logging, Bunyan epitomized what people think is the spirit of the logger. But he never existed. Created by a logging company in Westwood, California, because the management needed a logo, Bunyan, because he was needed by the folklore of the loggers, assumed mythological proportions, no matter what his origins and accomplishments. Other heroes have their proportions puffed and spun by the popular media. Abraham Lincoln, surely one of our greatest heroes, was created partially through the mass media of his day: the dime songsters, the joke books, the burlesque books, newspapers, every form of popular culture. The hero almost always stands on a platform, of his own making or that erected by others, of dissembling and deceit. Most heroes, it goes without saying, have done less than they have received credit for—regardless of their time of action. An excellent case in point was Johnny Appleseed, patron saint and hero of the Ohio Valley in the nineteenth century. Johnny was heroized for having walked from one end of the Ohio Valley to the other distributing what the people needed most—material to read, conversation and gossip, and apple trees. Johnny apparently did supply the Ohio Valley with these cultural necessities but he did not quite fill the role that mythologizers created for him. All heroes are more the product of their press agents than of their own actions.

In the argument over the proper media for the development of the hero, it is hardly realistic to ask that heroes be self-developed. The true hero is, presumably, too much interested in being heroic to publicize himself, and often his acts of heroism are too private and unnoticed ever to be known by anyone. There are, to paraphrase the English poet Thomas Gray, many heroes "born to blush unseen and waste their sweetness on the desert air." An excellent case is ex-President Jimmy Carter, who has been a much more heroic ex-president than he was while sitting in the Oval Office.

Romantics and folklorists (especially library romantics and folklorists) think that heroism is circulated exclusively by word of mouth. Such an attitude is hardly tenable. Heroes have always been created by the media of that day. If the operating medium is the bard around the campfire talking or singing of the deeds of someone in the hunt, that is the existing form of mass communication. If it is the illustrated manuscript of pre-movable type days, that is the means of communication. If it is the newspaper or the dime novel, or the TV camera or computer, that is the means of mass communication. If it is today's gossip, that is the means of communication. The main difference among all the media is one of intensity. Some burn cool and relaxed; some are hot and hurried. In the cool media the hero takes a long time developing and therefore can last a long time because his fire, never very hot, remains banked and can be drawn forth when needed. In the hotter media the life expectancy is much shorter. The hero serves his purpose and is then passed over, being left in the minds and hearts of the populace if he merits it, for a newer model. The media do not destroy so much as they just allow to die through inattention. Like the eighteenth century deistic belief of God as creator who wound a cosmic clock and then sat back to see it unwind, they create and then move on.

Conventional definitions of the hero as necessarily demi-god are based on very little faith in the people the hero serves. These people assume that the hero cannot survive in the light of reality in a democratic and technological society. There is, of course, a lot of hocus-pocus and mystery about the role of the hero. It is axiomatic that the more ignorant the society, the more heroic the hero. The needs of society demand and often want less than full revelation of the facts about the hero. No doubt had there been news media present when Odysseus returned to Ithaca from his odyssey, newsmen would have told him that it was poor navigating to spend ten years wandering around in the small lake of the eastern Mediterranean, and they would have suspected that his adventures among the unnatural creatures and gods and goddesses for ten years were merely an excuse to stay away from home. But had they searched around for background and in-depth interpretation they would have been able to confirm that the voyage, meaning more than it seemed, was symbolic and mythological and therefore true. More actuality about the voyage would not have destroyed its meaning but it would have made it less elevated, and greater circulation might have terminated its importance sooner, though it would not have negated its importance. In our own history, for example, Thomas Jefferson's stature as American hero has not been diminished, except among the Jefferson cultists, by historian Fawn Brodie's breaking the revelation that he had a longtime affair with Sally Hemings, his slave, and had several children by her. This weakness of the flesh, under the isolated circumstances in which Jefferson lived, explained and justified the behavior. America's Camelot of the early 1960s may have been strengthened not weakened in the long run by more closely associating it with the mythological world or King Arthur, through their revelations that John F. Kennedy, like Lancelot of old, had his Guineveres traipsing up and down the backstairs of the White House.

To assume that the people of a modern, technologized nation are too simple minded, too thoughtless to be able to appreciate a hero, warts and all, is to underestimate both the importance of the hero and the intelligence of the people. In an advanced civilization there is less room for and patience with the misty, part fake-phony hero, the anthropological culture hero of the past, because there is less dependence placed on him. People have less need for demigods. The kind of hero that is still needed—the down-to-earth, realistic role model—still serves contemporary society. To serve society, the individual needs to be known. The people in their slow but ultimate wisdom will recognize the difference between the heroic and well-knownness and distinguish between the hero and the mere celebrity. And the hero will benefit.

Heroes, somewhat like fads though of longer life, come and go. They are "in" and they are "out." They are "national" in influence or local. The Puritans of New England are not much revered these days; sometimes one has to remind the untutored of the greatness of Benjamin Franklin, Washington, Jefferson, and the others who broke the colonies from the mother country.

But the hero, even the transient heroes of the last quarter of the twentieth century, still represent on a passing or eternal scale a star in the distance, bigger than life and bright enough to attract imitation. They still serve as chinning bars on which are exercised the hopes and aspirations of individuals, groups, and nations.

Heroes can by nature be either conservative or radical, can serve as havens of refuge or as sharp swords to draw the blood of progress. As stereotype and formula they have two edges, the drag edge and the cutting edge. Both serve useful purposes as counterbalancing weights to keep the pendulum of society from running amok and swinging too far either way.

Heroes come in different sizes at different stages in a nation's development. When a nation is admittedly young and naïve, heroes stand ten feet tall. But when that people are more advanced, more sophisticated, more cynical, they like their heroes more of their own size—at times even the dwarfs of antiheroism. In the more sophisticated societies the heroes serve more as only role models.

Of all the media undoubtedly movies and television have been the most instantly important in shaping or reflecting the changed faces of the heroes in contemporary society. These media reveal individuals little more "heroic" than ourselves but with greater abundance. This attitude is well exemplified in the joke about the husband (wife) who asked his wife (husband) what her lover (mistress) had that he (she) didn't have and was told "Nothing"; she (he) just had it "better developed." Or the one always told by the woman in the country occupied by American soldiers who has abandoned her former boyfriend and taken up with one of the soldiers because "he has it here."

What we see in movies and TV is a direct reflection of the changed heroic role, which is perhaps best stereotypically and formulaically exemplified by soap operas. Soap operas are the Big Rock Candy Mountain of present-day American dreams, the lotusland of body's desires. They reflect the contemporary pragmatism, the new materialistic bent. They represent wealth, power, beauty, self-indulgence, all the things that people now think are the real goals in life.

In the print medium best-selling fiction represents one of the most obvious forms of our heroes. Best-sellers must be timely, must give desired information, must be readable, must present some appeal just beyond our fingertips. Heroes in these best-sellers are only slightly distanced from ourselves. In our narcissistic age when TV commercials blare that we deserve only the best, we are inclined to be self-indulgent. We are therefore caught up in the various best-selling diet and self-help books because they insist that our rainbow is just over the hill and easily attainable. Potentially we can climb above the need for heroes by becoming heroic ourselves.

Other kinds of popular fiction—not so widely sold but equally important—such as the various kinds of crime fiction, Westerns (which are enjoying a comeback in popularity), sports, and others, make us reach for the heroic. But one type, the Romance, is for sales and influence in a world of its own. Romances are, of course, not new. Dating at least from the eighteenth century in England and America, in the Gothics of the Bronte sisters and Charles Brockden Brown, Romances flowered in the seventies and eighties in the United States with a future that no one can predict. They come in numerous bindings and illustrations and story lines, all portraying particular kinds of heroes and heroines. The Harlequins, popularized in the 1950s, spawned other series by authors and publishers: Silhouette Books, Ecstasy, Second Chance at Love, Circle of Love, Regencies, Rendezvous, Desire, and so on. It is estimated that by September 1982 there were sixty contemporary romance books published each month, with sales running into the millions, perhaps some ten every second of every day of the week. Perhaps surprisingly, the readers of these dreams are generally rather traditional-minded women who find life somewhat boring and who therefore want to escape into the make-believe. They are middle-class matrons who are looking for heroes with whom they can associate.

Along with TV, movies create the most vivid, powerful, and long-lasting heroes and heroines because their theatrical productions and daily lives are constantly kept before us in the popular magazines and on TV. It can hardly be said that heroes and heroines of the movie-house and television screen are here today and gone tomorrow because, despite the immediacy of the media, the public has a long memory and can keep stars of yesterday in mind for a long time. There is something of the actor or actress in each of us and we like to heroize what we wish we could accomplish.

In the world today different societies still have various mythologies and heroes, all very strange to people of other cultures. If it is true in the present world, where, despite the obvious vast differences among societies, there are fewer major differences than there have been in the history of mankind, try to imagine how vastly and unrecognizably different the mythologies have been throughout history. The wonders that Marco Polo saw on his trip to Cathay pale into sameness when one considers the differences throughout history. Obviously heroes had many faces.

It is unrealistic then to imagine that the heroes and mythologies of old have not had to be stretched mightily and completely modernized, to make them serve the needs of the present, when technology has made the world more different now from anything of the past than at any other time in history. Heroes and heroines in the early twenty-first century have thousands of faces. With the obvious changes in the function and appearances of heroes and heroines, it seems clear that it is time to change and modernize definitions. Failure to do so is being unrealistic and blind to the function of the form in society.

Reprinted with modifications from *The Hero in Transition,* eds. Ray B. Browne and Marshall W. Fishwick (Bowling Green, OH: Popular Press, 1983).

SUGGESTIONS FOR FURTHER STUDY

1. Check the various media that are developing heroes and heroines today. Which are most powerful?
2. Watch a section of a soap opera or read a Romance and see how the hero and heroines are developed.
3. What effect have the concepts of heroes had on your development?
4. Developments of heroes and heroines are done on formula. What formula would you use?

The Real Life Adventures
of Pinocchio

REBECCA WEST

"Once upon a time there was . . . 'a king,' my little readers will say right away. No, children, you are wrong. Once upon a time there was a piece of wood." Thus begins *The Adventures of Pinocchio,* starring a long-nosed puppet who has been one of the world's most immediately recognizable characters since his creation more than a century ago by a Tuscan writer, Carlo Lorenzini, known as Collodi.

The latest references to Pinocchio are to be found in what seems at first a rather unlikely place, a film by Steven Spielberg. The film is *A.I.: Artificial Intelligence* (2001), based on Stanley Kubrick's project, cut short by Kubrick's death, in which a robot with emotions longs to become a real boy. In an essentially negative review, *New Yorker* film critic David Denby wrote about *A.I.:* "The story is based explicitly in *Pinocchio,* but it gives us a queasy feeling from the beginning. Have the filmmakers forgotten that Pinocchio is a scamp? He's disobedient and lazy, he lies, he has a nose that rather famously gets longer. Pinocchio wants to be a real person because he's tired of being knocked around as a puppet. He is redeemed by love for his wood-carver 'father' just at the very end of the tale."

I would wager that this fairly simplistic reading of *Pinocchio* is based more on memories of Walt Disney's 1940 film version than on the original tale, published first in serial form and then as a book in 1883. In Collodi's complex story, there are many stimuli for "queasy feelings," as well as for other diverse emotions and intellectual responses, which careful readers, including prominent Italian and American authors, have experienced and used in order to shape Pinocchios of their own. Was the original Pinocchio merely a "scamp" who was simply "redeemed" by his putative father? Did he wish to be a real boy only because "he was tired of being knocked around as a puppet"? I don't think so, nor do the many writers and filmmakers who have been inspired by the world's most persistent puppet.

The story of *Pinocchio* has not only entertained generations of children around the world—according to several sources, it is outsold worldwide only by the Bible—it has also provided fuel for many Italian and other writers of adult fiction and has been the inspiration for cinematic references that are instantly recognized more than one hundred years since Collodi first created the puppet. A contemporary archetype, the long-nosed, not quite human boy figure has entered into global popular culture (how many countless Pinocchio puppets, toys, statues, cartoons, references in ads, and so on must there now exist?), as well as into high literary culture, most visibly in his homeland but also in the United States and all over the world.

Although he created one of the most famous sets of fathers and children, Carlo Lorenzini was a life-long bachelor. Born in Florence in 1826, he chose to take the pen name Collodi, which is the name of his mother's native town near Pescia in Tuscany. Collodi came of age as a writer in the so-called *decennio di preparazione,* the "Decade of Preparation" from 1850 to 1860 when Italy was moving toward unification. Like many of his generation, he was a participant in the 1848–49 battles for Italian national independence and unity, and throughout the 1850s he was active as a journalist, writing under a variety of names and on many topics, including politics and music. One of his first books, published in 1856 when he was thirty years old, is a kind of curious tourist guide, one of the first examples of a literary work dedicated to train travel—Italy's first train, a short trip from Naples to Portici, opened in 1839—called *Un romanzo in vapore: Da Firenze e Livorno* (A Novel in Steam: From Florence to Leghorn). In 1857 he began a vast work about Florentine social life that he called *I misteri di Firenze* (The Mysteries of Florence) in homage to a popular book by the French writer Eugène Sue called *Les mystères de Paris* (a work that fascinated Umberto Eco, who wrote an important semiotic analysis of it). When Italy became a unified nation in 1861 Collodi began work as an administrative officer in the new government, but he continued to write fiction, publishing a translation of Charles Perrault's *Mother Goose Tales* and several successful pedagogical books that recount the adventures of little boys named Giannettino and Minuzzolo.

Pinocchio was written in the final phase of Collodi's career, the decade before he died in 1890. Although he was well respected during his lifetime as an Italian writer and social commentator, his fame didn't really begin to grow until *Pinocchio* was first translated into English in 1892 and then in a widely read Everyman's edition of 1911. In Italy his fortunes were bolstered by the powerful philosopher-critic Benedetto Croce, who discovered *Pinocchio* and praised it. There is now a "Collodi industry" in academic culture that mirrors the popular-culture production of toys, movies, and such, and each year scholars worldwide produce hundreds of books and articles devoted to Collodi, most of which have to do with *Pinocchio*.

Collodi lived in a complex period of Italian history, when there was both a great push for unification and much ambivalence about what unity would bring to a country deeply tied to local tradition, style, life, and customs. The writer lived in a reality of a unified nation, a unification that he, who was a republican against the monarchs, had supported with true ambivalence. Collodi's beloved hometown, Florence, was the first capital of the newly formed nation, and Collodi disliked intensely the effect it had on the place that for him had been "a great big house in which all of the inhabitants knew one another very well." He liked the close, comfortable, domestic quality of the pre-capital Florence. Attracted to order, discipline, structured educational practices, he also dabbled in the occult and in mesmerism, and he was attracted to the inherent disorder of life and things. After Italian unification, there were many programs initiated with the goal of making the Italian people; in the famous phrase of Massimo d'Azeglio: "We have Italy, now we need to make the Italian." But in spite of his interest in pedagogical writing, Collodi was suspicious of these efforts to create the ideal Italian citizen, seeing many of them as a threat to individuality and personal freedom, in which he very much believed. The clashes within Collodi between freedom and disorder and, on the other side, structure and unity find expression in his story of Pinocchio, which is possible to read as a tale both of transgression and of the necessity for conformity.

Children's literature was a relatively new genre in Collodi's time. The idea of such a genre was really unknown until the mid-1800s, when children became identified as a particular class of being. *Pinocchio* is, however, a book for both children and adults. *Pinocchio* can be read as a kind of fairy tale, but it can also be read as belonging to a very Tuscan tradition. The Tuscan tradition of the novella, or short story, goes back to Boccaccio's *Decameron* and also to classical sources such as Homer and Dante—not to mention the Bible. The critic Glauco Cambon has written, "Storytelling is a folk art in the Tuscan countryside and has been for centuries. *Pinocchio*'s relentless variety of narrative incident, its alertness to social types, its tongue-in-cheek wisdom are of a piece with that illustrious tradition." Cambon also highlights the importance of the *Odyssey*, the *Aeneid*, and *The Divine Comedy* to *Pinocchio*'s structure and style, and he concludes, "In a place like Italy, the cultural background would insure a deep response to this aspect of Collodi's myth and guarantee its authenticity." Indeed, from its very first publication, the tale has been read and enjoyed by children and adults, both of whom find different pleasures in it.

Written and published serially, much as Charles Dickens's fiction was published, the book we now think of as a unified tale was published in two distinct parts over a three-year period. The first part, "La storia di un burattino" (The Story of a Puppet), was published over several months in 1881 in the *Giornale per i bambini*, a popular children's magazine. The first fifteen chapters of the unified book are made up of these pieces, and in the last of them Pinocchio is hanged. Collodi killed off his character, evidently with no plans of resurrecting him. But the editor of the *Giornale* pleaded with him to continue the popular story, and so in 1882 and 1883 Collodi published piecemeal the second part, "Le avventure di Pinocchio," which became chapters 16 to 36 of the book. There was a further continuation of *Pinocchio*—hardly known to anyone outside Italy—another serialized story called "Pipì o lo scimmottino color di rosa" (Pipì the Little Pink Monkey), published in the same children's magazine from 1883 to 1885. In this Collodi story the protagonist is a wealthy, obedient, very good little boy named Alfredo who seems to be Pinocchio transformed into a boy. But Alfredo is as boring as can be; it's not a good book; and it's not the good little Alfredo that we remember, but rather the naughty, willful Pinocchio.

Indeed, Collodi's original contains few positive, educational, peda-gogical, or moral elements—especially in the first part, which is made up mostly of negative adventures, Pinocchio getting himself into trou-ble. There are no lessons drawn from these experiences. Only in the second part is the idea that Pinocchio wants to be a boy introduced, and this introduction occurs just ten chapters before the book ends; it does not dominate the story. Instead we have the sense that Pinocchio for the most part is perfectly happy to be a puppet. There's a narrative reason for this: negative adventures—danger and so on—are much more fun to write and to read than are a series of moral lessons.

Pinocchio's long nose and his predilection for lying are not at all highlighted in Collodi's original tale. Pinocchio does have a long nose, but he is *made* with a long nose, *born* with a long nose. The emphasis that we remember so well from Disney's version of the drastically growing nose is not there, nor is there much emphasis on the fact that Pinocchio lies. He does all sorts of things, but they are seen as typical children's peccadilloes: he loafs, he's disobedient, he skips school.

A significant addition to the book's second half is the figure of the Blue Fairy, a civilizing female influence on the unruly puppet who had, until her appearance, lived in an entirely masculine world. The puppet's "birth" is accomplished without any maternal involvement, but his "re-birth" as a real boy takes place under the sign of the mother, as if Collodi somehow realized that a motherless creation is inevitably monstrous (à la Frankenstein) and doomed to exclusion from the human family. The Blue Fairy is an extremely interesting character, moving from a little girl who is dying to a grown-up who appears at times to be a sister, a love interest, and a mother. She is a complicated figure: she's mean to Pinoc-chio, she punishes Pinocchio, and of course she disappears at story's end. She has a role, a function, but she doesn't stay. There is no push for a happy family ending. Some Italian critics, however, have found a family of sorts in *Pinocchio*, reading the book as Christological allegory: the Blue Fairy is a Virgin Mary, since blue is the Virgin's iconographic color; Geppetto is the nickname for Giuseppe, or Joseph; and the little puppet, the son of a carpenter, must die in order to be reborn as a transfigured being.

The Blue Fairy is not the only disquieting figure. Pinocchio himself (itself?) is mysterious from the word go. He is *in* a piece of wood. He is not carved into a puppet who then begins to talk. The *piece of wood* talks, before it has taken on form, an event that links the tale with various traditions of myth, especially Celtic myth—of talking trees, of creatures that hide in material, waiting to emerge magically. In fact, Pinocchio has a failed father, the man who first decides to carve the mysterious piece of wood. However, he wanted to carve it into a table leg. This pragmatic carver is nicknamed Ciliegia, or Cherry, because he has a very big red nose—he's a drinker. (Collodi's interest in the nose as a sign of character is apparent: in *A Novel in Steam,* he was already meditating on the nose: "I would rather like it if physiologists could tell me which sympathetic nerves exist between the heart and the nose and how it comes to pass that the seat of affections and passions finds itself in direct correspondence with that fleshy protuberance, of infinitely variable form and size, which divides the surface of the human face into two more or less equal sections!" Clearly, Collodi had a fascination with the nose—a fascination that has given Freudian critics great delight.)

Cherry, however, is unsuccessful in his carving because the little piece of wood begins to cry out, "Don't hit me so hard! Stop! You're tickling my belly!" Frightened, Cherry decides to give it to his friend Geppetto, who decides that he will make a puppet. However, his reason for making a puppet is not Disney's reason. He doesn't want a little son figure. He wants the puppet to earn his living. Geppetto's primary problem is poverty, dire poverty. He says, "I will make a puppet who can dance, and fence, and make daredevil leaps, and then we shall travel the world, seeking our wine and bread." He names his little puppet "Pinocchio"—a Tuscan variant on *pignolo,* or pine nut. Within the name itself is the message that food is extremely important in this peasant world. In fact the theme of hunger and of looking for something to eat dominates *Pinocchio.* It's a book about a poverty-stricken, peasant rural class, looking for food, looking for sustenance.

There are many eerie elements in Collodi's book: Gothic night scenes, Pinocchio's hanging, funereal images surrounding the dying little girl with blue hair. However, *Pinocchio* never becomes a truly scary Gothic tale simply because of its lively narrative tone, a grandfatherly, vernacular Tuscan that carries Pinocchio ever onward through his varied adventures. Combined with the ancient, recognizable themes of Pinocchio's journeys—initiation into maturity, the overcoming of hardships, and the search for a mother's love—the result is a book with mainstream appeal.

Over the past half century *Pinocchio*'s narrative verve and its darker, more transgressive qualities have appealed to numerous contemporary writers. Unfortunately most of the works by Italian authors have not been translated in this country. But readers may be familiar with Italo Calvino's first novel, *Il sentiero dei nidi di ragno* (The Path to the Nest of Spiders, 1947), the story of a little boy's view of the Italian resistance. The protagonist's name is Pin—obviously, a shortened form of Pinocchio—and the novel is structured very much like *The Adventures of Pinocchio*. In fact Calvino has said that Pinocchio is one of his all-time favorite books; by that he doesn't mean children's books, he means *all* books.

A wonderful little volume called *Povero Pinocchio!* (Poor Pinocchio!) is made up of linguistic games that Umberto Eco created for his students at the University of Bologna. One game, "Poor Pinocchio!" was to re-write an episode from the tale using only words that began with the letter P. Eco's goal was to improve his students' vocabulary: to do the assignment obviously requires using a dictionary. But he loved the results so much that he took all of the student pieces and put them together into a complete *Pinocchio*. Here are the story's final lines in English: "Paradoxical! Possible? Puppet, primate? Proteoform pest, perennial Peter Pan, proverbial parable practically psychoanalytical!"

Another variation on the Pinocchio theme comes from the American writer Robert Coover. In 1991 Coover—a postmodern, experimental prose writer who teaches at Brown University—published a novel called *Pinocchio in Venice*. In it Pinocchio is a very old emeritus professor at an American university, going back to Venice to complete his magnum opus, a tribute to the Blue Fairy entitled *Mamma*. There he gets into every single fix that he got into as a puppet, as a boy, as he slowly disintegrates into sawdust. Coover's Blue Fairy is as protean as Collodi's original. She appears as a gum-chewing, big-breasted, bubble-headed college student named Bluebell who wears blue angora sweaters, as the classic Blue Fairy, and as a true, physical monster. It's only at the very end of the book that she, in all of her guises, and Pinocchio are reunited, as he finally understands their bond as monsters, excluded from full human existence—he as a piece of wood at heart, she as the lack that women have represented through the ages.

Many filmmakers have wanted to bring Collodi's tale to the screen, including Federico Fellini and Francis Ford Coppola. Neither ever did, though Fellini's final film, *La voce della luna* (The Voice of the Moon), starring Robert Benigni, has overt allusions to the puppet's story. However, hundreds of films and television versions have been made in every culture imaginable: Italian, French, Russian, German, Japanese, African, and so on. Even Japanese anime cartoons owe a partial debt to Pinocchio: the popular character AstroBoy is based on the puppet. The latest cinematic reincarnation has already occurred in Italy and will occur in the U.S. on Christmas Day: The premiere of Robert Benigni's *Pinocchio*. Benigni, the comic actor who wrote and directed *Life Is Beautiful* (1997), is a native Tuscan who has been working on his film version for years; in fact he says he has been preparing to do such a film all his life.

Although it opened in Italy to mixed reviews, one effect of its opening has been a frenzy of Pinocchio presence. A recent article in *The New York Times* reported that Rome has been overrun by Pinocchio—everywhere you look, every toy store, every department store, has Pinocchio statues, posters, and books. A young woman has written her feminine version, *Pinocchia;* there's also been a theatrical presentation called *Pinocchia*. Political parties are even using the omnipresent puppet. The National Alliance, Italy's rightist party, has plastered posters all over Rome with a picture of Pinocchio and accusing the left party of lying. So, great film or not, Benigni's offering has stimulated once more the great interest in Pinocchio.

Like Robert Benigni's film, Walt Disney's animated version of Collodi's tale received mixed reviews. But it was universally hailed as being amazing in its technical innovation. Film critic Roger Ebert has described several groundbreaking techniques in *Pinocchio,* including breaking the frame, by means of which it is implied that there is a world outside the screen. This common technique of life-action film had never been done in animation until Disney. One scene in which you see this very clearly is when the whale is sneezing out Pinocchio and Geppetto. All we see are Pinocchio and Geppetto being sneezed out and then sucked back, sneezed out and sucked back. But there is the palpable sense that the monstrous creature is right at the edge of the frame, just beyond our sight. Another innovation that Ebert notes is the use of the "multiplane camera," a Disney invention that allowed drawings in three dimensions. The camera seems to pass through foreground drawings on its way into the frame, creating a sense of depth. This technique is seen in the opening aerial shot of Pinocchio's village, passing through several levels of drawings, taking us deeper into the village, until we arrive at the closeup of the interior of Geppetto's cottage.

Disney's work is an odd and sometimes disturbing combination of American and European elements. The character of Jiminy Cricket, a kind of insect Will Rogers, is perhaps the most important American note. But the settings are very European, although they look more like a Bavarian village than an Italian village, and many of the characters are Old World, Commedia dell'Arte types. One of the most disturbing Old World characterizations is that of the greedy puppet master Stromboli. In the book he is simply a gruff Italian man. But in the Disney film, he is clearly a Jewish gypsy. His accent is Italian, but from an anti-Semitic perspective, Stromboli's gross facial features and his long black beard are recognizably Jewish, as is his tremendous love for money. It has been suggested that Stromboli is "a burlesque of a Hollywood boss," that Disney hated a lot of the Hollywood establishment. Although some of Disney's closest colleagues were Jewish and insisted that they were unaware of any prejudice on his part, Stromboli does disturb a viewer today, for it is impossible to ignore the anti-Semitic implications of his characterization. And it is all the more disturbing when one thinks of the period in which the film was made.

The Blue Fairy is also disturbing or "queasy making," though much less deeply so. The complexity of the book's character is gone. Disney's Blue Fairy is a bimbo, something like a 1930s starlet. There's nothing mysterious—or maternal—about her. She flits in and out of the film and mouths a lot of simplistic, moralistic stuff, but she has no real function. Her single goal is to get Pinocchio to be a good, obedient boy, back in the warm protection of Geppetto's fatherly space where mothers are simply not needed.

It is nonetheless a great movie, wonderful to watch, and it is a film with an allegory of itself embedded in it: it is an *animated* film in which the main character is precisely a nonhuman who is *animated*, thus becoming a simulated "human." There are several scenes in Geppetto's workshop in which the little wooden toys that he has made—the clock, the toys, the moveable puppets—are all turned on. In this pre-film world, little carved mechanical figures are made to move just as drawn figures will be made to move on the screen. To me this is a symbol of the tremendous love for animation that went into the film, a collective effort when the world of animation was just opening up. In these scenes without any narrative function, Disney and his team of artists were revealing something of the fascination that animation exercises perhaps as much on its creators as on those who enjoy the fruits of their labors.

However, there is a dark side to this urge to create life (even if only simulated life). While Geppetto is the version *in bono* of the artist as benevolent God, delighting in his "son," Stromboli is the version *in malo*, the evil puppetmaster God who creates the illusion of life for personal gain and glory. The ancient theme of the dangers of hubristic creativity hovers around this film, but there is also the sheer joy of creation that seeks to animate lifeless things and to endow all objects and animals with such "human" qualities as the capacity to live with conscious pleasure and direction.

The fascinating question of what constitutes the boundary between humans and non- or post-humans informs Spielberg's recent film, *A.I.: Artificial Intelligence*. In addition to the film's explicit references to the tale of Pinocchio—the human mother reads the puppet's story to her robot or "mecha" son, who then decides he wants to be human and, upon his expulsion from the home, he has a series of Pinocchio-like adventures as he searches for the Blue Fairy—it is possible to see the film, like Disney's *Pinocchio*, as a self-allegorical work. In Collodi's tale, in Disney's film, and in *A.I.* the puppet (or robot) is created by Godlike fathers as a child figure to serve the needs, material or emotional, of the parent. Collodi's Geppetto wants his puppet to help him make a living, Disney's Geppetto wants his puppet to give him companionship and love, and Spielberg's mecha, David, is created specifically and uniquely in order to love his human parents unconditionally. Geppetto is a craftsman, while the mecha's creator, Dr. Hobby, is a scientist. Nonetheless, they are, artists and scientists, all figures of the male creator who appropriates the pro-creativity of the maternal realm, as they singlehandedly "give birth to" their "sons," effectively excluding women from their worlds except in highly idealized and symbolic roles. In *A.I.* when an associate of the apparently benign designer of mechas makes what critic J. Hoberman calls "an obscure moral objection" to Hobby's creation of "a robot child with a love that will never end," Hobby's reply is, "Didn't God create Adam to love him?" Hoberman comments, "Yes, of course, and look what happened to him." In fact, the mecha David is also expelled from Eden and futilely looks for the fictional Blue Fairy to make him a "real boy" so that his mother will want him back.

Such elements make the story of Pinocchio much more than a simplistic lesson in the importance of obedience and conformity. Human creativity, whether an art, a craft, or a technology, can yield astounding results, but the power to bring into being real or simulated versions of ourselves is fraught with dangers, not the least of which is the illusion of total control over the creatures we make. The anomalous, the abject, or the sheer excess of individual desire—all historically associated with the feminine sphere—cannot be tamed or repressed merely by admonishments to conform to the Law of the Father, to be "good little boys." So, happily, Pinocchio goes on fleeing his destiny as a "good boy like all the others," until, sadly, that destiny catches up with him. Collodi enlisted the aid of the feminine in the taming of the puppet, but it is worth remembering that, at the end of the tale, the Blue Fairy only appears in a dream to Pinocchio, as the perfect mother he would wish her to be. What or who in fact she may truly be or truly desire is known only to her. Similarly, the mecha David is "reunited" briefly with the mother of his dreams at the end of *A.I.*, but neither she nor he is real, and their "perfect day" of mother-son bonding is disturbingly hollow. Pinocchio's and David's "dreams come true," as Disney's Jiminy Cricket so movingly sings, but at what price? Who put these dreams of perfect goodness and filial bonding into their heads? In reality, boys' dreams of idealized mother-figures might be comforting to them, but the dreams of their fathers or father-figures who are avid for total control of their sons can be, if realized, our worst nightmares come to life.

From *University of Chicago Magazine,* December 2002. Reprinted with permission of the author.

SUGGESTIONS FOR FURTHER STUDY

1. The author distinguishes between high culture and popular culture. Do you think she succeeds, and is the distinction necessary?
2. Puppets are popular worldwide, especially in folk communities that use them for various purposes. They are especially popular in Japan and especially among the elderly to provide an attachment to the past and to bygone days. Is that one of the functions of Pinocchio?
3. Why are puppets not as popular in the U.S. today as apparently they are elsewhere?

HEROES AND HEROINES

Myths are closely associated with and supported by the concepts of heroes and heroines, those people among us who are in some way superior. Heroes live close to the land of myths and serve as gatekeepers showing the rest of us the way to greatness. They are larger than life and feed our desires to be more than we are, to succeed in being superior. They inspire us and lead the way for us to develop outside the limitations of our own skins and circumstances and become greater and more important individuals. Spiritually and physically they are our role models.

Heroes are created by and used to fill the needs of individuals and society. They come in two ages—those of the past and those of the present. Heroes and heroines of the past fill the needs of maintaining traditions, of bringing the past to us, and tying us to that past. They help maintain the continuity of life, society, and nationhood. It would be more difficult for us to feel American if we did not have the great men and women of the past looking over our shoulders and speaking into our ears. But heroes and heroines are also our own creations to serve our own needs. Just as we sustain the heroes of the past, we also create our own in our time. The hall of heroes and heroines is large, and the impulse and need constantly to create new ones—and to shift the old ones around—seem endless.

The period of incubation for development of heroes and heroines changes. Those of the past were developed locally, and their growth and reputations spread slowly. Thus Washington was not the hero of his time that he is to us, not a giant among American fathers. FDR among many people of his time was a monster during his presidency. As such national models developed slowly—and sometimes falsely and without justification—they disappeared gradually. The shelf life of such heroes was long in the archives of history and cultural collective memory.

Our times are fast paced and changing. Our heroes are therefore created rapidly, widely, and at times mistakenly, and often are replaced by those of tomorrow. On the electronic mind of today they are deleted rapidly. Our heroes and heroines are more of us, not giant figures to be revered and placed on pedestals out of our reach but individuals among us who merely are better and more successful at what they do than we are. Democracy needs heroes and heroines but they must, in the words of Lincoln's Gettysburg Address, be of the people, by the people, and for the people. But they are also of the media, by the media, and for the media, coins to be stamped by the people in need of new figures and discarded as soon as they are no longer good, effective coin of the realm. Thus, though our shelves in the various halls of fame are large, they house constantly changing figures, as those of yesterday who no longer serve their purposes are pushed back into the halls of memory.

While they live, however, the heroes and heroines come in many faces and guises. Just as every impulse and challenge needs its heroes, so every field of endeavor must have some leaders. We have heroes and heroines of families, small groups, cults, and children, in politics, finance, sports of every description, and religions, among environmentalists, gardeners, hairdressers, and fashion designers, and so on. Even among outlaws, murderers, and terrorists, perhaps especially among those fringe groups.

The question inevitably arises as to the true definition and identity of heroes and heroines, and whether they play different and even dangerous roles in our lives. In the past, heroes and heroines were from us and for us but not among us. They stood on our shoulders—or other pedestals—and gradually receded from us as we worked toward them. In other words, they served as inspiration though not necessarily as accomplishment. Today they are created differently and are more of us. Democracy does not like or care to support the unattainable. The very definition of democratic is equal and attainable. If my neighbor can do something, so can I. The media daily place the spotlight on the unusual accomplishments of somebody not much unlike myself. All I have to do is dream hard, work diligently, and push myself into success on an equal footing with my hero.

But is this success truly heroic or merely unusual? Many observers—the conservatives, to be sure—feel that today heroes are heroic merely because they are well known and famous. Or famous merely because they are well known, and as such do not qualify for the description *heroic*. But societies create and nurture the heroes they need. Primitive peoples demanded primitive heroes. Cultures of the past that moved at a slower pace and were less media-driven and controlled than our own created and nurtured heroes and heroines who did not immediately flash as brightly as ours do and who survived longer. Heroes and heroines are the creations of their times just as they also help shape and create their world. As you examine the many aspects of today's cultures in the following pages you will need to distinguish between the various aspects of the heroic in cultures and to satisfy yourself as to which definitions and uses are the more valid. Heroes and heroines must undergo close examination and stand up under it. They are different kinds of creations now and serve different purposes.

It seems obvious that heroes and heroines appeal to the "less read" members of society, those who are interested in the various aspects of sports, and the heroes can in fact be people, vehicles, or actions involving both. As such they take on a kind of mechanical heroics which ties a person to mechanism and makes the two dependent on each other. Such a tie makes the study of the hero doubly—perhaps trebly—complicated as it involves the study of the person controlling the vehicle, the vehicle itself, and the tie-in of both to society. The following essay indicates how complicated these studies will become.

NASCAR Racing Fans

Cranking Up an Empirical Approach

M. GRAHAM SPANN

The death of Dale Earnhardt on the last lap of the 2001 Daytona 500 brought unexpected media attention to NASCAR fans. Media sources showed fans gathered at racetracks, churches, and other memorial services where they prayed, cried, and talked to each other about what Earnhardt meant to them personally, and to the quality of their lives. Nearly four thousand people attended a service at the Bristol Motor Speedway in Tennessee, and the governor of South Carolina declared the week of March 13, 2001, "Dale Earnhardt Memorial Week." These examples illustrate the connection between NASCAR fans and the American popular culture. NASCAR racing fans are some of the most loyal sports enthusiasts and represent a population ready for increased analytical consideration.

Social scientists have paid little attention to fans of automobile racing in the United States. Of particular note is the lack of empirical research on NASCAR fans. On any given weekend from the middle of February to the beginning of November social scientists can find hundreds of thousands of people gathered at automobile race venues across America. The Memorial Day Winston Cup race in Charlotte, North

Carolina, for example, typically draws in excess of 180,000 people. NASCAR (National Association of Stock Car Racing) is an organization that governs a set of rules regarding the technical and engineering components of racing cars, as well as race rules, regulations, logistics, marketing, and general business practices of the sport. NASCAR, founded in 1947, held many of its races in the southern part of the United States, but it is no longer constrained by southern consumers or venues. In the past five years, construction of racetracks has taken place in decidedly nonsouthern places like Chicago, Illinois; Las Vegas, Nevada; Loudon, New Hampshire; and Fontana, California. Clearly people from many different geographic regions now go to the races, making racing one of the most attended cultural and sporting events in America.

The search for patterns among groups of people is a basic task of social scientists, and this paper suggests a five-fold approach for discovering patterns among NASCAR fans. All sports are embedded in the general patterns of social interaction and organization in society, so the premise here is that NASCAR fans are people participating in collective behaviors that have consequences for individuals. These consequences may range from unwittingly perpetuating inequality to the development of identity in a (racing) social context. As such this paper suggests gathering data on (1) the demographic composition of NASCAR fans, especially class, race, and gender; (2) the cultural and subcultural phenomena of fans, including the role of heroes in fans' lives; (3) fans' sense of community; (4) how fans create their identities around racing norms and values; and finally (5) the organizational structure of fans. The hope is that scholars of popular culture, sports sociology, and the like will gain some insight into fans of NASCAR racing that will help them set forth a productive research agenda.

Demographic Composition

Fans are enthusiastic admirers of a person, organization, or movement. One popular myth about NASCAR fans is that they are all white, working-class males. Concomitantly, some assume that racism and sexism also flourish among these males given that the Confederate flag is a widely displayed symbol at race venues. Social scientists need good information about socially sanctioned exclusivity, intentional or otherwise, among NASCAR fans. We need to critically examines the demographic composition of fans. It is not the case that NASCAR fans are only from one social class position. An increasingly large number of dominant group members from higher classes enjoy the sport. Business executives are now using skyboxes at racetracks to entertain clients, just as they do in professional basketball or football. Furthermore, though income is only proxy measure of class position, it is worth noting that nearly 13 percent of NASCAR fans have a household income above $75,000 a year.

Most social scientists agree that it is difficult to separate social class descriptions of Americans from their racial composition. That is to say, racial and ethnic minorities disproportionately occupy status positions near the bottom of the class structure. Clearly, an athlete's race is an organizational feature of most professional sports. Some suggest that overt racism exists when whites occupy more leadership positions and blacks occupy more subordinate positions. The notion of "stacking" comes to mind here. [John W.] Loy and [Joseph F.] McElvoge show how racial segregation in professional sports is positively correlated with the centrality of position. Black athletes are often forced to compete among themselves, rather than with members of other ethnic groups, for team membership and playing time because they do not typically occupy the most powerful positions.

Wendell Scott is one of the few black drivers in NASCAR's history, but NASCAR teams currently have limited minority representation. This might partially explain the mostly white fan base. Fans of professional sports typically identify with members of their same racial and ethnic background, but NASCAR, as represented by its top series, the Winston Cup, currently has no drivers from underrepresented groups. Crews who work on the racecars are more racially diverse, but crews typically receive less media and promotional attention than drivers do. Ask any NASCAR fan that you know who their favorite "right tire changer" is and you will likely get a blank look of confusion. If, however, we compare racing crews to football linemen, then the stacking hypothesis is useful.

[Howard L.] Nixon points out that when elite sports organizations use exclusive social and economic membership criteria, they reinforce historical segregation lines. The appeal, then, of certain sports to dominant group members may be a basis for boundary maintenance. The social class of sports fans may vary over time within a nation or community, as well as across nations and communities. Collecting data on the demographic composition of NASCAR fans should provide some interesting cross-cultural data because other race organizations in other countries (i.e., Formula One) may have a more diverse fan base in terms of class, race, and gender.

The gender composition of NASCAR fans could also be included in any demographic investigation. Women drivers have historically been a part of NASCAR racing, but currently only Shawna Robinson is a competitive driver. [Michael A.] Messner argues that the propensity for men to be more involved in sports than women is part of our socially constructed cognitive images of what men and women are supposed to be and do. Dominant ideologies of what it means to be a woman or a man typically reflect deep-seated structural arrangements of society, especially patterns of power, status, and social class. Interestingly, nearly 39 percent of NASCAR fans over eighteen are women. Given generally acknowledged differences in socialization practices between females and males, we might partially explain the rather large proportion of female sports fans to changing gender expectations in society.

About 40 percent of NASCAR fans have attended college, but investigating how level of education affects NASCAR fan participation, their attitudes and beliefs, or other areas of sociological interest has yet to be empirically tested. The same is true for political affiliation. There are, of course, many other demographic variables available for our theoretical propositions, but discovering basic demographics like class, race, gender, education, and political affiliation is a start to an empirical approach of NASCAR racing fans.

Cultural and Subcultural Phenomena

The second empirical approach is examining NASCAR racing fans from a cultural standpoint. Culture is all human-made products, either material or nonmaterial, associated with a society. Culture is the framework within which society's members construct their way of life. [Mark D.] Howell chronicles the cultural history of the NASCAR Winston Cup Series and posits that the "regional strength projected by NASCAR racing history—its ties to southern culture and folklore—creates a stereotypical depiction of drivers." These stereotypes are reinforced in movies like *Thunder Road* (1958), *The Last American Hero* (1973), and more recently *Days of Thunder* (1990) starring Tom Cruise. But whether these images help constitute a real world subculture remains to be discovered.

Is it the case that NASCAR fans constitute a subculture? [Christopher Bates] Doob defines subculture as the "culture of a specific segment of people within a society, differing from the dominant culture in some significant respects, such as in certain norms and values." Two major subcultural patterns may be present among race fans. The first pattern is usually mutually exclusive: fans of General Motors racing cars, fans of Ford racing cars, and fans of Dodge racing cars. Currently, NASCAR teams field Chevrolet, Ford, Pontiac, and Dodge racing cars. This phenomenon is of particular cultural and symbolic interest because all of the cars, regardless of make or model, are hand-built, track-specific race cars. Major automobile producers manufacture few of the mechanical parts; rather, fabricators create cars that look like the major automotive brands. Some teams switch brands by simply putting a different body and name on the same chassis. As [Peter] Berger once said, things "aren't what they seem." Fan loyalty to a particular brand of car may be relevant to the study of NASCAR fans, but we also need to discover if different norms and values exist for fans of the different makes. More importantly, we could discover the boundaries that people maintain which perpetuate the division between fans of the various makes.

Beyond automobile make, the second subcultural pattern among fans is loyalty to, and identification with, a particular driver. This loyalty also takes on symbolic meaning. Readers may have noticed small round window stickers with numbers on people's cars. These numbers correspond to NASCAR drivers' car numbers and are symbolic representations of driver support. For example, the number twenty-eight matches up with the Texaco-sponsored Ford of Ricky Rudd, and the number twenty-four represents the DuPont-sponsored Chevrolet of Jeff Gordon. Most of us have seen sports news reports of Jeff Gordon winning a race, but many drivers have active fan clubs and loyal, lifelong fan followings. Fans of Dale Earnhardt, for example, have already catapulted him to a hero to be worshipped in the folk religion of NASCAR. As a hero, Earnhardt becomes a symbolic representation of the dominant social myths and values of society.

Clearly sport and culture are interdependent. Sport is bound to society and structured by culture. Connecting symbolic patterns is an important part of an empirical approach to NASCAR fans. Social scientists could discover if patterns exist between types of fans and the driver(s) they follow. Are fans willing to support their favorite driver if he/she switches to a different make of car? By looking at fan automotive brand and driver loyalty, we can better identify cultural and subcultural patterns and discover if NASCAR fans really are a subculture.

Senses of Community

The third empirical approach includes studying fans as members of friendship networks who share a "sense of community" with other fans. Both [F.] Tonnies's work on community typologies and [E.] Durkheim's insight into social integration (conscience collective) stress the importance of community in human life. Similarly, sense of community ought to be important for NASCAR fans. Sense of community is where people believe their needs can be and are being met by the collective capabilities of the group; feel that they belong; believe that they can exert some control over the group; and have an emotional bond to the group. Sport spectating is a social activity and if NASCAR fans are a subculture then we should find a higher sense of community among them. [Merrill J.] Melnick sees sport spectatorship as enhancing people's lives by "helping them experience the pure sociability, quasi–intimate relationships, and sense of belonging that are so indigenous to the stands." [Elmer] Spreitzer and [Eldon E.] Snyder found that 75 percent of women and 84 percent of men viewed sport as a good way of socializing with others. We might then inquire whether sense of community among NASCAR fans exists only at the track or is it pervasive throughout the fan base.

Identity

Studying identity formation among NASCAR racing fans centers on subcultural norms and values. Identity "refers to who or what one is, to the various meanings attached to oneself by self and others," say [Karen S.] Cook, [Gary Alan] Fine, [James S.] House. Do NASCAR fans build their sense of self around being a Chevy or a Ford fan? Fans might reinforce such an identity by cheering for a particular brand, rooting for and belonging to fan clubs associated with a particular driver, and finding themselves in social settings where other people have similar identity characteristics. We could look at how racing fans construct a sense of self and how that sense of self affects behavior.

Organizational Structure

Finally, social scientists could examine NASCAR auto racing fans from an organizational perspective. We can look at the degree of commitment to racing as a determinant of placement within a hierarchy. Examining the cultural and subcultural beliefs of fans, their commitment to particular automotive brands and drivers, their sense of community, and their identity may give us the social organizational "picture" we need to determine a series of outwardly expanding concentric circles; with the most committed fans occupying the core, inner roles (these will probably be family members and friends who make up the actual teams), and the least involved fans composing the periphery.

Conclusion

As [Allen] Guttmann notes, sport as a social institution includes a number of qualities such as secularism, the ideal of equality of opportunity, specialization of statuses and roles, bureaucracy, quantification of achievement, and the keeping of records. By critically examining differences in social class, race, and gender, and by determining cultural and subcultural patterns we garner insight into the structural foundations of fans' identity, their sense of self, and their sense of community. All of these areas point to the interplay of structural conditions and human action. Why do this? As social science moves into the twenty-first century, we must study topics people not trained in science can understand. We must continually emphasize the importance of social science and show that the theory and methods of our disciplines can make seemingly ordinary events, like automobile racing, understandable as part of the larger structural and institutional fabric.

From *Journal of Popular Culture* 36, no. 2 (Fall 2002). Reprinted, without bibliographical information, with permission of the author.

SUGGESTIONS FOR FURTHER STUDY

1. Collective sports like auto racing produce their heroes. How do these heroes differ—if at all—from what we ordinarily mean when we use the term?

2. If it is important to study and understand heroes of collective sports like auto racing, is it equally important to understand the individual social and physical heroes that are used to satisfy the hunger of people?
3. What are the specific outstanding points the author of this article makes that you would immediately extract for use in studying conventional heroes and heroines?

As society becomes more democratized and equal, the definition and role of the hero or heroine change so much that they tend to disappear. In their place come people who are famous merely because they are famous and have done nothing except exist to merit their elevation to heroic stature. In the eyes of many believers in democracy and equality this form of the heroic is false and destructive because it delays the development of true democracy. The concept is perhaps debatable, as demonstrated by the following essay, written by the author of one of the earlier papers outlining the role of the hero/heroine in society. It will benefit the student to think over the arguments from both sides of the matter and decide which, if either, is the more valid.

The Concept of Hero against Democracy

RAY B. BROWNE

The historical definition of the role of heroes is out of date in a democracy. A democracy grows beyond the need for the conventional hero. Historically the hero has been a servant of the people, has tried to wrest privilege from the powerful and give it to the powerless. For example, Prometheus stole fire from Zeus and gave it to the people. Dionysius gave civilization to people through wine. Thus the hero, the hero-god, was created to help mankind escape the restrictions imposed by human nature.

Historically and culturally, heroes and heroines have encouraged the development of mankind. They have been used as chinning bars on which people can strengthen their spirits and their culture, raise themselves above their environs so that they can see farther and escape those who seem to be hold them down and back.

Although heroes have always seemed to be held in high repute, above and superior to the common body of mankind, actually they have played a somewhat different role. They have occupied the position that Confucius's wise monarch should have occupied, of being, though

47

superior, the wise servant of the people, although the hero has been wiser than the good monarch and often has served a much greater role.

The hero has known that his power flowed from recognition by the people and that therefore he had to serve them. Thus, though the hero has stood with his head in the clouds, his hands have been working for the good of mankind.

In a curious and seemingly paradoxical way the heroes have always been inferior to the people they served and subject to the people's granting of status and power. Heroes exist only so long as they are granted their superiority by the people, voted into office if you like. Once that license has been withdrawn, the heroes lose their power, their recognition, their status. They become historical references and has-beens. That's extraordinarily important. In their role then as stepladder, heroes have allowed mankind to climb toward something, and to feel superior to them; at the same time the heroes serve as a means by which a superior force descends to the world of humankind.

Up to a certain stage in a nation's development this two-way traffic is important. Growing boys and girls and growing nations apparently need role models, people and heroes they can look up to and emulate.

In such roles heroes and heroines serve useful purposes. But in the life of every person and nation there should come a time when these models of emulation should no longer be needed, should in fact act to inhibit and stifle rather than to develop.

When their rite of passage has been accomplished, people need to put away their youth and their immaturity. As one line from a certain good book said, "When I was a child I spake as a child, I acted as a child. But when I became an adult I put away childish things." In other words, heroes and superheroes, heroines and superheroines are really kid stuff and should hold no place in a properly educated and mature democracy.

A properly educated and mature democracy has no need for and no use for heroes and heroines. The people are able to stand on their own two feet and face reality, not try to hide their faces in nostalgia and make-believe and stand in the tracks and the shadow of superior people.

Theoretically, at least, a properly educated and mature democracy should not fear the present and the future and is not ravaged by emotional stress and anxiety. In fact, one could say axiomatically that the degree to which a people fear the present and the future is the degree to which they cater to heroes and heroines.

A people can tyrannize itself and tie itself down with this use of heroes and heroines. But there's a far greater and more terrifying purpose that heroes and heroines serve. They can be party to abuse of people. That is, the power brokers in society, the sophisticates who are, as they think, superior to all the heroic forces, are glad to use and abuse the concept and reputation and terrifying forces of heroes to manipulate the people who still believe in them.

The concept and device are age-old. People not subject to the power of certain ideas and forces, those who stand safely outside, use the assumed power of the force to keep in bondage those people who still believe in it.

The practice is as old and vicious as selling snake oil, a useless mixture sold as medicine. The mere naming of the snake oil and the ingredients make it magic by implication. So what's in a name? Everything. All the power and magic that people will allow to be forced into it; the more richly resonant the name can be made, the more it can be used and abused.

In addition to the rich resonance, names are endowed with the power of the abbreviated symbol. Originally, names, like those wonderful forty-word titles of books in the eighteenth century, were often comprehensive and revealing summaries. But people nowadays like short names and short titles. And just as brevity is the soul of wit, it is also the smoke and mirrors of disguise, deception, and abuse. Names are wrappers that can surround all kinds of poison, or flags which can signal all kinds of misinformation. Often outside forces manipulate these names and symbols for their own purposes. Personal names, especially those that resonate with power and have echoed through the corridors of time, encrust themselves with magic and innuendo and become the most awesome and misleading of all.

In fact, we can safely say that *every* name, especially those of heroes, is loaded with pseudo-facts, outright falsifications, and the potential for corruption. People generally don't live up to the potential in their names. Names breed exaggeration and abuse.

So the concept of the hero in all societies is filled with make-believe, no matter how useful that make-believe might be, and is fraught with the potential of self-serving abuse. In a well-educated and mature democracy, the concept should be recognized for what it is and discontinued as being no longer needed. If the concept of hero is needed, then the mantle should be placed where it belongs. Not on the shoulders of single individuals, but on the real heroes, the people. Heroes don't make history, don't move mountains. People do the moving and the naming, but heroes get the credit.

It is particularly distressing to have history load all the glory, almost never the infamy, of so-called great events on the shoulders of individuals who generally don't deserve it. It is imperative that we move the bit players to center stage. They are the heroes. The nominal stars are only the players.

Let me give you two examples, safely from ancient history. Those of us who make heroes of the warlords who caused the building of the Great Wall of China turn history and reason upside down and shake out the wrong conclusions. It is said that every stone laid in the Great Wall cost the life of one worker. Some people are recognizing that credit, if that is the word, for the wall must be spread among those who physically built it, not the ones who sat in their castles and ordered it. For example, the editors of the book *Popular Culture in Late Imperial China* say, "The emphasis on the elite in Chinese history has led to grave distortions in our visions of Chinese history and culture, distortions that can only be remedied by serious systematic study of the world beyond the boundaries of the ruling class."

Let's take another example, which because of its opulence and wealth has become everybody's favorite during the last couple of decades, King Tut. Although Tut apparently lived a short life of tyranny and opulence, he was not the hero of the age. His tomb and the symbols of tyranny and robbery surrounding his sarcophagus do not make a hero of him. That has been done by the elitist archaeologists of today who when they open a tomb run for the gold. They are interested in the opulent and golden symbols of power and wealth. But gold ornaments do not cover the true heroes. The heroes, on the contrary, were the thousands of workers whom he exploited for his own glory, those people who endured the shifting sands of time and died in the process. Today there are at least four thousand mummies of Tut's contemporaries extant, in the sand surrounding the Egyptian pyramids. From x-rays of the mummies we can tell the number of children the women had, the diseases everybody suffered from, the food they ate, the causes of death. Often only Egyptologists and mummologists are interested in those nondescript mummies. But those thousands, not Tut, are the real heroes of the day. They should have precedence over Tut as the real heroic people of the time.

In our own country and especially in our own time, we should be careful how we place the mantle of heroics on individuals. Individuals are less creators of their age than they are creations of and spokesman for that age. If Thomas Paine had not written *Common Sense*, somebody else would have and stated the same principles. If Thomas A. Edison had not developed the electric light somebody else would have. People were hopping all around the skies when Charles Lindbergh flew solo to Paris.

To admit these facts is not to diminish the feat of the individual, but only to put it in perspective. Heroes are as often pushed forward by the wave of events as they are creators of the waves. Thus, in our chronicles and descriptions of heroes, we should be careful to give credit where credit is due, to recognize the proper heroes.

If I were looking for a title to properly describe the heroes of the American Civil War, for example, I would not choose the title *Lincoln Agonistes*. A better title would be the *Civil War and Lincoln*. But an even better one would be the *People of America during the Civil War*. There must be even more encompassing titles which would knit together the ragged edges of truth and reality. It is, I think, improper and perhaps dangerously erroneous to put the spotlight only on Lincoln, no matter how great his accomplishment in holding the nation together.

Thus, we should do away with the station of individual hero and heroine with its superiority and inferiority. For every hierarchy there is a lowerarchy which tiers people into layers of importance and unimportance. At its silliest, the notion of the hierarchy leads to royal-watching. At its best it provides an incentive for everybody to climb the ladder. But there is no excuse for the rungs of the ladder somehow to be reserved for the strong and powerful.

The concept of hero is large and strong enough for all to become heroic in mind and spirit, if not in wealth and fame. And I am convinced, again I emphasize, that in a *properly educated and mature* America, there would be no need of heroes and superheroes. The concept is contrary to the things we Americans as a nation must hold dear and desirable. The ultimate conclusion, of course, is that in a properly educated and mature America, we wouldn't be studying heroes except as historical subjects. In America the study of heroes is properly a historical subject rather than one for people looking into the future.

As historians we should study in a context of re-created life. We should re-create the life and culture in which the heroes and heroines existed. Otherwise we are in many ways distorting and misrepresenting the whole concept of heroes. Like Lincoln I'll stick with the people rather than the academics, the intellectuals, who often create papier-mâché heroes that don't last long or use criteria that are too subtle and unreal. The people, on the other hand, collectively know what they want. We hear warnings that people should not be allowed to create their own heroes; they know not what they do, what they need. But their concepts, their movements, their institutions are no worse or weaker than the intellectuals', whose may be high-sounding but surely lack the legitimization of consensus—and consensus is the backbone of creation and perpetuation of heroes and the concepts of heroes.

All heroes are figures of fantasy. The only hero who is not a figure of fantasy is that person who sees somebody in trouble, relieves him of that trouble, then goes silently on his way. We never know the event. It is never recorded. We never know the name of the hero. Most people who do an extraordinary deed call a press conference. That's the way heroes are created and live these days. And ultimately the heroes' purposes are ulterior, used for their ego or for self-aggrandizement. If we are going to have heroes in their proper place in a democratic society, sooner or later we need to get to the point where the press is so wise that when the person who does a heroic deed calls a press conference nobody comes. The press doesn't need the copy and we the public do not need the news. The force of the concept of heroism is recognized and taken for granted. Therefore we do not need it individualized and demonstrated.

The names of individuals, although they are easy to put in the pantheon and remember, don't identify the true heroes. The heroes are the forces which alter, change, keep together, animate, make us Americans, or whatever. They are the dynamics which remain heroic and are the result of the forces which American cultures create and direct. They are the subjects we should study. And we forget the named individuals since they are merely the incarnations of the forces. If on the road to the generalizing of heroes into concepts one studies the individuals, then those individuals can only be properly studied in deep and full context, as nameplates on the forces.

As we read about the lives of heroes around us maybe we see some growing sophistication in the development of our individual heroes and heroines and of the cultures in which they live. If so, perhaps, just perhaps, they demonstrate that American society is weaning itself from the need for heroes, and in so doing illustrating that society can get along without them. Perhaps, just perhaps, we are moving toward being properly and sufficiently educated and mature that heroes are or sooner or later will become unnecessary in our society. Perhaps.

Original essay.

SUGGESTIONS FOR FURTHER STUDY

1. This is a radical approach to the study of the role of heroes and heroines in society. Do you agree with the author or radically disagree?
2. Choose one of the many studies of heroes in the library and compare the arguments of the authors with those in this essay.
3. Look at some of the heroes or heroines around you today and evaluate their purpose and accomplishment in society. Could we get along with fewer or do we need more?

ICONS

All peoples apparently have used icons as a part of their spiritual existence. Religious icons have been reflections of a spiritual world made real on earth in objects such as pictures, statues, remnants of holy bodies, places where exalted people have been, and objects that have been touched by holy people.

The secular world also has objects which reflect what people hold dear, important, and valuable and in their own ways are therefore "holy." The icons of a capitalistic society reflect both the spiritual and the economic sides. Thus many icons—Coca-Cola, Barbie, Michael Jordan, movie stars, leaders of grand capitalist organizations, presidents of the United States and leaders of other countries, grand houses, expensive automobiles, fashionable wardrobes—represent wealth. Others—like the fruit of labor, excellence in sports, etc.—symbolize what hard work can accomplish and therefore should be held dear. To a punctilious society, a dependable clock, computer, or automobile and flawless artistic performances and those who perform them are iconistic.

Perhaps the icons that rise and fall most rapidly are in the world of entertainment. We often ask—sometimes wistfully—where are the stars of yesteryear, and we frequently look around for the stars not of yester-year but of yester*day*. We examine an old newspaper or magazine of a year or two past and begin to see faces and to read of reputations long forgotten. Examples will be found throughout the articles in this book, and you are invited to draw up your own list and try to trace them back to their crowning glory when they were genuine icons, phony icons, general or limited icons. They can be all at the same time since our view as worshippers of icons is both limited and general. Just as they rise to great heights as icons in people's hearts and minds, they also fall at varying speeds. Except for religious or politically holy icons, most will fade from view and memory.

One icon seems that it will never fade because it represents most of what people wanted to believe in or see in themselves: Marilyn Monroe, the ever-lasting goddess—or princess—of America and the world. She is the Elvis Presley of the movies and will always remain so. She embodied all that women—and fathers and suitors—seemed to value. Though we have had movie queens before—ever since we were able to use the media to put them on pedestals—all have had to sit at Marilyn's feet. We have touted Betty Grable with the million-dollar legs, pictures of which decorated the foxhole of every soldier during World War II, and the sexy movie star Rita Hayworth and many others, but all have lacked the versatility, the overall charm and the charisma of Marilyn. Rita, Betty, and the many others have gone because they were taken seriously only by their financial backers and those who thought them mere entertainers. Monroe is considered more than a mere entertainer, a tragic figure who was destroyed by the society that she helped create but could not control once she had created it. The following essay perhaps sufficiently describes her many strengths. The reader should notice how carefully the author, like Sherlock Holmes the famous detective, analyzes all clues available.

Just the Right Touch

By Introducing a Note of Modesty,
Marilyn Monroe's Gloves Actually Heightened
Her Come-Hither Allure

DAVID H. SHAYT

"Diamonds Are a Girl's Best Friend," Marilyn Monroe asserted in
1953's *Gentlemen Prefer Blondes*. The screen siren might have added that
another, less dazzling accessory also held a place in her affections—a
pair of gloves, usually opera-length, worn seductively scrunched at the
elbow. Whether dancing the night away at the Coconut Grove nightclub or attending an opening for one of her thirty films, Monroe was
often spotted wearing this ladylike accoutrement. Suggestive contradic-
tion was the name of the game. Monroe's gloves, invoking a coquettish
nod to modesty, were belied by the plunging neckline.

Now, forty years after her death at age thirty-six, one pair of the
actress's gloves, a recent bequest from an anonymous donor, add spice
to the holdings of the Smithsonian's National Museum of American History (NMAH). "Decades before stars would not make a public move
without the services of platoons of stylists and designers, Marilyn was a
truly great stylist," writes Meredith Etherington-Smith, director of
Christie's International, the London-based auction house, in *The Personal
Property of Marilyn Monroe*. The gloves, she notes, constituted an important
element of the Monroe look. "She had many pairs of immaculate beige

56

kid [skin] gloves, and she always wore dramatic and beautifully made rhinestone earrings which cascaded in flashing rivers of light. . . . All this was carefully contrived to increase the effect of her uniquely luminous quality."

The pair ceded to the NMAH Entertainment Collection are evocative emblems of Monroe's carefully orchestrated image. Exquisitely stitched in soft white kidskin, the elbow-length gloves bear a faintly detectable blue stain, most likely ink, lightly smudged on the outside of a cuff.

This tantalizing imperfection bespeaks a lost history. Whence the stain? Did Monroe perhaps sign an autograph for an adoring fan wearing these gloves? Scribble observations on a program note? Jot down her phone number for an admirer, even a future husband?

Joe DiMaggio? Arthur Miller?

While the story of the intriguing smudge is consigned to oblivion, there is little doubt the gloves possess symbolic significance as well. They function, says costume historian Shelly Foote of the Smithsonian's Division of Social History, as a talisman of a vanished era. "Marilyn Monroe and Jackie Kennedy were among the last prominent glove wearers. In the '50s, high school girls at proms or debutante balls would not be caught dead without gloves on. But after the mid-1960s, they would not be caught dead wearing them." (The former first lady might well have taken exception to this linkage to the woman who so seductively crooned "Happy Birthday, Mr. President" to JFK—with whom several biographers allege she had an affair—on the occasion of his forty-fifth birthday, in May 1962, at Madison Square Garden.)

These days, Monroe mementoes of any kind are among the hottest Hollywood collectibles around. When Christie's sold off a raft of Monroe's belongings in New York in 1999, prices exceeded even the wildest expectations. Hundreds of glitzy possessions, everything from necklaces and cocktail dresses to cigarette lighters, were snatched up in a bidding frenzy that grossed some $13.4 million. The flesh-colored Jean Louis sheath, hand-stitched and ornamented with six thousand beads, worn by Monroe for that presidential birthday fete, went for $1.3 million. (Afterward, the bidder who snared the prize, entrepreneur Robert Schagrin, claimed he was prepared to go "to at least $3 million" for the dress.) As for her gloves, one lot of three pairs fetched $6,900.

The Monroe memorabilia also offer an intriguing, and touching, glimpse of a woman who was more vulnerable and more complex than her besotted public perceived at the time. She was a perfection-obsessed professional who sometimes rewrote her own lines, as her notated scripts attest. She was also an omnivorous reader whose personal library contained the works of authors such as Joseph Conrad and Graham Greene. As an actress, Monroe founded her own production company, a bold act of self-assertion in a Hollywood that was indisputably a male preserve.

The provenance of Monroe's gloves reflects, too, a profound shift in an unexpected arena—industrial America. During the 1950s, most clothing worn in this country was still manufactured on home soil. And most leather gloves were stitched in one corner of upstate New York, near Albany. For some two hundred years, from the 1780s to the 1980s, a great deal of America's leather hand wear originated in a little town christened, appropriately enough, Gloversville.

The town was also home to a young glove cutter who would, several decades before Monroe transformed herself into a Hollywood legend, take over tinseltown. In 1925, Samuel Goldfish, a forty-three-year-old Polish immigrant who had started out sweeping up leather scraps in a Gloversville workshop, decided to seek his fortune in California. Following a move to Los Angeles, he changed his name to Goldwyn and began a meteoric rise within the ranks of the fledgling film industry, ultimately forming partnerships that would evolve into Paramount, Metro-Goldwyn–Mayer, and United Artists.

As for Monroe, the tension between style and substance, between glamorous façade and private anguish, increasingly shadowed her days, until she was found dead, a likely suicide, of a barbiturates overdose at her home in Hollywood on August 5, 1962. The seductive image, conjured out of the pearls and silk sheaths, the fur stoles and spiked heels—seem somehow summed up by the pair of gloves, an artifact at once elegant and forlorn of a tragic trajectory. "She could have made it," her ex-husband Arthur Miller once said, "with a little luck."

From *Smithsonian*, December 2002. Reprinted with permission of the author.

SUGGESTIONS FOR FURTHER STUDY

1. Does the Smithsonian Institution seem genuinely interested in owning Monroeiana for its historical cultural value or for display of its commercial value?

2. As you understand it, what really makes Monroe artifacts more valuable than those of, say, Betty Grable?

3. The Smithsonian used to be known as the nation's attic. Now it is striving to become the world's greatest museum. Does the addition of such artifacts as Monroe's gloves help achieve that goal?

4. Evaluate the importance of icons in your own life. Would you be a different person if you had other icons? Evaluate the role of icons in your particular small or large group—religious, cultural, or national. Do you think life would be different if history had dictated different icons?

Honky-Tonk Poet

Fifty Years after His Death at Twenty-nine,
the Music World Still Marvels at
Hank Williams's Homespun Hits

GEOFF BOUCHER

New Year's Eve, 1952. The Cadillac and its hired driver were waiting in the frosty Tennessee night when the hotel porters guided an ailing Hank Williams into the backseat. He was on his way to yet another show in yet another state, but he was in ragged shape, battered by the bottle and sedatives and heartache. He was painfully skinny, and his angular face looked far older than his twenty-nine years. It was about 10:45 P.M. when they closed the sedan door in Knoxville. When they opened it the next morning, in Oak Hill, West Virginia, the year was 1953 and the greatest country singer of them all was blue and cold, his spirit long gone on the dark highway.

The exact moment of Williams's passing is, like his music, a lonely brand of mystery. The paperwork tells us he died fifty years ago this month in Oak Hill and the cause of his death was a heart condition. All of that, though, is about as solid as the snow that fell past the headlights that night. What is certain is the unmatched resonance of the Hank Williams songbook, a collection whose echoes can still be heard not only in today's country music, but also in rock, folk, rockabilly, blues, and pop. The impact is all the more impressive because the man's career was

so brief: his breakthrough hit, a reworking of "Lovesick Blues," was released in 1949, and his last recording session was only three years later.

Williams's original songs, such as "Hey, Good Lookin'," "Cold,
Cold Heart," "Your Cheatin' Heart," "I Can't Help It (If I'm Still in
Love with You)," "Move It on Over," "Long Gone Lonesome Blues,"
"Honky Tonkin'," and "(I Heard That) Lonesome Whistle," defined
the elemental sound of country music. They also made the sickly kid
from Alabama a superstar, a pioneering crossover artist who delivered
regional "old timey" music to mainstream America with a staggering
thirty-seven Top Ten hits.

"Hank is generally considered the greatest songwriter in the history
of country music," says John Rumble, senior historian for the Country
Music Hall of Fame in Nashville, Tennessee. Williams's songs endure
because of their candor, their appeal to universal emotions, and their
rustic, Bible-tinged Southern flavor. He may have looked like other
Grand Ole Opry stars in his crisp, fancy western wear, but his songs
were often hand-drawn maps of despair.

"It was the honesty, that's what set Hank apart and why people still
listen to his music," says country singer Ray Price, who was a roommate
of Williams's and one of his best friends. "His music wasn't over anybody's head," Price adds. "He was one of the people. And they loved
him for it." In a 1953 interview, Williams spoke of his "folk music," saying, "I like to think that folk songs express the dreams and prayers and
hopes of working people."

Willie Nelson, the songwriter and country singer, always performs a
Hank Williams song or two or three, and he says the beauty of them is
their simplicity, "just a voice and a guitar and a lot of great words."

A Hank Williams song, embroidered by his sometimes joyful, sometimes haunting yodel, is a model of rustic poetry, as in the lyrics of his
1949 recording "I'm So Lonesome I Could Cry":

> Hear that lonesome whippoorwill
> He sounds too blue to fly
> The midnight train is whining low
> I'm so lonesome I could cry
>
> I've never seen a night so long
> When time goes crawling by
> The moon just went behind a cloud
> To hide its face and cry

When Williams was buried in Montgomery, Alabama, an estimated twenty-five thousand people showed up for the funeral. "It was incredible," says Kris Kristofferson, the singer-songwriter (and movie actor) who was a teenage Williams fan in distant California when his idol died. "The reason all those people came was the same reason I have sung his songs my whole life. He moved people to their soul. And when he died, all those people—people in the South, outsiders, the poor people, the losers, the heartbroken folks—everyone who identified with him, they took it hard. They felt like they had lost a guy who had been on their side."

Hank Williams's music was the sound of Saturday night staggering into Sunday morning, a lonesome shuffle between the roadhouse bar stool and the church pew. He learned how to perform for a crowd and drink by himself in the "blood buckets"—rough, Alabama honky-tonks—but the Bible he loved as a boy is where he got his rhythms. On the radio shows that would make him famous, in fact, Williams always performed at least one hymn, and the spirituals he wrote, such as the mesmerizing "I Saw the Light," are often overlooked.

"There are Baptist churches all over the country that have Hank Williams–penned songs being sung right now," says New York Times reporter Rick Bragg, author of Grammy-nominated liner notes for a 1999 Hank Williams CD collection. "I guess Hank had as much claim on God as anybody, maybe more so than some."

Bragg, an Alabama native, says Williams was as wounded and spiritual as the region that created him: "They were sad times. We went from Reconstruction to the Depression to World War II to Korea, to Vietnam, to the pain of the civil rights era. What he did was he spread that pain out enough that we could stand it."

He was born Hiram King Williams, a name inspired by Scripture, in Mount Olive West, Alabama, on September 17, 1923, the second child of Elonzo H. Williams and Jessie Lillybelle Skipper Williams. He had a birth defect, a mild form of spina bifida, which would cause him back pain his whole life, and was a rather sickly child. The boy's father had fought in World War I and returned to work in logging camps and strawberry fields, but by 1930 his health was failing. When Hank was six, his father was taken to a veterans' hospital in Louisiana with partial paralysis and a diagnosis of dementia. Hank sold peanuts and shined shoes to help the family.

Years later, Hank would say his first memory was watching his mother play the organ. Religion, too, impressed him early. As the story goes, "He would tell his mother, 'Get that Bible in this bed,' and he would fall asleep with it," says Kira Florida, coauthor of a biographical scrapbook, *Hank Williams: Snapshots from the Lost Highway*. The boy marveled at the music floating through the humid air from the local black churches. His mother, a resourceful if severe woman, gave eight-year-old Hank a second-hand guitar that, according to one account, she had bought for $3.50, a considerable sum for a woman who earned about 25 cents a day as a seamstress and nurse. He didn't go past the ninth grade, quitting after his sixteenth birthday.

Hank learned to play the guitar from a bluesman named Rufus Payne, also known as Tee-Tot. Payne and two other black men, one playing a bass fashioned from a broom and tub, were buskers, or street performers. Payne had in young Williams an unofficial protégé who would not be deterred, no matter how the wandering musician, weary of the boy's ceaseless questions, tried to put him off. "All the musical training I ever had," Williams would say later, came from Payne.

In his mid-teens, he won a number of local talent shows—acting contests with his own composition, "WPA Blues," after the Works Progress Administration—and formed a band soon to be called the Drifting Cowboys. The name reflected the influence of singing cowboy Gene Autry and other stars of "Hillbilly Hollywood," but it was the rough-hewn blues that Williams had learned from Payne, along with songs by Grand Ole Opry star Roy Acuff, that shaped the young musician's sensibility.

Williams became a regional favorite on radio and in traveling shows and, after a wartime detour as a welder, was in Alabama in 1943 performing with a touring medicine show. There he met his future wife, an aspiring singer, who spurred his career and gave him plenty of anguish to draw on. The painful candor of his later hits "House without Love" and "Why Should We Try Anymore" are believed to reflect his stormy marriage to Audrey Sheppard Guy.

They met in Banks, Alabama, and Audrey seemed an unlikely candidate for Hank's affections: she was married, had a two-year-old daughter, and reportedly dreaded Williams's drinking. In a 1979 interview, though, she recalled the potential that drew her to him. "If some woman, equally as strong as I am, had not come along, there would never have been a Hank Williams. He did not want to live when I met him. He was an alcoholic." The first time the singer took his new girlfriend home, Hank and his mother "fought like men would fight," Audrey recalled, over the new romance. The screaming match prefigured a tension between Audrey and Hank's mother that would dominate much of his remaining life.

In December of 1944, a justice of the peace who owned a local gas station presided at Hank and Audrey's marriage ceremony near Andalusia, Alabama. The singer was twenty-one. If his mother and wife bedeviled young Hank, they also pushed him to fulfill his promise.

The other shaping force in Williams's career was Fred Rose, the Nashville songsmith who owned Acuff-Rose Publishing with Williams's hero, Roy Acuff. Audrey set up a meeting with Rose, who became Williams's manager, producer, songwriting collaborator—and goad. "Hank, anything I've written you is for your own good," Rose wrote in a 1948 letter to the singer, "as I know what a fool a man can make of himself with drinking."

Those years were pivotal, with Hank's recording "Move It on Over" establishing his reputation in 1947, and his live performances on the *Louisiana Hayride*, a Shreveport radio show broadcast throughout the South, fueling his rise in 1948. Despite binges and a volatile marriage, Williams was living a dream in Nashville by the middle of 1949, performing on the Grand Ole Opry. His hit recording of "Lovesick Blues" held the number one spot on the U.S. country music charts for an astonishing sixteen weeks. Williams and the Drifting Cowboys commanded $1,000 a performance and upstaged even Bob Hope when they shared a bill with him in a caravan show.

Williams was an electrifying performer—sober. "I remember one night in Richmond when he was pretty well lit up," says Price. "We got him offstage before it got too bad." The next night, Price goes on, "the place was packed to see what he would do. And he was amazing." At a time when Elvis Presley was a schoolboy, Williams gyrated suggestively onstage and flashed dark, flirtatious eyes. Women screamed his name and scuffled for his attention. "He was the first man to move," Oscar Davis, the concert promoter, once said. "He'd move sexually, and the women would love him."

Williams marveled at the adoration. "I've been to some places where it's impossible to walk across the stage without having the major portion of my outfit torn off," he said in a 1951 interview. "They even grab fistfuls of hair. When you get to be a success, folks have a habit of writing you and telling you their troubles. If their husband dies and they're left with eight starving kids, they write. If their sweetheart done them wrong, they write. If they feel sorta blue, they write. I dunno, I reckon they think I'm something like the Red Cross."

But he had plenty of his own troubles. By 1951, his back was causing severe pain, despite surgery and the steel braces he wore, and he was drinking so heavily that his handlers checked him into a sanatorium in Madison, Tennessee, where he was confined to a cabin with barred windows that he called "the hut." His marriage collapsing, he said in a divorce filing in 1952 that he had "suffered every humiliation, abuse, and mistreatment that a man could possibly take from a woman." For her part, Audrey said he was an abusive drunk. As Ray Price remembers it, Williams's split with Audrey left him reeling: "The strange thing is he told me that he told her, 'If you don't take me back, I won't make it a year.' And he told her one year to the day before he died."

In August 1952, the Grand Ole Opry fired Williams for missing performances and behaving erratically, and he returned to the Louisiana Hayride, making yet another hit with "Jambalaya." He married again, to Billie Jean Jones Eshliman, but was pining for Audrey, to hear Price tell it. "He was so torn up you never got to see him be himself," Price recalls. In October, Williams hired a quack personal physician—a parolee with a "medical license" from a traveling salesman—who gave Williams prescriptions for chloral hydrate tablets, saying the powerful sedative would help him overcome his drinking problem.

The circumstances of Williams's death are the stuff of legend. But he is known to have received morphine shots that day from a Knoxville physician, supposedly to ease chronic hiccups, and Colin Escott, author of the 1994 book *Hank Williams: The Biography*, concludes the artist "died from the combined effects of alcohol, an undetermined number of morphine shots, and chloral hydrate."

The music, of course, is what matters now. Williams, with Rose, was supremely successful at crafting a signature sound that was more tradition-bound than that of other country superstars, such as Red Foley or Eddy Arnold. "The high steel guitar of Don Helms—that was something Fred Rose insisted on, to cut through the noise of beer joints and taverns where Hank Williams's music was played on the jukebox," Rumble says.

As with most country acts of the day, there were no drums, but the sock rhythm guitar and other accompaniment laid down a percussive sound as basic as a heartbeat. "Hank instinctively knew that he had to keep things simple, to be 'vanilla,' as he called it," Rumble says. "He didn't let his guitarists get too intricate or too complex. It was really simple to create a rhythmic platform for his lyrics. In country, the lyrics are always out front. Country music is storytelling."

While most country singers relied on others' storytelling, Williams saw himself as a songwriter first and singer second. No matter that he never learned to read music. His talents went beyond honky-tonk, as became evident when Tony Bennett recorded "Cold, Cold Heart" in 1951, which solidified Williams's reputation as a great American songwriter, period. His songs would be recorded by scores of artists of all musical stripes, from Johnny Cash to Louis Armstrong, Rosemary Clooney to the Grateful Dead, and Henry Mancini to the Bee Gees.

Perhaps more telling of his legacy, Williams appears as sort of a mystical presence in numerous songs by other artists, including Lou Reed. "We all wanted to sing with him, but instead we sing *about* him," Kristofferson says. "He was maybe the best white soul singer ever, and there is something a little magic about him."

Williams remains deeply influential and much celebrated five decades after his death. "He was a wonderful songwriter, but it was very simple in what it was," says Willie Nelson. "The songwriter Harlan Howard used to say a great song is three chords and the truth—and that's pretty much Hank Williams." When Nelson plays "Jambalaya" or "Move It on Over" in concert, he says the music affects young fans "the same way it affects me."

In 1961, Williams was among the inaugural class of inductees into the Country Music Hall of Fame and was elected to the Rock and Roll of Fame in 1987, even though he died before the genre barely existed. *Life* magazine declared in 1994 that he was the most important performer in country music history.

He had one child with his first wife: Hank Williams, Jr., who was three when his father died and became a country music singer, performing his father's music for years. The son then moved into his own as an artist, incorporating a rock sensibility and joining the "outlaw" country movement, a reaction against slick Nashville productions. Now fifty-three, he may be best known for his role as official theme-singer for *Monday Night Football.* Hank Williams's second child, born to Bobbie Jett five days before he died, is Jett Williams. A country music performer since 1989, she has recorded three albums and written a 1990 autobiography, *Ain't Nothin' as Sweet as My Baby.*

Grandson Hank Williams III is also in the family trade, playing country music and a hybrid he calls "punkabilly." Critics have given him favorable reviews, and the rail-thin guitarist, whose second album is 2002's *Lovesick, Broke & Driftin'*, is said to look and act a lot like Hank, Sr. Only thirty, he has already outsurvived a grandfather as tragic as he was gifted.

Out on the Interstate between Montgomery and Birmingham, a sign saying Lost Highway pays tribute to the gawky Alabama boy who grew up to be arguably the most influential practitioner of an indigenous American art form. The man seemed to expect that the road he traveled was not going to be a long one. The last song released in his lifetime was a lament with the tragic-comic title "I'll Never Get Out of This World Alive." On the floor of the Cadillac in which he died was a piece of paper with lyrics to another song, several cryptic, elegiac lines ending:

> Tonight we both are all alone
> and here's all that I can say
> I love you still and always will
> But that's the price we have to pay.

From *Smithsonian*, January 2003. Reprinted with permission of the author.

SUGGESTIONS FOR FURTHER STUDY

1. Compare Williams's music with that of another country singer.
2. Defend or question the placing of Williams in the Rock and Roll Hall of Fame.
3. It might be a good idea for one or more students to sing one of Williams's songs in class and then lead a discussion of its merits.
4. Why, do you think, do many musicians, especially country musicians, turn into alcoholics?

Before icons fade, many people exploit the public's interest in them, and the public at large—often the younger elements—maintain their interest. Often this interest is really more nearly idolatry, if only for a month, a particular event, or a year.

Icons, myths, and heroes are blood siblings. They reflect the striving of people toward what they consider a more nearly perfect or improved individual or society. They embody humankind's effort to stand straighter and taller, to improve. Rituals are the machinery that keep them alive and working. Rituals are the actions—sometimes nearly thoughtless, sometimes religious, sometimes political, often barely thought about. Like the Declaration of Independence trying to establish a more perfect political union, icons try to establish a better human society by holding dear those aspects which beg humanity to improve.

Icons represent the good, the positive. But they are countered by the dark side of humankind's aspirations, to be the most negatively powerful. Throughout history—beginning with the Bible and other holy books—society has taught that there are two major forces in the world: good and evil, light and dark, heavenly and hellish. Icons have generally been used to represent the positive and good. But there are icons of evil and lesser tokens of the forbidden, like taboos, things you cannot do, those which are forbidden—all of which at times seem like mirror images of the icons, closely associated though distinctly different. Both have powerful attractions and lead and direct people's lives.

Icons extend from subjects that are considered important in everybody's eyes to those which are felt to be merely valuable antiques or trinkets in the eyes of most but considered important to at least some people. An excellent example is the some thirty-five hundred items auctioned off at the estate of the late Roy Rogers and Dale Evans in Apple Valley, California, in April 2001. Among the items were the electric cart, called Trigger 3, that Rogers used to get around in during his last years (which sold for $10,000), replicas of Rogers's six-shooters (which sold for $8,500), Dale's butterfly vest ($900), and Roy's shirt ($5,500). Twelve hundred people attended this auction and bid on even more valuable objects, such as the Rogerses' four-bedroom horseshoe-shaped house. The value and power of individual icons, like beauty, are in the eye of the beholder. Some of us see one thing, some another. Each person needs to recognize his or her own icons and be able to evaluate them. Some value one aspect, some another.

Today many magazines, such as *People*, focus on individuals, sometimes devoting entire issues to one person. The cover of a year-end *People* magazine (December 30, 2002) was emblazoned with "2002 Twenty-five Most Intriguing," and included young men and women, as well as some older and unexpected: the Osbournes, Halle Berry, Britney Spears, Martha Stewart (who descended from queen of cookery and fashions to defendant in court), Jimmy Carter, and Charles Moose (who caught accused snipers John Allen Muhammad and Lee Boyd Malvo). See the December 30, 2002 issue of *People* magazine for the full range of icons.

Such treatment by magazines can elevate individuals from the ordinary to the status of icon, or leave them as ordinary people and raise the status in which they reside to the iconic. Can an individual become an icon by simple acts of doing everyday things only slightly better than anybody else does them? If so, then the term may be meaningless. It is up to each of us to decide whether these persons merit the status of iconic or, like heroes and gods, have feet of clay.

Life has its dark side, and icons can demonstrate a fatal attraction that leads believers down what Shakespeare called the "primrose path" to disaster. Parents can hold icons responsible for many of the evils of everyday culture, as the following essay demonstrates.

Measuring Up

Obesity in Young Boys Is on the Rise, and
So Are Eating Disorders. Whose Fault Is That?
Try G. I. Joe

AMY DICKINSON

Women my age know whom to blame for our own self-loathing, eating disorders, and distorted body image: Barbie. So we're raising our
vulnerable, body-conscious girls to beware the perpetually pointy-toed
goddess with the impossible body and perfect face. Now it's time to take
a good look at our sons and their plastic influences. Studies show that
boys increasingly suffer from eating disorders, and if that fact is surprising, the root cause is not—after you take a good look at G. I. Joe.

   G. I. Joe, for those of you who haven't raised an eight-year-old
boy lately, has evolved from a normally proportioned grunt into a buff,
ripped, megamuscular warrior who, if he were a real man, would have
twenty-seven-inch biceps and other proportions achievable only through
years of bench presses, protein diets, and the liberal use of steroids.

   A recent study shows that 36 percent of third-grade boys had tried to
lose weight. In the past ten years, more than a million males have been
found to have eating disorders. In addition to suffering from anorexia
and bulimia at increasing rates, boys are falling victim to a newly named
disorder: muscle dysmorphia (also called bigorexia)—the conviction
that one is too small. This syndrome is marked by an obsession with the

size and shape of your body, constant working out and weight lifting (even if you aren't involved in sports), and the use of supplements to "bulk up." Parents might tell themselves their kids' spending hours in a gym working on "six-pack abs" is better than hanging out on the corner and drinking six-packs, but a true case of bigorexia can be just as ruinous to a boy's health and future.

Dr. Harrison Pope, co-author of *The Adonis Complex,* a helpful book on male body obsession, says parents should look at the world through their sons' eyes. "Boys are fed a diet of 'ideal' male bodies, from *Batman* to the stars of WWF," he says. "So parents need to tell their boys—starting when they are small—that they don't have to look like these characters." Pope, himself an avid weight lifter, says parents should also educate themselves and their sons on the uses and dangers of supplements such as adrenal hormones. "Any kid can go into a store and buy 'andro' [formerly Mark McGwire's bulk-up drug, androstenedione] legally," he says, "but we still don't know what long-term use will do to a boy's health." Pope believes that up to 15 percent of high school boys use andro, often in dangerous megadoses. A large percentage will then move on to anabolic steroids.

Boys are hampered by their tendency to stay silent about their anxieties, but parents can help them open up by asking questions rather than making statements. The media are full of unattainable images, so an Abercrombie & Fitch or a Gap ad can spark a discussion about what the proper build for a boy is. Parents of kids involved in such weight-sensitive sports as wrestling should know that crash dieting can trigger health problems and eating disorders.

Danger signs include extreme mood changes, compulsive behavior, and depression. Parents of very young boys can take a page from the Barbie playbook by asking their sons to compare muscle-bound action figures with real people they know, like Mom and Dad. When we did this in our house, it got a big laugh—maybe too big. But at least it's a start.

From *Time,* November 20, 2000. © 2000 Time Inc. Reprinted with permission.

SUGGESTIONS FOR FURTHER STUDY

1. Before you become too critical of youngsters following the lead of their icons, ask yourself how much you are swayed by the lifestyles, habits, and appearance of your media stars.

2. Is America a people of copycats forced by custom and fear of being different lead to do what is common in society? Are we bound by customs and rules?
3. Choose your favorite media personality and outline his or her commendable characteristics.
4. Search your mind for persons—including yourself—who paid too high a price for being different in our do-alike society.

In a free-market capitalistic economy such as the United States, people with money to spend on items other than the necessities of life are likely to be extravagant in their "conspicuous consumption." Not only are they self-indulgent but they insist on standing out from their fellow human beings, above the ordinary and being the "royalty" of society. This is especially true of their fixation on cars, since the earliest days. The following article demonstrates how expensive it is to own the outstanding icon in the automobile world.

Ferrari's Latest Toy Goes for a Cool $675,000

DAN NEIL

You want the Enzo? First you have to find one.

The Enzo is Ferrari's latest exotic sports car, a $675,000 missile powered by a 660-horsepower V-12 engine capable of exceeding the top interstate speed limit by, oh, 147 miles an hour.

"I would love to tell you that I have the capability of driving this car to its maximum performance," said Jorge Carnicero, fifty, an investment banker in Washington who put down his $150,000 deposit in May. "But I don't."

Only about four hundred will be available worldwide. When the first of about ninety Enzos allotted to the North American market begin arriving this month, the car will corner the market in superlatives: the fastest car in current production; the most expensive Ferrari ever made; the car most likely to induce hysterical aphasia in parking valets.

Every few years Ferrari, based in Marandello, Italy, produces a limited-edition model that translates everything it has learned in Formula One racing—the world's most popular motor sport and the most technologically advanced—into a street-legal production car. The Enzo—officially rolled out last fall at the Paris Motorshow and named after the company's late founder—is actually fourth in the series, which began with the 288 GTO in 1984, followed by the F40 in 1987 and the F50 in 1995.

"For Ferrari, racing is always the most important thing; this is our passion," said Ferrari's president, Luca di Montezemolo, who called on everyone from the Ferrari Formula One team technical director, Ross Brawn, to the current world champion, Michael Schumacher, to help develop the Enzo.

The sports car division of Ferrari has expanded over the years, helping the company's revenue quadruple the last decade, to about 1.1 billion euros (about $1.2 billion) in 2002, on sales of about seventy-five hundred cars. That figure includes cars built by Maserati, which Ferrari bought in 1997.

The Enzo is by far Ferrari's most important product, even though it represents less than 5 percent of its annual vehicle production for the next two years.

Despite all the hoopla surrounding the Enzo no one would list it among Ferrari's most esthetically pleasing cars.

"It's ugly, hideously ugly," said Brock W. Yates, an editor at large at *Car and Driver* and the author of a biography of Enzo Ferrari.

"It's radical, aggressive, unique," countered Mr. Carnicero, who expects to have his car delivered in March. He chose Ferrari red, one of three available colors that also include yellow and black. An avid collector, he already owns three Ferraris, including a limited edition 2001 550 Barchetta, which cost $273,000, a pittance compared with the price of the Enzo.

The design—more technical than sensuous—was done by Ferrari's styling partner Pininfarina. Like a Formula One racecar, its body conceals "tunnel" to produce aerodynamic downforce so the car won't fly off the road. Unlike a Formula One car, which is prohibited from having movable spoilers, the Enzo uses speed-sensitive air foils and a rear spoiler to increase downforce at speed. At 135 miles an hour, the car generates almost one thousand pounds of downforce that hold it to the road like an invisible hand.

Most distinctively, the car's lower lip—a little like the hinged wings of the Vought Corsair fighter plane—echoes the front air foil of Ferrari's Formula One car.

Raise the gull-wing door, and you will also find a cockpit that dispenses with civilian niceties—stereo, carpet, air-conditioning, electric windows—in favor of a race-bred minimalism so severe it's practically Zen-like. For example, the seats, custom-fitted for buyers, are rigid shells lined with thin leather upholstery, and the steering wheel is studded with buttons, like the wheel of a Formula One car.

The Enzo's motor is mated to a six-speed gearbox, built by the design company Magneti Marelli, which uses an electrohydraulic mechanism activated by paddles behind the steering wheel, rather than a traditional stick-shift and clutch pedal, to change gears. And, thankfully, it has enormous braking power—four brake discs (14.6 inches in diameter) made of composite carbon and an antilock brake system that prevents the wheels from locking up under heavy braking. The A.B.S. is part of the car's drive assist system that includes traction control, which steps in if a driver's intemperate right foot should spin the rear tires with too much power. The system has three settings—normal, sport, and race. Only the most skilled drivers, though, will want to handle the Enzo with the system switched off.

Still want one? You missed the boat by about six months. Last summer, Ferrari asked its dealers (thirty-three in North America) to submit lists of potential buyers drawn from among their best clients. The company first selected 349 clients whose requests would be honored. In October Mr. Montezemolo announced that Ferrari would build another fifty cars—but no more after that. These lucky few buyers like Mr. Carnicero represent the most ardent "Ferraristis," well-known collectors with whom the company has been dealing for many years.

"Primarily, we were trying to avoid speculation," said Luca Del Monte, a spokesman for Ferrari North America in Englewood Cliffs, N. J. Ferrari's image was tarnished somewhat when F40's were snapped up by speculators who sold the car on the open market at inflated prices to anybody with the cash in hand.

"We want the cars to remain in the hands of people who are loyal to Ferrari," Mr. Del Monte said, "collectors who have a special relationship with the factory and especially their dealers."

Eventually, Enzos will begin showing up at exotic cadre dealerships. It's not difficult, for instance, to find an F50 for sale in California or Florida, though well above the original list price of $480,000. Hugh Steward, general manager of Ferrari of Atlanta (whose dealership was allotted two Enzos), said the market price for an F50 is about $800,000. While many exotic sports cars depreciate in value, limited-edition Ferraris, usually "are great investments," he said.

As for whether Enzos will ever be seen on the street anytime soon, Mr. Steward says he thinks they will. "Ferrari makes cars that are very drivable, very friendly," he said. "But with this kind of car one needs a certain amount of experience."

SUGGESTIONS FOR FURTHER STUDY

1. No matter how owners defend their ownership of such a car, how can it be other than "showy" when it drives too fast to be allowed on the road?
2. What does Mr. Steward mean when he says that drivers of the Ferrari "need a certain amount of experience"?
3. Do you think that men are more likely than women to desire and own such an expensive icon as this automobile?

Walt Disney and his creations are American—and world—icons. He created small people who have through the years satisfied the desires and needs of people worldwide. Mickey Mouse is America, just as it is childhood, adulthood, the tie between people and other animals and inanimate objects.

The Masks of Mickey Mouse

Symbol of a Generation

ROBERT W. BROCKWAY

From time to time in his later years, Walt Disney tried to explain the enduring popularity of Mickey Mouse. The animated cartoon character he created in 1928 always baffled him. Mickey continues to baffle critics today. Over the years since Mickey Mouse first appeared, just before the Wall Street crash, he has undergone a series of metamorphoses, and has actually grown up with the generation born during the teens and twenties. He was still popular when Disney died in 1966, and his fiftieth birthday was celebrated by national festivities including a black tie party at the Library of Congress attended by the president of the United States. In part the continued popularity of Mickey Mouse has been whimsy, in part nostalgia, but some critics find deeper significance in the little chap made of circles and clad in red short pants with white buttons. He has become an archetypal symbol, not only to Americans but to people everywhere, especially to the generation that was young during the thirties. They are the Mickey Mouse Generation.

The meteoric rise of Mickey Mouse and Disney astonished the film industry. In later years Disney sometimes mused over the vastness of his corporate empire and murmured, "We must never forget that it was all

79

built by a mouse." The phenomenal success of his character never ceased to fascinate him and his critics. Mickey was instantly popular not only among ordinary people young and old, but with intellectuals, artists, and heads of state.

In 1933 the Mickey Mouse craze was global. George V decreed that there must be a Mickey Mouse cartoon at all film performances attended at the palace by the royal family and their guests. The Emperor of Japan wore a Mickey Mouse watch. Known by names in many languages, Mickey was adored by the whole world. He was listed in *Who's Who*, and *Encyclopedia Britannica* devoted an article to him. What is most intriguing, the global fondness for Mickey Mouse has endured more than five decades. What is most fascinating is his complexity. Disney once tried to account for Mickey's appeal by his simplicity, saying that he is easy to understand. He is not. He is as complex as Disney was himself and as profound in his symbolic and mythic implications as any mythic or fairy tale character. He is what Harold Schechter calls a "new god."

Being composed of wafers, he also evokes the mysteries of the circular design which some authorities find profoundly significant as an archetypal figure. Such a phenomenon can scarcely be dismissed as frivolous. While technical innovation and commercial promotion account for some of Mickey's popularity as a film star, his remarkable endurance shows that his creator unwittingly touched something deep in the human psyche.

Although the ultimate origin of Mickey Mouse may have been a cute field mouse named Mortimer, whom Disney tamed when he was in Kansas City, and mice appear in an early *Alice's Wonderland* film, Disney claims to have conceived the Mouse during a train trip back to Los Angeles from New York in March 1927. He had just lost his Oswald the Rabbit series and nearly all of his animators to the New York distributor Charles Mintz. "But was I downhearted?" he later wrote. "Not a bit! For out of the trouble and confusion stood a mocking, merry little figure. Vague and indefinite at first. But it grew and grew and grew. And finally arrived—a mouse. A romping, rollicking, little mouse. . . . The idea completely engulfed me. The wheels turned to the tune of it. 'Chug, chug, mouse! Chug, chug, mouse!' The whistle screeched it. 'A m-ousa-ouse,' it wailed. By the time the train had reached the Middle West I had dressed my dream mouse in a pair of red velvet pants with two huge pearl buttons, had composed the first scenario and was all set."

On his return to California, with all of his staff of animators but one signed up Mintz and producing Oswald films, the Disney brothers and the one loyal animator secretly created the new character. He called the mouse Mortimer until his wife, Lillian, persuaded him to change the name to Mickey, which she thought was less pompous. (According to another version of the story, the name was suggested by a distributor.)

Mickey Mouse was drawn by Ubbe Ert Iwerks, the son of a Missouri barber from Holland with a first name which sounds odd even to most Dutchmen. Iwerks shortened it to Ub. Walt and Ub, who were the same age, met in 1919. Both were trying to become animators. Of the two, Ub was by far the more talented at the drawing board. In fact, Disney was never able to draw his own creation, Mickey Mouse.

Ub secretly drew the first two films, producing seven hundred frames a day. They were *Plane Crazy,* inspired by the Lindberg flight, and *The Gallopin' Gaucho,* in which Mickey was a swashbuckler like Douglas Fairbanks. Both animated cartoons were silent films. None of the distributors were interested in Mickey Mouse, and Disney decided to make an animated cartoon with sound. Although Lee DeForest had developed a practical sound system for film in 1923, none of the studios showed interest until Warner Brothers staved off bankruptcy in 1927 by producing *The Jazz Singer* with Al Jolson. After that all the studios produced talkies, but none of the animators except Disney dared try the new technique. Disney made another trip to New York and contracted use of the Cinephone sound equipment from a freebooter in the film industry named Pat Powers. On his return to Los Angeles, the Disneys hired a new staff of animators and, after much experimentation, developed a workable technique for making animated cartoons with sound. They made *Steamboat Willie* in which Mickey and Minnie Mouse cavort aboard a boat carrying animals, piloted by Pegleg Pete who was to become Mickey's arch-rival. Mickey rescues Minnie from Pegleg Pete's unwelcome advances and, in the course of the river journey, plays a cow's teeth like a xylophone, her udder as bagpipes, and Minnie twists a goat's tail and plays him like a hurdy-gurdy.

Steamboat Willie opened at the Colony Theater in New York on November 18, 1928. And thus Mickey Mouse was born. He appeared in theaters all over America during 1930. Powers, the distributor, contracted for more Mickey Mouse cartoons. Disney studio hired more staff and remade and released *Plane Crazy* and *The Gallopin' Gaucho.* They

also agreed to make six more and soon were producing Mickey Mouse
reels at the rate of one every four weeks. Early in 1931 a syndicated
Mickey Mouse comic strip drawn by Iwerks appeared and Hermann
(Kay) Kamen, a New York merchandiser, licensed the manufacture of
figurines, dolls, and other items, including a Mickey-Minnie handcar on
a circular rail and Mickey Mouse watches. The first saved the Lionel
Company from bankruptcy and the second the Ingersoll-Waterbury
Watch Company. The tiny, obscure Disney studio became a corporate
success and Mickey Mouse was popular throughout the world.

Mickey's chief rival was Pat Sullivan's Felix the Cat, created by Pat
Sullivan and drawn by Otto Messmer. Felix was sometimes called the
Charlie Chaplin of cartoon characters. "Like Chaplin, Felix is a loner in
a hostile world, who combines resourcefulness and a touch of vicious-
ness to survive."

According to Max Langer, "What was most appealing about Felix
was his personality. He had his distinctive pensive walk, head down and
hands clasped behind." His versatile, prehensile tail could be a baseball
bat, fishing rod, or telescope. The stories concocted by Raoul Barre
were good. Leonard Maltin considers Felix to have been the equal of
Mickey Mouse in every respect save sound. "Felix is as recognizable
and rounded a character as any later cartoon character." Mickey's only
initial advantage was sound. As the aging Iwerks recently told John Cul-
hane, Mickey "was the standardized thing. . . . Pear-shaped body, ball
on top, couple of thin legs. You gave it long ears and it was a rabbit.
Short ears, it was a cat. Ears hanging down, a dog. . . . With an elon-
gated nose it became a mouse." Iwerks's comment is overly modest.
He improved the animating style of the day. The conventional style of
drawing originated with animated cartooning itself, an art invented at
the turn of the century by French and American pioneers such as J. S.
Blackmore. During the teens the art was developed by animators such
as Winsor McCay and his "Gertie the Dinosaur." Little progress was
made in drawing style during the twenties until Ub Iwerks (who is sometimes called the forgotten man of animation) introduced a more fluid
style as well as more refined drawing technique.

The cartoon style of the twenties was slapstick. While it has ancient
and medieval antecedents, slapstick as a comic film style originated in
France at the turn of the century; it was enormously popular among the
urban proletariat. According to Durgnat, "French comedies swarmed

with [comics] called *cascadeurs* who, in Nicole Vede's words, 'really did perform the plunge from the third story into a tub of washing, and at the exact moment that the floor of a room fell through, each man knew precisely where to leap—one onto the piano, another onto the aspidistra—silk hats still on their heads, lorgnettes dangling, beards a-quiver.'"

The comic style which Disney exploited in the Mickey Mouse films of the early thirties was derived from Mack Sennett's slapstick comedy. Sennett studied the French slapstick films and adapted the technique to produce the "Keystone Kops." According to Durgnat, "American comedy continued to derive its poetry from coupling simple and violent attitudes with a delirium of physical and mechanical knockabout." With Sennett there was a shift from the American music hall's older style of character comedy to that of mechanized man. "Thus Sennett's films register not only the shock of speed but the spreading concept of man as an impersonal physical object existing only to work rapidly, rhythmically, repetitively. But Sennett parodies the conception, to concoct a universe where authority, routine, and the monotony of factory days are shattered as cars burst into bedrooms and beds race down the highway. Comedy, by exaggeration, veers toward revolt, an orgy of disorder, a Saturnalia of chaos."

According to Durgnat, slapstick emerges from childlike impulsiveness, dream fantasy and visual poetry. The "slapstick comedians are childlike, and . . . act out impulses which as adults we suppress." That was the style of comedians who delighted audiences during the twenties. Chaplin, Arbuckle, Keaton, and Lloyd learned their craft from Sennett's Keystone Kops and went on to develop their own styles. The early animators such as Sullivan and Fleicher exploited the same slapstick style and so did Disney.

During the thirties, tastes changed. Durgnat notes that "if anything, the comic tone took an upbeat turn. The earlier movies took poverty matter-of-factly. But when it became a national problem too, and the subject of optimistic pronouncements from complacent Republicans as from dynamic New Dealers, a more optimistic frame of reference was introduced. The cinema had, from its very beginnings, been steadily rising in the social scale, and the middle classes are far more decorous and squeamish about the seamy side of life than the lower classes; the Hays Code (1933) marks the middle class dominance. Further, the grimness of life made everyone all the more responsive to sentimental escapism."

While slapstick continued to delight, there was public demand for new comic modes and so Disney started *Silly Symphonies* in 1932. These short cartoons were masterpieces of charm, sentiment, and escape.

By 1934 Disney was complaining that Mickey had become a problem child. "He's such an institution that we're limited in what we can do with him. If we have Mickey kicking someone in the pants, we get a million letters from mothers scolding us for giving their kids the wrong idea." The problem was solved by introducing a supporting cast which included Donald Duck, who made his debut in *The Wise Little Hen* in 1934. He soon upstaged Mickey as slapstick comic and the latter became a straight man. Mickey was born again. The barnyard bratty kid gave way to the likeable small town fellow in oversize coat with brass buttons and braid who conducts the band in the town park on a Sunday afternoon. He is plagued by a bratty Donald Duck who keeps playing a flute while the band is trying to perform "The William Tell Overture." If *Steamboat Willie* was the *rite de passage* marking Mickey's birth, *The Band Concert* was his initiation into maturity. There was a new Mickey Mouse audience, and Mickey was born again.

In later years, Disney said that the Mickey Mouse film was addressed to an audience "made up of parts of people; of their deathless, ageless, absolutely primitive remnant of something in every world-wracked human being which makes us play with children's toys and laugh without self-consciousness at silly things, and sing in the bathtub, and dream."

The Mickey Mouse film was primarily addressed to the inner child in the adult rather than to actual children, few of whom had money of their own for theater tickets. While Mickey was ostensibly reborn for commercial reasons, the change had profound psychological implications. Disney often said, "There's a lot of Mickey in me." There was. There was also a lot of Mickey in the Mickey Mouse audience. He and they were growing up.

As Jacob noted in 1939, Disney exhibited rare artistic idealism and integrity for a business man, especially during the thirties. "Money is important indirectly," Disney said, "experimentation comes first. Quality is the thing we have striven most to put in our pictures." He added, "I don't favor much commercialization. Most producers think it is better to get while the getting is good. We have not operated that way."

Disney was attuned to the soul of Middle America; he shared its values himself, and was exceptionally sensitive to its changing moods. A theater-going public which liked Andy Hardy, the bashful Jimmy Stewart of *You Can't Take It with You,* and, above all, the Chaplin of *Modern Times* wanted a kindhearted and gentle, youthful but grown-up Mickey Mouse. The new Mickey of the middle and late thirties was sometimes the heroic dragon-slayer who rescues Minnie from the pirates, the desperadoes, and Pegleg Pete. More often he was the bourgeoisie do-gooder. He moved from the farm to the small town and from there to the suburbs. He became the neighborly Middle American young fellow who lives next door, "Mr. Nice Guy."

New, in-house instructions for drawing Mickey were prepared in 1934 by Ted Sears and Fred Moore. They wrote: "Mickey is not a clown . . . he is neither silly nor dumb. His comedy depends entirely upon the situation he is placed in. His age varies with the situation . . . sometimes his character is that of a young boy, and at times, as in the adventure type of picture, he appears quite grown up. . . . Mickey is more amusing when he is in a serious predicament trying to accomplish some purpose under difficulties or against time." Moore adds, "Mickey seems to be the average young boy of no particular age, living in a small town, clean living, fun loving, bashful around girls, polite and clever. . . . In some stories he has a touch of Fred Astaire, in others of Charlie Chaplin, and in some of Douglas Fairbanks, but in all there should be some of the young boy."

Fantasia (1940) was Mickey's finest hour. Here Mickey is the apprentice in Paul Dukas's *The Sorcerer and the Apprentice,* a story by Goethe. Mickey is the sorcerer's cap who commands the sea, winds, clouds, and stars like a god.

No Mickey Mouse films were made during the war years. The few films made during the late forties and early fifties portray him as the likeable suburbanite in pastoral settings with the comic roles entirely taken over by Pluto and other supporting characters. His last was *The Simple Things* in 1954. The short film had become too expensive to produce, and the thirties type presentation with short subjects and cartoon followed by feature gave way to the double feature just before Hollywood succumbed to television. Again, Disney and his alter ego Mickey were quick to adapt to the new medium and the Mickey Mouse Club appeared.

During the mid-fifties, as the genial host of Disneyland in tails, Mickey underwent a third *rite de passage* in his life journey. He climbed to the top of the Disney empire as the corporate image. This was his most recent metamorphosis. The middle-aged Mickey mirrors the world of the corporate executive. He became an "organization man." He also became the King of the Magic Kingdom and his appearances took on the mystique of monarchy. He acquired *noblesse oblige* and patrician charm. He became avuncular; he was often seen nuzzling small children with nurturant affection on Main Street, U.S.A., in Disneyland. He became gentle and sentimental.

Disney was often taciturn in his later years. Mickey was not. When Disney died in 1966, *Paris Match* featured a cover in which a sad Mickey has a large tear in his eye.

The recent founding of Magic Kingdoms in Japan and France attest to Mickey's continued popularity abroad. He remains well beloved throughout the world. By no means all of his loyal devotees are either very old or very young. Many are youthful and middle-aged. Many experience something akin to mystical experience in his presence.

Recently he was in trouble. Trade articles with titles like "Wishing upon a Falling Star at Disney" lamented, "What a great studio Disney used to be." The crowds who attended Disneyland during the Los Angeles Summer Olympics in 1984 fell below corporation hopes and expectations. But both Disney Studios and Mickey have since recovered. Mickey continues to be a symbol. To test this point, Donald Bains showed the cartoon title card with Mickey's beaming face in a sunburst to an infant who reached out for the cheerful image which made him feel happy. He invites anyone to try the same experiment. During the late fifties, Dr. Tom Dooley, who ran a hospital ship off the cost of Southeast Asia, found that he could not entice children to come for medical help until he obtained permission to paint Mickey Mouse on the hull of the ship. The children never had seen Mickey before but were drawn by the figure. Such experiences as these, and they have been numerous, intrigue commentators familiar with the archetypal theories of C. G. Jung.

Among those who have attempted to interpret the popularity of Mickey Mouse in terms of analytic psychology are the aging Ub Iwerks, who drew him, and John Hench, until recent years the Vice President of W. E. D., the Disney corporation which manages Disneyland and Disney World. According to Iwerks, "Mickey's face is a trinity of wafers— and the circular symbol, as C. G. Jung has told us, always points to the single most vital aspect of life—its ultimate wholeness." "Simple round forms portray the archetype of self which, as we know, in experience, plays the chief role in uniting irreconcilable opposites and is therefore best suited to compensate the single-mindedness of the age."

Hench, who came to the Disney studio in 1939 as an artist, suggests that Disney art was able "to exploit very old survival patterns, a case in point being Mickey Mouse who is composed of circles." Mickey "has been accepted all over the world, and there is obviously no problem of people responding to this set of circles. I'm going to oversimplify this, but circles never cause anybody any trouble. We have bad experiences with sharp points, with angles, but circles are things we have fun with — babies, women's behinds, breasts. So Mickey was made this way, while a contemporary known as Felix the Cat didn't get anywhere. He has points all over him like a cactus. He has practically disappeared while we couldn't get rid of Mickey if we tried." Circles are "very reassuring — People have had millions of years experience with curved objects and they have never been hurt by them. It's the pointed things that give you trouble. Imagine putting a set of dynamic curves together in a design that has the power that this one does, so that he goes all around the world and no one thinks of him as an American import. They give him a name and then it's all a déjà vu experience. They respond to the curves."

According to Harold Schechter, who interprets popular culture in Jungian terms, Mickey is a trickster, the archaic and universally encountered god who, according to Jung, evokes the shadow, the seamy side of the personal unconscious, kin to the Freudian id. According to Jung, the shadow refers to impulses "which appear morally, aesthetically, or intellectually inadmissible and are repressed on account of their incompatibility." When the shadow appears in dreams it represents that which is bestial. "The dream confronts the individual with the very thing which he resents; it is presented as an integral part of his own personality and as one that may not be disregarded without danger."

According to Edward Whitmont, "The shadow can also stand for the less individualized part of the personality, the *collective* shadow which corresponds to the most primitive, archaic level of the human mind — the level which links us with our animal past — often symbolized by a beast or some sort of anthropomorphized animal."

In myth the shadow is encountered as the trickster. The latter is an archaic and virtually universal mythic figure such as Coyote among some American Indians and Loki among the ancient Norse. According to Jung, the trickster has persisted from archaic times to the present in the medieval jester and Punch and Judy. Since the antecedents of slapstick comics such as Sennett's Keystone Kops are of this tradition of farce, it follows that Krazy Kat, Felix the Cat, and Mickey Mouse are as well. Because of his various metamorphoses in the course of the development,

Mickey Mouse is much more complex than the other animated figures, none of which progressed past the slapstick stage.

Disney posed as a philistine and often ridiculed intellectuals and their theories about his characters and creations. He always insisted that he was only an entertainer. Yet, though inarticulate in the expression of ideas, he frequently disclosed deep intuitive understanding and philosophical wisdom. He, too, recognized the archetypal nature of Mickey Mouse, though he did not put it in theoretical terms. Disney realized that he had unwittingly touched a very deep chord in the human psyche and that Mickey Mouse was far more than a comic-strip character.

Mickey may live to see the year 2001, the centennial of Disney's birth, but he may not survive much beyond. As an archetypal form, Mickey Mouse seems to be temporally bound to those generations who grew up during the teens, twenties, and thirties of the present century. Only they seem to respond to him. In essence, the Mickey Mouse Generation is the Depression Generation. Mickey has some impact on younger people but far less than upon those born during the inter-war years. That generation is now senior and it is also diminishing. All gods eventually die, and Mickey is no exception. But, being immortals, all gods rise. Mickey, too, may be reborn in some future imaginary character of the popular culture of which he is an avatar. In past ages we knew him as Dionysius and Pan. Future generations will encounter him again.

From *Journal of Popular Culture* 22, no. 4 (1989). Reprinted, without bibliographical information, with permission of the author.

SUGGESTIONS FOR FURTHER STUDY

1. Since Mickey Mouse is synonymous with Walt Disney, will the mouse's name and influence live as long as his creator's?
2. Disney's name has reached outward with theme parks, which continue to expand. Currently a new giant one is being built in Beijing, and it is expected to draw more customers (worshippers?) than any other, even the one in Tokyo. Does that mean that Mickey's name and influence are guaranteed as long as theme parks continue?
3. Pinocchio's name and influence are not as widespread as Mickey's. Does that mean that he is a less important cultural-literary figure?

PREOCCUPATION WITH CHILDHOOD

There is always a little of the child in all of us. With some there is always a great deal, taken out in various childlike activities that we practice all our lives. Sports, for example, though we play them in hard, adult fashion and for great amounts of money—both earned and bet—are still holdovers from the free activities of young people. Another example is the delight we adults take in getting on the floor and playing with our children or grandchildren, becoming for the moment one of them. Toys are not only great commercial enterprises but, as Kathy Merlock Jackson points out below, icons of our attitudes and manifestations of our commercial drives and our dreams for continued youth.

From Control to Adaptation

America's Toy Story

KATHY MERLOCK JACKSON

The child's toys and the old man's reasons are the fruits of the
two seasons.

William Blake

Nothing defines us more than our toys. From infancy, when we clutch
brightly colored blocks and cuddly teddy bears, to adulthood, when our
toys of choice are fast cars, electronic games, and cute or expensive collectibles, toys say a great deal about who we are and what we value.
Some toys, such as kites, jacks, and hoops, are inherently recreational,
enabling us to have fun. More often than not, though, toys also serve a
larger purpose as they exemplify our cultural truths: what skills we hope
to develop, what attitudes we want to cultivate, and what possession we
wish to flaunt. Toys reflect the interplay between our society's view of
play and its opposite, work.

All societies have had toys, affirming a basic human need to connect
with an object—perhaps a doll or a ball—in some form of play. However, it was not until the late sixteenth century that the word "toy"—
which was associated with triviality, delusion, and lust—began to refer
to children's playthings. In America by the end of the nineteenth century, the notion of "toy" took on new meaning. Prior to this time, toys—
which were almost always homemade, usually of wood—were few, as

children endured endless hours of chores, leaving little time for play. The toys and games that they did have frequently embodied moralistic messages. By the Industrial Age, this began to change as mass-produced, affordable toys became available, and workers had the income to buy them. At the same time, children, who previously were regarded as little adults and treated accordingly, entered a new sphere. Deemed different from adults by virtue of their innocence, children warranted special care, protection, nurturing, and instruction as they moved through a distinct stage of development known as childhood, characterized by their own books, clothing, and playthings. In essence, they won the right to be children and to play, and toys became part of this formula. This attitude became even more entrenched by the 1950s, when, during the post–World War II baby boom, television invaded American homes, attracting children with shows and advertising geared to them and espousing a child-centered, family-oriented agenda.

In such a culture, where children are highly valued, the role of toys takes on greater importance, and several questions emerge, some practical, others ideological. What functions do, and should, toys provide? What messages do toys and the narratives that accompany them impart to children? How do toys reflect and affect attitudes and values in a dynamic, increasingly technological, careerist, and consumerist mass culture? Do we ever outgrow our toys? As artifacts of popular culture, toys embody the controversies of their time. Sites of philosophical struggle, they form a text that invites a discussion of contemporary issues regarding empowerment, control, social roles, and consumption.

Then and Now

One way to address these issues is to consider how toys have changed. In the summer of 2000, the Francis Land House in Virginia Beach, Virginia, which dates back to colonial times, presented an exhibit of American toys from the first half of the twentieth century. Titled "Memories of Childhood," it was made possible through the contributions of various friends and members of the Francis Land Houses Historic Society, who scoured their attics for treasured childhood playthings. In one corner of the exhibition hall stood a large white dollhouse with painted green shutters that Henry Nichols Horton built in 1925 for his daughter Doris. An exact replica of the Horton Family home in Providence, Rhode Island, the dollhouse contained furniture and accessories that Horton had crafted. Other toys in the exhibit included a Shirley Temple doll in a blue dress, a porcelain tea set painted with red flowers, a pair of rusty roller skates with a key, a clay marble game, two tattered brown teddy bears, a cowboy shirt and spurs, a Little Orphan Annie stove previously used to bake mud pies, and several tin toys, such as a bus, train, and plane. Many of the toys were categorized along gender lines: one case for boys' toys and another for girls'. The fact that people kept these items for over fifty years suggests their value, a sentiment shared by the exhibit's visitors, who upon seeing the artifacts launched into stories of their own fond toy memories.

If we progress to the toys that children play with in the twenty-first century, we see many of the same items—dolls and dollhouses, stuffed animals, cars and trucks. In its first three years of operation, the National Toy Hall of Fame in Salem, Oregon, inducted several toys that remain as recognizable today as they were decades ago: the hula hoop, Frisbee, marbles, Play-Doh, Barbie, Lincoln Logs, Lego, Monopoly, Slinky, the jump rope, the bicycle, jacks, and Mr. Potato Head. Nevertheless, differences in toys and play from yesteryear abound. Plastic has replaced smooth polished wood or metal as the most popular toy material, a subject much lamented by Roland Barthes in his 1957 essay on French toys. Skateboards have overtaken shiny metal roller skates that had to be laboriously buckled over a child's shoes. Instead of Shirley Temple and Little Orphan Annie, superheroines from popular toy-based television series and blockbuster movies such as *Pokemon* and *Star Wars* dominate modern children's toy lines, providing schoolchildren with a shared culture they can discuss each day. These later items are often marketed in a series, spawning a collectible mentality that did not exist previously. Dolls (especially Mattel's Barbie) and trucks still sell, as evidenced by the rows of each at Toys 'R' Us; however, affluent, modern parents are more likely to eschew gender-specific toys, and the children who do play with them tend to outgrow them more quickly. Increasingly, though, the major change in childhood play is that today's toys of choice, even for the very young, are electronic—video games, computer simulations, and virtual reality scenarios—often with violent, politically charged narratives. Given the rate at which toy technology is progressing, one doubts if fifty years from now these hi-tech toys will ever grace a museum exhibit, for the devices on which to play them will have been long phased out. Nevertheless, these toys have given new meaning to the concept of play.

Theories of Toys and Play

Although individual toys have changed over the years, their overall importance has remained constant. While the words "toy" and "play" suggest activities that are neither serious nor useful, John and Elizabeth Newson are correct when they define play as "perhaps the most serious and significant of all human activities." Toys are not, of course, necessary for play, but they do provide a vehicle for it and encourage children to relate to their environment and others in particular ways, ones promoted by adults who typically provide the toys. Perhaps Roland Barthes says it best when he writes that "toys *always mean something,* and this something is entirely socialized. . . . [They] *literally* prefigure the world of adult functions." Toys, Barthes posits, introduce children to a wide range of questionable concepts—war, bureaucracy, ugliness—and in doing so, they reflect a culture's values towards childhood and reveal what one generation believes the next must learn.

While philosophers as early as the ancient Greeks have speculated on the nature of toys and the types of play they evoke, only during the last half of the twentieth century have theorists really begun to consider toys seriously. This initial flurry of attention coincided with the post–World War II baby boom, which reached its peak in America in 1957 and marked a period of child-centered thinking, new methodologies regarding teaching the young, and unprecedented affluence which enabled many parents to indulge their children with toys. For example, Erik H. Erikson includes in his seminal work *Childhood and Society* (1950) a chapter titled "Toys and Reasons" in which he coins the term "micro-sphere" or "small world of manageable toys" to which a child returns for comfort and refueling. Erickson proposes the theory that "the child's play is the infantile form of the human ability to deal with experience by creating model situations and to master the reality by experiment and planning." In a later book, also titled *Toys and Reasons,* based on his series of Godkin Lectures at Harvard University, Erikson refines his theory of toys, noting especially their role in the establishment of the child's political imagination. Other significant works of this period that explore the primacy of play and toys include *Homo-Ludens: A Study of the Play Element*

in Culture (1949) by J. Huizinga; *Man, Play, and Games* (1961), by R. Cail-
lois; *Encounters* (1961) by E. Goffman; and *Play, Dreams, and Imitation in
Childhood* (1951) by J. Piaget.

Psychologist Brian Sutton-Smith, who also began studying toys and
play theory in the 1950s, produced his major work *Toys as Culture* in 1986.
In it, he outlines three major categories of toys: "toys of acquaintance"
that are short lasting and designed only to display consumption; "toys of
identification" that children bond with and find comfort in; and "age
and sex stereotypical toys" that are designed to promote imagination but
ultimately socialize their users. Sutton-Smith argues that a pattern exists
by which children play games to allay the stresses brought about by
child-rearing practices, but these very games enculturate them into society's ways. Termed the conflict-enculturation hypothesis, it explains
the dynamics between culture and play. Sutton-Smith also concerns
himself with the ways in which toys prefigure work, arguing, "The rise of
the toy as a child's gift in modern society can also be seen as the rise of an
instrument that would accustom children to . . . solitary preoccupation
and solitary striving for achievement. . . . [The] toy is a model of the kind
of isolation that is essential to progress in the modern world. . . . With the
toy we habituate children to solitary, impersonal activity; and this is a
forecast of their years to come as solitary professionals and experts."

As more researchers began to study how children play with toys, several writings appeared examining the functions that toys and play serve.
In *Why People Play* (1973), M. J. Ellis divides over two dozen theories of
play into three categories—classical, recent, and modern—including
such explanations as surplus energy, relaxation, instinct, catharsis,
learned behavior, psychoanalysis, and stimulus-seeking. The breadth of
his approaches attests to the substantial interest that scholars in various
disciplines exhibited in the study of play. William C. Ketchum Jr., in
Toys and Games (1981), focuses on the function of toys to encourage children to mimic their elders, thereby adopting their values, and cites the
many toys, from board games to knights to dollhouses to model kitchens,
that were designed to train boys to be "brave, honest, and hardworking"
and girls to be "kind, dutiful, and attentive to their elders." In *When Toys
Come Alive* (1994), Lois Rostow Kuznets associates toys and play with not
only amusement and education but also with "religious rituals, social
mores and values, gender definition, commerce, technological experimentation, and artistic expression." Finally, Hartley, Frank, and Gold-
enson in *Understanding Children's Play* offer a concise list of the functions of

play: 1. to imitate adults; 2. to play out real roles in an intense way; 3. to reflect relationships and experiences; 4. to express pressing needs; 5. to release unacceptable impulses; 6. to reverse roles usually taken; 7. to mirror growth; 8. to work out problems and experiment with solutions.

Play, then, rather than being trivial, can really be quite essential, offering a forum for children to explore the roles, situations, and relationships they will face as they mature.

The cultural studies movement of the 1980s and 1990s, with its emphasis on interpreting symbols, rituals, events, ideas, and artifacts of both high and low culture, yielded a plethora of new theories of toys, occurring at the same time that the toy industry underwent a revolution of its own, spearheaded by the rise of video and computer games, the development of toy-based programming, and increased conglomeration and merger in the toy industry. In 1993, two important works appeared. Stephen Kline's *Out of the Garden: Toys, TV, and Children's Culture in the Age of Marketing* and Ellen Seiter's *Sold Separately: Children and Parents in Consumer Culture.* Kline argues that marketing strategies in the age of sophisticated television advertising and toy-based programming have shaped not only the design of toys but also the ways in which children play, noting, "The particular malaise within market-industrial society that arises when the privileged position we give to marketing within media begins to undermine and threaten our aspirations for a more civilized society which would promote the full development of children." Seiter, while criticizing the low quality and gender and racial stereotyping that occur in advertising geared to children, takes a more positive view of television, theorizing that the medium and the toys that it promotes provide children with a shared culture. She also defends parents—especially overworked, lower-status mothers pressured by their more educated, middle-class peers who believe that children's consumption should be limited to the "right" products and that good parenting is equated with only expensive, educational toys.

Addressing parents, children, and advertising messages, Seiter explores toys through the lens of gender, race, and class, an approach embraced by many contemporary theorists. In *From Barbie to Mortal Kombat: Gender and Computer Games* (1998), Justine Cassell and Henry Jenkins propose a theory of the regendering of digital technology. They assemble a series of essays that describe and analyze the computer games currently on the market, observing that the majority are violent, designed by men for boys, and frequently carry misogynistic messages and images of females in primarily objectified, victimized positions. These games have limited appeal to girls, who prefer stronger female characters and more cooperative, relationship-oriented fare. The authors advocate the development of more games geared to girls, who need to hone their computer skills in order to remain competitive with their male peers. While "Barbie Fashion Designer" broke ground as the first popular computer game marketed to girls, it perpetuated many stereotypes, signaling the need for and accessibility to new games that better socialize diverse groups of children, including the less advantaged, regarding gender, race and ethnicity, and technology issues. Mary F. Rogers delves into many of these same areas in *Barbie Culture* (1999), a title in the Sage Publications Core Cultural Icons series that combines theoretical and practical analyses of key elements in contemporary consumer culture. Rogers's work, representing a trend of studies that show how particular toys are imbued with the values of a culture, takes Barbie seriously. To understand Barbie, she writes, one must "look at how childhood has been changing over the past century or so; how toys and their manufacturers have established themselves in consumerist cultures; how adults as well as children nurture themselves on fantasy; how gender, social class, race, sexual orientation, ethnicity, and age continue mapping out the contours of people's identities; how fetishism and fashion and eroticism interplay alongside mass advertising and other elements of media culture; how cyberspace is as much cultural and psychological as it is technological; and how modernist and postmodernist elements co-shape our worlds today."

As Rogers's assessment of Barbie confirms, toys reflect a myriad of complex social concerns. *Powerplay: Toys as Popular Culture* (1996) by Dan Fleming expresses a similar point of view by combining both psychoanalytic and cultural theories. In an attempt to explain how toys function as objects and what they reveal about culture, he focuses on narrativization of toys, especially the hegemonic, often violent stories that accompany media-related toy lines such as Mighty Morphin' Power Rangers, Teenage Mutant Ninja Turtles, Transformers, G. I. Joe, and Star Wars. Such stories, Fleming argues, combine the human form and machines and reflect cultural tensions, especially regarding power, male identity, and the uneasy balance between individuality and teamwork. In *Kids' Stuff: Toys and the Changing World of American Childhood* (1997), Gary Cross also examines conflicting attitudes about toys and the changes that have created them, citing the confluence of unresolvable issues regarding childrearing, the American family, and twentieth-century manufacturing and marketing. In particular he investigates effects of the toy industry's practice of producing television advertisements aimed directly to children coupled with the desire of parents to share the world of consumption with their children.

Given business practices of the late twentieth century, one cannot consider toys without addressing the complex corporate structure that produces them; thus, another theory of toys encompasses the organization of the industry, the way decisions are made, and their impact on the marketplace and the American mindset. *Toyland: The High-Stakes Game of the Toy Industry* (1990) by Sydney Ladensohn Stern and Ted Schoenhaus and *Toy Wars: The Epic Struggle Between G. I. Joe, Barbie, and the Companies That Make Them* (1998) by G. Wayne Miller take this approach. Both of these books imply that the power relationships inherent in contemporary toy play simulate the political nature of key players in the toy industry in an era of aggressive marketing and corporate takeovers. Also, a reality in toyland is that toys promoting aggressive behavior and traditional gender roles sell, triggering a troubling socialization process and dissuading toy makers and merchandisers from redirecting their efforts to toy lines, advertising, and displays that are not gender-based and do not promote violence.

Related research assesses the various appeals that advertisers use to attract children and their effectiveness. As Jean Kilbourne asserts in *Deadly Persuasion: Why Women and Girls Must Fight the Addictive Power of Advertising* (1999), advertisers teach children that their most important relationships are not with people but with products, contributing to a culture characterized by addiction to consumption. Kids 'R' Us president Mike Searles notes, "If you own this child at an early age, you can own this child for years to come. Companies are saying, 'Hey, I want to own the kid younger and younger.'" Thus toys often provide children with their first important relationships with products, equating consumption with happiness and teaching brand loyalty at an early age.

Toys, then, as research has shown, provide a mechanism for understanding larger concerns. They have been at the center of controversies regarding the nurturing and teaching of the young; the dynamics of gender, class, and race; the explosion of media merchandising and television advertising; the corporatization of America; the work ethic and need for recreation; the consumer society and display of wealth; and the role of violence in entertainment and play. Increasingly, though, the issues of the day are technology and its effects on culture; toys belong in this discussion too.

Theorizing Toys in the Twenty-first Century: Constructing Identity and Learning to Adopt

America in the twenty-first century has been transformed by affluence, transience, more leisure time, and digital revolution, all of which have affected people's relationship with toys. Children's lives have become more structured as family patterns change, creating greater need for planned day-care experiences, and Americans' worship of achievement becomes more pronounced. In an era in which elaborate pre-school, kindergarten, and elementary school graduations ritualize the importance of progress and accomplishment, the average child spends more time with a computer, often at the encouragement of parents who hope to instill occupational skills, than with a bicycle, the traditional symbol of childhood independence away from home with the neighborhood gang. Both children and adults are prone to regard computer literacy as essential to their happiness and livelihoods. They are also more likely to be engaged in solitary activities than they were a century ago, with electronic toys frequently filling the bill. In a postmodern world of rapid technological change, children and adults often share toys and play patterns. They immerse themselves in video and computer games such as *Mortal Kombat* and *Space Invaders,* collect Beanie Babies and *Star Wars* figures, and use their toys for conspicuous consumption and to assert status. Thus, while toys fulfill many of the same functions they always have, the landscape of play has changed in sync with the culture.

In the twenty-first century, just as words remain the language of adults, toys remain the language of children. Through toys, children express who they are; they construct an identity of their current and future selves. Many toys still have to do with role playing, enabling children to gain confidence as they try out and practice their roles, often gender-based, in society. Classic toys trained children to weave their own narratives and control their environment through play as diverse as manipulating cars and trucks, maneuvering army figures, dressing and simulating adventures for Barbie and her friends, or arranging facial features on Mr. and Mrs. Potato Head. This process, which empowered the child, often involved creation. Iona and Robert Opie speak to this when they write: "It is a truism that when children play at living with wooden bricks, model soldiers, toy cars, ships, farms, and railways spread out on the floor, their pleasure comes from creating a world entirely their own and under their control. They decide what goes where, and what happens when. They make the geography and the scenery from corrugated paper, cardboard, papier mache, silver paper, cushions, and the less prestigious books. If, as is usually the case, their world resembles the real world, they pretend they are organizing real events and making real decisions: they take families in trains for holidays on farms in the country; they crash cars and arrange for the occupants to be taken to the hospital; they pitch camp, and line up opposing armies to shoot at each other with matchstick-firing cannons; they build houses and bridges and decide to knock them down."

While toys that teach children to control their environment still abound, especially for the very young, older children and adults increasingly seek out another type of play experience. In recent years, toy store sales have decreased. While this is partly due to changes in the marketplace with the growth of superstores such as Wal-Mart and K-Mart which usurp toy sales, it also has to do with the fact that consumers are more likely to bypass the toy store for the computer store. Digital devices have become the mainstay of modern play, curtailing children's hours spent with classic toys and even with television. And this type of play is decidedly different. In computer and video game scenarios, the element of control that was so essential to early play patterns is taken away. Now with virtual reality, players are controlled by the software, which determines the narrative. Although they try to assert control through making certain choices, they no longer dominate; thus, with virtual reality, the meaning and process of play change.

In traditional play, children could be masters of their own fates, learning to control their roles in this. However, digital play creates a sensation of the randomness of life. One cannot control the outcome in *Mortal Kombat* in the same way one can when playing Barbie or army or cowboys. This calls for a new skill: adaptation. Thus, while classic toys—which developed in the Industrial Age—taught control and creation, electronic toys—emblematic of the Information Age—teach adaptation. Training to adapt begins in childhood and continues through adulthood.

Virtual reality also presupposes a new concept of time; everything is speeded up, serving as an electronic metaphor for modern life. Change is fast; thus, one must respond and adapt to sudden threats. Many of the most popular computer games address survival; the player who cannot immediately solve problems posed by the developing narrative dies. This sense of urgency becomes another metaphor for modern life in the informative age; one must act quickly and be able to adapt, a process that does not empower in the same way as creating but does instill confidence. While the nineteenth and twentieth centuries were ages of control, the twenty-first century contains computers that think faster than people, who have lost control; they require the confidence necessary to respond to the rapid change that permeates their world.

Intrinsic to technological change is an overload of information easily accessible in a digital society. However, this magnitude of information requires another kind of adaptation: the ability to collect, order, and organize. The toy collecting trend, attributable today to both children and adults, reflects this mindset. Schoolchildren learn that he or she who has the most valuable Pokemon cards has the greatest status on the playground, and adults, who are just as likely to collect Beanie Babies and Holiday Barbies as their children, exhibit the need to acquire items that are perceived to be in limited supply and "have them all." These behaviors demonstrate another response to the modern age: adaptation through ordering and collecting, making sense of the barrage of messages and images by identifying objects that provide familiarity and comfort and acquiring, classifying, and arranging them. In the process, a collector identifies with his or her desired objects; thus, part of oneself is what one collects.

Conclusion

In modern America, many forms of play and toys co-exist, reflecting diverse value systems and often cultural conflicts. Play has become as important as work, as people are as likely to define themselves through their leisure activities and their toys as through their livelihoods. This lifelong process begins in childhood, teaching important lessons and skills. In 1996, Pixar Pictures released the first fully computer-animated feature-length film, the immensely popular *Toy Story*, which tells the story of a classic cowboy doll named Woody who risks being displaced by a space-age action figure, Buzz Lightyear. Woody eventually learns to adapt to the change in the playroom, befriending Buzz, realizing that anything can be forgotten and phased out, but ultimately enjoying himself and his place. This scenario belies the role of toys in our culture. Toys enable us to construct who we are, appreciate our personal and collective pasts, prepare for the future in a world of constant flux, and live for the moment, having fun.

From *Journal of American and Comparative Cultures* 24, nos. 1 and 2 (2001). Reprinted, without bibliographical information, with permission of the author.

SUGGESTIONS FOR FURTHER STUDY

1. None of the authors in these many studies discusses religious dolls and games (and play) and the roles they play in the lives of many people. Such dolls are religious icons and have deep and religious meanings. How do secular dolls and the role they play in society resemble the religious icons?
2. Secular games and their instruments (toys) are one way of keeping history before us, of bringing cultural patterns of the past to the present. In that way they play a major role in perpetuating culture. In what way do you think your own playthings and games influenced or directed your development as a child and as an adult?
3. Why do you think the authors of these many studies of toys and games—for both children and adults—omitted any discussion of them as religious or secular icons?

STEREOTYPES

Stereotypes are the generalities of life cut down to a fine point concerning a particular subject and directed usually toward a special goal. Ordinarily they concern people or people's behavior. Their purpose can be toward either the good or the ill of a particular people or group, and although they can be intended to favor or disfavor a particular group, more likely than not they will be used for negative purposes. Stereotypes are the short-hand of description and are nearly always incomplete.

They usually pick up from a most obvious characteristic, real or imagined, and generalize from that particular. For example, in my own stereotype, throughout history the English, being very insular about the sanctity of their island, have disliked other nations and have therefore tended to generalize negatively about them. The author of the first English dictionary, Dr. Samuel Johnson, for example, stereotyped all Scots in his famous statement, "The noblest prospect which a Scotchman ever sees is the high-road that leads him to England." French author Andre Maurois double-stereotyped both the Irish and the English in his comment, "If in the eyes of an Irishman there is any one being more ridiculous than an Englishman, it is an Englishman who loves Ireland." Yet, though there is usually more falsity than truth in a stereotype, there can be uplift and a modicum of truth, as in the brief profile of the typical American by the nineteenth century French cultural philosopher Alexis de Tocqueville, in one of his many stereotypes of the American: "The love of wealth is therefore to be traced, as either a principal or accessory motive, at the bottom of all that the Americans do." Thus, stereotypes are to be recognized, questioned, approved, or disapproved, with the realization that although they smooth the course of conversation, provide the muscle of all entertainment, and are the wheels on which civilizations move, they are in fact a minefield in which truth is often blown to bits or twisted into ugly-seeming reality. One must always step carefully among those explosives.

The stereotype about the evil of the lawyer goes back at least to Shakespeare. He (now she) is a friend who helps you protect yourself and your interests or a monster who invades your territory and tries to take it from you. Because of this threat and because of the effect of advertising, lawyers, like doctors, until recently have been forbidden to advertise. But in their clever ability to interpret the law to their own benefit they now are perfectly safe—and respectable—in their advertising, as the following article demonstrates.

Have You Been Injured?

The Current State of
Personal Injury Lawyers' Advertising

PEYTON PAXSON

As part of the professionalization of the legal field that began in the late nineteenth century, nearly every state licensing authority enacted prohibitions against lawyers' advertising, arguing that advertising demeaned the profession and tended to mislead consumers. Defying these restrictions, two Phoenix lawyers ran an advertisement in the *Phoenix Republic* in 1976, for which they were disciplined by the Arizona Bar. The case ended up before the U.S. Supreme Court, which held in *Bates v. State Bar of Arizona* that the First Amendment's protection of free speech also protected lawyers' advertising.

Within the decade following the *Bates* decision, nearly a third of all lawyers said that they had advertised. Of those who had advertised, 86 percent had done so in the yellow pages and 12 percent had advertised in newspapers. In 1992, lawyers spent $419 million on yellow pages advertising and almost $130 million the following year on television advertising; the president of the Association of Trial Lawyers of America estimates the current annual spending on television advertising to be $750 million. An important factor driving this advertising is the burgeoning number of American lawyers; in 1983, there were 612,000 attorneys in the United States; in 1998, there were 912,000. The growth of the profession has caused many practitioners to rely on advertising to compete and to expand the market for legal services.

The Commission on Advertising of the American Bar Association (ABA) found that the smaller the law firm, the more likely it was to advertise. For instance, while 57.5 percent of lawyers polled in a 1992 survey said they had placed display advertisements in the yellow pages, solo practitioners comprised over 40 percent of that total. Overall, law firms with three or less were responsible for nearly 60 percent of lawyers' advertising, while firms with over twenty lawyers comprised only 2 percent (ABA). This is not surprising, given the fact that most small firms and solo practitioners primarily serve individuals, while medium and large firms tend to have commercial practices.

The leading specialization among advertisers is personal injury law, its practitioners representing victims of automobile accidents, medical malpractice, and "slip and fall" injuries; a calamity for the prospective client provides a business opportunity for the legal professional. These so-called plaintiffs' attorneys, almost without exception, charge a contingent fee for their services, usually about a third of the amount recovered for their client. Since contingent fee percentages in personal injury cases are fairly uniform, there is little price competition, and indeed, much of the public perceives discount lawyers to be as trustworthy as discount sushi. Personal injury lawyers essentially offer the same product to each of their clients, obtaining money to recompense the client for his/her losses, while assuring the client that s/he deserves that cash. If money is the product of personal injury lawyers, then the service advertised is actually a standard commodity, with advertisers offering consumers neither pricing flexibility nor other bases of competitive positions. Thus, the primary objective of lawyers' advertising is establishing and maintaining name recognition, with the result that most personal injury advertising possesses facile messages (and often, simplistic production values).

Although the bulk of personal injury lawyers' advertising seems relatively crude, some sophisticated marketing research has been conducted by the organized bar (comprised of regulatory authorities such as the ABA and mandatory state regulatory authorities, both of which tend to be dominated by large firms and a status quo ideology) as well as academics and consultants. This work has investigated such factors as the demographics, channel effect, and efficacy of content. Much of the research focuses on advertising targeted at victims of automobile accidents. For instance, one marketing consultant advises: "An analysis of automobile accident statistics by state and county indicates 50–60 percent of all injury-causing accidents occur between Friday morning and midnight Sunday. Soft tissue damage produced by automobile accidents can represent up to two-thirds of all injuries. Because soft tissue injuries become symptomatic twenty-four to seventy-two hours after the accident, the audience availability begins on Monday morning and extends through Wednesday afternoon."

The consultant states that women comprise between 60 and 70 percent of those who make the initial call to a lawyer regarding automobile accident injuries, regardless of who is injured. The consulting firm points out that women with children are the predominant audience of television programming during the daytime segment, and goes on to claim that "women respond to legal ads immediately during morning viewing, but will delay calling during afternoon hours—those calls generally come in after a favorite show concludes."

A 1993 survey conducted for the ABA found that those who had the most favorable opinion of lawyers tended to be female; African American or Hispanic; with an annual family income of less than $20,000; and between the ages of eighteen and twenty-nine. Those with the least favorable opinion of lawyers tended to be male; white collar; college graduates; had an annual family income of more than $50,000; were between the ages of forty-five and fifty-nine; and received most of their information about lawyers from newspapers.

Consumers with the most favorable opinions of lawyers tended to be those that have had little or no personal contact with lawyers, and most lawyers' advertising is aimed at these first-time users of legal services. These consumers are predominately blue-collar and rely heavily on advertising to select a lawyer when they need one, citing television as their primary source of information. As one advertising consultant points out, "Your prospect from TV advertising is not just someone who needs a lawyer. Your prospect is someone who needs a lawyer and will hire one from TV. This usually means someone who does not already have a lawyer, and does not know any lawyers."

As is true of other advertised products and services, channel effect proves to be a significant factor in lawyers' advertising. Studies published in the *Georgia State University Law Review* and *Pacific Law Journal* found billboards to be the least favorable medium for generating a positive perception of lawyers among consumers. Television was almost a dead heat in the Georgia State study, generating a favorable impression among 44 percent of consumers surveyed, and an unfavorable impression among 48 percent, although the Pacific study, using a Likert scale, found largely unfavorable results for television.

Newspaper advertising did well in both surveys, but the most favorable medium for lawyers' advertising was the yellow pages. The Georgia State study found that 79 percent of those surveyed had a favorable impression of lawyers' advertising in the yellow pages and only 13 percent did not. Another study conducted for the Yellow Pages Publishers Association found that consumers are more likely to view advertisements in the yellow pages as information rather than as advertisements per se, and nine in ten consumers see lawyers' advertisement in the yellow pages as providing useful information.

Today many members of the legal profession view the yellow pages as so important to their practices that the medium has grown cluttered with dozens of pages of lawyers' advertising in many communities' telephone directories. In an effort to stand out, some lawyers have resorted to full-color advertisements, fourth (back) cover locations, tabbed advertisements, and two-page spreads. Paradoxically, the yellow pages, praised as the most dignified channel for legal advertising, have become yet another source of discomfort for the organized bar, which has traditionally asked its members to refrain from "distinctive" advertising.

Even more disconcerting to the organized bar are those lawyers who engage in brazen gimmickry. In Madison, Wisconsin, a three-hundred-pound attorney named Ken Hur, who proudly referred to himself as "the advertisingest lawyer in America," sponsored a car in a demolition derby, promoting his personal injury services for accident victims. A law firm in Los Angeles hired an actor to portray Tommy the Tortoise, who passed out handbills on Rodeo Drive. In 1999, a personal injury lawyer in Minnesota won federal court protection of his right to fly the Jolly Roger flag outside his office to promote his practice.

Advertising methods such as these continue to draw the wrath of the organized bar, which since the *Bates* decision of 1977 still carefully monitors lawyers' advertising activities and pursues alleged violators in disciplinary hearings and court trials. The United States Supreme Court has revisited the matter of lawyers' advertising several times since *Bates*, but has not significantly scaled back its holding in that case, despite repeated requests by state and local bar associations to do so. The only post-*Bates* case to limit lawyers' advertising saw the Court allow state licensing agencies to impose thirty-day waiting periods after accidents before attorneys could send direct mail to possible claimants.

On the whole, the organized bar has continued to resist lawyers' advertising in most forms, believing that advertising degrades the profession. Some reactionary factions of the organized bar have warned practitioners that although proscription of lawyers' advertising is unconstitutional, the prudent lawyer should avoid challenging state bar associations' regulatory efforts. As Albert L. Moses, at the time the ABA's Legal Economics Editor, cautioned: "Even if our local rules are more restrictive than what is constitutionally permissible, to violate local rules is to invite trouble. Lawyers who want to test unduly restrictive local rules should remember the definition of a pioneer as the person lying beside the trail with an arrow in his back. Successfully testing local rules may be personally satisfying, but how long will it take to outlive the image of a lawyer accused of unethical conduct by the local bar or court?"

On the other hand, research by the ABA's own Commission on Advertising has found that "while the legal profession strongly believes that advertising contributes to the decline of the profession's image, the public rarely mentions advertising as a factor." In addition, the Commission notes the fact that advertising by lawyers is relied upon most heavily by people of modest means and concludes, "Advertising is a viable vehicle to enable low income families to find legal representation. The importance of this finding cannot be ignored as the organized bar continues to pursue its goal of improved access to all persons regardless of their income."

Faced with such information, with the *Bates* decision still intact after nearly a quarter century, and with competitive forces in the legal profession intensifying, at least a few factions within the organized bar have gradually come to accept advertising as an immutable activity among lawyers. Rather than continue strident attempts to prohibit lawyers' advertising and marginalize advertisers, a current approach is to establish standards of accepted advertising practices. The ABA's "Aspirational Goals for Lawyer Advertising," adapted in 1988, advise that "Since advertising may be the only contact many people have with lawyers, advertising by lawyers . . . should uphold the dignity of the legal profession." The ABA goes on to counsel against "the use of inappropriately dramatic music, unseemly slogans, hawkish spokespersons, premium offers, slapstick routines or outlandish settings in advertising." Some state and local bar associations have published stylebooks with extremely conservative examples of print advertisements that are little more than traditional "tombstone" advertisements or institutional advertisements that proclaim the merits of the legal profession at large rather than the particular skills of an individual lawyer or law firm.

The advent of the Internet offers both a powerful new medium for lawyers' advertising and another source of uneasiness for the organized bar. The alleged misuse of the Internet has already led to the suspension of at least one lawyer, Laurence Canter, who maintained offices in Tennessee, Arizona, and California and sent thousands of unsolicited e-mails to listserve and usenet groups in 1994. This "spamming" prompted an immediate online "flaming" campaign against Canter, and the filing of formal complaints from as far away as Europe and Asia. Canter had also authored a book, *How to Make a Fortune on the Information Superhighway*, a fact used against him at his 1997 Tennessee disciplinary hearing.

Most attorneys who advertise on the Internet employ more subtle techniques. Soon after the October 31, 1999, crash of Egyptair flight 990 in the Atlantic Ocean, R. Jack Clapp & Associates, a Washington, D.C., law firm, registered the web domain egyptair990.com. The site purports to be sponsored by the law firm "on behalf of the victims of Flight 990 and their families." Clapp & Associates promises to update the site periodically "to provide a short and objective summary of the latest news in relation to the tragedy and the legal theories which might be used to recover from the responsible parties." The firm concludes that "those responsible for the crash need to, and will be, held accountable."

Other websites have appeared that are supported by fees or commissions from participating lawyers. These sites include Americounsel.com, promoted by celebrity law professor Arthur Miller, and TheLaw.com, featuring former New York Mayor Ed Koch; another is the tactfully named Sharktank.com. Visitors to those sites may browse through a series of articles on legal subjects, link to other legal resources, and of course locate a lawyer to represent them. Because the Internet has (arguably) only recently moved beyond the innovator and early adopter stages of consumer adoption, lawyers' advertising on the Internet tends to be more urbane than much of the lawyers' advertising in other media. This will probably change as the Internet continues its market penetration, and the demographics of Internet users broaden.

In the face of an increasingly crowded and competitive field, heavy investment by lawyers in established and emerging advertising media will continue. Lawyers will continue to rely on yellow pages advertising, in light of positive consumer reaction to lawyers' advertisements in telephone directories. Given the heavy consumption of television among the target market, television will remain a favorite medium of personal injury lawyers. The Internet will likely prove to be another important medium for lawyers as more and more households go online. Since the bulk of personal injury lawyers' advertising continues to target working-class consumers who are first-time users of legal services, there seems to be little reason to expect advertising messages to evolve much beyond their current rather unsophisticated state.

From *Journal of Popular Culture* 36, no. 2 (Fall 2002). Reprinted, without bibliographical information, with permission of the author.

SUGGESTIONS FOR FURTHER STUDY

1. Has your opinion of lawyers and the laws they write been changed by this article?
2. If you were a juryperson on a case involving personal injury would you be inclined to award the person vast sums of money (say in the millions) just so you could "stick it to" the big wealthy company who can afford the cost?
3. Some lawyers have achieved great reputations mainly by getting wealthy as trial lawyers. Would you listen to their counsel and the lobby they generate to give them more power in government?
4. Lawyers—all the way from Congress down to your local attorney—write laws for the nation to follow. Knowing that, do you have more respect for the laws of the land?
5. If you needed a lawyer, where would you look for him or her? In the yellow pages or elsewhere?

Some of the most severe criticism of dramatic entertainment today is directed at the television soap opera. Its critics say that the characters are unnatural and unrealistic, the episodes are repetitious and simplistic, and the behavior presents dangerous portraits for average citizens, mostly women. *Days of Our Lives* has been one of the more popular soap operas for ten years. The following digest of scripts reveals the development of this particular "soap."

Days of Our Lives

Belle Learns That John Is a Spy . . .

Philip informs John that he can get information on Maya by using Shawn. John notes that Victor might be involved in the diamond smuggling, but Phil is ready to bring down his dad. Later, Philip prods Shawn about Maya. . . . Belle vows to find out what's up with Philip. She follows him to the pier; Shawn tails Belle.

DiMera Image

At the police station, Cassie is freaked about Rex's reveal that Roman is their pop. Cassie is brought in for her arraignment; she blurts out "my father" when she sees Roman, but then recovers. Tony learns that Maya has been playing him. He asks Rex to go into the diamond business with him. . . . Rex has Mimi collect data so he can uncover who his mom is.

Ice Princess

Brady moves into the Kiriakis manse. Larry's henchman, Russell, plans to move Rolf's body and meets with Nicole in the stables. Brady thinks that they're having an affair. Later, Nicole lures Larry's police escort off the road, while Russell gets Larry out of the car. Russell swaps bodies and sets the car on fire. Larry vows to make good on his promise to kill Victor.

The Write Stuff

Tony goes to see Sami at the hospital. She tells him, via writing on a white board, to go to hell. Tony then asks her to recover in his mansion, but she refuses. . . . Lucas kisses Cassie, but pulls away when she wants to sleep with him. Cassie then picks up a man at the Brady Pub; John stops them. An angry Cassie says that Marlena's not her mother. . . . Sami dreams that Tony tries to kill her and Lucas rescues her. Later, a visiting Lucas admits he wishes that he'd saved her; they share a hug.

Salem Scene

Jack is led to believe that Jennifer is pregnant, but she denies it. . . . Hope learns that she has no trust-fund money. . . . Vin threatens Bo. Later, Bo and Hope follow a perp, Jesse, and fight him.

Body of Evidence

Nicole hides Larry in the Kiriakis stables. She then takes a shower; Brady walks in on her. She tries to seduce him, but he urges her not to use her body. Later, Larry insists that Nic have sex with him, but she heeds Brady's advice and refuses. She begs Brady to persuade Victor to let her go to the Blue Note.

Going Overboard

Phil trails Maya to a ship; Belle surprises him on-board. Shawn is almost caught by a henchman, but knocks him out. Maya picks up vials of mysterious goop, then hears Belle and drops one. Shawn distracts Maya by calling out to her. Phil discovers diamonds and collects some goop. As he and Belle leave, they're held at gunpoint by some thugs; Philip fights them, but Belle is injured. She recovers in time to knock out their attacker with a cargo hook. They escape through a porthole. . . . Shawn and Maya meet at the Brady Pub. She wants to be alone, but John interrupts them. Soon, Tony arrives. John asks about Maya, but Tony lies that she is an antiques dealer. Alone, Tony discusses business with her; he informs Rex and Lucas that she's double crossing them. Tony urges Rex to speed up the diamond-making process so he can make a purchase. They make plans to send the laser to South America. . . . John threatens to get Phil out of the ISA, but Philip states that he completed the mission. Belle hears them talking and learns that John's a spy. After, Belle finds Shawn with Maya at the Pub and wants answers.

From *Soap Opera Digest,* July 8, 2003. Reprinted with permission.

SUGGESTIONS FOR FURTHER STUDY

1. Watch a soap opera—preferably *Days of Our Lives*—and see what characteristics of the stereotype, both in plot and action, it contains.
2. What are the strengths and weaknesses of this kind of stereotypical entertainment? Is there risk in so much real or implied sex and danger?
3. What harm or good does such entertainment provide?
4. If soap operas are easy to write, could you provide one?

FORMULA

Formula is one of those general categories which cover a large movement. Formula is something like a cooking recipe. It outlines the ingredients to be used in the cooking and generally how they are to be mixed and cooked. Or more properly, perhaps, formula is like a road map. It tells in general where one wants to go and what roads to use to make the journey. Formula is somewhat similar to myth, at least in some of its generalizations. That is, stories and behaviors have been developed around mythological creatures and people. Myth develops its characters in a way common to all: miraculous birth, outstanding mental or physical achievements, beneficial results to society as a whole, and a mysterious (usually youthful) death which promises a return when the mythological character is needed.

John Cawelti, one of the leading authorities on the subject of formula, theorized in *The Six-Gun Mystique* (Popular Press, 1970) that formula is a sophistication and narrowing of the concept of myth into the realization that all cultural expressions develop in a mixture of the old and new, the well established and the newly developing, that is, conventions and inventions. Conventions are the framework on which much or most of the cultural product develops and depends; inventions are new and develop in different and new ways, and in so doing advance the general body of convention one step. Convention provides stability to the cultural aspects of life; invention, although it tends to de-establish, does so only so that new conventions can be tested and worked out.

All cultural expressions, especially those having to do with the common aspects of life, combine convention and invention. Some people condemn the former and praise only the latter. Others realize that both are necessary for the order and stability of culture, and neither is superior to or inferior to the other. They are simply different, serve different purposes; to wish for the dissolution of convention in the interests of invention is to ask for the dangerous deregulation of orderly culture. In the essays in this book you will be asked to examine these concepts and decide where reality and truth lie.

The following essay about the western genre demonstrates how formulaic stories depend on universal myths, motifs, and conventions as bases for their development and invention. The essay also demonstrates the universality of the conventions for their general appeal and intercultural appeal. The same conventions are the bedrock of all popular literature and of most activities of life. In effect, the romance, crime novel, adventure novel, and all others are like the western; only the names, characters, and atmosphere are different. They grow out of the cultures that support them and reflect those cultures but their underlying roots tie all of them into one life-support system.

Dick Francis's Six-Gun Mystique

RACHEL SCHAFFER

In *The Six-Gun Mystique,* John Cawelti analyzes the conventions and themes of the western genre, including how the types of characters help create the familiar patterns that make this genre unique. He describes the tripartite division of characters found in the typical western: the townspeople, representing the advance of civilization into the wilderness; the Indian or outlaw, representing the lawlessness, violence, freedom, and male camaraderie being encroached upon; and the hero, serving as mediator between and possessing qualities of both of the other groups. The hero may be a lawman, gunman, or cowboy, with special survival skills and a capacity for violence that the more domestic and peaceful townspeople initially disapprove of but inevitably discover they need. He also holds a sympathetic view of the goals of the townspeople, i.e., of the advance of civilization itself. The hero's role in the western, as Cawelti describes it, is therefore as a middle-man, in a "mediating role . . . between civilization and savagery."

The close relationship between the cowboy hero and the private detective has been noted by more than one critic of the mystery genre. George Grella, for example, states the parallel broadly: "The private detective of the hard-boiled thriller is yet another version of the cowboy who symbolizes the pastoral dream of America." Glenwood Irons observes that "the popular representation of this male detective-as-urban-cowboy who stands out against the rottenness of society has a powerful appeal. From the outside, he restores order in the midst of the murderous chaos to which we are exposed in the popular media . . . and carries the work of the Western hero into twentieth-century urban centers." And T. J. Binyon observes more specifically that in order to create Race Williams, one of the earliest private eyes in fiction, Carroll John Daly "simply moved the cowboy hero off the prairie and on to the streets of New York or Chicago."

While the setting and themes of Dick Francis's British racing mysteries are half a world away from those of a typical western—and almost as far removed from those of a hard-boiled American private eye novel, as well—there are some striking similarities between a Francis protagonist and a western hero. If honesty and integrity are seen as signs of civilization, while violence and crime represent a mental and emotional wilderness, then the Francis hero, like the western hero before him, can be seen as mediating between the two, supporting the victory of civilized behavior over criminal savagery. Both western and Francis heroes are often outsiders, usually arriving on the scene from elsewhere and, in Francis's novels, also exhibiting attitudes, values, class characteristics, or personal traits that separate (and usually alienate) them from those around them. In addition, both types of hero at times clearly do not fit in with the "townspeople" populating the story yet have skills that others lack and need to solve the central plot conflict. In a Francis novel, those skills, as with the western hero, usually include physical prowess and fighting ability (or at least stamina and an impressive ability to withstand pain), but they also extend at least as often to internal strengths such as tenacity, honor, integrity, cleverness, confidence, and modesty, strengths which are even more sorely needed in the protagonist's role as mediator and problem-solver in a time and place far different from the American Old West. The six-gun mystique of a Francis hero is loaded not with bullets but with the kind of personality traits that enable him to comply with modern limitations on violent actions and still emerge victorious.

The majority of Francis novels are set in England, and the townspeople of the small frontier settlements of the western find a modern realization in the racing communities that support the Francis hero in whatever occupation he happens to hold in a particular novel, often jockey or trainer in the earlier mysteries, but expanded to a wide variety of professions (architect, painter, wine merchant, etc.) only tangentially related to the racing community in the later ones. Just as the western's townspeople need protection from a threat of violence, so too does Francis's racing community need protection from a villain threatening the well-being of the racing game in some fashion.

Cawelti describes the "basic situation which various Western plots tend to embody" as developing out of "the epic moment when the values and disciplines of American society stand balanced against the savage wilderness." The conflict between society and wilderness gives rise to a "formulaic pattern of action," involving the elements of capture, flight, and pursuit in various permutations. The hero's role in the pattern is as a supporter of "the agents and values of civilization." serving in the process as protector, rescuer, and destroyer of evil.

These elements of plot and the hero's role as protector can be seen in many of Francis's novels, especially where horses are concerned. David Brion Davis describes the cowboy's horse as "his link with the cavaliere and plumed knight" of medieval chivalry and states that the cowboy's "love for and close relationship with his horse . . . show his respect for propriety and order." In this framework, the "horse thief becomes a symbol of concentrated evil" by threatening the desired social order. The same symbolism and a close relationship between protagonist and horse can be seen in the majority of Francis novels. The well-being of the race horses, even more than the jockeys, is of paramount importance to any Francis protagonist, and the integrity of the races they run in comes a very close second. In *Dead Cert*, for example, the protagonist, jockey Alan York, discovers and puts an end to a conspiracy to pay off jockeys to stop horses from winning, spurred to investigate by the death of a close friend whose horse was tripped in mid-steeplechase when he refused to go along with the plot. There is also a chase involved as the hero takes off cross country on a steeplechase, pursued by the gang of crooked taxi-drivers who do the villain's dirty work. At the very end of the novel, during a race, Alan has a chance to punish one of the worst of the villain-jockeys, but he expresses reservations that reflect the basic integrity that goes along with his role as protector of the racing game: "I had got to unseat him without hurting his horse. I was being unfair enough already to the owner in trying to lose him the race by dislodging his jockey: if I could not do it without damaging his horse, I must not do it at all."

For Kicks also centers around a threat to horses, this time in a plot by a trainer determined to turn winning races into a sure thing. His technique, as protagonist Daniel Roke discovers, is to condition horses through a fright reflex, using a flamethrower to singe their hind legs and provide a burst of adrenalin that later, when triggered during races by a high-frequency dog whistle only the horses can hear, gives them a winning edge. Daniel spies on one conditioning session, and his deep love and concern for horses is clearly expressed by his reaction to the villains' close use of the flamethrower on the horse being trained: "I nearly cried out, as if it were I that was being burned, not the horse."

Odds Against and *Decider,* on the other hand, offer examples of the protagonist taking action to protect racecourses, rather than horses, but the threat to the racing community remains the overarching theme. In *Odds Against,* ex-jockey Sid Halley is recruited by his ex-father-in-law to discover and foil the plans of businessman Howard Kraye to sabotage Seabury Race Course so he can take it over to sell for housing, as he had done earlier to another racecourse. In *Decider,* the threat comes from a member of the wealthy Stratton family, which owns Stratton Racecourse. Some of the family members want to sell the racecourse, and one of them actively sabotages the course's grandstands by blowing up a section of them. Architect Lee Morris, who holds shares in the racecourse, is brought in by the course manager and the Clerk of the Course to try to "knock some sense into them" and save the course.

Knockdown offers a different segment of the racing community in need of protection and rescue: horse owners and breeders are being scammed by crooked bloodstock agents, who demand kickbacks for working together to bid up the price of horses at auction. In this story, agent Jonah Dereham truly seems like the one honest man awash in a sea of criminals. He refuses to go along with the gang of crooks, even when he is physically attacked and his stable and house set on fire. Jonah acknowledges the ambiguity of some of the common fiddles in the business, observing that "sometimes it was difficult to perceive the honest course, and more difficult still to stick to it, when what I saw as dishonesty was so much the general climate." He also admits "that dishonesty was much a matter of opinion. There were no absolutes. A deal I thought scandalous might seem eminently reasonable to others."

However, just like the cowboy hero of the Old West, who Davis says "values his code of honor and his friends more than possessions," Jonah has a strict code of honor of his own that prevents him from going along with the thugs and harming the integrity of the racing game. He sees first and foremost not the opportunities to get rich but the unfairness of the kickback system and the harm it does in particular to small horse breeders and buyers. In the kind of laconic understatement so typical of Francis heroes—and the western cowboy—Jonah tells another agent, "I don't like what they're doing" and affirms to readers the bloodstock agent's "duty to the seller." His refusal to go along with the crooked practices of his colleagues costs him a dislocated shoulder, part of his home, and his brother's life, but he stands by his values, unwilling to sacrifice his integrity and the well-being of the racing community for mere monetary gain.

Whether it is horses, racecourses, or some human segment of the racing community that needs saving from the forces of evil, in each and every case it is the Francis hero who rides to the rescue (sometimes literally), not with guns blazing, but with a full complement of more abstract cowboy-style skills and traits at his disposal, parallel to Cawelti's description of the hero: "a horseman . . . possess[ing] skills of wilderness existence." The "horseman" trait—being able to ride well and having a love for horses—is an obvious similarity between cowboy and Francis hero: most Francis heroes work in some segment of the racing business or were raised around it, and almost all of them have a great deal of riding experience.

The "skills of wilderness existence" are a less obvious area of similarity between the two types of heroes, however. Some obvious survival skills differ: while cowboys are noted for their ability to live off the land and use firearms, Francis protagonists are rarely called on to participate in cattle drives or gun battles, and no Francis protagonist carries a gun. However, there is one Francis protagonist who possesses a great many survival skills: John Kendall of *Longshot,* who writes "travel guides to harsh terrains" and knows all about surviving in all kinds of wilderness. His expertise enables him to spot the clues and eventually solve the novel's central mystery. Edward Lincoln in *Smokescreen* also remembers enough basic survival tips to live through three and a half days in the South African wilderness with an empty plastic baggie and a rubber band as his only resources.

Although Francis protagonists operate in a different time and place from the cowboys of the nineteenth century Old West, their attitudes toward violence, as part of their moral code, are much alike. The western hero, Glenwood Irons says, "only reacts to violence and is not the cause of it," and Cawelti says, "The cowboy hero does not seek out combat for its own sake and . . . typically shows an aversion to the wanton shedding of blood." Most Francis heroes are reluctant to get into a physical fight (although they hold their own when pushed to it) let alone kill someone—not just because of the modern legal ramifications of such an act, but because, for the most part, their own moral codes forbid the use of violence to solve their problems except as a last resort. Thus Jonah Dereham, the *Knockdown* bloodstock agent, when faced with a safe opportunity to finish off the villain who has just killed his brother, is tempted but refrains: "The urge to finish off what I'd started was almost overwhelming. . . . Killing someone who was to trying to kill you was justifiable in law, and who was to guess that I'd killed him ten minutes later? The moment passed. I felt cold suddenly, and old and lonely and as tired as dust. I stretched out a hand to the telephone, to call the cops." Granted, a few Francis heroes have killed a villain out of necessity or by accident—like the western hero, "killing is an act forced upon [them]"—and one, Henry Grey in *Flying Finish,* actually kills a cold-blooded killer in cold blood, but their survival skills take different forms from the cowboy's, helping them to cope better as *victims* of violence than as perpetrators of it; as Marty Knepper puts it, "They suffer a great deal of violence but administer very little." All are true fighters in more psychological ways: they aren't easily intimidated, have endless resources of stamina, endurance, and tolerance for pain, and they never give up. Time after time in Francis's novels, a seriously hurt protagonist manages to hang on long enough to be rescued, to reach help, and above all, to protect the innocent and keep safe crucial information that the villains need.

A vivid set-piece involving this kind of self-sacrificing suffering and endurance is described in loving detail in *Smokescreen.* Actor Edward Lincoln has gone to South Africa to investigate the poor performance of horses owned by a close friend and at one point is handcuffed to the steering wheel of a car abandoned in the wilderness, left to die. Like a cowboy of old, he draws on his inner reserves of strength and stamina, as well as his knowledge of survival skills, to survive for three and a half days until help comes. And then, in order to lure the villain back to the scene and obtain sufficient evidence to convict him, he further sacrifices his own comfort by refusing to wash or change his clothes and returns the next day to face the ordeal of being handcuffed to the steering wheel once again; he confesses, "The hardest thing I ever did was to get back into that car."

Sid Halley, ex-jockey turned detective, is probably the most archetypal Francis hero and the one best illustrating a range of traditional cowboy characteristics. In each of the three novels he stars in, he exhibits stoicism at its most heroic and self-sacrificing. In *Odds Against*, he faces sadistic villains who smash his previously crippled wrist "to smithereens" in an effort to extract information from him, inflicting pain worse than any he has experienced; even then, in order to convince his captors that they have finally broken him, he still hesitates, bringing himself yet more pain, before telling them where to go—straight into a trap. As a true hero, he is willing to accept the price of losing his hand in order to protect others.

In both sequels, *Whip Hand* and *Come to Grief*, Sid undergoes similar threats to his one remaining hand; facing a life of helplessness, his single biggest fear, he still refuses to give in to the villains' demands and to his own fear. Like the laconic cowboy, use of silence is not just a personality trait but one of Sid's strongest weapons, employed over and over again in his job, to protect clients and the racing industry, and in his private life, to hide his fears and insecurities from the outside world because, as he says succinctly, "I don't like pity."

The villain in *Come to Grief* says Sid's nickname from his racing days is "'Tungsten Carbide'—that's the hardest of all metals and it saws through steel." Although Sid says that he feels just the opposite, that he has "water in [his] veins," it is his silent stoicism in the face of danger and his refusal to compromise his own strict moral code that give him his reputation for unbreakable toughness. Sid's ex-father-in-law once told him that "I had a vision of honor that made my life a purgatory and I'd said he was wrong, and that purgatory was abandoning your vision of honor and knowing you'd done it. 'Only for you, Sid,' he'd said. 'The rest of the world has no difficulty at all.'" Exactly: that difference in adherence to a moral code is what sets a Francis hero—and the cowboy hero—apart from the rest of society.

The code of honor of the Francis protagonist and the role of silence as part of it can also be seen in how he uses the information he discovers about the crime being investigated. In most of the novels, the hero uses his hard-won evidence to bring the villain(s) to justice, as in *Odds Against* or *Driving Force*. But in others, he uses his own sound moral sense to decide when more damage would be done to the innocent by revealing the truth, as in *Longshot* or *Decider*, where the villains can do no more harm and family members would only be hurt by learning what they had done. John Kendall in *Longshot* explains his decision to remain silent and keep the now-dead murderer's secret: "No child would become a secure and balanced adult with a known murderer for a father.... All of them [the family] would live more happily if they and the world remained in ignorance, and to try to achieve that I would give them the one gift I could. Silence."

Finally, the mediating role of the western hero can be seen literally in several Francis novels. Cawelti's description of "the most basic definition of the hero role in the Western," "the figure who resolves the conflict between" two groups, also fits the Francis hero as representative of the typical detective, by definition one who finds the link between criminals and the innocent. In the case of Francis heroes, they usually take on the role of mediator with reluctance, but their firm moral code compels them to do what they see as right—they cannot just stand by and do nothing. The fact that many of them are also outsiders in some sense, whether because of family, professional, or ethical differences from the other characters, makes them even more likely candidates as mediators, since they are more likely to be objective observers detached from the emotional connections that may blind members of the other groups and therefore be better able to detect clues and decide how to handle evidence.

Jonah Dereham in *Knockdown* and Lee Morris in *Decider* are quintessential mediators. Rather than resort to violence and illegal tactics to fight back against the ring of crooked bloodstock agents who are trying to coerce him into joining them, Jonah attempts instead to "negotiate for permanent peace" by working out a complicated arrangement in which some minor villains escape punishment in exchange for information he can use to blackmail the ringleaders into not only leaving him alone but also ending their criminal activities.

Lee Morris, the architect who renovates ruins and saves Stratton Racecourse from being sold, is misleadingly big and strong, making people think he wins arguments through brute force. Lee, however, knows otherwise: "There were times when to tread softly and shrink one's shoulder-span produced more harmonious results, and I leaned by nature more to the latter course. Lethargic, my wife called me. Too lazy to fight. Too placid. But the ruins got restored and left no trails of rancor in local officials' minds, and I'd learned how to get around most planning officers with conciliation and reason." It is these qualities, plus a great deal of self-restraint under provocation, that eventually win most of the Stratton family over. Although Lee is at first reluctant to be drawn into the affairs of the family his mother had warned him to stay away from, he eventually agrees to try, attracted by the thought "that I might against all the odds tame the dragon and sort out the Stratton feuds peacefully"—the voice of a natural-born mediator.

There are, of course, a number of basic differences between the Francis hero and the frontier hero, as well as between him and the classic hard-boiled detective, for where, as Grella says, the latter excels at *both* "dealing out and absorbing great quantities of punishment" and "requires physical rather than intellectual ability," the Francis hero is more complex, intelligent, pacifist, and above all vulnerable—and far more willing to *admit* his vulnerability and weaknesses. He lives in a different time and place from cowboys and hard-boiled dicks, and his coping strategies differ accordingly—but they are just as effective at achieving his goals of righting wrongs and re-establishing order.

The parallels between western heroes and detectives have been noted in countless critical articles over the years, and Francis, although coming from a background far removed from both westerns and hard-boiled detective fiction, captures those qualities of the hero that appeal widely to readers and that underlie both westerns and mysteries—those that Davis claims form "an expression of common ideals of morality and behavior." Whether the protagonist is a western, hard-boiled, or Francis hero, it is his courage, physical skills, personal integrity, and willingness to do things in the cause of justice that go beyond the capabilities of the average person that make him someone to admire, respect, and emulate. Both westerns and mysteries provide fertile ground for the blossoming of heroic qualities, and in both genres the goals are the same: to further the cause of civilization and protect the innocent from harm. [Dixon] Wecter sees the hero's "overruling passion" as "a sense of duty," and judging by the actions and sentiments of so many Francis protagonists—honorable men doing their best to resolve conflicts and protect the innocent—Francis would agree.

From *Clues: A Journal of Detection* 21, no. 2 (2000). Reprinted, without bibliographical information, with permission of the author.

SUGGESTIONS FOR FURTHER STUDY

1. It is generally agreed that crime fiction, especially the so-called hard-boiled type, is western fiction moved into urban districts. Is the strength of western fiction and crime fiction its using as its roots folk and mythological background and bases?
2. Read one of the Francis novels and see if the author of this article has read it properly.
3. Read one of the classic hard-boiled crime stories and compare its bases and development to a western story you know.
4. Increasingly critics are insisting that there is no difference between formula-fiction and so-called elite stories except in perhaps artificial aspects. Read a crime novel or western and compare it to one of the best-sellers or most highly respected novels of today and make your own comparisons and evaluations.

RITES AND RITUALS

Rituals are stereotypes and icons in action. They are segments of our patterns of behavior which we have inherited and practice and pass on to our descendants. Like most aspects of life, rituals are both secular and religious. Religious rituals are held sacred, or at least semi-sacred. Secular rituals are passages from one stage of life to another—such earth-bound activities as passing from childhood to adulthood, graduating from high school, entering a profession.

Rites are used to strengthen actions, sometimes consciously, sometimes almost unconsciously. Though they occur in all institutions, they are particularly apparent in sports, where they are strengthened by financial backing. Professional football, which culminates in Super Bowl Sunday, is perhaps the most obvious example of how sports takes on the flavor of religion and has come to replace religion on the Sabbath. It is interesting and significant that the following article occurs on the religion page of the newspaper from which it is taken.

Religious Fervor Is Building for Pro-Football Fans

Pageantry, Ritual of Big Game Have Spiritual Tone, Experts Say

JUDY TARJANJI

A super-sized religious event is about to occur in American life, antici-pated by millions with the kind of eagerness felt by children before Christmas.

It is Super Bowl Sunday, that annual ritual exalting sport, muscle mass, and territorial conquest and celebrating everything Americans truly love: entertainment, food, athletic competition, gambling, excess, and consumption.

The day on which some churches even cancel their evening services to accommodate the Big Game packs enough symbolism, pageantry, and ritual to make it a significant religious festival for American culture, said Joseph L. Price, author and editor of *From Season to Season: Sports as American Religion,* and a professor of religious studies at California's Whittier College.

"It's more than a sporting event," said Dr. Price, a sports fan who has been to seven Super Bowls. He sees in the annual championship game and its attendant hoopla a convergence of symbols from sports, entertainment, and the corporate world that give the entire event a highly religious flavor.

Add to that the way Americans show their faith in a particular team by wagering large sums of money on the game's outcome, and you have the makings of a religious experience accessible to millions of people.

Dr. Michael Marsden [provost and vice president, Saint Norbert College, De Pere, Wisconsin] also considers Super Bowl Sunday a sacred national celebration. He thinks it evolved because it fills a gap in the American holiday cycle between Christmas and New Year's and Valentine's Day.

"I've said for a number of years now that if Super Bowl didn't exist, it would have to be invented.

"It was created to sell TV time, but if you think about it in terms of a whole culture that needs to celebrate cyclical events, this is one of the most significant sporting events because it is equal to the World Series in draw. Also, it's closure to a season and a bridge between holidays. So it has all those things going for it. The only surprise to me is why as a culture we didn't do something about that earlier."

Dr. Marsden said the Super Bowl has become a quasi-religious event because Americans take their sports so seriously.

"If you listen to the hushed tones of the announcers prior to the game, you'd think they were announcing Midnight Mass from Holy Name Cathedral in Chicago. It's that level of awe and all that goes with it."

Bob Bentz, a producer for the Sports Spectrum Christian radio show, said he even has noticed commentators using religious imagery in their play-by-play. For example, he said, commentators will talk about the contest being a "David and Goliath" match. "The hyperbole is thrown around quite easily and often includes biblical references, whether they know it or not."

Dr. Marsden, a former professor at Bowling Green State University, said he considers it significant that the game takes place on a Sunday, the traditional day of rest for Christians.

"It consumes a Sunday and the Sabbath is given to celebration, not rest and reflection. That's the other side of traditional Sunday activities. . . . I would not want to count on having a large church attendance Sunday evening."

Rather than compete with Super Bowl, many churches decide to bow to the game.

In his latest book, Dr. Price traces decisions to cancel or change the times of Sunday services because of the Super Bowl to the late 1960s in Richmond, Virginia. There, he said, "They changed the time of the services to accommodate deacons who wanted to see the game. Actually, I think the pastor wanted to see the game. But there was a shift early on."

Dr. Price said such cultural accommodations by churches are not new and also have been seen in a trend toward holding Sunday morning services earlier so that congregation members can eat out afterward, have more leisure time on Sunday afternoon, or in the case of churches in Dallas, to get home in time to see the Cowboys on TV.

In recent years, some churches have gotten into the spirit of the Super Bowl themselves by holding their own parties. A few even capitalize on Super Bowl fever by seizing the occasion to pitch an evangelistic messages to fans.

Locally, the Rev. Richard Isaiah, director of the Fellowship of Christian Athletes in Northwest Ohio, will give a halftime talk at a Super Bowl outreach for youth at Berean Fellowship in Point Place.

Also, through an eight-year-old program developed by Sports Outreach America, churches and other groups can sponsor "Power to Win" parties at which fans gather to watch the game and view a Christian sports video during halftime.

Since the program started, more than fifty-five thousand people have made faith commitments at such parties, 70 percent of which were in churches. Michael Wozniak, executive director of Sports Outreach America, said about three thousand of the parties are expected to be held tomorrow for about two hundred thousand people.

"We're trying to show people that you can take [the Super Bowl] and use it as a ministry opportunity," he said.

This year's twelve-minute Power to Win video will feature testimonies from Aeneas Williams of the St. Louis Rams and Darrell Green of the Washington Redskins. "Unfortunately, we have to make decisions about the video at the beginning of the season," Mr. Wozniak said. "This year of all years, we guessed wrong. We bombed and we're showing two players for teams that didn't even make the playoffs."

Mr. Wozniak said fans who are invited to such parties are told up-front that the video will be shown. "We don't try to ambush anybody. . . . In no way, shape, or form do they come in the door and we lock the door behind them and hit them over the head with a Bible. This is nonthreatening, friendship-style evangelism."

The idea, he said, is to have friends watch the game together. "At the same time, we want to show that to many of these athletes, there's something more important than winning a Super Bowl ring and that's having eternal life and a relationship with Christ."

Dr. Price said the phenomenon of using or expressing faith as an athlete is part of a movement known as "muscular Christianity." "It's not a new phenomenon. [Evangelist] Billy Sunday was one of its archetypes at the turn of the twentieth century, but it is not uncommon for sports to become a vehicle for expressing faith."

He said although Christianity is the most prominent religion in many sports, increasingly a number of Jewish athletes have used their success in sports as a forum for expressing faith.

In studying the relationship between religion and sport, he said, he has sometimes been accused of being sacrilegious. "I'm not trying to belittle religion or elevate sport; instead, I'm trying to help us understand what it is about human behavior that might be inclined toward religious behavior. If we can more thoroughly understand the devotion of people to causes, and teams, and identified religious traditions, then perhaps we can make better progress and move towards justice and peace."

From *Toledo Blade*, January 25, 2003. Reprinted with permission.

SUGGESTIONS FOR FURTHER STUDY

1. What do you see in the future if sports—especially professional sports—and religion continue to merge into one form of activity?
2. Celebrity worship of sports giants may be blinding and coercive. Are your favorite heroes from the sports world?
3. Do the women in the class see that women sports figures are in fact liberating for women and a kind of effective feminism?

More serious—religious—rituals are so-called rites of passage, those religious or semi-religious events in life that mark the passage from one natural stage to another: birth, christening (if it is done in a family), religious conversion, finally death.

Death, since it is the termination of life, the closing of the chapter that opened with birth, and the opening of the big question of what follows, is especially awesome, dreadful to some of us, promising to the religious. Throughout history, it seems, civilizations have varied in the way they buried their dead but have always made it into a meaningful and impressive ceremony. Especially well known for their preoccupation with death and the hereafter were the ancient Egyptians, the South American Mayans, and the Incas because they thought of death as the passage to life in a hereafter.

Americans too have always been preoccupied with the hereafter. For religious or other reasons, Americans have been reluctant to consign the dead body to the earth and oblivion. Before the Civil War the matter of death and consignment of the corpse was largely a domestic and private affair. People "sat up" with a corpse at night to make sure it was dead (often bodies went prematurely to the grave), to protect it from evil spirits, and to show a certain amount of respect for the dead. A ceremony at home or church was followed by a graveside ceremony, where a short sermon was preached, grief was expressed, and the casket was covered. Though the ceremony seemed directed toward the expression of grief only, sometimes it had a practical purpose of deterring robbers who stole corpses and sold them for medical studies.

During the Civil War professionals began to take over the care of corpses. Nowadays disposition of corpses is left to funeral homes, many of which charge excessively high prices that take advantage of the emotions and weaknesses of the bereaved at a particularly vulnerable time.

Looking back into America's past is becoming increasingly popular, urged by professional historians and others interested in what history can teach us about today and tomorrow. Sometimes this study seems to get off track and become more interested in objects than in what they can teach about the society that used them. Antiques, for example, which are promoted by dealers and at least one national TV show, must be in perfect shape to be valuable; that is, they are art objects rather than cultural artifacts. Archaeology, paleontology, Egyptology, and numerous other scientific disciplines use objects—especially those of the Egyptians and South American Mayans and Incas—to reveal the secrets of the past.

Such things as headstones and antiques can tell us much about our history. As in Egypt many American headstones have disappeared, but maybe it is not too late to hear the whispers echoing down the corridors of time among the ghosts that inhabited them. Care of the corpse and satisfaction to the bereaved has always been for the benefit of the latter, driven only partially by the need to dispose of the corpse. In the last decade or two of the twentieth century some funeral homes offered drive-by viewing, whereby people need not leave their automobiles in order to pay their respects. At the beginning of the twenty-first century one funeral director, in order to increase his already fantastically high income, suggested "theme funerals" at which the total environment (as at a theme park) would reflect the personality of the deceased. Thus, if the deceased had been a great sports fan, the funeral might have a sports theme, with sports memorabilia (rented at very high cost) strewn around the room. If the deceased happened to like food (or the bereaved liked food) it might be appropriate to have a banquet theme at the side of the casket. And so on. As one proponent suggested, the theme funeral suggests futurity and relieves the pain of the occasion. In a fast society that demands newness, perhaps it not surprising to see innovation in the final and unalterable act on earth.

Forgotten Cemeteries Unearth Buried Treasures

LIZ SIDOTI

POWELL, OHIO. Amid long grass and fallen leaves three small, moss-covered stone tablets poke crookedly from a rolling pasture where New Case's three children were buried in the 1840s.

Little is known about Case, a farmer who was the original settler of part of southern Delaware County. However, the tiny cemetery gives clues to three tragedies in his life—sons Ervin and Martin and an unnamed infant all died before age two.

"Who were you? What did you do? Why were you here? Those are all the questions these little places can help us answer about those who came before us," writer Judy Brozek said as she bent down to examine the intricate carvings on the stones. Brozek has researched the seventeen Liberty Township cemeteries near her home in Powell.

It is unknown how many similar small cemeteries have been destroyed since the state was founded two hundred years ago or how many still exist but have not been discovered. Preservationists working to locate, protect, and restore them say the cost is lost history. "They tell our individual stories of ancestry but they also tell the one story we all have in common—the history of the state," said Melanie Pratt, a state historic preservation officer.

In September, a legislative committee began examining whether Ohio should create a program to preserve cemeteries and unmarked human burial grounds. Such a program is unlikely any time soon because the state has little money for such projects.

Because there is no statewide preservation effort, local community groups and individuals have taken the lead in preserving cemeteries throughout the state, especially those where veterans and notable Ohioans are buried.

The Ohio Genealogical Society, which has spent the past thirty years locating cemeteries, says there are at least sixteen thousand in Ohio.

The state did not keep track of the graveyards until a law passed in the mid-1990s required all active cemeteries—those with burials in the past twenty-five years—to register annually beginning in 1995.

About 3,300 cemeteries are registered, meaning that an estimated 12,700 are inactive.

Thousands of those are pioneer and soldier graveyards from the 1800s with no more than a dozen burial plots. Families who had buried their own on their property eventually left such cemeteries behind.

Under Ohio law, ownership fell to local governments, which often were not aware such cemeteries existed or that they had become responsible for upkeep, such as mowing lawns and fixing broken headstones.

"So many have been lost or forgotten," said Lolita Guthrie, a Bowling Green resident who is the Ohio Genealogical Society's state cemetery chairwoman. "Part of the reason is that society is so transient now. Families used to go back and take care of their plots, but that doesn't happen in a modern generation."

The plots have been discovered through the years as the state grew. While some cemeteries have disappeared as housing subdivisions, golf courses, and office complexes have been built, others have been saved and—in some cases—restored by developers.

In Cuyahoga County, Carnegie Management Co. built a shopping center around a Middleburg Heights cemetery that has at least seven graves, including those of the Hickox family—the city's first settlers— and a Civil War veteran.

Once an overgrown plot fifteen hundred feet from the nearest road, the cemetery is in the middle of a parking lot and has a wrought-iron fence, glossy markers, and trimmed landscaping.

"It was either move the cemetery, and I don't think anyone wanted that, or fix it up," said Rustom Khouri, the company's president. "We're good neighbors. We try to do right by the community . . . even if it looks a little odd sometimes."

Preservationists say the cemeteries must be protected because a headstone may be the sole record of a person's life, especially if the person lived in the nineteenth century, when paper birth and death records often were unintentionally lost or destroyed.

In Cleveland, the Erie Street Cemetery dates to the 1820s and is considered to be the city's oldest.

It has the remains and memorials of some of the city's first families.

"It's the only physical evidence left for the people who first settled Cleveland," said Katie Karrick, who has been dubbed "The Cemetery Lady" because of her nationally distributed historic cemetery newsletter, "Tomb with a View." "Their houses are gone. Their possessions are gone. Their little hamlet is gone. All that is left is a stone with their name on it.

"If we don't keep that type of history up close in the front of our minds, we're going to lose sight of where the city has come from," said Karrick, also founder of the fledgling Ohio Cemetery Preservation Society.

In Sinking Spring in Highland County, Nick Ewing has led a massive cleanup of the Governor Byrd Cemetery, where Charles Willing Byrd, the governor of the Northwest Territory in 1802, and thirteen Civil War veterans are buried.

"Before, you couldn't hardly see that a cemetery was there because the brush was so high," Ewing said. "I thought 'Good grief, if he's that important, shouldn't he deserve better?' It started with just me, and then it kind of snowballed, and now the whole town's involved."

In southern Ohio's [Gallia] County, the Lambert Land Preservation Society raised nearly $20,000 for a memorial in a Morgan Township cemetery where the graves of thirty blacks and fifteen Civil War veterans do not have headstones.

The marble memorial lists the names of the thirty former slaves of Charles Lambert, Jr., a Virginia man whose will in 1843 freed them and granted them 265 acres.

"We wanted our kids to have something to look back on so they could know where they came from and that they have a great heritage," said Corliss Miller of Bidwell, whose husband, Glenn, is a descendant of one of the slaves.

From *Cleveland Plain Dealer,* January 5, 2003. Reprinted with permission.

SUGGESTIONS FOR FURTHER STUDY

1. Neglected cemeteries like the one in Ohio exist throughout the United States. Is it important that graves in these cemeteries be found and marked for future generations?
2. In Washington, D.C., and state capitals throughout the land giant marble statues and gravestones are erected to those people considered by politicians to be important. Are they more significant in history than the common citizen who has done most of the work?
3. At the moment growing interest in veterans is driving interest in monuments to them and the restoration of their graves and cemeteries. Are veterans more important in the development of society than nonveterans? Are Civil War veterans more important in our study of the past than others, say, scientists, business people, ordinary citizens?

Though they make up only a little more than 1 percent of the population, American Indians occupy an important and growing position in American society. They are having their land returned to them, are being granted the right to operate casinos (which are highly profitable), and enjoy certain other privileges. One of their major concerns is perpetuation of their religious beliefs about treatment of their ancestors. This treatment is also a major concern of the rest of society.

Descendants of Ohio's Earliest People Fight to Save Mounds

LIZ SIDOTI

COLUMBUS. Mound Street runs through the state capital. Indian Mound Mall is a spot in Heath, Ohio. And Newark is home to the Moundbuilders Country Club.

The places and their names—symbolic as well as literal—are testaments to the state's rich American Indian legacy. It is a history that descendants say is increasingly disappearing as development disturbs Ohio's numerous American Indian burial and earthen mounds.

"There's no way to get back what's lost, but what we can do is try to preserve what's left," said Barry Landeros-Thomas, a member of the Native American Indian Center of Central Ohio.

Descendants of American Indians say most mounds in Ohio have been disturbed, so they are fighting to protect the limited, albeit unknown, number that remain untouched.

American Indian burial mounds on public property are protected by federal law. However, there are no laws protecting those on private land, where many are located.

A state legislative committee is examining how Ohio could better preserve such burial grounds as well as cemeteries, but a lack of state money is likely to hinder development of such a preservation program.

"Mounds are part of a very rich, deep, and complex history of native people that's tens of thousands of years old," said Landeros-Thomas, who is of Cherokee and Lumbee ancestry. "But they've been bulldozed over, dug under, or manicured into an eighteenth green."

Since 1910, the private Moundbuilders Country Club has leased part of the Octagon Earthworks in Newark for use as a golf course. The property was purchased with public money in 1893 and eventually turned over to the Ohio Historical Society, which still owns the ancient mounds. The country club's lease expires in 2078.

It is believed the Hopewell people built the eight-foot-high earthen mounds, which were not used for burials, about 1,650 years ago in an octagon connected to a perfect circle to identify lunar movements for religious and other ceremonies.

The club says it restricts public access to the mounds during golfing season because of safety concerns.

Visitors are supposed to view the site from a wooden stand near the parking lot or from a short trail that borders one side of the course. The club also offers a few golf-free days to accommodate those wanting to pray at the site.

However, the Historical Society and club officials are considering ways to improve access, such as additional paths or viewing towers.

In November, Barbara Crandell, seventy-three, of Thornville, was convicted of trespassing for praying at a mound there in June. The Cherokee descendant says she has prayed there for twenty years.

Crandell, a member of the Native American Alliance of Ohio, argues that the land is public and she has a right to be there as a descendant of the people who built the mounds.

She said that many Ohio mounds that were at one time American Indian graveyards now are piles of dirt. She blames archeologists.

"The remains aren't in there anymore. They're up on a shelf at the Historical Society and at universities, probably in shoeboxes," she said. "How about just letting us bury our dead? How about just leaving the graves alone?"

From *Cleveland Plain Dealer*, January 5, 2003. Reprinted with permission.

SUGGESTIONS FOR FURTHER STUDY

1. Should the special requests about treatment of Indian remains be respected?
2. Ohio Indian mounds are only a part of those throughout the United States. Many have been returned and all are under some question as to whether they should be returned to the Indians or declared national lands. Is this the proper way to treat them?
3. Should American Indians be treated differently from other minorities just because they were living here when the Europeans came and occupied the land?

HOME AND ENVIRONMENT

Americans have always had a special place in their hearts for home and the concept of what it supplies in comfort and psychic reassurance for a restless people. Poet Edgar Guest said, "It takes a heap o' livin' in a house t' make it home," but for that living there must first be a home. One reason the 1982 film *E.T., The Extra-Terrestrial* was so popular was the longing the being had for home, expressed in his sigh, Home!

Perhaps because of our restlessness and the size of America home has been a place that we, like homing pigeons, could always fly to as the need arose. Home also has presented us with a movable myth that could be adjusted as one wished. America has always been a society in which the future is brighter than the present, the distant is more pleasurable than the nearby, and bigger is better. We aspire to larger organizations, bigger cars, wider highways, longer vacations, ampler wardrobes, and larger houses which make for happier homes. We progress through house size as our financial resources and family size grow, with definable borders that make possible the physical community and spirit that we are at the same time trying to build. Is it possible to have a community without borders—like Doctors without Borders, which provides worldwide medical expertise—to achieve the new sense of global outreach?

What kinds of new attitudes must we generate to reshape the many myths of the American home, the many reassuring attitudes and poetic remarks about it—"Home is the place where, when you have to go there, / They have to take you in," "In love of home, the love of country has its rise." Or have we turned on its head the cliché that one's home is one's castle and made it one's castle is one's home, and the more stately the castle the more comfortable the home? Is the icon of the home in jeopardy of becoming tarnished or broken, as it should be, or is it in our best interests to maintain and defend the icon? Must a larger house be required with every additional child in our drive toward what might be called conspicuous comfort?

We always long for retirement years—when the children have left home and return only for visits—and the big house with a three-car garage, and the mansion with so many rooms that we can hardly count them and seldom visit some of them. In our expansion past invisible and undefinable limitations, do we push out and give up the Home, which though primarily the residence, is also a group of many related and unrelated spiritual and physical aspects: the garage, the lawn, the porches (if any), the patio (with its equipment), fences, lawn equipment, outdoor toys. All these elements make up the total environment. But these aspects of the environment are related only secondarily to the individual's immediate surroundings.

The inside of the dwelling constitutes the immediate and most compelling environment. The number and makeup of the rooms are significant because that part of the environment reflects the personalities of the residents. Large rooms and high ceilings demonstrate their desire for spaciousness, perhaps one of the undying desires of people of all cultures, especially Americans. Americans don't like to be fenced in. In the forties, Bing Crosby sang, "Give me land, lotsa land, under starry skies above, / Don't fence me in." To Mark Twain's Huckleberry Finn, home was a threat to the individual. "Aunt Sally will try to civilize me, and I been there before," he says as he escapes the clutches of civilization.

Is that fear derived from the thought that the larger the home the stronger the restraints? When four walls, ceiling, and floor surround one on all sides it sometimes is difficult to feel "free." Sometimes the most oppressive and yet most promising is the ceiling, which reveals the desire of the person living beneath it to reach for the stars and heavens, especially with a cathedral ceiling, and to decorate it in any of a thousand ways that suits him or her. Perhaps most important are the four walls. They create the environment, making it large or small, beautiful or bare. They may be covered with all kinds of pictures, three-dimensional objects, paint, wallpaper, or ceiling decoration.

To the author of the following essay about home, bigger does not mean better. But whatever its size, home not only contains and defines us but becomes an extension of our bodies and psyches. A person is truly a part of these aspects of his environment and they a part of him.

We speak of "my home" and "my room," and if our homes and walls could speak they would probably talk of their people, their inhabitants, those who live with them and in them. Houses and rooms and all other aspects of our domestic existence are very much a part of our culture, shrines, and other cheap or expensive belongings. But behind these are the settings against which we move and live.

When Half as Big Is More than Enough

BARBARA STITH

My conversation with the insurance agent went as I'd expected. She assumed, correctly, that the house my husband I were buying was protected by deadbolt locks and smoke detectors. She was satisfied the wood stove had been properly installed. She wasn't concerned about the lack of hydrants on our country road; a pond a quarter mile away would provide plenty of water in case of fire.

Only one fact troubled her. "You've got the size of the house listed as twelve hundred square feet," she said. "That's just the first floor, right?"

No, I said. That's the whole house, first and second floors. She paused. "That can't be," she insisted, unable to accept that our family of four could fit in so small a space.

I could understand her skepticism. Our house is small, especially by modern standards. The average new home is almost twice as big as this one, according to the most recent U.S. Census statistics, built to accommodate a home office, a wide-screen TV, and restaurant-size kitchen appliances. Such luxuries would never fit in our house. When we bought a piano, we had to take out the wood stove to make room for it.

A small house isn't an easy sell, even in the brisk housing market our town enjoys. Skaneateles is perched on a pristine lake in upstate New York, a vacation destination for many, including Bill and Hillary Clinton. A house that's for sale draws a fair amount of traffic. Our house, however, had sat vacant for months.

We had driven by a dozen properties that day: stately Victorians in the nearby village, a handsome reproduction saltbox, a ranch that was nondescript but boasted a breathtaking view of Skaneateles Lake. Each of them had merit—more practical merit in terms of living space and lake access and resale value than this house.

But I was certain I would live here as soon as our car eased down the long driveway, flanked on one side by a row of towering sugar maples. The house sat on six acres of lawn and meadow, a mile and a half from the village. Its simple lines gave the appearance of a house a child would draw—a square bottom, a triangle for a roof. Inside we found cut-glass doorknobs, windows with a kind of glass that makes a ripple of the landscape, and a bundle of tattered blueprints. Ours is a kit house, ordered from the Sears catalog in 1929, with batches of shingles, lumber, and lath delivered by rail car. Like so many kit houses, it looks immediately familiar. You've seen our house a hundred times in any small town with a tree-shaded street.

We've met half a dozen people who were searching for a house at the same time we were and looked at this place. They all expressed their enthusiasm for it, then explained, somewhat apologetically, that it just wasn't big enough for them. To me, that's like turning down a date with the kindest, smartest guy you know because he's too short.

The only thing that's big about our house is the front porch. It's as wide as the house and eight feet deep, the kind for which porch swings were invented. Downstairs, there's a living room, dining room, and kitchen. The upstairs has three bedrooms and a bathroom. That's all.

We don't have an entrance hall, a laundry room, or a family room. "You only have one bathroom?" asked my six-year-old daughter's friend when she arrived to spend a week with us, fearful of the hardships ahead.

She survived, and so do we. Four people and one bathroom is not ideal, but it's a ratio that teaches us how to schedule and to wait. The living room needs to accommodate many activities, often simultaneously: playing, reading, my nine-year-old son practicing drums. Sometimes it feels very loud, very cluttered, very small. Sometimes three or four of us end up on the couch at the same time, and it feels exactly right. If we had a different room for each activity, we wouldn't be together.

We've talked about adding on: even a modest addition could yield a family room, a bathroom, and a more spacious kitchen. Yet it's been nearly seven years since we moved in, and our house is not one inch bigger. Something holds us back—thrift or indecision or the nagging fear that we could end up with a house too different from the one we love. It might end up bigger, yet somehow diminished.

When we bought this place, we disregarded the overarching principle of modern homeownership: to think of our house as the biggest investment we'll ever make. We'd have made a wiser financial decision if we'd bought any of the other houses we saw during our search. We'd have had more personal space, more room for more things. If we'd grown dissatisfied, we could have easily sold and moved on. An enormous house that sprang from a farmer's field since we moved here has changed hands three times already.

Our house's limited resale value probably means we're stuck with it. What we're stuck with, though, is a house that feels as if it's always been a part of the landscape and a part of our lives. The reason we bought it is the only one that makes sense to me. It felt like home.

SUGGESTIONS FOR FURTHER STUDY

1. Stith seems to favor what might be called the "old ethos" of home that is expressed in such sentiments as "Home is where the heart is," or "Be it ever so humble, there's no place like home." What are the values and results of such feeling in modern America?
2. Does small-scale housing make a family more closely knit?
3. Become for the moment an interior decorator. Examine the walls of the room in which you sit and in which you live, and assess the effect they have on your thinking and behavior. How would you change if your environment changed?
4. Design physically or verbally your ideal kind of room and house.

5. As a long project read a short account of an architect's life and work and comment on his or her contributions to society in general.

6. In trying to visualize an existence with too-close walls and one without walls, imagine the prisoner on death row or in a dungeon staring constantly at cold gray walls, or the freedom that could come from a life without walls of any kind. Would wall-lessness satisfy all needs?

YOUTH, AGE, AND
CHILDREN

Popular culture throughout the world is with all the people all the time. It is the society they live in while awake and what they occupy while asleep. It is the living atmosphere they breathe and exist in. It is with them from the cradle to the grave, in fact, before the cradle and after burial. Before birth, fetuses are cared for in either time-honored folkways or by modern medicine. After birth, whether at home or in a hospital, infants begin life surrounded by the elements of culture that are found, to one degree or another and in one way or another, throughout the general society. After death the bodies are disposed of in conventional ways, and the grief expressed for the departed is that common to the society. They live on in the culture of the individuals or family groups or in the wider and most lasting history.

Two of the more important elements in the human environment have to do with major elements of domestic existence. One is the folklore of our lives. Life at home is made up of all those activities that hold people in families and communities and allow them to carry on daily existence, including such domestic actions as cooking, housekeeping, crocheting, quilting bees, yard sales, bodily cleanliness, and others.

Of all the practices in human society often the most powerful in shaping a person's thought patterns and actions are those of everyday society, the folk. The folk are generally thought to be the people who are largely untouched by modern, outside influences—especially the media. But in fact all people have their roots in folk practices and attitudes of the past and to one degree or another have their thoughts and actions dictated by or influenced by the unwritten, traditional lifeways of their ancestors and of the community in which they were reared and live.

In many ways not recognized or admitted we are what we inherit and our descendants are what we pass on to them. Our traditions come to us with our mother's milk—no matter what form our sustenance takes—and the activities we pursue because of the attitudes of our associates. The public and private influences of the new world that we gradually move into have great effect on shaping our lives, but, at least at the beginning and for a long time thereafter, traditions reshape the messages of the outside world—especially of the media. These traditions of nurturing childhood and continued shaping of character come to us in many forms. All are influential. One of the more important is nursery rhymes, childhood versions of the important realities of life.

American society in general always has looked beyond the accomplishments of the adult generation and banked on its future; America was, in the words of the Puritan divines who established the original nation the "Citie on a Hill," a paradise on earth, with accomplishments and dreams that people throughout the world could hope to attain. With a great deal of this paradise in the present, there was even more in the future. That future was invested in the accomplishments of the next generation, the children who would take over the nation. Building on the adult society in which they lived they might reach the paradise the adults had aimed for but not achieved.

Ours is a society in which authorities and "research" dictate behavior. Like our Puritan ancestors we have been taught by the authorities to begin early and make children little adults, to cram adult knowledge, experience, and proper behavior into them as early as possible to prepare them for Harvard, Carnegie Hall, wealth, and power—those aspects of the good life we might have attained if only more opportunities had come our way—or been appreciated when they did. The myth of unlimited attainment for children is built on the icon of a golden childhood.

But America is a land of changing theories of personal achievement. Yesterday's theories of perfectibility in children—and society through that perfectibility—is undergoing change. Today's theory encourages indulgence, to let children be children and enjoy childhood, to play in their own way when they want for as long as they want. They can be happy even if they don't become Mozart or Einstein or Bill Gates or Johnny Cochrane. Perhaps we want a life less tense than that of the rich and powerful and more happy for children and therefore for adults.

The following essay reflects another concern about children.

A New Battle over Day Care

BARBARA KANTROWITZ

Are young children more aggressive when they spend a lot of time in day care? That appeared to be the disturbing conclusion of a study of more than eleven hundred children in ten U.S. cities released last week by the National Institute of Child Health and Human Development. Researchers found that 17 percent of children who spent more than thirty hours a week in nonmaternal care had behavior problems (such as hitting, interrupting others, or bullying). These findings generally held up whether families were rich or poor. Only 6 percent of children who spent less than ten hours a week in day care had similar problems. The study reignited a long-term debate over the effects of child care and made many working parents anxious. But researchers caution against an overly simplistic interpretation of the results. "The easy answer is to cut the number of hours children are in care," says Sarah Friedman, scientific coordinator of the study. However, Friedman says, scientists do not yet know whether the hours in child care alone or other factors caused the children to behave more aggressively. For example, she says, children in extended care may not get as much attention from stressed-out parents at home, which could also cause behavior problems.

The study, which began ten years ago and is ongoing, also found positive benefits for kids who are in day-care centers (rather than in family day care or with babysitters). These youngsters had stronger language skills and better short-term memory—both of which would help them do better in school. Researchers said that was probably because caregivers in centers have more training and education than home-based care providers. Nationally, about 30 percent of children are in day-care centers, while 15 percent are in family day care (in the provider's home) and only about 5 percent are cared for in their own homes by babysitters.

Faith Wohl, president of the Child Care Action Campaign, a non-profit advocacy group, said that she hoped policymakers would be guided by this positive evidence as well as data showing behavior problems. "The Bush administration is in the budget process right now," she says. "They have already sent a signal that they are diverting funding that was for child care. This might encourage more of the same, depending on what kind of constituent mail they get."

From *Newsweek*, April 30, 2001. © 2001 Newsweek, Inc. All rights reserved. Reprinted with permission.

SUGGESTIONS FOR FURTHER STUDY

1. This article obviously does not give all the details of the several studies referred to. Is the piece sufficiently detailed to change your feeling about child care?
2. More and more "scientific" reports and reviews are being published in the popular media. Do you think they are helpful, or since they are all incomplete and ongoing do they perhaps do more harm, creating more anxiety, than good?
3. Thinking about your growing up and your observations of children today, what suggestions do you have about ways to care for young children?
4. With more than 50 percent of mothers now working, and with the economic world built on two-income families, what is the future of day care for children and for the society which forces it upon us?

The houses in which we live are, after all, only the setting—the geography—of family life and happiness. Though at times we seem to forget it, the far more important aspect of life—and culture—is the people who live in the houses. Historically, it has been considered the role of women—mothers—to take care of the house, family, and family life. The women's movement of the last two decades, however, has to a certain extent freed women from the apron strings of the kitchen and child care, placing more and more importance on the role of the father, as the following article demonstrates.

Oh Dad Poor Dad, Your Daughter Has Looked in Your Closet and I'm Feeling So Sad

Daughters Dissing Daddy in the Memoir

ROGER NEUSTADTER

In the past decade there has been an explosion of sociological research on fathers. Today the academic research and media stories on deadbeat dads and fatherlessness either blame fathers for their children's problems or warn of catastrophe if fathers make a wrong move. There is now a broad spectrum of literature which holds that the absence of fathers is an important factor in negative childhood outcomes. Many neoconservative social scientists, in particular, have claimed that fathers are essential to positive child development and that the lack of father involvement has catastrophic results. These neoconservative social scientists have replaced the earlier "essentializing" of mothers with a claim about the essential importance of fathers. [H. B.] Biller and [J. L.] Kimpton have even used the term "paternal deprivation" in a manner parallel to [John] Bowlby's concept of maternal deprivation. These authors have proposed that the roots of a wide range of social problems (i.e., child poverty, urban decay, societal violence, teenage pregnancy, and poor school performance) can be traced to the absence of fathers in the lives of their children. Several sociological jeremiads focus on the social and psychological cost of father absences and, by implication, the potential redeeming features of father involvement.

While there has been an explosion of research on fathering, there has also been an explosion of memoirs. (Of course no causal relations between these two social trends is suggested. However, there is a significant convergence, although not agreement, on the substantive issue of fatherhood.) The literary genre of the memoir has become a particularly robust trend in recent years. The arrival of the memoir boom and its proliferation on the shelves of bookstores and in our collective consciousness has been noted by numerous observers. James Atlas notes that "the triumph of memoir is now established fact." "The memoir," Patricia Hampl asserts, "has become the signature genre of the age." Interestingly, many of the current crop of memoirs are characterized by judgmental attacks and revelations of fathers by their daughters.

Ironically, at a time when the notion of the father as a necessary link to physical and emotional well being is rapidly expanding, and there has been a deluge of public condemnations of absent fathers, there have appeared descriptions of present fathers as defective persons in several notable contemporary memoirs written by daughters. This kind of negative reflection of fathers seems gendered. Frank McCourt sees his ne'er-do-well father as a person with redeemable characteristics in *Angela's Ashes*. "I think my father is like the Holy Trinity," he writes, "with three people in him, the one in the morning with the paper, the one at night with the stories and prayers, and the one who does the bad thing and comes home with the smell of whiskey and wants us to die for Ireland." McCourt, who seemingly has many reasons to be unforgiving, is forgiving. He feels "sad over the bad thing," but feels "the one in the morning is my real father," the one he wishes to tell "I love you, Dad." (A similar forgiving sentimental attitude towards problematic fathers is sounded in Philip Roth's *Patrimony*, Geoffrey Wolff's *The Duke of Deception*, Art Spiegelman's *Maus*, and Tony Hiss's *The View from Alger's Window*.)

Significantly, a number of recent notable memoirs that have been published during the current memoir boom are written by daughters who are critical of their fathers, not for their absence, but for the lives they led, the particulars of their lives, and for the "bad thing" they did in their lives. The titles of many of these memoirs about fathers use the imagery of darkness and shadows. Indeed, a number of recent memoirs suggest that some contemporary women feel under no compunction to make their peace with dads or support recent arguments on the social and cultural importance of fathers. They reject the value of their patrimony and repudiate their fathers in their memoirs. If much of the academic literature describes the deleterious effects of life without father, many female memoirists describe the deleterious effects of life with father. In searching their family closets they found and revealed skeletons of their fathers' past in their memoirs.

Kathryn Harrison's *The Kiss* narrates the incestuous affair she conducted with her manipulative and obsessive father. The father, a minister, left the family when she was only six months old, and Harrison saw little of him until she was in college. The father remarried, had children, and had a church. It was when he came to visit his now college-age daughter that he began his seduction. She tells the story of a powerful man with a consuming desire to ravish his daughter. She tells how her father, banned from the household since she was a baby, comes back into her life when she is a twenty-something student and lures her into a four-year-long relationship.

It begins with a kiss when she is taking him to the airport. "My father," Harrison writes, "pushes his tongue deep into my mouth: wet, insistent, exploring, then withdrawn." Ultimately, he successfully makes his daughter his sexual partner. The story that follows is her long passionate affair with her father, a saga of turpitude. Subsequently he courts her by letter, phone, and tape recordings. There are meetings in airports and motels, in cars, and even in his ministerial office. Harrison never gives a full description of her father. He is the force of lust, she describes his eyes, his tongue, his probing hands, and his penis. She likens him to a poisonous insect; "In years to come, I'll think of the kiss as a kind of transforming sting, like that of a scorpion; a narcotic that spreads from my mouth to my brain."

If Harrison narrowly focuses on her father's incest, Louise Kehoe in *In This Dark House* focuses on the overarching breadth of her father's overbearing, cruel torment of the members of his family. A successful architect in London, he moves the family to a farm he calls "World's End" in rural England in 1939. Although Kehoe's mother wanted children, when she became pregnant "my father insisted categorically on her getting rid of them," even though abortions were "illegal, extremely difficult to obtain, and terrifyingly unsafe." Her father compels her mother to wear lipstick and high heels around the house to satisfy his whims. When her mother intercedes on behalf of her children, "this would cause him to turn the full force of his wrath on her like a water cannon, for, as he saw it, she was willfully opposing him—an act that showed her to be as shallow and disloyal as the children themselves."

Much of the book is a description of the torments he inflicted on his children. Kehoe's father is described as psychotically cruel, as "tyrannical and overbearing as the very worst sort of Victorian patriarch." His children call him "The Fuehrer." He raises his children in an atmosphere of "resolute misanthropy." He constantly compared, criticized, and disparaged his three children. He forbids his children to socialize with children of well-to-do families. He polices their activities, listens to phone conversations, and reads and withholds Kehoe's mail. He nurses grievances over abnormally long periods: "Hidden behind the books on the top shelf in his study he had a series of notebooks—dubbed by us the Book of Grievances—in which he chronicled our wrongdoings, omissions and shortcomings." By playing the children against each other he "strangled trust and turned us into strangers, eroding our ability to identify with one another and leaving us largely untroubled by one another's sorrows."

Many sentences begin with "Dad," followed by descriptions of what her dad did. When Kehoe makes intellectual overtures her father uses the opportunity to tell her that he considered her too stupid to understand anything more challenging than Mickey Mouse. He accuses her of histrionics and calls here "Sarah Bernhardt." A lover of beets, he viciously berates his daughter for not eating beets. When Kehoe begins to excel at painting at art school, she notes that "Dad shot me down in flames." When a painting of hers is displayed at school he dismisses her painting as "pedestrian and unimaginative" while shamelessly purloining a painting of a classmate which he framed and hung on the living room wall. When her father forcefully strikes a blow against her, which sends her reeling to the floor at the age of seventeen, Kehoe leaves World's End forever.

Later, years after her father's death, Kehoe discovers that her father had a secret past. Under what she calls a "mountain of careful, interlocking lies" she finds that her father was not the secular Polish student that he claimed to be, nor the son of a Russian admiral, as her mother had told her sister in what turned out to be a carefully concocted cover story, but a Polish Jew whose parents had died at Auschwitz. As she uncovers her father's past, Kehoe finds that she has a cousin living in New York to whom her father had "denied the existence of his own children." He had even surreptitiously visited the cousin while visiting Kehoe in Boston. Kehoe finds a convoluted trail in which he covered up his past. She finds her childhood to be the result of the debilitating effects of growing up with parental deception. Susan Cheever, Margaret Salinger, Mary Gordon, and Germaine Greer also open the closets of their fathers' secret pasts.

In *Home before Dark,* Susan Cheever focuses less on her father's works than on her father's private journals to reveal that his façade of an aristocratic New England background was a fiction and that he was tortured by his own nature—isolated from family members, a closeted and tormented homosexual and an alcoholic, "the worst kind of alcoholic . . . intent on destroying himself." Cheever describes her father's relationship with other family members as cold and distant: "On parting, we aimed kisses at one another's cheeks, and there were brief hugs for special occasions. We shook hands a lot." He is petty, refusing to visit his dying father-in-law. He is critical of his daughter's weight and appearance. His marriage is unhappy—there are fights, poor communication, and an absence of physical intimacy.

Cheever shines the spotlight on the details and the self-hatred of her father's clandestine homosexual life. His homosexual desires were, for much of his life, charged with a revolting lewdness. "My father," Cheever writes, "was a man of intense and polymorphous appetites that caused him tremendous guilt and self-loathing. His desires could poison his image of the pure life he wanted." When he was overpowered by his desires, "he paid for his pleasure with agonizing periods of guilt." In the last decade of his life, Cheever describes how her father became close to a series of younger male "proteges," taking a male lover in his last years who supplanted his wife.

Margaret Salinger, another daughter of a famous writer, also reveals details of her father's private life in her memoir *Dream Catcher.* Although the memoir is focused on her childhood and adolescence, Salinger reveals many personal flaws of her father. After his service in World War II as a combat soldier, Margaret Salinger reports that her father married a woman who she claims was a minor Nazi party official. The marriage was short-lived.

She describes how her father courted her mother at age sixteen, while she was still in high school. He is pictured as reclusive, inconsiderate, eccentric, and selfish. J. D. Salinger's marriage to her mother, Claire, resulted in her mother's increasing isolation "to the point where she felt she became a 'virtual prisoner.'" Her story chronicles an environment of extreme isolation and neglect. The whole family is brought up in the isolation of her father's refuge; friends and visitors are discouraged. She describes her mother in despair, subject to her husband's "lacerating criticism" when he felt she failed to come up to his standards. When her mother's pregnancy became obvious her father's attention turned to "abhorrence."

Margaret Salinger notes how her father was often "in the thralls of his private fads." She describes her father's flirtation with Zen Buddhism, Kriya yoga, Christian Science, Scientology, and microbiotics; his speaking in tongues; and his macrobiotic fasting. Many of her father's "health regimens," such as drinking urine or sitting in an orgone box, he practices alone; however, when his children became ill some of his experiments were extended to his family. She reports that almost from birth she was subject to her father's spiritual enthusiasms. When she fell ill as a baby, she writes, she wasn't taken to a doctor because her father "had suddenly embraced Christian Science and now in addition to being forbidden any friends or visitors, doctors were out." Later, J. D. Salinger's belief in illness as error became the cause of the break between daughter and father.

Mary Gordon's father died of a heart attack when she was seven years old. Her book [*The Shadow Man: A Daughter's Search for Her Father*] recounts her quest as an adult to discover and understand her father. Gordon represents herself as having completely idealized her father. When she was ten she began to write his biography. She began it, "My father is the greatest man I have ever known." Well into her adulthood she describes her father as an "untouched figure of romance." "He was the handsomest man in the world, as handsome as the movie stars I loved: Jimmy Stewart, Fred Astaire." He was charming and erudite, "urbane and elegant," an intellectual, a writer and publisher of a humor magazine, a brilliant, eccentric man who loved her.

Who and what David Gordon really was is the object of his daughter's search. In her archival and family research she found her father's whole enterprise to be a "charade, a costume drama." Gordon describes how her idealization of her father "led to a kind of memorializing that amounted to a kind of entombment." The book is figuratively and literally about the disinterring of her father. It concludes with his re-burial in a different cemetery from the one where he had been reposed with his Catholic in-laws. In disinterring her father, Gordon finds the deception of his life, the horror of his ideas, and the weakness of his style.

At the age of forty-four, Mary Gordon finds that her father is not the person she thought he was. Gordon began her search believing her father was born in Lorain, Ohio, went to school in the Midwest, studied at Harvard and in France, was a writer, and then married her mother. Thus it was a shock to discover in the course of her investigations—which consisted in part of reading her father's works in libraries, checking his family's birth records, and traveling to his hometown, Lorain, Ohio—that the life story her father told was a sham. Her father had lied about the date and place of birth, and his native language. Her father was born in Vilna, Russia; his native language was Yiddish. He was not an only child—he had several sisters; he had not graduated high school, there was no Harvard and Paris, and he had been married before. He had worked for the B & O railroad. His stories of study in Oxford and Paris were pure fantasy. He learned not in the classrooms of Harvard, but by stealing time from his office job to read at the public library. She also finds that her father had abandoned his mother and sisters and allowed them to die as paupers in state charitable institutions.

At the beginning of her quest she knew that "I might find things that I wish I hadn't, but I didn't know the extent to which this would be the case." Gordon goes to the Columbia library and the Brown University library to know her father as a public man, to look for her father as a writer. She finds that her father published words, held ideas that make her feel that she cannot love him in memory. She concludes that "what he wrote, and what I have made myself read, what I have waited so long to read properly, has taken away what I used to have, my joy in being with my father, with the man who took me to the city, who bought me books, wrote me poems."

He wrote with a "fascist bite." His writings show a man who was obsessively anti-Semitic. After his conversion to Catholicism he became stridently right wing, admiring Father Coughlin and Father Feeney. He describes Einstein as "this genius of a Jew-boy." He supports McCarthy and believes that the Rosenbergs deserved to die. Reading her father's political writings she finds him to be "full of aggressive and obsessive parochialism." In his writing she finds "nothing that I can find myself in, nothing that doesn't alienate or scandalize me."

His writing for "Hot Dog," a soft core pornography magazine, reveals a man whose sexual tastes were vulgar, a man who lived on the fringes of pornography. Looking at the pictures, Gordon becomes "furious" "to think of him screwing girls who want to get into the magazine" and appalled at the "jokes whose titillations are merely pathetic, with the sadness of sexual jokes that don't travel well." She wonders how her father thought of her breasts.

She censures not only what he wrote, but how he wrote: "Everything he wrote or edited was patched together, cobbled together not very smoothly, not very well. I'm not even left with the pride of the daughter of a fine stylist. He was far from great, he wasn't even good." His writing is tedious, careless, full of gross misinformation. Ultimately, Gordon censures her father for his work, and for his life.

Like Gordon, Germaine Greer embarks on the path to discover her father's past. In *Daddy We Hardly Knew You*, Germaine Greer at mid-life feels an emotional urgency to know her father and makes what she calls a "detrimental pilgrimage" to uncover her father's past. She finds not only that many aspects of his past were deliberately hidden, but that "a certain little girl mis-remembered" aspects of her father.

Greer examines her father's origins and eventually discovers that her father had faked his identity to her mother and all family members. After many attempts at tracing his origin she finds that his name had not been Reg Greer but Eric Green. He had been raised by a foster family and had not known who his biological parents were. "Gotcha," Greer writes, "I'd never have found you liar. Just didn't lie quite enough." She finds that he was "barely literate" placing twenty-ninth out of thirty-one students on the qualifying examination for state high school.

Her search for British military records yielded that her father had been a code officer, who, working underground at Malta, had cracked under the pressure of German bombs. He was the one who lost his head when, all around him, others were keeping theirs. He tried to chicken out; he exaggerated his symptoms to the investigating officers, and they believed him. He is diagnosed as having an "anxiety neurosis" and is given a medical discharge. Germaine Greer is "troubled" that his anxiety neurosis "was a calculated performance." Even sick, Greer remembered himself well enough to distort truth. He lies about his weight and weight loss to get a medical discharge.

Greer focuses on the pattern of deception which became part of her father's life. He claimed a career as a bank manager. She finds that he never was a manager of advertising, but a sales representative. She uncovers unpleasant details of his behavior in the office where he pressed unwanted attention on the secretaries. Her father was not the gentleman she thought. He was the "office masher" who "couldn't keep his hands off" his secretary.

In *Falling Leaves: The True Story of an Unwanted Chinese Daughter*, Adeline Yen Mah tells the story of her childhood as "the least loved daughter." Although the major nemesis in her life is her stepmother, the father is often the instrument of the new wife. So beguiled is her father with his new wife that he never intervenes on his children's behalf.

When Adeline goes to a new school after the family moves from Tianjin to Shanghai, her father forgets to pick her up, reprimanding her, "You wouldn't be lost if you had taken a map with you and studied the location of the school and your way home." He enforces an austerity program in which the children of the first wife are fed congee, a soupy gruel made of rice and water and pickled vegetables, while the children of the new wife feast. "Hunger was my constant companion," Mah wrote, "and my pockets were always empty." She is only allowed old-fashioned haircuts, and must walk to school because her father won't give her tram fare. Her father beats her, sends her away to schools, and never visits. To show that his prize German Shepherd had benefited from obedience training, her father tests the dog's obedience by having it sit by Adeline's beloved pet duckling. The test fails. The result is that the dog maims her pet duckling. Mah's memoir is a case study of an evil stepmother and fatherly abuse.

Like many memoirists, those discussed in this paper triumph over the adversity of their childhoods and their fathers. Mah becomes a physician. Kehoe becomes a dentist. Salinger graduates Phi Beta Kappa from Brandeis, and from Harvard Divinity School. Harrison, Cheever, Gordon, and Greer become successful writers. These memoirs celebrate the capacity to triumph against the odds. The daughters become what Lillian Rubin calls "the transcendent child," adults who overcome the deficits of their pasts to transcend a difficult childhood. From their perches of triumph and success, their memoirs look back on their deficient fathers at the very time when celebrating life with father is in such vogue. In looking into their family closets they find and reveal the skeletons of their father's past, past identities, and their fathers' relationships with their daughters.

From *Journal of Popular Culture* 36, no. 2 (Fall 2002). Reprinted, without bibliographical information, with permission of the author.

SUGGESTIONS FOR FURTHER STUDY

1. Though these studies are of women who became successful and somewhat well known, do you think all women could benefit from digging into their pasts, especially their relationships with their fathers?

2. Read one of the memoirs discussed here and see if there is more in the development of the authors than the author of this article reveals about her.

3. Read a memoir of a happy childhood and growing up and compare it to one of the books discussed here.

4. Are the authors of the memoirs discussed here unusually sensitive and therefore their accounts of women growing up not typical? Or are they really representative?

NOSTALGIA

Another important element in human association is nostalgia, especially the appeal of the past—and particularly the golden years of youth, when life as remembered was rich, pleasurable, and seemingly endless. Giving up the umbilicus cord that ties us continually to the rich sustenance of the past and moving into the more vulnerable years of adulthood is not easy. The following essay, written by a college student for college students, demonstrates the tug of the past on the heartstrings of the present and future. The lure of the past and the hold it has on people of all ages can be seen or felt in many expressions of adults as well as youths, and should be watched out for.

Don't Let Your Childhood Die

ERIK DUNHAM

STILLWATER, OKLA. Do you believe in magic? I don't think I ever did—some kind of cynical gene in my DNA—but a lot of people did growing up.

And for those people, there was the McDonaldland crew. It seemed like not a single Saturday morning would go by that I wouldn't see their crazy hijinks at least twenty times between such greats as *Garfield and Friends* and *The Real Ghostbusters*.

Hamburglar would steal all the food and Ronald and Grimace would save the day with the Fry Guys. All the while, Mayor McCheese would try to restore order in the magical world.

Personally, I always wanted to see Hamburglar try to pull a kidnapping/ransom situation with the good old mayor—I mean he was a giant burger. Sadly, my commercial episode ideas were always rejected. Since then I've never donated a cent to the Ronald McDonald House. He who laughs last, ha ha.

Anyway, I was actually getting to a point with this column. Where are they lately? I expect to see a show on VH1 sometimes—the McDonaldland characters, where are they now?

I mean, occasionally you'll see Ronald and Grimace passing out Happy Meals on TLV, getting kids hooked on that heroin in a box (it's the prize that keeps 'em coming back), but their glory days are in the past.

I remember when they used to incorporate all the characters into the commercials. Birdie would run in like Chicken Little saying something's wrong, then Ronald and Grimace would go outside to see the Fry Guys in a bind or Hamburglar running off with Happy Meals. Then Mayor McCheese would scratch his head a little and Ronald would pull off some clown magic or MacGuyver ingenuity to save the day.

That's one problem I always had with that gang—why was Ronald so magical? He's the clown. Leave the magic to David Copperfield. Clowns are supposed to be funny and sometimes evil—all clowns are inherently evil.

And what was Grimace anyway? I mean, Birdie lays eggs for breakfast, the Fry Guys were um, fries, the Hamburglar was a hungry drug addict, and Mayor McCheese was a big cheeseburglar. Later came the Nugget Buddies (six naked guys living in a box together—yikes) who were Chicken McNuggets. Ronald was the ringleader, but what was Grimace?

I've heard shake gone wrong, grease trap leavings, and even Ronald's retarded brother, but nothing seems to make sense with him. Why is he named after a reaction you have to bad food?

Anyway, I got off the point again. Even the rare times when you see these characters anymore, it's usually only Ronald, Grimace, and some kids. Where'd everyone else go and why is even Ronald so scarce?

I have this theory about the disappearance of such childhood icons and the increase in adolescent violence. It seems to kind of go hand in hand. Kids look for icons on TV to steer them in the right direction, but Sugar Bear, Cap'n Crunch, the Cookie Crook, and even Count Chocula are nowhere to be found.

Yes, these characters were often violent ("it's got the crunch with punch") and maybe in some cases a little evil, but that was the small dose kids needed. We all gain exposure to violence and evil in different ways growing up. If it comes in small doses at a time in the form of a cartoonish character, we can sort it out easier and say, "That's bad." Then we grow into good little slackers.

When you have the cartoons of today that are mostly real-looking characters in real situations, kids go, "Do I look up to him even when he's fighting?"

The cartoonish characters of our childhood didn't evoke as much confusion. Plus, they were just fun (not to say that Batman isn't, but Batman has always been around so it's an exception).

So, even though these cereal and food sponsor characters were annoying, and even mysterious (in the case of Grimace), they were an important part of childhood. And now they're all gone. Food corporations have grown up and killed them.

I guess that's what comes with getting older. Age is supposed to bring wisdom, though, so be smart and don't let these legends fade into forgotten history.

Always remember the lessons you learned from a fast-food clown. Pass on the stories of Cap'n Crunch defeating the Soggies to your kids and grandkids someday, because it just might save mankind. This is especially important if Soggies come from outer space one day thinking we've forgotten how to defeat them.

It could happen.

From U-Wire, May 7, 2001. Reprinted with permission.

SUGGESTIONS FOR FURTHER STUDY

1. Americans constantly try to lay the blame for their undesirable behavior on other people or institutions. The fast food industry has always drawn fire, now even more so, in light of medical studies. Yet all civilizations have relied on fast food of some sort. What would American society be today without the fast food industry? Better or worse? Healthier or still, from some cause, obese?

WHAT TO DO WITH
THE OLD PEOPLE?

Though raising children to be happy and productive members of society should take the forefront in questions relating to age, the problem—if that is the right word—of the elderly deserves serious attention because of their role in society and in the hearts and minds of individuals.

N. R. Kleinfield reports in the *New York Times* (January 20, 2003) that centenarians are the fastest growing age bracket. "According to the 1900 census, 1,455 people who were at least one hundred lived in New York City. The 2000 census identifies 1,787, an increase of nearly 23 percent, with 58 of them 110 or older. Nationwide, fifty thousand people are estimated to have made it to one hundred, and demographers project that there might be close to one million in triple digits by 2050. Centenarians here, there, everywhere." Though the last Civil War veteran has just died, thousands of World War I and World War II veterans still live. Finally, the aging baby boom generation threatens to strain Social Security and Medicare to the point of bankruptcy.

Meanwhile conflicting drives work against one another. Relatives of the elderly say they want to keep their own relatives alive as long as possible, but they do not feel quite as strongly about the elderly in general. Medical research and doctors and hospices and retirement homes want to keep older people alive, but they all have economic interests at stake. Recognizing the growing number of elderly voters, Congress passed a bill forbidding the forced retirement of workers over seventy years of age. Meanwhile the younger generation, seeking jobs in various fields of the work force, wish that people over seventy would leave their jobs to make space for them.

The lotusland of old age has always been painted over with myths and the mists of inevitability. Seniors are icons of wisdom, luxuriating in leisure, "doing what they have always wanted to do." But the folklore of the joys of age is filled with contradictions. America, at least since the Industrial Revolution, has belonged to the energetic and strong and young. Now the old, rich, and healthy are reluctant to give up control. The scene of embarrassing conflict will continue to grow, as more and more people reach old age. Meanwhile, it is heating up, as the following essay demonstrates.

After a Full Life, at Seventy-five, One's Duty Is to Die?

THOMAS SOWELL

WASHINGTON. Our betters have been telling us how to live our lives for so long that it is only the next logical step for them to tell us when to die. We have grown so used to meekly accepting their edicts, even on what words we can and cannot use—"swamp" has virtually disappeared from the English language, replaced by "wetlands," as "bums" has been replaced by "the homeless," "sex" by "gender"—that it seems only fitting that they should now tell us when to die.

Now the new phrase is "the duty to die." The anointed have proclaimed this duty, so who are we ordinary people to question it? Former Colorado governor Richard Lamm has said that the elderly should "consider making room in the world for the young by simply doing with less medical care and letting themselves die."

In the Hastings Center Report, described as a journal of medical ethics, a medical ethicist says that "health care should be withheld even for those who want to live" if they have already lived beyond the politically correct number of years—which he suggests might be seventy-five. He says that after such a "full rich life" then "one is duty-bound to die."

Another medical ethicist would consider extending the limit to eighty years but, after that, medical care should be denied to all who have "lived out a natural life span."

There was a time when Americans told people like this where they could go. But today, everything is everybody's business. The next step is for it to become the government's business.

How did we get sucked into collectivizing decisions that were once up to individuals? Purple prose is one factor: One of those who wants to see old-timers removed from the scene declares that the costs of keeping them alive is "a demographic, economic, and medical avalanche."

Collectivism takes on many guises and seldom uses its own real name. Words like "community" and "social" soothe us into thinking that collectivist decision-making is somehow higher and nobler than individual or "selfish" decision-making. But the cold fact is that communities do not make decisions. Individuals who claim to speak for the community impose their decisions on us all.

Collectivist dictation can occur from the local level to the international level, and the anointed push it at all levels. They want a bigger role for the U.N., for the International Court of Justice at the Hague, and for the European Union bureaucrats in Brussels. Anything except individual freedom.

Maybe they will and maybe they won't. Maybe we are all destined to give up our freedom to those ruthless enough to take it from us—or glib enough to soothe us into handing it over to them.

From *Toledo Blade*, April 28, 2001. Reprinted with permission.

SUGGESTIONS FOR FURTHER STUDY

1. Sowell obviously has a larger issue to discuss than proposed deprivation of life of the old. Does he manage effectively to move from the immediate issue to the larger one?
2. Is the idea of voluntary death of the elderly tied in with other social relaxations in society?
3. Assuming that you are a lawmaker, social worker, or advocate of the elderly or the young, what outside elements of popular culture would you marshal in your arguments pro-life or pro-termination for the elderly?

FADS

America is a nation of faddists. Always on the move, we do not like to remain for long in the same place, to do the same things, to have the same experiences, even to wear the same clothes. We enjoy change, whether it is moving on to new and better things or just changing for the sake of change. We are therefore dedicated to having and enjoying fads, even being controlled by them, those generally short-lived crazes in which we pour our unconscious and conscious attention for a while before moving on to another. We seem unable to live without fads—in fashions, music, art, movies, cars, sports apparel, beauty contests locally and worldwide, foods—every aspect of life that has come-and-go possibilities. In fact it is hard to say whether changes in society develop fads or whether fads develop society.

We are always interested in ourselves, in our self-interests and enjoyments. Perhaps nowhere else is it so obvious as in our worship of our own bodies and appearance, our health, our longevity and happiness. In personal appearance, both male and female—especially the latter—we resort to almost any trick both to conform to the latest fads in personal appearance and fashion and to use other fads to stand alone, different from others.

Personal beauty and health begin with food, in exercising care in what and what not to eat, and in health supplements and medicines to enhance beauty. Such medicines and health supplements have been with us in America since the early days when they were recognized as "snake oil" but consumed by the thousands of gallons. Today all media spread word about the latest discoveries of the most useful foods in getting and remaining slim and for living the long and happy life. Though medical science constantly reminds us that these supplements are unneeded and useless, drugstore shelves continue to bulge with them, and we spend billions a year to consume them. One of the latest—perhaps silliest—is bottled "spring" water that has come to be accepted by the public as more healthful than tap water. We are willing to pay large sums for this water. In the New Orleans airport, for example, ice-cold water drinking founts are everywhere but people pay $1.75 for a bottle of water, when Cokes and coffee can be bought for $1.25. It has been proved that most of this bottled water comes from the tap and contains all the impurities found in regular drinking water. But we treasure the bottle of water we carry around with us and drink from at will. The fad of living by the fad seems irresistible. When the fad can be linked to a reliving of the present and past through looking at photos of oneself and one's friends, the desire takes on much greater attraction, as the following essay demonstrates.

Delight in Disorder

A Reading of Diaphany and Liquefaction in Contemporary Women's Clothing

DENNIS HALL

That fashion in the postmodern era has lost its authority is a well known and documented story. In the 1990s, while the marketing and consumption of clothing, especially women's clothing, may still fall into recognizable patterns, fashion is no longer able to impose an annual "Look" to which there are no or few alternatives. This year's New Look, which carries the codes of prestige—principally exercises of money and power—is simply no longer able to supplant last year's Old Look, which bears the burdens of advancing dowdiness and disadvantage. As Ted Polhemus describes the situation: "Instead of the authority of *the* fashion, one is today more likely to see pluralism, with different designers proposing radically conflicting New Looks. While some fashion pundits may strive to reduce this cacophony of different colours, shapes, hem lengths, and so on, into a consistent trend—a single direction—anyone viewing the photographs of the Paris, Milan, London, or New York shows can appreciate that difference rather than consensus is the order of the day." The market delivers to the consumer a profusion of fashion elements out of which she may—no, she is forced—to construct a look or—much more likely in this era of protean identities—a variety of looks for herself.

One of the many general strategies in women's clothing—often called fashion themes—has long played with the ever-shifting boundaries between revealing and concealing the body, and in the 1990s many designs exhibit a nearly unprecedented disclosure of the body by one device or another in play upon common expectations about dress and nakedness—a play that seeks and often captures an experience of the erotic.

This general strategy of body disclosure is routinely executed through four distinct although related clothing tactics, which may appear alone in a fashion look or, perhaps more frequently, in various combinations. Indeed to find all four in a given outfit or magazine fashion feature or in a designer's runway show or as the object of a fashion writer's attention is not uncommon.

The first tactic is the practice of turning what once passed for underwear into outerwear so to transfer the associations of nakedness to dress, even though the body remains covered: the evening gown that looks like a slip, the bustier, the halter top that looks like a bra, the blouse that wears like a camisole, the night dress as day dress.

The second tactic is a fairly direct matter of exposure: plunging necklines, often to the navel, bare midriffs, skirts slit to the thigh, extremely short skirts, open waist bands and unbuttoned blouses, dresses with revealing cutouts, thong underwear—all exercises in exposing skin, skin once ordinarily covered when one dressed.

The third tactic I want to call diaphany; it is the use of transparent materials, stuff of such fineness of texture as to permit seeing through. Sheer fabrics, of course, have a long history, but diaphany, the use of sheer fabrics in the explicit service of "body consciousness," is principally an undertaking of the '80s and '90s. In 1983 Jean Paul Gaultier shrouded bustiers in blouses of sheer horsehair netting and in 1988 Karl Lagerfeld, as Suzy Menkes explains, "first made legs take the veil in chiffon. . . . Chiffon, georgette, and organza have also been used as transparent curtain for body-conscious fashion by Gigli, Dolce, and Gababana and other designers in the vanguard." Writing in May 1993, Suzy Menkes, at the time fashion editor of *The International Herald Tribune*, observed that "for three years, high-fashion designers have been transparently in love with see-through fabrics. Models on the runway reveal lightly veiled breasts, midriffs, thighs, legs—and then turn to show the bare derriere. Although this sheer story started with the avant-garde, now even the fashion establishment is making indecent proposals. For spring, Bill Blass showed the ultimate uptown evening dress: pin-striped chiffon, sheer at the rear, to be worn over nothing but a thong." Diaphany is a similarly employed fashion tactic into 1998.

And the fourth tactic I want to call "liquefaction"—the use of opaque fabrics, yet stuff so fine and pliable that it clings to the body of the wearer, as if a layer of skin, so revealing every contour, the very texture of the body of the wearer, while still covering her skin: clothes made of fish scale and fine metallic knits, Lycra, spandex, rayon or silk jersey, ultra fine and closely fit knits of all kinds. These clothes, perhaps as much a technological as a tailoring wonder, seem to defy the nature of cloth, often looking as if poured upon the wearer. Some of these clothes can have a startlingly erotic effect while completely covering the body. I call this fashion tactic "liquefaction" after Robert Herrick (1591–1674) who, in "Upon Julia's Clothes," succinctly describes this effect:

> Whenas in silks my Julia goes,
> Then, then, methinks, how sweetly flows
> That liquefaction of her clothes.
>
> Next, when I cast my eyes and see
> That brave vibration each way free,
> Oh, how that glittering taketh me!

Since roughly 1980, one or another of these tactics has been at one time or another a more conspicuous player in the fashion arena than the others, but none has been totally eclipsed. These tactics will likely remain routine tools in the designer's repertoire and available to the consumers of the signal commodities that are women's clothes. Body disclosure, I think it important to keep in mind, has never been a dominate fashion strategy, constituted *the* Look of any year, but it has always been an option, *a* Look. More likely, one of several looks a woman might adopt as the mood suits her or as social context demands.

Although in some ways related, body disclosure in mainstream fashion is a cultural exercise that represents a body consciousness distinct from the more explicit sexual codes of the boudoir wear offered by Frederick's of Hollywood or Victoria's Secret and the like or the codes of the Naugahyde and chains fantasies sold in shops with names like "Worn to Be Wild" or through the Intimate Treasures catalogs offered in the back of *Cosmopolitan* magazine.

As a glance about will confirm, body disclosure has yet to become a ubiquitous element in the clothing of the masses; it remains primarily on the runways of Paris and New York and in the pages of *Vogue, Mademoiselle, Glamour, Elle, W, Cosmopolitan, The New York Times Magazine.* Dramatic body disclosure may sometimes be seen on the streets or in the dining, bar, and ballrooms of big cities. These traditional arbiters of the popular taste, however, are having their usual effect. Sometimes it is only a metonymic flicker of fashion's brighter light, but body disclosure, particularly through the tactics of underwear and simple exposure, is increasingly a part of athletic costume and informal summer wear even in Peoria, and diaphany and liquefaction have become common features of evening wear, the dress for those special occasions when and where the play of between nakedness and dress are part of the pleasures of the fashionable social text.

The vast bulk of discourse on the fashion of body disclosure, doubtless because it makes saleable copy, focuses upon extreme manifestations of this fashion theme, is concerned with degrees of exposure — what body bits can be observed. The discernable nipple is a particular concern. But it is well to keep in mind that body disclosure, on the fashion runway as well as off, manifests itself in many different ways and in varying degrees, ranging from the Sister Margaret Mary school of the demure to the undeniably revealing, but none of the clothing on offer to women in the name of fashion, even the most extreme, suggests the topless dancer.

To date the more serious discourse on body disclosure in women's clothing has focused on four other, often overlapping, concerns.

First is the concern about the propriety, even the safety, of wearing such clothing in the age of AIDS and in an era of reputedly increasing sensitivity to issues of sexual harassment and violence, in a decade when sexual restraint is or ought to be making a comeback, despite, perhaps because of, some of the more notorious demonstrations to the contrary.

Second is the concern about whether such clothing is good or bad gender politics. The fashion press maintains a solidly postmodern schizophrenia on questions of this kind. Suzy Menkes writes in January 1992, in *Vogue*, that "fashion's bra-and-lingerie look has a message — just as Yves Saint Laurent's bared bosoms did in 1968, when their appearance on the runway signaled the start of the Permissive Society. Women have come a long way, from burning bras to flaunting them. If a woman now chooses to look sexy, that is her right. And if a man chooses to misinterpret the signals, that is his problem. Corsetry on the runway is not about fashion titillation but about a world in which sexual harassment is a burning issue." However, in July 1993, in *The New York Times,* in an article headlined, "On the Riviera, Exposure Ebbs and Chaste Is Chic,"

the same Ms. Menkes cites the sexual harassments in New York swimming pools, AIDS, and tilting against a sexist society in her approval
of "the youngest women [who] are leading the revolt against exposure."
A major concern: what kind of political statement does wearing transparent clothing make?

Third is the question about when and where might one appropriately wear such clothes, and what degree of revealing the body will work
on which occasion? "Anyone can understand," Menkes notes, "a chiffon dress for evening: the look has been around for years. But . . . blow-
away dresses, bias-cut in chiffon over brief underpants . . . the flimsy,
filmy dress has been proposed as everyday clothing." For this summer,
designers as diverse as Helmut Lang and Isaac Mizrahi sewed totally
transparent dresses over bikini underpants, prompting one fashion wit
to suggest that the international collections should be renamed "ready-
to-where?" A major concern: can these clothes be worn to work? In
what kinds of public places?

And fourth is the concern about aesthetics. Are these clothes beautiful or pretty? Do they flatter the wearer? What sorts of people can wear
them? How might one or another of these tactics be included in a wardrobe? Is body disclosure one of those trends that produces more than
the usual number of fashion victims?

Remarkably absent from the discourse about the fashion of body
disclosure, however, is any serious concern about its erotic character.
There are, of course, the requisite declarations that this clothing is
daring or provocative or sensuous, but these largely unelaborated as-
sertions seem to depend more upon the description or the photo-
illustration of body disclosure than upon any analysis of the communication of sexual feeling that is requisite to noncommercial senses of the
erotic, whatever else the term may mean.

On the advice of Mary Douglas, I think it fair to see clothing as an
extension of the human body and to treat it "as an image of society" and
so to see fashion of body disclosure as a cultural element that "sustains a
particular view of society." I want also to suggest that a culture's sense of
the erotic, as for example the one expressed in the fashion tactics of diaphany and liquefaction, works to sustain a particular view of society.

Extremely helpful in understanding the erotic in the realm of clothing is a compelling article entitled "Between Clothing and Nudity," by
Mario Perniola, who argues that "in the figurative arts [into which category I am inclined to put fashion design and the exercise of wearing

fashionable clothing], eroticism appears as a relationship between clothing and nudity. Therefore, it is conditional on the possibility of movement—transit—from one state to another. If either one of these poles takes on a primary or essential significance to the exclusion of the other, then the possibility for this transit is sacrificed, and with it the conditions for eroticism. In such cases, either clothing or nudity becomes an absolute value."

"The metaphysics of clothing and the metaphysics of nudity," Perniola explains, "correspond to each other by assigning an absolute value to visibility, but in opposite ways." In Western thought's Hellenistic roots, on the one hand, we have a reverence for nudity based upon the ability to see the "naked truth," "the metaphysical ability to see beyond all robes, veils, and coverings through to the thing itself in its exact particulars." In good Platonic fashion, we have often seen our naked bodies as imperfect replicas of the ideal, have taken them not only as symbols but as indexes and icons of truth. Getting to "the naked truth" is a process of getting undressed, getting free of clothing. From this perspective, being clothed is a privation.

In Western thought's Hebraic roots, on the other hand, we also have a reverence for the condition of being clothed as a mark of humanity. "Clothing prevails as an absolute," Perniola suggests, "whenever or wherever the human figure is assumed to be essentially dressed, when there is the belief that human beings are human, that is distinct from animals, by virtue of the fact that they wear clothes." In good Hebraic fashion we have often seen our clothed bodies as robed in the glory of God, as putting on the armor of righteousness and truth. To be clothed is taken not only as a symbol but as an index and an icon of the truth that will set you free. Getting to the truth is a process of getting dressed, putting on clothing. From this perspective, being naked is a privation.

The absolute dominance of either of these cultural positions, to the exclusion of the other, makes experience of the erotic impossible, for the erotic is less a static condition than a dynamic process; sexual arousal is more a matter of "becoming" than of "being," a distinction that explains, for example, why both nudist camps and monasteries are not ordinarily erotic. In Perniola's account, this process, this becoming at the heart of eroticism, is perceived in the dynamic tension often created between the Hellenistic and Hebraic conceptions of the human figure that makes possible the transit between clothing and nudity. "The metaphysics of clothing and nudity have had a continual influence on

Western culture into our times. They return whenever the conflict between the body's dignity and its freedom is posed in absolute terms." Perniola illustrates "the erotics of dressing and undressing" and the use of "nudity as veil and clothing as nudity" in convincing readings of Reformation and Mannerist and Counter-Reformation and Baroque art.

Fashion's play in the boundary between nakedness and dress can be understood in similar cultural and social terms.

That body disclosure should play a significant, though clearly not dominant, role in women's clothing reflects in a small but clear way a renewed tension between the surviving Hebraic and Hellenistic strains in American culture. While never completely static, American society's view of the relationship between dignity and freedom is in greater ferment in the 1990s than it has been since the late '60s and early '70s, the result of a variety of forces like the shift in Republican rule from the White House to the Congress; radical changes in economic structure and practice and an unprecedented run of prosperity; the rise of religious and other forms of "fundamentalism"; multiculturalism and "rights" movements of every description; the apparent collapse of monolithic world communism and its attendant destruction of the notion of a monolithic capitalism and democracy; the crises in education and health care; and many others. The '90s is proving an era of considerable turmoil—one might even say arousal—and is providing a social and cultural context rife with the possibility of transit between dignity and freedom. The second generation of feminism, sometimes called "post-feminism," is just such a force: a collection of concepts, dispositions, and actions far less fixed than fifteen or twenty years ago and reflective of the diversity, indeterminacy, and decenteredness of the present era, commonly characterized as postmodernism. It is a tough time for -isms.

And it is a tough time for women buying clothes, as Cathy Guisewite reminds us *ad nauseam*. For women—unlike men who may escape into the sartorial pablum of a dark suit or khakis and a blue blazer—there is no neutral position, there are no unelaborated codes in dress. Whatever a woman chooses to wear—her "look," in fashion parlance—is loaded with social, professional, political, economic, and sexual messages. "Nothing is less certain today," Baudrillard notes, "than sex, behind the liberation of its discourse. And nothing today is less certain than desire, behind the proliferation of its images." Women's clothing can be a difficult process of composition even in a context of relative social and cultural consensus, but in a context of social and cultural indeterminacy, to dress is to enter an hermeneutical jungle.

To wear clothing that employs the tactics body disclosure represents a desire, at least in part defined by pursuit of an experience of the genuinely erotic, an experience denied many women who consider their options constrained by polarities that tend to be mutually exclusive, even absolute in their demands, by what amounts in the 1990s to a salient binary code. On the one hand, there is feminism's almost Hebraic demand for dignity that seems to require a clothing of the body so to signal such notions as independence, self-determination, agency, deliberation, self-consciousness, and sense of control. On the other hand there is—for want of a better term—the feminine's almost Hellenistic demand for freedom that seems to require a disrobing of the body so to signal such notions as social and economic interdependence, a "conception of the self divided, at odds with itself, ambivalent" [Joel Whitebook], collaboration, social construction and direction, unconscious understanding, and a sense of abandon.

In the fashion strategy of body disclosure, however, an oscillation occurs between the conditions of being clothed and being naked, indeed, a transit between the processes of robing and disrobing, the putting on and the taking off. Just as medium-rare flirts with the difference between the cooked and the raw, this form of body consciousness operates on the boundary between the clothed and the naked so to provide a concrete experience of the play of difference so honored by contemporary critical theory. And "difference," Jacques Derrida suggests, "produces what it forbids, makes possible the very thing it makes impossible." The pleasures of body disclosure's text, however, derive less from opening up the limited possibilities of exhibitionism or voyeurism than from a constant undoing and preserving of both feminism and the feminine and their respective associated ideas.

In a piece that begins decrying the scandalous degrees of exposure in diaphany on the fashion runways as dangerous as well as undignified, Suzy Menkes concludes by saying: "There is another way of looking at see-through. If the skirts and tops are worn over a layer of stretch or opaque fabric, fashion becomes not more revealing but more covered up. Instead of marking the high water line of sexual provocation, the light chiffon, to be followed by heavier wood gauze for next winter, may bring a return to chaste concealment. The fashion for sheer clothes then becomes a signal of something that doesn't seem so out of place in the age of AIDS, aggression, violence, and rape: women's bodies may be starting to take the veil." Fashion conscious women, then, may have the freedom of style and the dignity of responsibility that style seems to forbid; in "chaste concealment" they may reveal their modesty while being modestly revealing.

Both diaphany and liquefaction are processes at once of covering and uncovering, of dressing and undressing. "There is," Perniola observes, "a threshold to undressing, and once it is passed all motion stops. Like the veil, [however], the incompleted act opens and maintains the intermediate space between clothing and nudity." The tactics of diaphany and liquefaction bear the codes of greater sophistication and social prestige and are, I submit, more intensely erotic than the more extreme and relatively fixed tactics of underwear and direct exposure which often violate what Perniola describes as the limits of undressing. The body clad in underwear in American culture is in a state of undress, a condition so much a part of the ordinary syntax of love making as to be an index of sexual engagement. Likewise, the body exposed with necklines plunging to the navel and skirts slit to the thigh and the like is a body available not only to visual but to tactile access. In American culture, touch is a prelude to sexual possession, one that rather quickly goes a long way toward closing the gap between the initiation and the fulfillment of a sexual conversation that leads to the pleasures of the flesh. Moreover, "seeing is touching" is one of the metaphors we live by, but one, because of its representative character, that tends to open the gap; indeed, the metaphor of sight need never lead to actual touching in order to provide the pleasures of the text.

Fashion's strategy of body disclosure, especially through the tactics of diaphany and liquefaction, rather forcefully restricts clothing's sense of touch to the realm of metaphor. Fashion is finally a visual eroticism; the garment—no matter how much like underwear, how strategically cut, how sheer, how clinging—remains a tactile barrier. The experience of the erotic arises from the transit between clothing and nakedness, between the invisible and the visible, and between sight and touch; neither condition becomes an absolute value.

Fashion's disclosure of the body, then, may be seen as an effort to represent and so to experience in a sufficiently satisfying way a continual movement between becoming clothed and becoming naked. Diaphany and liquefaction especially are symbols of the turmoil of indeterminacy of the late modern era, are indexes of the particular turbulence women experience in this context, and are icons of the desire on the part of many women to reclaim the erotic; that is, to reestablish the transit between constraints of dignity and the permissiveness of freedom.

From *Journal of Popular Culture* 34, no. 4 (Spring 2001). Reprinted, without bibliographical information, with permission of the author.

SUGGESTIONS FOR FURTHER STUDY

1. Do the women in the class try to dress according to fashion or are they content to wear the clothes common on campus—and be comfortable?
2. Do you think that "fashion" is only clothes deep and therefore care nothing about it? Or does it have an important function in American society?
3. Do you think that psychiatrists and philosophers—as in this article—make too much of something that is, after all, only clothes and the way to wear them?

Beyond the Quilting Bee

DIRK JOHNSON

It was a night off from the husbands and the kids. In a suburban Chicago rec room, as stereo speakers cranked the beat of Bare Naked Ladies, a crowd of eighteen women were cutting loose. Scissors in hand, they hovered over photo albums and fitted their memories for the ages. It is the great scrapbooking trend sweeping America, the twenty-first-century version of the quilting bee.

"Somebody, please, give me an idea!" cried out Jenny Johnson, thirty-four, looking for help in designing a page that commemorated her four-year-old daughter's visit to a beauty shop. Across the folding table, three women lifted their eyes from their own projects. "Bubbles," offered one of the scrapbookers, "cut out cute little bubbles." With an approving nod, Johnson set to work on pink bubble cutouts that framed pictures of little Cassady having her hair done. "She got her hair washed in the big bowl," her mother explained. "It was a very big deal for her."

Scrapbooking has become a big business. *Creating Keepsakes*, the leading scrapbook trade magazine, estimates that four million people, almost all of them women, gather for "crop-alongs" every month. One company alone, Creative Memories, has sixty-five thousand "consultants" who visit these gatherings offering expertise and, of course, plenty of equipment to sell, like treated paper and adhesives that preserve forever that special trip to the Wisconsin Dells. Creative Memories estimates sales of $300 million this year. One avid scrapbooker says she has spent more than $10,000 on the hobby in two and a half years, a sum she was not eager to share with her husband. Meanwhile, there are now about two thousand scrapbook stores across the nation, up from three hundred five years ago. And that doesn't count the burgeoning scrapbook aisles at Wal-Mart—or the hours of television programming. Last month one cable network held an eight-hour scrapbooking marathon, which including a one-hour special called "Croppin' USA."

These are not your grandmother's humble albums. These are extravagant creations: titled pages, journal entries, love letters, artwork, color-coordinated doodads. And they are meant to be exhaustive records of family life. Ashwini Karnik, twenty-six, has a picture of her son eating, under the headline "Arnav Having His First Mango." The scrapbook of Paula Fabbri-Morrow, thirty-eight, includes DNA from her two-year-old daughter, Julia, taken from amniocentesis.

Jenny Johnson claims to have recorded "everything" in the life of her daughter through the age of two starting with the ultrasound. "I mean everything," she says. "Tell me what you want to know." There is Cassady's first bath in a tub, her first trip to the park. "I'm on the lookout for photo ops every day," she says. Scrapbooking is a hobby that suits the nesting instincts of baby boomers and even Gen-Xers, drawn to the simple pleasures of home life. Besides all that, Johnson acknowledges another appeal. "To be very honest," she says, "it's nice to be out and doing something without my children under my feet."

Scrapbookers typically meet in somebody's home, but there are scrapbooking cruises to the Caribbean and Alaska, weekend sessions at resort hotels. Often the meetings have a theme, such as pajama-party sessions or Hawaiian-wardrobe nights. Depending on the group, there might be a little wine. At Laura Brown's home the fare was more wholesome: finger bowls filled with pretzels and M&M's.

Some say they took up scrapbooking because they felt guilty about having so many boxes of photographs gathering dust in the attic. Others say they're a bit miffed that so few pictures were taken of them as cute little tykes—and they want to make things better for their own children. Cassandra Vickas, thirty-six, is already teaching her five-year-old, Veronica, to cut and paste: "She got a scrapbook for her birthday."

Sitting elbow to elbow, sometimes into the wee hours, the scrapbookers cannot help but compare their talents. And that can cause a little anxiety. "I'm really competitive," says Mary Young, thirty-seven, "and I've got a lot of friends who say, 'I did ten pages last night, how about you?'" She'll sheepishly confess that she did only one page. But she is not about to give up. And that might give pause to her husband, Jeff.

She might consider having a second child, she has told him. But not until she's caught up on her scrapbook.

SUGGESTIONS FOR FURTHER STUDY

1. Are the mothers who scrapbook looking for individual or group immortality in fixing photographs of themselves and their children in these permanent places?
2. Is the scrapbooking evidence that American women have too much—and potentially dangerous—time on their hands?
3. What would be the difference between female and male scrapbookers if men took up the activity?

FASHION

Fashion comes in more forms than clothes. The act of following or setting the latest trends is also a form of fashion. With women, especially, fashion is being at the forefront of visibility. Through the centuries, fashion for women has turned on having the body and actions visible to both women and men, especially when women can be sexually suggestive without being too obvious or blatant. Belly dancing, especially in countries other than the United States, accomplishes such desires for women.

Shakin' All Over

MICHELE ORECKLIN

To understand why belly dancing is enjoying such popularity today, it's important to set aside certain preconceptions. Banish the image of nubile harem girls undulating under an Arabian moon for the amusement of sheiks. Envision instead women of expanding waistlines and advancing ages finding their inner goddess under fluorescent lights at the local Y.

In the current resurgence of belly dancing, its reputation as a seductive art is played down. Rather, it is promoted as a way for women of all shapes and ages not only to tone their obliques but also to deepen their souls. The success of this message explains why sales of videos by "belly twins" Neena and Veena are soaring and gyms in New York City and Los Angeles are scheduling belly-dancing classes during hours once reserved for Pilates. It's why dance studios from Omaha to Anchorage can't accommodate everyone seeking to enroll.

For many, belly dancing is chiefly notable as the one endeavor outside of a wedding in which women are encouraged to wear veils. But it has changed the life of Nebraskan Faith Erdei, fifty-one, a mother of twelve who works at a nuclear-power plant. Every week she drives the fifty miles to Lincoln to attend class because it's the one place she can feel feminine. Roni Flory, twenty-seven, of Carrolton, Texas, says learning to express herself through belly dancing has made her more effective at her sales job by giving her the confidence to talk to anyone.

Improved self-esteem was probably not why belly dancing evolved thousands of years ago. Though its origins remain murky, it was probably first performed in the Middle East, then spread through that region and North Africa. The term *belly dancing* is a misnomer adopted in the West in the nineteenth century: in ancient Middle Eastern societies, women would have been forbidden to show their midriffs. Most modern practitioners contend that belly dancing was designed not for sexual enticement but as a fertility ritual or for birthing ceremonies for and among women. There has also been speculation that the rotating pelvic moments arose from the action of stirring soup.

It's much easier to pinpoint how and why belly dancing has caught on at this moment in the U.S. Following the 9/11 attacks, people began seeking knowledge about Middle Eastern society: Marta Schill, president of the twenty-five-year-old Middle Eastern Culture and Dance Association, says membership has grown more than 30 percent, to one thousand, over the past year. This desire to learn about Arab traditions coincided with the release of music videos by pop stars Shakira and Britney Spears, who bared their stomachs and belly danced with abandon, sparking the interest of teenagers and young adults.

"When the room is packed, I say, 'Thank you, Shakira and MTV,'" says Mesmera, who teaches belly dancing in Los Angeles. Mesmera (real name: Laurie Rose) began belly dancing twenty-seven years ago and in recent months has seen her class sizes swell. She says she doesn't care what brings people in; she's just happy to get out the message that belly dancing "gives you a stronger sense of self," even if that self doesn't look like Shakira. "We're all different shapes and sizes, but Mesmera makes everybody feel beautiful," says Monica, a high school teacher. Echoes Suzy Roan, forty-four, a divorced bartender who teaches belly dancing in a suburb of Anchorage: "It's one of the few dancing arts where it's totally acceptable to be yourself. If you're plump, it's O.K."

Mesmera's classes resemble those taught nationwide. Even in a beginner's class, most of the twenty students wear flowing skirts in cotton or gauze and scarves adorned with coins tied low on their hips. After breathing exercises, the students are instructed to twist their hips slowly in a figure eight while extending their arms to the side. Later come side-to-side sways, pelvic thrusts, and serpentine torso waves done to a rhythmic drumbeat. Occasionally classes are accompanied by live percussionists, and women play finger cymbals called zills, though CDs with Middle Eastern music and singing are often used.

Belly dancing can be an effective cardiovascular exercise that helps strengthen muscles by isolating different parts of the body, but the moves are gentle, not pounding like other forms of dance or aerobics. Diana Stone, fifty-four, an instructor in Asheville, North Carolina, explains, "This dance feels right for the body of a woman."

Feeling feminine but not weak is a strong draw from Barbara Sorenson, fifty-five, who teaches in Lincoln, Nebraska. She says belly dancing indulges her desire to wear jewelry, makeup, and billowing fabrics, to be "female but also strong and feminist." Sorenson says the style she teaches, Tribal Fusion, is "a dance of attitude, strength, beauty, and the celebration of a woman's spirit." (Despite the emphasis on femininity, some men do belly dancing but with sharper, less rolling moves.)

Americans tend to treat ancient rituals like new cars, customizing them for convenience, then trading them in when something more exciting comes along. But that isn't the way belly dancing is seen by people like Don Gold, president of StudioWorks, a Thousand Oaks, California, video distributor whose parent company gave the world Tee-Bo. Gold just signed a deal with belly dancer instructor Dolphina, who teaches in Los Angeles, to distribute her Goddess Workout Fitness Video series because "we think we're ahead of the curve of a new revolution." It's possible that the practice will become classic, like yoga, but there's always the danger that it could end up in the used-trend lot, discarded and rusting like step aerobics.

From *Time*, October 28, 2002. © 2002 Time Inc. Reprinted with permission.

SUGGESTIONS FOR FURTHER STUDY

1. How widespread is belly dancing among the women in this class?
2. Do men view it as exercise and shaping of the female body or as sexual provocation?
3. Men should remember that Elvis Presley was banned from television at first because of his sexually explicit hip gyrations.

4. Would mixed classes of males and females change the nature of belly dancing?
5. If you were a parent would you encourage your daughter(s) to take these classes?

FOODS

Through the centuries food—which for millennia was mere fuel for the human machine—has become a medium through which people express and demonstrate degrees of sophistication and esthetic differences among social classes. Primarily eating has remained a family bonding ritual and a classroom in which lessons and traditions and lore of one generation are passed on to the next. Through the ritual of the family meal the members of one generation—one immediate or extended family—bond with another. It is also an occasion for generations to learn from each other: the older generation not only passes down history and traditions but absorbs new attitudes and practices from the younger generation. Around the table people of two or more generations blend their lives empathetically.

One prized characteristic of mealtime has always been the length of time needed for the intermixing and developing of social intercourse. Generally, however, the relaxed and discursive mealtime has been as much a fantasy as a reality. For one reason or another people have always been in a hurry—they eat and run. Correspondingly, people have always had to grab a bite from some source outside the family dining room. Throughout history there have been suppliers of prepared food waiting for the hungry passerby. In ancient Athens and Rome, food was available on the streets. In London, Paris, and elsewhere beef pies and steamed chestnuts—and fish and chips—and other food were handy. Most of the time the ready foods were cursed as necessary evils though they were occasionally romanticized and made the subject of glamour and pleasure in story and song, as in the steaming chestnuts of Parisian streets. In our own day this fast-food industry has been generalized under the four-letter word McDonald's and its numerous imitators.

The dishonor of the American fast-food industry may be undeserved. The food is certainly cleaner and tastier than that provided years ago, and it serves a societal need or it would not prosper. Furthermore, the industry offers numerous benefits to society. The billions and billions of hamburgers sold in the United States encourage democracy, as the Cadillacs and Jeeps parked outside or at the pick-up window demonstrate. Even greater benefit results in other countries, where fast-food restaurants weaken established hierarchies and social establishments. They bring together groups of people—young and old—who can for a short time at least be together in a semi-"foreign" setting to eat and talk. The political results may be even more powerful symbolically. McDonald's and other fast-food emporia overseas are living testimonials to what can happen to at least one segment of society if people are allowed to exercise their individual freedom and desire to live different lifestyles.

If the American Dream is to be recognized and realized as the Human Dream, and the two aspects of that dream are a full stomach and freedom for individual enterprise and accomplishment, then the fast-food industry has a compelling positive effect. McDonald's and McDonaldization-like American movies, TV, and other manifestations are not four-letter words that reveal America at her worst but are instead examples of the fruit of Americans—and everybody worldwide—for at least portions of life, nutrition, and mobility.

Meanwhile back in the home, the kitchen is no longer the private sanctuary of the cook who prepared her meals according to tradition or the latest guides in newspapers and books. Now frequently her guide is a radio or TV chef who takes the snobbishness out of cooking and recalls the pleasure of eating. Julia Child has been replaced by such people as Emeril Lagasse, who is the McDonald's of TV chefs.

Students are becoming a more knowledgeable and demanding bloc. Universities and colleges look upon students' eating habits as a source of income; therefore they must be satisfied. If that satisfaction comes from McDonald's and other fast-food restaurants in the student unions and dormitories, universities will install them. If, as is becoming increasingly evident, students are becoming more sophisticated and careful about their eating habits, the universities will supply different kinds of food. Still, for one reason or another, students want fast food at their disposal. Such food can be berated and criticized for causing obesity—the second most common cause of death in the U.S.—but educated students still demand it.

An intriguing question remains: If the American fast-food industry is bringing about democratization around the world, is democracy causing more harm worldwide than good?

Suppliers work hard to keep up with the demands of the fast-food public. The kitchen is now more a scientific laboratory where every food and every mixture of chemical with it is tested to see if it satisfies the public taste.

Inside the Food Labs

JEFFREY KLUGER

There are a lot of different factors Michele Kester has to juggle when she invents your next scoop of ice cream. Right now she's not as concerned about flavor or texture—although those are important—as she is about architecture. Kester, a food technologist in the Burbank, California, labs of ice cream giant Baskin-Robbins, has been fooling around with an idea for a flavor she calls Cinnamon Bun, but first she has to make sure the stuff will hold together. If you're not careful with the size and number of your chips, nuts, or bun bits—what the ice cream techies call inclusions—even the densest scoop of the richest brand can fall apart. "Any inclusion larger than three-quarters of an inch may be too big," says Kester, scooping up a handful of cake pieces and tossing them into a bowl of white ice cream base. "Sometimes it's guesswork."

But Kester doesn't really have the luxury of guessing. Baskin-Robbins' trademark list of thirty-one flavors has expanded to almost one thousand since the company was founded nearly sixty years ago. To keep that number growing, eight food technologists in the Burbank facility each come up with about twenty new flavor brainstorms a year; of all those, perhaps three or four make it to the big leagues.

The shelves of canisters filled with Oreos, M&M's, and other colorful inclusions that line the laboratory walls certainly keep the ideas flowing. So too does the dream of being the person who develops the next Pralines 'n Cream—perhaps the most celebrated member of the company's flavor roster. "It's a fun job," says Kester. "I get to play with food all day."

Of course, play, as Kester is the first to admit, is only part of it. The food trade is a $500 billion industry in which uncounted new products jostle for space on overstocked shelves. Fully 25 percent of all meals are now consumed in restaurants, and of those eaten at home, two-thirds are either prepared entrees or restaurant takeout. With all that, Big Food has had to become Big Science. Companies that want to stay in the game can't afford to drift along with the same product line year after year until someone in R and D dreams up another Pop-Tarts or Pringles. Nor can they afford to have a good idea and then let it die from poor execution—simply that the corn in the corn puff was the wrong texture or the cavity in the cupcake crowded the filling.

As a result, the food industry has become a place where product design is micromanaged as never before—where flavors are built literally by the molecule, salt crystals are measured by the micron, manufacturers agonize over which side of a chip is the best place for the flavoring, and any new product under development must be focus-grouped and taste-tested down to its last scrap of fiber and last drop of corn syrup.

"The eating experience has so many different factors—smell, texture, taste, and different combinations of all of those," says Nicole Ifcher, a marketing manager at Nestlé. "If the idea doesn't resonate with consumers, they won't buy it."

Complicating things further is the speed with which American food fashions change. No sooner do manufacturers devise the perfect product for the perfect niche than new categories open up. What's a U.S. food company to do when Latino consumers—13 percent of the U.S. population—begin clamoring for the *aguas frescas* and spicy tamarinds they grew up with? Where do foodmakers turn when kids—who never met a food they wouldn't prefer sweeter, saltier, chewier, or bluer—create a whole new demand for so-called extreme flavors? And what do they do when all those new choices begin contributing to an exploding American obesity epidemic and the same people who have done all the consuming suddenly demand the foods they love in lower-fat formulations?

"I always look at what's missing in our portfolio," says Vida Lelong, a food developer at Nestlé's thirty-four-hundred-square foot test kitchen in Glendale, California. "You have to ask, What are the hot buttons? And do we have a product that will fill that need?"

Over the years, there is perhaps no company that has done a better job of pushing hot buttons than McDonald's—nor any company that has been better at transforming vaguely defined culinary arts into sharply defined food science. Witness the tale of the McGriddle.

For all the power and ubiquity of the McDonald's brand, the company always had a weak spot when it came to breakfast. The Egg McMuffin has been successfully wooing the breakfast crowd since 1973, but salty, savory foods touch only part of the morning palate. "We found that there was a real demand for sweeter breakfast foods," says Gerald Tomlinson, the company's executive chef.

Tomlinson's answer: An egg, sausage, or bacon sandwich with pancakes instead of a bun. For a company that lives and dies by the one-handed-eat-behind-the-wheel-and-don't-drip-on-your-clothes meal, however, that presented problems. Tomlinson tackled the pancake puzzle in 1999 and first considered a muffin-shaped product with sausage bits stirred into the batter. But would consumers recognize a pancake with so unfamiliar a figure? And how do you add the syrup, the source of that all-important sweetness?

Tomlinson next considered two flatter pancakes sandwiching sausage, with syrup poured on top. That at least looked like a stack of pancakes, but it was an impossible mess to eat. That's when the McDonald's brain trust called in an even larger brain trust and invited the outfits that supply the condiments, bread, and other basic foods to a sort of flapjack summit.

As it happened, one of the company's suppliers had just patented a technology that allowed it to crystallize sugar-based concoctions like syrup. Stir crystals into the batter, and when the mix is heated, the syrup should seep through the entire pancake matrix. "You want that maple flavor in every bite," says Wendy Cook, head of R and D.

Getting that to happen even with the new technology turned out to be a challenge. The crystal size had to be calibrated precisely so it would melt uniformly and provide a smooth texture or, as the industry calls it, mouth feel. The weight of the syrup had to be determined so when it melted it wouldn't sink to one side of the pancake. Even the grilling time had to be fixed so the pancakes wouldn't look pasty and underdone or charred and overdone. "There are very tight specs on the color of the cakes," says Cook.

In June, when all those parameters had been set, the McGriddle was triumphantly introduced. "This is a product that motivates you to go out and have breakfast," Cook says. "We're actually growing the category instead of simply engaging in a share war."

That is the dream of any food manufacturer: invent a product so imaginative and irresistible that you don't have to hijack your competitors' customers or cannibalize your own to get them to buy it. Rather, you serve them something they weren't even aware they wanted until you introduced it to them.

Need proof that it works? Look at Pringles. In the closed community of snack-makers, few things inspire more awe than Pringles. Close enough kin to the potato chip that consumers have always been willing to try them, they nonetheless endure as a completely distinct species of snack. Few people know exactly what to call a Pringle—the company prefers "potato crisp"—and almost nobody can tell you how they're made. That's exactly how Procter & Gamble (P&G), the Pringles parent, wants things. The Miami Valley laboratory where Pringles varieties are developed, outside Cincinnati, Ohio, is not an easy place to find, located along a twisting two-lane road, beyond a landfill and behind a sign. People in the lab are not about to give product secrets away, but they are willing to share a few potato-crisp basics. Pringles are made from potatoes that are processed into flakes, pressed into sheets, and cut into precise shapes. They're placed in their signature molds, fried in an oil blend, and then salted and seasoned in two steps—which brings out a stronger flavor than performing both stages together. To prevent that flavor from becoming overwhelming, each Pringle is seasoned on only one side.

Where the true Pringles magic lies is in the composition of that seasoning. In general, there are a few rules anyone has to follow to create a flavor, and Pringles has mastered them. First, learn to distinguish your top notes from your back notes. For the company's massively popular sour-cream-and-onion taste, it's the sour cream that does the heavy lifting, with the onion riding lightly aboard. "The onion is the top note," says Yen Hsieh, the lead technician of the lab.

Just as important, you've got to research your market. There is a reason there's hardly a corner of the planet where you can't find a can of Pringles, and that's because P&G has taken the time to learn what people in those corners like to eat. Got a hankering for squid-flavored Pringles? No, and you're not likely to develop one. But the company is considering just such a product for the Asian market, where squid is big in snacks. Curry-flavored Pringles are popular in Britain, paprika is a hit in Germany, and a perfectly ghastly sounding ketchup Pringles is a smash in Canada.

Another challenge is knowing how to manage your flavors once you've got them. Onion, for example, is a very volatile taste, which means it tends to evaporate as the chip ages. One answer is bigger onion flakes, but they fall off the chip. P&G thus had to determine the precise micron measurement of each bit of onion flavor and make sure it never varies. It's also critical to listen to how consumers react to the flavor, even if they're not making much sense. P&G routinely tests products with focus groups and has learned to translate their feedback.

"We'll have someone say, 'It's too spicy,'" Hsieh says. "And you're thinking, It's sour cream and onion. What are you talking about? You have to interpret because they're not flavor experts."

Finally, as every food manufacturer knows, it's important to admit when you're licked. Sometimes a flavor simply defies duplication. At that point, it's time to call in the big guns from the big flavor houses. For a foodmaker looking for flavor help, the place to go is New Jersey. Commercial sailing vessels returning from the Far East used to unload their cargoes at the New York docks, and the spices and essential oils were sent to storage facilities in New Jersey. When technology made manufacture of synthetic flavors possible, the spice houses were in the best position to capitalize on the new science. Among the biggest of the flavor bigs is International Flavors & Fragrances (IFF), which has one of its global labs in Dayton, New Jersey.

IFF's plain headquarters, housed in an unremarkable industrial building in an unremarkable industrial park, belies the extraordinary things the company can do. Specialists here can duplicate almost any imaginable flavor, using technologies like gas chromatography and mass spectrometry. The principle behind the science is deceptively simple.

A sample of a food item—a strawberry, for instance—is burned at high speed and high temperature in a gas chromatograph, reducing it to its constituent elements. The resulting vapor is then channeled to a spectrometer, through which the strawberry molecules stream in order of weight and size. Because the scientists know the measure of the molecules they ought to see in food, they can interpret peaks and valleys on a readout and identify all the components as well as their concentrations. Eliminate the ones that have nothing to do with flavor, and you're left with a perfect schematic of the stuff that makes the strawberry taste the way it does. Using the same chemicals, you can then rebuild that flavor in the lab. "It may take a month to do it right," says IFF senior flavorist Kevin Miller.

Just how you choose which foods you burn in your chromatograph can make a difference too. A small strawberry may taste different from a plump strawberry; a just-ripe one will taste different from one that has gone pulpier and sweeter. For subtler flavorings, technologists may not want to touch the fruit at all, instead simply sampling the volatile gases it gives off. IFF scientists sometimes place a glass shroud around a carefully cultivated plant in a field or greenhouse, drawing off the sweet, rich air with a syringe, and use that as their flavor template. "It gives you a completely different flavor from what you'd get if you cut into the fruit," says Miller.

Once IFF's analysis labs are done taking the measure of a food and rebuilding its flavor, those flavors are sent out to other labs in the building to determine how they hold up in food products. In the dairy department, flavors are tested in ice creams, puddings and—most challengingly—yogurt. "Yogurt is a very dynamic system," says food technologist Dan O'Brien. "You start off one flavor at the beginning of the product's shelf life and get a very different one at the end." In the bakery department, the scientists fret over how flavors hold up when food is placed in an oven. "The flavor may be great in the lab," says O'Brien's colleague Brian Kelly, "but when we throw a little heat on it, adjustments may have to be made."

It's in the world of candy, however, that the challenges and rewards are potentially greatest—if the manufacturer can come up with something that appeals to the biggest flavor consumers of all: kids. "Children, on average, prefer 60 percent more flavor in foods than adults do," says O'Brien. This is no surprise to their parents, who once loved consuming now-classic candies like Red Hots and Atomic Fireballs. But what's on the market today is not your daddy's candy.

Nestlé does an especially good job of marketing to kids, particularly those from eight to twelve—the so-called tween group. Tweens enjoy such venerable tongue busters as SweetTarts and Laffy Taffy as well as such newer offerings as the Wonka candy line or the souped-up Sweet-Tarts Shockers. The Shockers are ultrasour SweetTarts in a chewy fruit base that may be unpalatable to parents but are catnip to their kids. Young consumers also like it if candies have what manufacturers call play value. SweetTarts Gummy Bugs offer all the flavor punch of ordinary SweeTarts, with the added value of coming in insect shapes. "First you see all the colors running together on the candy, and that's a lot of fun," Nestlé's Nicole Ifcher says. "Then you decide how you are going to eat it. Do you bite the head off? Then you put it in your mouth, and the sugar sanding signals something sour, but you have the chewy texture underneath."

Another food category in which high-octane flavors can be everything is Latino cuisine. Americans raised on the pasty fare of gentrified Mexican restaurants may know little about the fine and fiery food available south of the Rio Grande, but flavorists do—particularly when it comes to chili peppers. The spiciness in food is measured in Scoville units. A typical fast-food taco may reach 150 on the Scoville scale. IFF flavorists have developed chili essences that climb to one million. One drop, the scientists boast, can heat a giant pot—perfect when you're marketing to an audience unafraid of taste.

Sweet drinks are also big with Latino consumers, and Nestlé is planning to hit that market hard, beginning with its Kerns line of *aguas frescas*—fruity or milky drinks often made from scratch in Hispanic homes. There are dozens of varieties of *aguas frescas,* and before Nestlé technicians could begin to select three or four to sell ready made, they knew they had to understand their audience better. Company representatives began touring *taquerias* around Los Angeles, sampling everything from basic beans and slaw to more complicated *carnitas* and *carnes asadas.* More important, they made it a point to drink whatever beverages the customers were ordering.

Ultimately, Nestlé settled on three *aguas frescas:* a simple strawberry, a more complicated tamarind drink (made from a tart, vanilla-bean-like pod), and an exceedingly complex *horchata,* made from rice, cinnamon, and other spices. "Everyone has their own family recipe for *horchata,*" says food developer Vida Leong. "We mixed and blended for weeks until we matched what we considered the gold standard." So far, their efforts are paying off. The three *aguas frescas* have been doing well in California and Arizona and will roll out around the country in the months to come.

The problem with all these new food choices is that sometimes enough can be way, way too much. The obesity problem in the U.S. has reached epidemic proportions, with 65 percent of the population considered overweight or obese. The pressure is increasing on restaurants and manufacturers to get at least some of the fat out of food. The difficulty, of course, is that fat is often where flavor lives.

Researchers at IFF and other flavor companies have ways to get around that. A critical element in fatty foods is mouth feel—the creamy, palate-coating character of, say, thick pudding or cheesy lasagna. Scientists can mimic that feel with substances such as starches, polysaccharides, or lactones (a natural product of fermentation). These lower-cal alternatives can give food a higher-cal feel. "When you create the impression of fat," says Miller, "you also enhance flavor."

Other tricks are simpler. Stouffer's, for example, has found that crushed tomatoes in its Lean Cuisine line go a long way toward enlivening foods stripped of their fattier ingredients. "The tomatoes have more body and a riper taste," says Kathy Klingensmith, who works in R and D.

Also important is avoiding dryness. Fatty food is usually moist, and for consumers accustomed to gooey cookies and premium ice cream, something that's both dry and fat-free might well be tree bark. Developers thus fortify foods with substances known as humectants—glycerin, sucrose, or similar ingredients that hold moisture.

Certainly not everybody needs or wants to know about the humectants in snacks. Scientific reductionism is fine in astronomy or physics, but it's another thing entirely when your dinner is involved. There are few things more intimate than the preparation of food—an ancient, imprecise craft built on pinches and dashes and tasting things at the stove. What are old-style cooks to do when this quiet craft is elbowed aside by an industry in which flavor concentrations are measured in parts per billion and companies like IFF can sell, without irony, a product called Fleximint, "a tool kit for mint work"?

Traditionalists may abhor all this, but the food scientists are only doing what we ask them to do: respond to the needs of 280 million people all trying to eat at once and do so in the most enjoyable, affordable, and nutritious way possible. It's the industry's job to fill the national plate; it's our job to decide which parts of that vast meal we want to eat.

From *Time*, October 6, 2003. © 2003 Time Inc. Reprinted with permission.

SUGGESTIONS FOR FURTHER STUDY

1. With so much scientific preparation of our food, why are most Americans dangerously overweight?

2. With the data given here about scientific ways to keep food from being fattening, why do we continue to gain weight?

3. Do you believe that the businesses that provide food make changes to provide better food only when the public—or the courts—force them to?

4. If you were in a position to develop some kind of new food or an improvement on one that already exists, what would you work on?

5. In a food democracy where every individual is free to eat what he or she likes, should the guiding philosophy be to let everyone direct his own path to an enjoyable but early grave?

6. As the food labs develop foods that appeal to so-called minorities, where does the end come? Are they to develop foods now that will appeal to a growing minority when its purchasing power is sufficiently strong to make manufacture and sales profitable? Or should each company wait until some other company has developed a profitable line of minority food?

The food industry described above resulted at least partially from the emergence of fast-food businesses that supplied a need of people to eat on the run. Perhaps the dietary habits of the American public would be different today if the fast-food industry had not supplied that need. But in this country if there is a need or demand someone will rise to fill it, as the following article discusses.

Selling 'Em by the Sack

White Castle and the Creation of American Food

DAVID GERARD HOGAN

This story is about White Castle: the company, the man who started it, and the sequence of developments that it spawned. It is social history because it analyzes how and why fast food altered American life; it is biography because it is impossible to examine White Castle without discussing the achievements and tenacity of its founder, Billy Ingram; and it is "corporate history" because it follows the company's triumphs and failures since 1921. The White Castle story cannot be told without including any of these elements. Ingram founded the company, and the significance of the company is that it drastically changed American eating patterns and, hence, American life.

The creation of White Castle in 1921 greatly affected life in America during the twentieth century. White Castle marketed the hamburger to Americans so successfully that it became their most common meal and their primary ethnic food. White Castle's success also inspired a legion of imitators and gave birth to the multi-billion-dollar fast-food industry, which continues to thrive despite America's increasing obsession with fat content. In addition to providing America with a primary food, White Castle and subsequent fast-food companies taught Americans a new and different way to eat, leading to many changes in American culture and lifestyle.

White Castle's founder Billy Ingram successfully sold to the general public the hamburger sandwich, which in 1921 was a product considered disreputable and undesirable. Because of Ingram's marketing genius, by 1930 Americans in every corner of the country accepted the hamburger as a mainstream food and eventually made it a staple of their daily diet. Ingram did not "discover" or "invent" this food, but he did introduce it to Americans at an affordable price and deliberately marketed it to specific segments of the population. He sold his hamburgers in large quantities at five cents each, telling his customers to "buy 'em by the sack" and introducing and promoting both the food and the carryout format that became synonymous with fast food. Within a decade Ingram had altered the American palate and captured millions of customers. In fact, it could be said that what Henry Ford did for the car and transportation, Billy Ingram did for the hamburger sandwich and eating.

The immediate outcome of Ingram's marketing genius was that White Castle sold a lot of hamburgers. It quickly became apparent that Americans loved them and avidly followed White Castle's advice to "buy 'em by the sack." The longer-term effect was that Billy Ingram's success became well known and countless imitators started restaurant chains that were virtually identical to White Castle in product, architecture, and even name. White porcelain buildings appeared on many street corners, bearing names such as White Tower, White Clock, Royal Castle, or White Palace. This almost immediate proliferation of White Castle imitators was the beginning of the massive fast-food industry, which today ranks among the largest segments of the American economy.

Beyond the creation and promotion of a new food product and the founding of a new industry, White Castle had even greater—if less quantifiable—effects on American society. The fact that the hamburger that Ingram marketed so aggressively became America's favorite food had several important ramifications. First, millions of Americans consuming millions of hamburgers each day caused a major increase in beef production. Not only did the beef producers love the ever-growing demand for their product, but the fact that Americans were eating more meat also affected their overall diet and health.

For better or worse, White Castle started the massive consumption of hamburgers that continues unabated to the present. Its most significant contribution to American culture is that hamburgers came to be closely identified with American culture. In 1921, Billy Ingram promoted his hamburgers to an American society whose many subgroups were still deeply entrenched in and divided by their original ethnic traditions. The early 1920s was a time of intense ethnic and racial division in the United States, with few areas of "common ground" between the groups. One result of this division could be found at the collective dinner table. The diverse ethnic foods consumed by people from different backgrounds often were a persistent link to their past. Many recently arrived European immigrants and northward-migrating African Americans maintained their indigenous cuisines, whereas other Americans were divided gastronomically by region and class. These differences in backgrounds, customs, and tastes were a major obstacle in the formation of a homogeneous American ethnicity. One might also argue that in 1921 there was no true American ethnicity. Much happened in the next forty years, however, to bring American citizens together under a single ethnic identity. In this book I analyze the evolutionary "creation" of this new American ethnicity and discuss how Ingram's hamburger sandwich emerged as the country's principal ethnic food. I even contend that White Castle and its imitative progeny were instrumental in helping create a uniquely American ethnicity.

As a society, we still often do not consider that a unique American ethnicity exists or understand its defining characteristics. Nonetheless, there was a quiet, unheralded change in ethnic identity between 1920 and 1960, even though many Americans failed to notice it. Although we acknowledge the existence of American patriotism and nationalism, we generally do not ponder or revel in our ethnicity. In fact, many people deny the essential commonalities in our culture; indeed, some are horrified by the notion that the fast-food hamburger has come to be identified as America's premier ethnic food. If you find this hard to believe, just ask anyone from another country, "What is American food?" Nine out of ten replies will be "Hamburgers!" This outsider's perspective allows us to see what we so rarely ponder and often take for granted; the hamburger is all around us on a daily basis, consumed by many millions. The fact that it is so close, so mundane, and unextraordinary is exactly what makes it so important and central to who we are as a people.

In some ways, the hamburger is to America what fish and chips is to Britain or the tamale is to Mexico. Each of these foods helps define the country's ethnic identity yet is usually disdained or at least is downplayed by the elites in their societies. Fish and chips, for example, is savored by much of British working class, but rarely, if ever, is served at middle- or upper-class tables. Greasy and traditionally wrapped "to go" in old newspaper, fish and chips also became popular in the early twentieth century, appealing to the appetites of an increasingly busy British working class. These elements of speed and convenience closely parallel those of the hamburger. Common features of most true ethnic foods are that they are easily cooked, convenient, inexpensive, and tasty. Their ready accessibility and affordability, in fact, are what often identify them with the working or lower classes and hence often make them less desirable to the more affluent or more "cultured." Although usually plain and inelegant, such ethnic foods remain the sustenance of the majority of the world's population and—in conjunction with language, history, and belief systems—help define particular peoples and cultures.

In addition to documenting White Castle's extraordinary significance in terms of the American economy and ethnicity, this book also follows the company along its roller-coaster ride of business highs and lows. In essence, the history of White Castle reflects the history of twentieth-century America. Tracing the company's progress chronologically through the decades mirrors the prosperity of the 1920s, the upheaval of the Great Depression, the war years, the social explosion and demographic changes in postwar America, and the prosperity of modern times. Issues of class mobility and division, racism, changing gender roles, and demographic movements also are central to the White Castle story.

I have written about White Castle because most historians have ignored the founding of the fast-food industry and culture in America. Little scholarly work has been done on fast food, and most of what is in print focuses on the McDonald's phenomenon of the late 1950s. Although White Castle frequently receives a brief mention, or even a paragraph, in many food or cultural histories, it is often discussed interchangeably with its imitator White Tower, often confusing which chain and entrepreneur actually started the hamburger craze. For the most part, however, both White Castle and the formative years for fast-food hamburgers exist only as footnotes in scholarly works either in praising or criticizing Ray Kroc and his golden arches. This misplaced emphasis has led both academics and the general public to believe, erroneously, that fast food really started in the 1950s, thereby leaving any developments before that time in an undocumented haze. While books abound about far more peripheral issues in American life, a void exists in the explanation of the basic question of how and what Americans feed themselves. Being either forgetful or elitist, historians often overlook the history of American food in general, reserving a special blind spot for the history of fast food. Telling the White Castle story is just my attempt to clarify that haze.

From *Selling 'Em by the Sack: White Castle and the Creation of American Food,* by David Gerard Hogan (New York: New York University Press, 1997). Reprinted with permission of the author.

SUGGESTIONS FOR FURTHER STUDY

1. Every day you engage in the ritualistic pattern of behavior in eating food prepared by formula (either cultural or chemical). Discuss several aspects of these kinds of behavior in your own eating habits. Discuss the importance of the role of food and eating as a determiner of taste, standards, etc.

2. Students are demanding change in their ritualistic behavior of eating at colleges and universities. Discuss the changes in demands that you have seen and engaged in.

3. Are you concerned with eating too much "junk food"? Do you believe it is "junk"? Are you concerned that your university or college is probably offering more fast-food choices for lunch and dinner?

4. In your off-campus eating, what changes have you observed in the ritual of eating by nonstudents?

5. If you were allowed to establish and direct student feeding on campus, what would be your plans and means of reaching your goals?

6. Ask yourself, other students, or adults what they are doing to prevent obesity. Read up on what the fast-food industries are doing to reduce and prevent obesity. Discuss the role of the fast-food industry in the United States and overseas.

7. Try to envision the difficulties in an American society that had no fast-food industry. What would be the effects? A better or a worse society?

PERSONAL APPEARANCE

The conflict between the benefits of food and its dangers to the human body when taken to excess is probably as old as humankind. Consumption of food—overconsumption—is a part of the American Dream. If food is available it is an American right to consume it. Americans use food both as a form of conspicuous display—in other words making it a social occasion—and as mere fuel—to keep the body in locomotion. Increasingly food is being democratized and speeded up, so that every civilized community has an oasis of fast-food restaurants that offer virtually every kind of food that can be supplied quickly and profitably. These fast-food places have always been harshly criticized for dishing out greasy foods that severely stress the heart and health in general. They are blamed for causing two out of three Americans to be overweight or obese, with the number growing every year. One leading physician and diet expert, Robert C. Atkins, in half a dozen books has insisted—not with the concurrence of all other diet experts—that it is not the grease but the carbohydrates that are the cause of the obesity.

Diet is also tied closely to physical beauty. Beauty is the highest priced commodity on the market today, and both men and especially women will do almost anything to achieve it, even cut down on eating. Dieting is not easy. Drugstore shelves are heavy with the nostrums that are supposed to make one lose weight, as are the stacks of gadgets that allow one to exercise the pounds off. That slimness brings happiness is one of the great myths of modern civilization, and the many formulas for achieving that happiness are as numerous as snake oil salesmen and women.

The media are so saturated with messages about the importance of food and medicines to achieve beauty that there is no need to reproduce one here. They echo throughout our existence day and night.

Since time immemorial people have used their bodies for ornamentation. Ancient Egyptians decorated their bodies. Tattooing is an old form but newer alterations have been practiced since they have been discovered to be reasonably safe. Using the body as a canvas on which to practice art is in itself a form of advertising.

Another form of enhancing the body is aesthetic surgery, a practice that is growing in popularity and outreach. It is used not only to correct disfigurement of the face and body but also to "beautify" certain aspects of the human body, especially among females. But it is so visible, especially rhinoplasty, that surgeons must specialize to please an ever-growing public. For example, many Japanese women want to look like American women. Influenced by advertising and media images to believe that big American-style breasts are the key to happiness and that American women's eyes are more beautiful than Japanese eyes, they are undergoing breast augmentation and having their eyes "Americanized." Increasingly, however, ethnic groups within the United States recognize that in facial beauty one nose does not fit all, so they are having their noses rebuilt to conform to ethnic styles: idealized Latino noses for Latinos, African American noses for African Americans. Undoubtedly as other minority groups strengthen their cultural positions, their sense of ethnic identity and beauty will grow and they will want to reinforce their blood ties. Meanwhile the general movement is outlined in the article below.

Outside-In

Body, Mind, and Self in the Advertisement of Aesthetic Surgery

DEBORAH CASLAV COVINO

The American Society for Aesthetic Plastic Surgery (ASAPS) reports a 119 percent increase from 1997 to 1999 in aesthetic procedures performed in the U.S., to a 1999 total of 4,606,954. The American Society of Plastic Surgeons (ASPS), reporting over a longer period but drawing from a smaller group of physicians, advertises a 174 percent increase in total procedures from 1992 to 1999. For the ASAPS, the most popular procedure is the chemical peel; for the ASPS, liposuction tops the list. ASAPS also features a survey of "1000 American Households" which concludes that 57 percent of women and 58 percent of men approve of cosmetic surgery. These statistical histories can be read both as indicators of the striking and substantial growth of the aesthetic surgical industry, and as advertisements for the professional associations that cull the numbers. Alongside the proliferation of web pages, media ads, and television news stories about the promise and perils of aesthetic surgery, these statistics tell us that we are in the midst of a very persuasive and pervasive cultural phenomenon.

Because the aesthetic surgical industry so often defines and legitimates itself by asserting that changing the body changes the mind, I am prompted to ask to what extent and under what dispensations it continues and adapts conventional and longstanding conceptions of the body-mind relation. An understanding of the industry's stake in the history of this relation can inform current debates over medicine's interest in normalizing the body and psyche around aesthetic considerations. Historically, conceptions of the body-mind relation have preserved a hierarchy that favors the mind; the aesthetic surgical industry holds to this longstanding dualism, in which the inner self is primary and higher, the body a recalcitrant aspect that must be controlled. However, the industry also views its aesthetic administrations as a way of revaluing the body, faulting those who attribute vanity and superficiality to surgical beautification, and urging that the body be given the importance that it warrants. This valorizing of the body, I will argue, is only an apparent disruption of the mind-body hierarchy, since the industry values only the body that defies its mutable nature, and accords with received beauty ideals. Altering our perceptions about aging and physical difference is not an industry concern; rather, its persistent objective is to rehabilitate the body so that it reflects the happiness and goodness of the inner self.

The Body-Mind Relation

Aware that it must vigorously promote an identification with established medical disciplines, the aesthetic surgical industry focuses heavily on better mental health as a primary outcome of aesthetic intervention. Because aesthetic surgeons often cut into bodies that are functionally sound, the industry has legitimated its status within the medical profession by arguing that it is improving the patient's psyche. Mario Gonzalez-Ulloa's 1985 *The Creation of Aesthetic Plastic Surgery*, written under the auspices of the International Society of Aesthetic Plastic Surgery, historicizes the profession with particular reference to this claim for what we might call the outside-in benefit of aesthetic surgical intervention: "We have always known that inner psychic and spiritual changes bring about a new external radiance, but we are now discovering that the process also works in reverse: Change the external appearance— restore the lost years—of a person struggling continually against indifferent or negative social reactions, and the inner light that has died begins to glow once more." Though the mind is more stable than the body in this premise, psychological and even spiritual health are influenced by the social and cultural challenges presented to persons who are no longer perceived as young and beautiful. When a good appearance goes, the strength of the internal self gives way to external conditions.

In this connection, Elizabeth Haiken gives substantial consideration to the role that the popular concept of the "inferiority complex"—derived from Alfred Adler—played in the aesthetic surgical industry's successful legitimation of itself as a healing art. As Haiken concludes, "The inferiority complex, in fact, became the final link in the self-reflexive argument plastic surgeons formulated to justify the practice of cosmetic surgery." The industry's continuing acknowledgment of this idea that a body fix transfers itself to the mind comes forward in its specialized use of the term "psychosurgery" to indicate the ultimate destination of the surgeon's scalpel. [Thomas] Pruzinsky and [Milton T.] Edgerton, in their scholarly study of body image, buttress the industry position by observing that "in fact, the only rational for performing aesthetic plastic surgery is to improve the patient's psychological well-being." Restore external appearance, and the inner life is also restored, so the reasoning goes.

In general, the industry maintains a conception of the relationship between mind and body much like that articulated in Plato's *Phaedrus*, where the body appears to be an obstacle to the manifest virtue of the inner self. Developing its own neo-Platonic formula, the industry relies on a tri-partite model of the individual, positing an *essential* self, a *susceptible* mind, and an *amendable* body. The essential self is not often explicitly or alertly distinguished from mind, but does emerge in statements by industry advocates such as [Kimberly A.] Henry and [Penny S.] Heckaman: "Remember, changing your outer appearance will not change who you are inside. . . . It may, however, result in greater self-confidence and a sense of security about yourself"; here, the mind grows happier in response to the body's improvement, while the essential self remains unchanging. The body is always both correctable and in a state of failure, and the mind—mediating between the eternal self and the amendable body—can be directed by the aesthetic improvement of the body to construct an image that preserves the myth of the unchanging self.

Besides being fundamental to an industry that features the individual—rather than society or culture—as the unit of positive change, this concept of an unchanging self is tied up with the industry's affection for a spiritualized rhetoric of physical renewal. Aesthetic surgeon Alan Gaynor pronounces cosmetic surgery not just "a practical and necessary adjunct to life, but far more importantly, [a practice that] . . . resonates from some of the deepest, most important and even spiritual parts of us"; and Alan Engler declares that when "the gap between body and state of mind is bridged by plastic surgery . . . patients' spirits are uplifted along with their bodies." Gaynor's and Engler's reliance here on a spiritualized image of renewal warrants the proposition that, in a post-religious age, it is aesthetic surgery that guarantees the unchanging self. Also, this unchanging self—which contains both one's uniqueness and the indicators of eternal youth—coincides with what Western religious terminology recognizes as the soul. Describing the power of the surgeon who alters the body to effect at once mental health and a sort of spiritual revival, Engler represents the industry suggestion that fixing the body brings about the harmony of body, mind, and spirit, so that aesthetic surgery becomes an activity invested with physical, psychological, and religious resonances.

Our growing confidence that the body can enjoy the blessing of deep and lasting therapeutic change accounts for the increasing popularity of the term "aesthetic"—rather than the term "cosmetic"—for describing procedures that improve appearance. [Sander] Gilman prefers "aesthetic," as I do, because he recognizes that all attempts to alter body appearance are tied to cultural and racial conceptions of beauty. Stress on the aesthetic function of body alteration is evident in growing numbers of aesthetic surgery "institutes" or "centers," and in advertisements that picture classical artworks such as the *Mona Lisa* and Michelangelo's *David* to suggest the affinity of the surgeon and the artist. As one ad for a South Florida surgeon says, "When choosing a plastic surgeon, an artistic touch means as much as great credentials." Many of the monikers of today's procedures emphasize this artistic dimension: Three Dimensional Liposculpture, Permanent Lip Enhancement, and Feathertouch Skin Resurfacing. The aesthetic surgeon, then, is both priest and artist, whose work is no longer to be understood as merely cosmetic, that is, superficial. While "cosmetic" products and procedures are associated with temporary remedies, "aesthetic" reform—accompanied often by the metaphor of sculpture—is featured as lasting, concrete alteration. Where "cosmetic" suggests surface disguise and the erasure of the self, "aesthetic" indicates principled reconstruction and the remaking of the self in psychological and spiritual, as well as physical, terms.

The good effects of aesthetic surgery touch the soul, or, in latter-day terms, elevate the inner self. This idea that the body is an obstacle to inner grace materializes in aesthetic surgery advertisements for restoring an outward appearance that reflects the "you" inside. One typical ad, for instance, urges consumers to "rediscover the beauty in your eyes," positing an originary beauty that emerges through the alignment of an internal quality or vision that is not lost forever, but can re-emerge when the external body around the eyes is aesthetically improved. The argument here is that the beautiful inner self must be allowed to speak through the body rather than be muted by the ugliness of aging. Pressing this point further, by offering an implicit parody of the Keatsian adage that "beauty is truth, truth beauty," advertisements for facial procedures note than an unbeautified face can give a false impression of the inner self; those who suffer from drooping brows, for instance, sport "horizontal lines and furrows that can make a person appear angry, sad, or tired" ("Forehead Lift"). The disjunction between an "angry" face and a "happy mind" is best remedied by making the outside a vision of psycho-emotional truth. This authentic, originary self exists in the epistemological frame that distinguishes the natural from the unnatural: by promising that aesthetic surgery can "uncover the natural beauty you thought you lost," a *Palm Beach Post* ad effectively features the wrinkle-free face as natural, the wrinkled one as unnatural, setting a true and beautiful self in opposition to one's deteriorations. The unnatural muting of the inner self is featured as imposing devastating losses on human history by Henry and Heckaman, who add historical and medical legitimacy to this view by quoting the famous late nineteenth century rhinoplasty surgeon John Orlando Roe: "How much valuable talent had been buried from human eyes, lost to the world and society by reason of embarrassment caused by the conscious, or in some cases, unconscious influence of some physical infirmity or deformity or unsightly blemish."

The importance of a well-maintained body to a "life that is worthwhile and free of inconvenience" (Athanaeus in Michel Foucault) legitimates advice on the care of the self early in the history of medicine, as Foucault explains: "The increased medical involvement in the cultivation of the self appears to have been expressed through a particular and intense form of attention to the body. . . . The body the adult has to care for, when he is concerned about himself, is no longer the young body that a needed shaping by gymnastics; it is a fragile, threatened body, undermined by petty miseries—a body that in turn threatens the soul, less by its too-vigorous requirements than by its own weaknesses." The "rapprochement (practical and theoretical) between medicine and ethics" (Foucault) leads to greater alertness to the imperfections of the body, insofar as such alertness involves one constantly in the process of correction and improvement, and results in detection through the body of "diseases of the soul," which may otherwise "pass unnoticed" (Foucault). From the Western history of the body, then, the aesthetic surgical industry derives a moral philosophy of medical purpose, as well as an obsession with physical imperfection, that maintains the body as the agency of the soul, and appeals to the longstanding and paradoxical desire to both transcend and retain the body, to both elevate and take along the full materiality of the self.

Focusing on the body as both reflection and facilitator of inner goodness, the aesthetic surgical industry makes its case for recovering the individual's good and true self. In this regard, the industry rejects any association of its practices with the mistreatment or mortifying of the body (what feminist commentaries on the industry largely maintain), characterizing surgical beautifying as a social and personal good that brings with it greater social acceptance and better self-regard, as with the well-known ads for L'Oreal that justify the extravagance of hair dying: "Because I'm worth it." Aesthetic improvement is an indicator of self-worth, and its denial or dismissal is implicitly associated with worthlessness: aesthetic surgeon Ronald Levine's slur of those who do not beautify the body as "granola heads" accuses them of preferring a pitiable asceticism to the good life.

Interestingly though, and perhaps in complication of Henry and Heckaman, we see in early Greek thought both suppression of the body and identification, through the body, with the mind and soul. Nicole Loraux observes a paradox in the form of Socrates' dying: his obsessive interest in his own body, whose gradual deadening he observes so explicitly and carefully, belies his stated indifference to getting rid of it. In effect, there is a kind of conflation of soul and body, inside and outside, so that Platonic philosophy—which does prioritize mind and soul—nevertheless remains fixated on the body. The characterization of spiritual redemption that takes place through an obsessive fascination with the body is commercialized by the aesthetic surgical industry. One recent ad for aesthetic surgery declares that "beauty is only *skin* deep," playing upon the familiar adage that beauty—and its associate goodness—is located both in and through the body, both on the surface and below or beyond it. The declaration here becomes not so much a denial of beauty's depth, which would risk trivializing its importance, but an insistence that the agent of one's beauty is the skin, and that skin features can be surgically improved. Another ad that asks, "How would it be to have the wisdom of the years and the face of youth?" intensifies the outside-inside relationship, and changes the association of wisdom with agedness, replacing agedness with rejuvenated beauty. The young face becomes the face of wisdom, wise not only by virtue of life experience, but also because it reflects the intelligence not to become a granola head. Wisdom lies in the care of the visible self, and also inheres in a repertory of maxims that both qualify (as with "Beauty is only *skin* deep") and reiterate popular adages. The Palm Beach Plastic Surgery Center ad that counsels consumers to "change the things you can" accords patients both power and wisdom, lest there be any doubt that the fate of the body is amendable; those who are not granola heads—whose heads are in fact filled with associations among beauty, virtue, wisdom, and good looks (and whose pockets are filled with enough money to maintain those associations)—are empowered individuals with bodies that reflect the quality of their minds.

Glorified Bodies

Because the aesthetic surgical industry postulates and prizes an inner self associated with timeless youth and beauty (and the wisdom to reclaim them) the exteriors it recommends often conform to an aesthetic conventionally associated with the canonical Western art of antiquity. Though industry spokespersons often make the argument that the clinic is not rigid in its determinations about what beauty is, acknowledging that beauty ideals change over time and across cultures, and making the case that beauty ideals are not strictly Caucasian ones, the use of familiar Western artworks corresponds with the advertisement of body types that maintain dominant models of the beautiful body.

Advertisements often picture classical representations of beautiful women, such as Venus or Aphrodite, and thus deliver the message that 36C breasts and smooth, tight skin render one the living version of a goddess. Though aesthetic surgical patients are endowed with the power to make choices among options (e.g., breast size), the argument predominates that certain beauty attributes are universal, and urges desire for a body that is "classically contoured." Benjamin Gelfant represents at some length the industry's conformity to time-honored models:

Many plastic surgeons have continued in the classic search to define beauty and have used the classical canons of beauty, as described by Albrecht Durer and Leonardo da Vinci and others, to aid in shaping the facial bony features to give an overall appearance of beauty. The argument is made that these proportions have universal appeal, and are seen implicitly in the forms of many beautiful things in nature (such as the spirals of sea shells) and in classically beautiful architecture such as the Parthenon. We respond to these proportions in the faces and bodies of individuals we consider to be attractive or beautiful. Balance and harmony provide a sense of completeness and stability, freed from visual tension and distortion. The Greeks believed that all beauty was based on mathematics and that beautiful objects could be analyzed by numbers. For them, a form such as a rectangle with sides of 1:1.6 was aesthetically the most satisfying. Unfortunately, absolute numbers are of uncertain value when trying to determine nose size and shape on a small thin face or large round one. Perhaps Keats was right when he declared, "Beauty is truth, truth beauty."

Setting aside the obscurity in the reference to Keats, we see that the argument here is unapologetic about its obeisance to classical aesthetics, positing "universal appeal" as the ground of its own visual value system.

As Gelfant's comments suggest, in addition to supporting physical/sexual dimorphism—conforming women to the appearance of fertility, and creating strong chins, noses, and calves in men—the aesthetic surgical industry tends to universalize Caucasian features as preferred. Speaking of equal proportions among the three parts of the face, well-aligned foreheads, lips, and chins, noses and upper lips at 100–110° angles, eyes separated by the width of a single eye, and heads measuring the width of four eyes across, Gelfant remarks that certain "overall facial shapes . . . would be considered unattractive, in any culture," and cites rhinoplasty as one procedure for those who feel "ethnically conspicuous."

Claiming that the desire for beauty is as ancient as the human race and urging the conformity to longstanding Western beauty ideals, the aesthetic surgical industry creates a majority politic for its practice, not only relating patient celebrations of successful surgical outcomes, but also reviewing the sociological and psychological research that verifies what [Deborah] Sarnoff and [Joan] Swirsky call "the halo effect" to describe the importance of good appearance to social and professional life. Most make blunt declarations that "for the majority of people, looks matter," and detail the range of patient motivations. Bingo Wyer is typical of trade-book authors who suggest that the relationship between just about everyone's inner and outer self can be improved by aesthetic surgery, further reinforcing both the psychological benefits of surgical intervention and its universal values:

> So who are you? And how would somebody who knows you really well describe you? . . . Make a few notes, then see if you can spot shared traits with the following groups:
>
> "I'm okay."—We all know people with a balanced self-image who tend to work well with others, even if they are extremely reserved and quiet. These types may be bothered by a physical characteristic that they would like to improve or change.
>
> "I'm okay, but . . ."—The line between this group and the former is almost imperceptible; both share many similar traits. However, for this group, the bothersome feature gains psychological importance over time. Fat thighs, for example, keep them from going to the beach with friends.
>
> "I'm okay, but help!" Invariably this group is made up of teenagers or young adults. They have a particularly high awareness of an appearance flaw. . . .
>
> "I'm okay, but I love my corporate earning power!" These cosmetic surgery candidates achieved significant career success early on. Now an equal number are keen on staying at the top; they view cosmetic surgery as a tool to help extend corporate tenure.

Here, we see that aesthetic surgery is for everybody: the well-adjusted, the maladjusted, and the overachievers are all motivated to a lesser or greater extent toward body improvement. And for Wyer—taking the industry line—they constitute a collective majority that will benefit from new bodies.

Echoing this view, Patricia Burgess even includes a "Motivation Continuum" that helps readers determine whether or not their surgery will turn out to be "one of the best decisions I've ever made." Such vigorous promotion creates a majority body politic consistent with capitalism's democratizing power to make its services available to the many. Thus, despite the fact that the clinic has the capacity to redouble the inferior status of the nonbeautiful, a phenomenon that will continue to show its disparities along racial and ethnic lines, it will no doubt also succeed in further homogenizing appearance as one prominent feature of the new millennium.

As the following account by Alan Engler suggests, the aesthetic surgical mythos trades in the centers of normalcy, and has become part of everybody's imagination:

> On a hot August day I was walking through a department store. It was during a heat wave—the type where everyone is advised to stay indoors and seek shelter in a shopping mall if air conditioning is not available. As I headed for the exit I passed through the cosmetics department. Walking toward me was a woman in her forties and a girl, presumably her daughter, about fifteen years old. As they approached, I saw that the girl was becoming a bit wobbly on her feet. I moved closer to them just as her eyes rolled back and she started to faint. I jumped forward, caught her as she was falling, and lowered her onto the ground. Her mother became hysterical and blurted out that her daughter hadn't eaten a thing for lunch. After determining that the girl had simply fainted and would be okay, I reassured her mother. I asked for some water. A store employee brought out an atomizer of designer water, which I sprayed onto the girl's face. She opened her eyes and looked up at the ceiling. Her mother, now calmed, turned to me and, noticing my beeper, asked if I was a doctor. I nodded. Next she asked what kind of doctor I was. "Actually," I said, "I'm a plastic surgeon." At that point the girl, apparently revived but still lying flat on her back, lifted her head up sharply and asked, "Oh wow! Do you do liposuction?" The mere mention of plastic surgery appears to have spurred her recovery.

"Plastic surgeon" acts as a magic word, raising the sufferer, and uttered here in a place where people take refuge from ordinary discomforts (August heat that makes our bodies swelter) in an artifice that has become normal (a climate-controlled exhibition of skin fashions). The damsel-in-distress motif prevails: the noble doctor happens to be "passing through" when the pressures of wretchedness—heat, hunger, and the unruly body—call him into action. He catches the falling, fainting girl, hears her mother's confession, dissolves the parent's hysteria, and revives the girl with water blessed by the beauty industry. He then restores the girl's vitality, not with nutrition, or even psychotherapy, but with the prospect of liposuction. Ironically, the girl is transformed into a more intensely enthusiastic and happy person by the excited imagination of having the material that supplies her body's energy sucked out. It is not at all clear that she is a candidate for liposuction, and the implication is that the prospect of that procedure has redemptive power for us all, that the very presence of plastic surgery and its agent can activate new psychic health, and cure us from the crisis of possessing ordinary bodies susceptible to mutability and social othering.

In the eyes of the industry, today's surgical beautifying is the effect of a long history in which the desire for beauty has prevailed. Both trade books and industry histories trace a verification of this fact back to ancient Egypt, often citing the Smith papyrus from circa 4000 BCE which "describes methods of dealing with wounds and scars, with particular attention of cosmetic results," though there is speculation that Nile-dwellers "used cosmetics to protect their skin from the sun as early as 10,000 [BCE]." It is our racial destiny, within this industry paradigm, to enjoy a trim body (through liposuction), youth (through breast and face lifts), conventional femininity and masculinity (through breast enlargements, permanent makeup, pectoral and penile enlargements), and Caucasian features (through rhinoplasty and skin bleaching). Through these procedures, psychic health is restored, selfhood rejuvenated. The practice of amending the body is aesthetic, then, in the traditional sense of that term, connected with the creation of beauty that is 1) located in rudimentary sensations, feelings, and intuitions (as in the meaning of Greek aesthesis), and thus an essentially psychic phenomenon; and 2) productive of imitation, that is, of copies, of simulacra. As Elaine Scarry notes with comprehensive attention to the history of beauty, "Beauty brings copies of itself into being." Though Scarry would no doubt recoil at the association of rhinoplasty with the aesthetic, she nonetheless reminds us that hegemonic cultural versions of the beautiful activate attempts at mass duplications. The menu of possibilities for aesthetic surgery advertises, in sum, the achievement of harmony, of past with present, desire with fulfillment, inner self with outer self, technological with spiritual, biological with psychological, self with other. These associations determine the range of our understanding of bodily beauty, and the aesthetic surgeon returns us to wholeness by cutting into body parts and effacing racial and cultural difference.

From *Journal of Popular Culture* 35, no. 3 (Winter 2001). Reprinted, without bibliographical information, with permission of the author.

SUGGESTIONS FOR FURTHER STUDY

1. The author seems to be condemning all the work of aesthetic surgeons. Do you think she would be against such surgery for

accident victims and soldiers? Or is it merely vanity surgery that the author resents and condemns?

2. In 2003 the most popular aesthetic surgery was rhinoplasty or what we might vulgarly call "a nose job." Has anybody in the class had aesthetic surgery? What is the general attitude toward it?

3. In an interview on television an aesthetic cosmetic surgeon once said that he always gives the would-be subject a short lecture on his art and a chance to refuse. Do you think that such specialists have taken up the practice out of greed?

4. Are you of the opinion that perhaps the whole of society would benefit from a kind of general aesthetic surgery, perhaps as a part of Medicare? Would the improvement in looks justify the expense?

CULTURAL EXCHANGE

Americans have always been a traveling people, from the earliest settlers who walked from spot to spot or moved on animal or in wagons and buggies. It was felt that travel accomplished several purposes: it informed people about geographical and cultural conditions in places other than their own and about the people in those places, reducing fear of and animosity toward them. People have long been looking for a One World globe, with the peace and understanding that was hoped would result. Thus with Marshall McLuhan's concept of the Global Village, many people's hopes again rose. But, as the article below indicates, the Global Village concept may have been just another mote in the dreamers' eyes, and humankind will have to wait for some other development beyond the unleashing of self-fulfillment and power in the rising nations around the world.

The Vanishing Global Village

RAY B. BROWNE

The rapid shrinkage of the cultural world and the intensified mixtures of peoples in political, commercial, and the resulting social activities make it necessary for all of us everywhere to appreciate the power of the huge electronic media that are driving the intermixing of the peoples and cultures of the world—the drive toward worldwide equality and democracy and its resulting popular cultures and powers. If we do not understand those popular cultures we leave the destiny of our own cultures and those of other countries in the hands of the politicians, rabble rousers, merchants, and media moguls who may or may not be the most reliable and trustworthy creators and custodians of desirable cultures. If for one reason or another the world does not appreciate the great power unleashed in the democratization of the world, then perhaps it deserves the turmoil and battling peoples and cultures that we will receive. As with the legal mandates, ignorance of the cultural laws is no excuse and no escape. We receive what we consciously or unconsciously create or have created around us.

But a misreading of the impact that the electronic media are exerting on the various cultures of the world can cause misleading and dangerous misassumptions on all societies, strong and weak, around the world. The slick spin to the story of the world for the last thirty years has that the media—TV, radio, movies, print, computers, etc.—are drawing the varied and extended communities around the world into a global village, presumably with citizens who are like-purposed, content, politically and culturally like-minded (at least to the degree that they can get along with one another), and happy. That's one reading of Marshall McLuhan's poetic vision of a global village, a concept that apparently promises peace and contentment to a world otherwise filled with wars, rumors of wars, obvious injustices, and people battling to overcome what they see as mistreatment.

The various peoples and cultures throughout the world make up pieces of a mosaic all of which fit into a large holder with the parts moving slowly to adjust to shifting conditions and developments. The important words are *slowly* and *evolutionarily*. The notion, and hope, that the elements will move rapidly to form a peaceful global village pits the power of electronic communication—instant outreach to touch other peoples and elements of culture which may be very desirable—against human nature—nationalism, regionalism, parochialism, tribalism, cultism, religion, language, fear of change and of the unknown. The same electronic impulses which on the one hand pull us all closer together at the same time give us identity and significance in our separateness—in small groups—and in so doing make it unnecessary for us to join the larger community. When one has the mobility to move into and out of the global village, from and back to his or her "native" village, many opt for the smaller unit where life is looser, freer, easier. It takes a lot of enlightened self-interest to overcome this reluctance to join larger communities. Only Americans seem to have a natural instinct to become part of a larger community. Human beings are capable of political and social revolutions on one scale or another. But cultural changes are more evolutionary than revolutionary, three steps forward and two backward.

More and more people are looking around them to try to locate the existence of their dreams but are discovering that having to cobble together their global village is more than electronic communication. Bringing people closer together through electronic and other means does not necessarily make them happy villagers. So let us examine the interacting of the conflict between global-villagers and the nation-staters.

There is nothing new in the intermixing of peoples around the world. According to Professor Alison Brooks, of George Washington

University, the history of intercultural trade is lost in the earliest traces of human societies. "Humans were using long-distance trading networks for the exchange of quality stone and other goods in Africa at least one hundred thousand years ago," she believes (*U.S. News*, May 20, 1996). In our immediate past, since the thirteenth century when Marco Polo traveled the spice trail to Cathay to establish trading and cultural relations, it has been assumed that trade is one activity through which people get to know one another. It has always been a given, also, that with travel has gone mutually beneficial interchange of cultures. Rusticiano of Pisa, who recorded Marco Polo's adventures, felt "it would be a very great pity did he [Marco Polo] not cause to be put in writing all the great marvels that he had seen, or on sure information heard of, so that other people who had not these adventures might, by his Book, get some knowledge." Sixteenth-century English philosopher Francis Bacon correctly observed, "Travel . . . is a part of education." He listed some two dozen kinds of activities the traveler should observe and advised that such a visitor to a foreign land should live among the locals in order to more fully learn from his travels.

The interchange of cultures, now driven electronically, has never been as powerful as it is now. There is no question that today the U.S. has the strongest, largest, and most diverse popular culture in the world and that it touches every land. According to scholar Peter Freese, American popular culture "is the most successful export article of the United States . . . [and] has effected an ever increasing 'Americanization' of daily life in Germany, as well as in many other countries around the world." Joseph Arpad bears out Freese's observation in stating that Hungarian popular culture today is virtually all foreign. "To see something that is Hungarian popular culture, not American nor Western European, . . . is more difficult." Media mergers, according to Joseph Tukrow, drive "the globalization of mass media activities." *Newsweek* commented on one aspect of this outreach: "Entertainment is not just one of America's largest exports, it's also our culture gone global." During the summer of 1996 American TV through CNN and NBC penetrated more and more deeply and widely into Mexico, and American professional football and baseball filled Mexican stadiums while playing preseason games in various Mexican cities.

But the flow of American culture toward reshaping the world in America's image is not all one way. In the *New York Times* John Rockwell reports that "American popular culture has never been more dominant internationally." But he suggests that this predominance of American cultures "is not so much emblems of American superiority as the simple acceptance by a developing world of a simple international standard of discourse. . . . They may represent not the monopolistic invasion by one country of all the others but the focal point of an international mass culture forming before our eyes."

But the various media—including travel—at the same time is fragmenting the world's popular cultures. The success of radio, TV, and the computer in making all people throughout the world into a general community has been at best qualified, as was that of newspapers and magazines before them. True, TV has furthered the movement that had been intensified by radio and travel in making people from various parts of the world aware of, imitative of, and culturally similar to those from other countries. TV by its very nature has been at least partially successful in separating people from their physical and cultural territory, which is necessary before people can all be joined into a single larger community.

In America, where the TV barrage has been most effective in breaking down barriers, regional differences in speech patterns, dress, food, entertainment, transportation, architecture have been democratized. But TV at the same time it is breaking down barriers between elements of culture is exerting a counter-thrust against the blurring of cultures as one cultural group discovers the perceived strengths of its own culture and an unwillingness to give it up. This strength may have renewed vigor and unexpected lasting endurance.

But it spreads and disrupts foreign cultures, turning them into "little Americas" at least in many respects after they have been adapted to local habits and customs. Foodways are one of culture's strongest forces for continuity in tradition. Knowing that, and benefiting from at times costly experience, McDonald's fast food restaurants though spreading rapidly around the world because they obviously fill a need have modified their offerings under the arches to satisfy those customers who want fast food from their own country. In Amsterdam, for example, because the snack is a vital part of Amsterdam's custom, McDonald's is known as "MacSnack." In Bolivia McDonald's offers concessions to the local cuisine in the form of Bolivian tomato sauce made from hot peppers and coca-leaf tea. On the future menu is a typical Andean dish of beef, potatoes, peas, and hot peppers, all rolled in pastry. On another level we all know Disney's gaff in Euro-Disney until it recognized that the

French are different from other people and started serving wine and otherwise Continentalizing its "world."

In the electronic medium, TV, long thought to be the final homogenizer of cultures, the drift is instead toward the electronic communicator being a strong stabilizer for those cultures which do not want to change and disappear.

When TV programs, especially such "domestic" ones as soap operas or musicals, for example, are imported for broadcast they serve as a reminder of home and in so doing encourage people to continue to think of and act in the ways of the old country. In London, for example, every Saturday, tens of thousands of Indians rush to the TV set in order to see Indian soap opera. These TV programs serve to perpetuate the old order and the ways of home.

Taking back or protecting cultures is being profoundly affected today by tourism, which is one of the strongest outreaches of the First World on destination countries. In accommodating tourism the vital program is to encourage the visitors with all their presumed benefits but to maintain one's own culture. In doing so a destination must accommodate to tourist culture by developing amenities that are alluring to tourists yet at the same time maintaining the integrity of the local customs in order to be attractive to those tourists once they are present. Though this accommodation may be driven by hard-nosed economics it is spiritualized and made more successful and peaceful if based on self-knowledge and pride in one's native culture.

The present and future impact of tourism on another country, say Mexico, is staggering and may be overwhelming. One kind of tourism to Mexico is American retirees living in that country. This group is expected to reach half a million to a million and a quarter people by 2025 and pour into the local economies perhaps a billion dollars *a month*. In return for their money, these retirees will expect a dual world sufficiently Americanized to provide familiar comfort and amenities while at the same time retentive of its historical cultures and charms to make living there different, exotic, and exciting.

Locals are, of course, caught in a bind. While wanting to lure the dollar into their economy, they do not want to do violence to their culture. The obvious tension and possible conflict can be eased and lessened if the local culture is strengthened by self-knowledge and self-respect. In other words, they need to stand tall and straight in their own culture. People who respect their own culture can more comfortably deal with what appear to be attacks or slights by an outside culture. With cultures as with individuals, if the people are comfortable and confident with themselves they are more likely to be secure and comfortable with others and can properly weigh their own cultures against those that might be threatening to invade or substitute. Local cultures in these circumstances do not so quickly and easily fall to the outside power. If, however, they are not properly matured and understood they might easily become bellicose and deadly toward those cultures which are not belligerent but friendly. The meeting of cultures in a militarily powerful world among nations trying to prove their standing is fraught with threat.

Among many examples perhaps one of the simplest but most obvious can be shown in the adventures of Mattel Manufacturing and their Barbie doll. In 1997 Mattel added a new Puerto Rican Barbie to its "Dolls of the World" collection. For the physical attributes of the new Barbie the Institute of Puerto Rican Culture was consulted. She has a mulatto complexion, almond eyes, thick nose, plump lips, raven hair, and a local folkloric dress. To round off Barbie's appeal to the Cuban population, who constitute a significant part of Mattel's market, the manufacturer printed on the doll what they thought would be an appealing nationalistic message: "Puerto Rico was granted permission to write our own constitution in 1952, and since then we have governed ourselves." The Puerto Rican Barbie, instead of uniting the population, has split the 4 million living on the island and the 2.8 million living in the Continental U.S. into opposing war camps. Gina Rosario, a forty-six-year-old art director at an Alexandria, Virginia, school, who is of Puerto Rican descent, perhaps epitomizes the anti-Barbie forces: "She looks very, very Anglo, and what was written on the package was very condescending: 'the U.S. Government lets us govern ourselves.' If you're going to represent a culture, do it properly. Be politically honest," she urges. Meanwhile, a magazine editor in Puerto Rico who collects Barbies says she was "honored" by the Puerto Rican Barbie, as outlined in a *New York Times* article by Mireya Navarra, "A New Barbie in Puerto Rico Divides Island and Mainland."

Such are the streams of conflict swirling around a doll, and representative of the streets and residences of cultures of the world today. If Barbie, whose main purpose is to sell widely and make people happy, becomes the center of a storm of controversy between like-cultured people, how can the worldwide populations live in a village, no matter how widely separated physically? Will the problems be solved when all cultures have achieved similar levels of political and military power? Or will such power only further separate the cultural communities into smaller and more threatening opponents?

From *The Global Village: Dead or Alive*, eds. Ray B. Browne and Marshall Fishwick (Bowling Green, OH: Popular Press, 1999). Adapted and reprinted, without bibliographical information, with permission.

SUGGESTIONS FOR FURTHER STUDY

1. Do you see benefits or threats as a result of the global communities coming closer together?
2. Of all the forces driving toward global harmony, which do you see as the most powerful? The most threatening?
3. Popular culture should present the least threatening forces in world harmony because it consists of everyday, common things. Do some of the everyday aspects of popular culture, however, threaten harmony?
4. How do such political forces as tyranny, dictatorship, and lack of freedom impose more threatening and lasting anti-global situations throughout the world?

AIR TRAVEL

P eople travel for many reasons: on business, visits with relatives and friends, and sightseeing. Though the automobile industry urges travelers to make the trip a part of the enjoyment, people generally want to reach their destinations as fast as possible, and air travel is the answer. The airline industry, however, faces massive problems. The growing horde of travelers forces airlines to expand and to offer lower rates. Lower rates encourage more people to travel and thereby increase problems at the ticket lines, on boarding planes, on demands for takeoff times.

Traffic demands more and larger planes, which require renovation of airports and runways. But the public stiffens its "not in my backyard" attitude and loudly resists new airports, extended runways, and almost any expansion that would accommodate the new demands. Already there are too many passengers in the existing airplanes. The seats are too small, and delays and cancellations of flights make schedules uncertain. Passengers are urged to arrive at the airport two hours before the flight, board the plane thirty minutes before takeoff, often sit on the runway for a half hour or more, and wait for luggage, which may or may not have been put on the plane.

The industry tries to overcome the troubles. In 2001 it proposed modification of the hub system, flying some passengers from origin to destination without having to change planes at the hub—no delays or continuations. It proposed larger planes. The British-French Airbus is developing a prototype that will carry 550 passengers, with a café, gym, and sleeping facilities on board. Boeing is countering with a Stretch 747 that will accommodate 500 passengers. Both will fly faster but require longer runways, renovated waiting rooms, double boarding gates, more time on the plane and waiting for luggage, and more irritable passengers. The airlines are at a crossroads. Now they must enlarge runways and/or reduce the size of "hub" airports. Some of the problems and possible solutions are outlined in the following article from *USA Today*.

Luggage-Transport Service Expects Growth

EDWARD IWATA

Like millions of weary travelers, businessman Jim Cox is sick of standing in nightmarish lines and lugging thirty-pound bags through the nation's clogged airports.

But during a recent trip in Las Vegas, Cox tried a new luggage service called CAPS, or Certified Airline Passenger Services. To his delight CAPS checked out his bags at his hotel, assigned him a seat and boarding pass, and trucked his luggage to his flight.

And all for a measly six dollars—less than a cheeseburger and garlic fries at airport prices.

"I saved an hour or two of headaches, just skipping the line and not having to schlep my bags around," says Cox, executive director of the American Association of Cosmetology Schools in Scottsdale, Arizona.

Those words are sweet music to CEO Jerome Snyder of CAPS, a three-year-old luggage service in Las Vegas that appears to be on the cusp of nationwide growth.

"We're going to revolutionize the way people travel," Snyder says in a telephone interview. "We're bringing the airport to the passenger."

Snyder is betting that CAPS will beat the odds, because its services seem to solve the problem of waiting in line—the number one or number two complaint of air travelers, according to industry analysts, marketing research firms, and the U.S. Department of Transportation.

In a recent survey of one thousand U.S. households by TNS Intersearch, 50 percent of travelers said that wasting time in lines was the top cause of stress for them on vacations and business trips.

One analyst predicts that CAPS will be a godsend for travelers. "You've gotta love it—they're providing a service where airlines are lacking," says Terry Trippler, an airline expert at OneTravel.com, a travel services Web site.

Trippler says it may be hard initially for CAPS to hook customers who will be reluctant to part with their luggage, fearing it may get lost or stolen. But once travelers try CAPS and it works, the firm will have customers for life.

"They may need a little marketing at first," Trippler says, "but this should spread quickly by word of mouth. Once customers see the advantages, business will explode."

So far, CAPS has signed on eight airline partners, including Southwest, United, and Virgin Atlantic, and a dozen Las Vegas hotels, including Bellagio, the Las Vegas Hilton, and Luxor Las Vegas.

For now, their service is offered only with airline partners at McCarran International Airport in Las Vegas. But CAPS is talking with the nation's twenty largest airports, and it has gotten the go-ahead to open counters this June at San Francisco International.

It's also negotiating with dozens of airlines, hotels, and rental car companies, but won't name them.

The brainstorm idea for CAPS came three years ago during a chance conversation between Snyder, a banker and commercial real estate developer, and Rex Jarrett, head of American Baggage and co-manager of CAPS.

"We just happened to be on the same plane from Dallas, sitting next to each other," says Snyder.

It turned out that Jarrett's firm already had approval from the Federal Aviation Administration to move luggage from hotels to the Las Vegas airport for large, regular air passengers.

Sensing a jackpot, they quickly raised money from family, friends, and financial angels. They worked their business ties in Las Vegas and the transportation and banking industries.

After many months of political wrangling, they won over the FAA, which was worried about security.

To appease regulators, all CAPS employees undergo FBI criminal checks and drug testing. They must pass the same FAA-approved training as airline employees, and are trained to spot suspicious people and luggage. What's more, CAPS uses security cameras and barbed wire at its sites. Its vans and cargo trucks are locked and monitored. And workers store luggage in large steel booths they call shark tanks, because they resemble shark cages used by divers.

While many small businesses flop, CAPS (www.capstravel.com) may have a better chance. The firm's management team has spotted a badly needed travel service with mass potential. Revenue is doubling each month, and CAPS should turn profitable by the third quarter this year, Snyder says.

It'll face competition from Travel Lite Enterprises and its Virtual bellhop.com service, which will pick up and drop off luggage from a traveler's home or office. But that nationwide service caters to executives who can afford the typical price tag of sixty-five dollars to two hundred dollars. Another possible rival: Direct Baggage, a British company that plans to expand into the U.S.A. soon.

In the meantime, CAPS hopes to grow nationwide over the next two years. It's hustling now to raise $18 million from venture capitalists and investment bankers. The economic climate now is scary for start-ups, but CAPS believes it has a rock-solid business model.

"We feel the momentum," Snyder says. "It's a win for everyone: the FAA, the airports and airline industry, hotels, and rental car venues. Ultimately, of course, passengers just love it."

From *USA Today*, April 10, 2001. © 2001 USA Today. Reprinted with permission.

SUGGESTIONS FOR FURTHER STUDY

1. Would you use such service, or invest in it if you were able?
2. What does this new service and the others like it imply for air travel and the airline industry? More satisfied customers, happier airways?
3. Would you be interested in a logical further development of these added services to customers? Why not have a service that you call to get your ticket, pack your luggage and transport it

and you to the airport, and pick you up on your return? Perhaps have someone pick you up at the airport and unpack your luggage for you. In other words house to house, and full trip, coverage? Such service would provide the ultimate in service and stress relief.

4. The terrorist attacks of September 11 may have done away with such service. What would you suggest as alternatives?

SIGHTSEEING AND
VACATIONING

Another major reason for travel is the pleasure of seeing and experiencing new things. People probably have been sightseeing since the beginning of time. They have always wanted to see what is just over the horizon, especially the glory of some unusual site or religious or holy place. In classical times people flocked to see what we now call the Seven Wonders of the Ancient World: the Great Pyramid of Giza, the Hanging Gardens of Babylon, the mausoleum at Halicarnassus, the temple of Artemis at Ephesus, the Colossus of Rhodes, the statue of Zeus at Olympia, and the lighthouse at Alexandria. In the thirteenth century Marco Polo visited Cathay (China) to see the exotic land and people and remained thirteen years. The published account of that strange culture stimulated the travel glands of Europe.

In America one of the remarkable growth industries in travel has been the development of cruise ships which are in fact traveling cities and sightseeing facilities that sail to favored tourist sites—mainly in the Caribbean—and back home again. In this country the business began modestly. The first cruise ship was the *Quaker City,* which sailed in 1867 to the Holy Land, with Mark Twain and seventy-six other eager sightseers, mostly from the congregation of popular New York minister Henry Ward Beecher. These cultural pilgrims, like most that have followed, were drawn to the voyage by the lure of sightseeing and the magic of the sea, and stayed abroad nearly five and a half months.

Since the turn of the century the cruise line business has had a phenomenal growth. At times it seemed to be threatened by airlines, which afforded faster and cheaper—though less elegant—transportation to distant sites. But the cruise ship business has undergone a startling comeback and growth. In 1965 the number of passengers totaled only 330,000. By the end of the century the number had ballooned to seven million, The lure of the cruise seems irresistible. It provides tours to all kinds of exotic—even dangerous—places. Like a turtle it carries its hotel facilities with it, encourages short safe excursions to tourist spots on shore, and acts as a continuous buffet, spa, casino, and theater to those who want to luxuriate on board all day or when they return from short activities.

At the beginning of the new millennium the Caribbean is the most attractive destination, but ships regularly tour the fiords of Scandinavia and sail among the ice floes of Alaska, the Arctic, and Antarctica. Growth of the business seems to have no end. At the beginning of the twenty-first century there were seventy-six cruise lines worldwide (twenty-nine American), with 223 ships (122 American), and a passenger capacity of 9.5 million (6.5 million American). Countless other ships cruise rivers worldwide, and numerous old salts and would-be salts enjoy the leisure and limited facilities of tramp steamers and cargo vessels.

The large cruise ships are as long as three football fields and twelve stories high. Each is a small city that pours out thousands of people per day into destinations both large and small. They are always registered under the flags of small countries—Nigeria, Panama—and though they operate in the coastal waters of the United States they are not subject to laws and pour millions of gallons of untreated wastes into the harbors of American ports and all others they visit.

At the end of the twentieth century at least five new vessels—511,000 tons with a capacity of 11,700 passengers—were under construction. They will join the fleet which today ply the seven seas. Tours are run by all kinds of people, from business entrepreneurs to highly respected educational institutions, universities, and museums. For example, in 2001 the American Museum of Natural History advertised fifty-six tours all over the world, from Ireland ($2,370, the least expensive), to the South Pole ($38,000, the most expensive).

Everywhere they go they leave the inevitable detritus of civilization. Yet destinations use every kind of ploy to attract larger and larger crowds. In 2001 seven million tourists went to Hawaii. You can walk from one end of Waikiki beach to the other on sun-bathing bodies and never touch your feet to the sand. Yet the officials are trying to get approval to spend sixty million tax dollars to attract more tourists. More tourists will need more facilities, and more facilities will need more tourists to utilize and help pay for them. The business is a never ending upward spiral with an inevitable conclusion: If you believe that space for travel is finite, the increasing range of tourism might give you pause but might also suggest that travel be used for more than pleasure.

Troubled Waters

KEN ALPINE

No ocean remains untouched by man. And that spells trouble for many of the world's waters. To document these facts, renowned photographer Norbert Wu, under a grant provided by the prestigious Pew Marine Conservation Fellowship, embarked on a three-year effort to document the oceans' most unique and beautiful places, and the substantial threats assaulting them. Using still photography and high-definition video, he visually chronicled three-quarters of the globe, turning an unblinking eye on the undersea world—its beauty and its blemishes—so that people will better understand what is happening in and to our waters. His hope is that by understanding, people will be encouraged to do their part to preserve a world both removed from our sight and critical to our survival.

Wu is one of the world's most talented and prolific underwater photographers, the author of fifteen books on wildlife and photography, a filmmaker (most recently a film on Antarctica's undersea world that aired on PBS), and winner of numerous awards, this year a nod from his peers at the North American Nature Photographers Association who named Wu Outstanding Photographer of the Year. We sat down with the man behind the camera to hear his words behind the pictures.

AMERICAN WAY. What are some of the most pressing problems facing the world's oceans today?

NORBERT WU. Unfortunately, the list can go on and on. Overfishing. Global warming. Pollution and runoff. Reef destruction. The incredible waste in by-catch. Shrimp trawlers scoop up wasted by-catch by the truckload. The National Marine Fisheries Service estimates that U.S. shrimp by-catch is close to one billion pounds a year. That by-catch is life, killed for no reason.

AMERICAN WAY. Is there any one issue that in your mind is paramount?

WU. Overpopulation is the biggest problem on earth. Everything else comes from that.

AMERICAN WAY. You've endured long, cold hours, seasickness, and travel to the farthest reaches of the globe to document marine conservation issues. Why?

WU. People protect what they know and love. Unfortunately, the world's oceans and their problems are not familiar to most people, and so they're ignored. I'm hoping I can help bridge this lack of awareness and help people understand the beauty, importance, and fragility of our oceans. Photographs can be powerful tools.

AMERICAN WAY. You work with still photography and, more recently, high-definition television. Why have you made your life in the visual world?

WU. Well, I'm a terrible musician. It would be a truly awful thing to hear me sing. And I can't hear well either. And I hate writing. So it's visual stuff or nothing.

AMERICAN WAY. You've photographed some haunting images— turtles caught on long lines, finned sharks, sea lions choked by gill nets. How does that affect you?

WU. I hate to say it, but at some point, when you are pursuing a subject, you are glad to get it. It's like trophy hunting. Still it is difficult, perhaps the most difficult thing that I've had to deal with during the three years of this Pew project. Basically I'm going places hoping to photograph bad things happening. That's not always fulfilling.

AMERICAN WAY. Many people think, *Oh, the ocean has no direct effect on my life.* What would you say to them?

WU. It is easy to distance ourselves from the ocean because, at a casual glance, it does seem like a distant place. But it impacts us all, on large and small fronts. The oceans regulate the earth's weather. Corals secrete calcium carbonate—limestone—on a scale so massive it affects carbon dioxide levels in the atmosphere and the very health of the planet. The ancient Greeks believed that the ocean flowed around the earth and into eternity. Before it does, the ocean flows into all our lives.

AMERICAN WAY. What can people do to help?

WU. A simple and good place to start is being aware of what you should and shouldn't eat. If you want to promote wise, conservation-oriented fishing practices, the best way to do so is to think about what's going into your mouth. Consumer demand for dolphin-safe tuna reduced direct dolphin deaths in tuna nets by 99 percent.

AMERICAN WAY. The oceans are still a beautiful place. What are some of the most unspoiled and beautiful oceans you have seen?

WU. My new book [*Diving the World,* Hugh Lauter Levin Associates, 2003] features some of the world's unspoiled ocean locations: Papua New Guinea, the Revillagigedo Islands, Palau, the Galapagos Islands, McMurdo Sound in Antarctica. The thing about the ocean is that its surface hides great beauty and problems. It's difficult to tell from a glance if there's something going on under the ocean's surface. You could be on a gorgeous reef in the Philippines and suddenly realize that there are almost no fish. There's no place in the world where man has not had an impact.

AMERICAN WAY. Tourism can be a powerful force. How can folks use ecologically minded vacations to benefit the world's oceans and perhaps promote positive change in the way countries treat their local oceans?

WU. Well, some problems are bigger than tourism. Coral reefs might perish due to global warming despite anyone's best efforts. But it's also true that in the diving community there have been many success stories where ecotourism has saved coral reefs. In Indonesia, for example, a resort called Kungkungan Bay Resort has been a great force in marine conservation efforts in North Sulawesi. Diving operations and the divers who travel to them seem to bring conservation efforts to any area where the two come together—the diving operations have a financial stake in seeing their clients dive on healthy reefs. Places like Bonaire and Grand Cayman, they've all established marine parks because of divers. But divers are a small minority of the population. I also wonder how many of these ecotourists tell other countries that they are polluting, then go home to huge SUVs and houses that are six thousand square feet and have to be air-conditioned against the summer heat.

AMERICAN WAY. Is there any hope?

WU. Sure. There are great things going on. People have shown that it's possible to produce an awareness campaign that can actually save a species of fish. A good example is Atlantic swordfish. An organization called SeaWeb got all the chefs in New York to stop serving this highly threatened fish. The chefs did so, and Atlantic swordfish rebounded. Unfortunately, they've since stopped the campaign and it's the same story now. But there's still plenty of good news. Completely off-limits marine reserves have been established, and they have helped protect reefs and fish. TEDs [turtle excluder devices, which let shrimp pass into the main net while ejecting the turtles back into the wild] installed in shrimp trawlers have helped turtle populations rebound in the Gulf of Mexico since they are no longer caught and killed in the nets.

AMERICAN WAY. What is it about our oceans that gives you the most joy?

WU. The feeling of being underwater, seeing a reef full of life; there's nothing like it.

AMERICAN WAY. What is it about our oceans that gives you greatest cause for sadness?

WU. It's not the oceans that give me sadness. It's the people who are around the oceans, and their hypocrisy. I am astonished and saddened by the hypocrisy. The governments' policies and the fishing industry in particular, but scientists, too. There needs to be more cooperation and less self-serving interest if we're going to solve these problems.

AMERICAN WAY. What have the oceans taught you?

WU. Working on the ocean teaches you nearly everything you need to know. It teaches you patience. It reveals mystery, awe for life. It teaches you respect

From *American Way*, August 1, 2003. Reprinted with permission of the author.

SUGGESTIONS FOR FURTHER STUDY

1. Since you probably are a devotee of swimming and the oceans, discuss their effect on you.

2. What effect is the typical visit to the beach having on American society?

3. Visits to beaches usually invite display of the body. Discuss what this practice leads to.

4. Through the years the oceans have become much more important in our daily lives. Discuss.

5. How do the rituals and ways of life of people who live on islands and near the beaches differ from that of inland people?

The Wonderful World of History

*Why Travel without Heritage Is like TV
without Color*

DAVID A. FRYSELL

I'm old enough, alas, to remember the days of black-and-white television. What a thrill it was when we finally got our first color TV (its immediate successor, I believe, was still in the basement of my frugal
parents' house until recently). Suddenly, the world on our small screen
sprang to life, and Captain Kangaroo, the Lone Ranger, and Lassie
seemed to pop right out into our living room.

For travelers, as I've come to think of it, history is a lot like getting
color television. Sure, you can visit a place and see the sights, dine at the
restaurants and buy your souvenirs. But without history, it's like visiting
a place in black and white. One destination is hard to tell from the next
(much as on our old TV, the Lone Ranger, who I later discovered
was clad in powdery blue, looked an awful lot like the dun-costumed
Rifleman with a mask). The place has no character because you don't
know how it came to be that way. It's just a collection of buildings, as
flat and dull as the Hollywood sets so many of my favorite shows were
shot on.

History puts the color into the places we visit. Once you know something about the why of a destination—the "backstory," to stick with my Hollywood metaphor—you're better able to appreciate what you're touring.

To use an extreme example, consider Mount Vernon. If George Washington had never lived there (or if you didn't know he'd lived there, or didn't know who George Washington was), Mount Vernon would be just a big old house. Impressive, sure, but nothing that would draw streams of visitors.

Not far from Mount Vernon, in nearby Prince William County, Virginia, lies another such place that fully resonates with visitors only when you know what happened here: Manassas battlefield, site of the first real battle of the Civil War (as well as the second, much larger battle). It's a beautiful place, rolling green hills and a prim, white farmhouse. But you have to know why the cannons picket the hills for this place to make you catch your breath: That long, bloody, bitter chapter of American history began here, as naive picnickers watched, thinking the war would be over by afternoon.

We tour Manassas and its history-rich region on page six of this issue [*Heritage Travel*, Summer 2003]—putting the color of history, we hope, into your picture of what otherwise would be just another stretch of suburban Washington, D.C., sprawl. Not far away, we also visit the National Archives, to show you how to get the most from your visit to the "nation's attic." Without their rich overlay of history, of course, the treasures in the archives would be, well, just stuff—not much different from what you'd find at a good neighborhood rummage sale.

But places don't have to lie in the shadow of the nation's capital for history to turn them into Technicolor experiences. . . . You can find heritage just about anywhere—down the Natchez Trail into the heart of the South, . . . or across the Southwest to Oklahoma City, Dallas–Fort Worth, San Antonio, and Phoenix. . . . If you have Irish ancestors, like so many Americans, even a place as distant as Ireland can come to colorful life—green, of course—with not only a nation's history, but also pieces of your personal past.

Trust me, once you've seen the world in living color, made vivid by history, you'll never again settle for that old black-and-white view.

From *Heritage Travel*, Summer 2003, a special issue of *Family Tree Magazine*. Reprinted with permission.

SUGGESTIONS FOR FURTHER STUDY

1. There can be no doubt that the more a tourist knows about the site of his visit the more he or she enjoys it. Yet tourists usually don't read the free brochures provided at tourist sites. Would you recommend that all tour sites provide informed guides to talk to the visitors?

2. Tourists are both welcomed and resented by the locals they visit. How would you try to modify this mixed feeling?

3. Most tourists tend to rush from one spot to another as quickly as possible, refusing to return to a spot already visited, saying "Oh, I've already been there." How would you suggest tourism be properly shaped?

4. Prized sites for tourists—such as Yellowstone, Yosemite, and others—are simply being overrun and destroyed by tourism, threatening eco-destruction. How would you handle the situation—provide quotes of visits, locate video "tours" at distant sites (such as hotels in cities, tourist centers), or somehow provide the pleasure of a "visit" without allowing the tourist to visit the site physically?

MUSEUMS

Museums have always exerted an important and powerful influence on society. In America the first museum was Peale's American Museum, established in Philadelphia in 1785 as an effort to exhibit and preserve the past and to educate through visual contact. Almost immediately, however, the question arose as to which elements of the past are worth preserving, which are too ephemeral and worthless to be preserved, and which are too shameful to display and keep alive. Increasingly through the years, especially in the twentieth century, the conflict between opposing points of view has intensified. Professional historians and museologists have grown more vocal in insisting what history and culture dignify the nation and should be preserved. They recognize that museums are powerful instruments in sifting history and culture and dictating what aspects of a nation should be displayed.

Opposed to this elitist point of view has been a rapidly developing school of culturists who insist that museums can educate a nation's people by displaying its culture—past and present—in ways that are relaxed and amusing rather than sober faced and solemn. Historians and museum experts with this point of view insist that such a nonprofessional historian as Walt Disney in his movies and theme parks has taught more history and the American way of life than all the classrooms in the country. Living museums, such as Williamsburg and Sturbridge Village, and historical reenactments demonstrate that participatory history is more instructive than classrooms.

As their expenses have increased, museums have turned to the general public for support and consequently have had to adjust to the desires of the public. The Smithsonian Institution, the finest museum in the world with its 142 million artifacts, has had to grow more and more public-conscious. Thus the many museums, halls of fame, memorials to interesting and uninteresting people, and causes are springing all around us like mushrooms. The question certainly arises as to whether they are growing too numerous and being situated in the wrong places. Do too many such institutions reveal a slowing down of forward movement in society and a turning to look at the past? Does such concentration picture a society looking in a rearview mirror and becoming more and more a theme park in itself? And is there some danger in such a point of view and action? The following article tells about one new way that museums are serving the public.

In Virtual Museums,
an Archive of the World

JAMES GORMAN

On a simple table, under a bright light, the fossilized skull of a protocer-atops is waiting for its close-up. Once the portrait is made by a high-resolution digital camera, it will take its place online with eight thousand other fossil images and more than two hundred thousand catalog entries of vertebrate and invertebrate fossils in the collection of the American Museum of Natural History.

And this is just the beginning.

The museum has two million to three million fossils (no one really knows how many), and sooner or later descriptions of all of them will appear online, many with photographs. And the fossils are not the half of it. In all, the museum has thirty million items—bird and animal skins, pickled frogs, pre-Columbian pots, diaries, field journals, and sketches of explorers and scientists who braved the midday sun and the polar nights. Four hundred thousand are now online.

So far, the museum has just scratched the surface of digitization, as the process is called, but the hope is to one day create a searchable on-line catalog of the whole museum, with images and text.

Many other natural history and science museums large and small are undertaking the same Herculean task of putting their collections, or as much of them as can be captured in digital form, online. The Smithsonian National Museum of Natural History, with nearly 125 million specimens, now has nine million of them catalogued online, some with images.

In Chicago, the Field Museum, the Morton Arboretum, and the Chicago Botanic Garden have created a virtual herbarium that allows botanists and gardeners not only to find information of area plants, but also to view photographs of the original specimen cards, including the plants and notes on their collection.

The goal, officials at several museums say, is to link many collections in cooperative databases. Ben Williams, the lead librarian at the Field Museum, said, "We're all heading toward a kind of digital global museum"—in effect, a catalog of the world.

Right now, anyone with access to the internet, whether a Ph.D. candidate or a seventh grader, can check the mammal collections of seventeen museums at once on Manis, the Mammal Networked Information System. While this may merely be a time saver for a biologist in Seattle, it can be invaluable for researchers in third world countries who lack physical access to collections. A great deal of information on African animals, for instance, is available in American collections.

Specialists in reptiles, amphibians, fish, and other animals and plants have linked or are linking their collections as well. In fact, just as collectors, largely American and Europeans, tried over the centuries to capture a sampling of the physical world for the great museums of natural history, those same museums are now working to make all the results of all those searches available online.

The size of the task is hard to imagine. Art museums have undertaken similar efforts, but the numbers are hardly comparable. The Metropolitan Museum of Art, for example has thirty-five hundred works of art online. Its total collection numbers more than two million.

The work at natural history museums has gained speed in the last five years, with the maturing of the Internet and of software to connect scientific databases. Still, there is wide variation, from museum to museum and within museums, in what has been accomplished.

In some cases only the information that would normally be on a catalog card is available. For instance, all an online visitor will learn about Item 8513 at the American Museum is that it is a fossilized tooth of a

Tyrannosaur-like dinosaur called Albertosaurus collected in Montana, no date. But, Item 6515, a velociraptor skull collected in 1923 in Mongolia, is represented by a vivid photograph.

Photographs and old field notebooks from a variety of fossil expeditions are also online. A bit of browsing leads to the field notebooks of the dinosaur hunter Barnum Brown. In 1908 he was exploring the Hell Creek bed in Montana. On June 10 he wrote: "Passed Wilbur Titus herding a band of sheep because the herder had left he said. He was just as dirty as ever." This was shortly after Brown had passed Dirty Woman Ranch. "Wind blew a gale all day; sand came like dust," he wrote after recounting the day's other events, which included a splintered axle.

In addition to the facsimiles of Brown's journals, volunteers have typed in the text so it can be searched online.

Many museums contain so much information that making it accessible is an immense task. Michel Novacek, senior vice president and provost of science at the American Museum, said its efforts "started as little islands of hot activity" as some departments surged ahead of others in cataloging specimens and creating software. Now the various efforts are starting to come together, although some areas are far ahead. Of the 3.3 million specimens of living vertebrates at the museum, Dr. Novacek said, 2.8 million are represented online, including the mammals, reptiles, and amphibians. The birds are next.

Mark A. Norell, chairman of the museum's paleontology division, said work on digitizing what is "by far the largest collection of fossil vertebrates in the world" was close to being finished. All the dinosaurs, reptiles, and amphibians are done and the mammals are next.

Anthropology is also well represented, with 140,000 objects online with images and descriptions. As with all computer databases, the value of this one is that it can be searched—by locality, by culture, by the sort of object—to pick just a few categories. For example, users can search for arrows of the Blackfeet culture, or for arrows, or for anything from the Blackfeet culture.

Just about everything from the museum's 1909–15 Congo Expedition, which collected annual specimens and cultural artifacts, is online. Complete field notebooks in facsimile and standard text, photographs, maps, and specimen information are there, searchable and linked.

Tom Moritz, the director of library services, has created an easily usable online world with many byways. A computer user curious about rhinoceroses, for example, can find where and when they were encountered, see photographs, and read what the explorers thought of the great beasts.

None of these efforts match the research networks developed for certain groups of animals. Seventeen institutions cooperate in Manis, the mammal network. This effort was led by the University of California at Berkeley and supported by the National Science Foundation. Reptiles are also well served. The University of Kansas has led the way in that effort, called Herpnet.

Some of these networks do not present quite as smooth a face to the world as the Congo Expedition Web site. They are designed for researchers, students, and dedicated amateurs—people familiar with scientific names and taxonomy.

But the value of these databases on living animal species is extraordinary for purposes of conservation, said Scott Miller, chairman of the department of systematic biology at the Smithsonian natural history museum. Maps that can be changed with a click of the mouse to show different patterns of information, such as the historical change in species numbers, are invaluable for conservation policy makers, though Dr. Miller said there were serious issues about disclosing "information about specific locations of endangered species."

For the curious and the browser, the collections are also invaluable. There are photographs to download and old arrows to examine, along with headdresses and medicine bags and kayaks. And the more surfers find on the Web, museum directors are certain, the more they will want to see in person.

If the value of putting museum collection information online is clear, so are the obstacles. For one thing, there is money. The American Museum has relied on grants from the National Endowment for the Humanities, the National Aeronautics and Space Administration, and the Andrew W. Mellon Foundation. The National Science Foundation has supported some of the networking projects.

The technological problems of making databases talk to one another are also formidable. Just as a physical museum is built with a certain architecture, museums have constructed different software frameworks to store the digital versions of their snakes and cockroaches. The challenge is to make data easily transferable in similar categories, much the way address and telephone information can be imported and exported among different personal computer calendars.

These cooperative ventures are on every curator's mind. "Everybody realizes that is where the future lies," said John Heyning, deputy director of research and collections at the Los Angeles County Museum of Natural History, which has more than thirty million specimens.

But the physical world resists easy categorization, especially given the human flaws of collectors. The Manis site offers a glimpse of the difficulties that can be encountered in a list of "localities" that the organizers found while putting the system together. These are descriptions of where certain animal specimens were first found. Among them are such mythical spots as "Alaska, off the coast of California," or completely useless locators like "Pet Store" or "Highway" or "Ranch."

For example, one specimen is described as coming from "Highway 17, Park Ave. off ramp, Oakland." The entry notes: "There is no Park Ave. Anywhere near Highway 17." The specimen was a boa constrictor, in case you were wondering.

When you are cataloging the world, you have to expect some glitches.

From *New York Times*, January 12, 2003. © 2003 by The New York Times Co. Reprinted with permission.

SUGGESTIONS FOR FURTHER STUDY

1. These efforts by the big museums, though admirable, seem to be making the mistakes of those of the past. They are looking backward rather than forward. They are spending vast amounts of government and foundation money studying what they have rather than interpreting what they possess. They completely ignore the popular culture of the nation that finances their study of the past—generally the very distant past. What is your feeling about their emphasis?

2. If you were a member of one of the groups financing these efforts, what would you tell them about the proper way to spend money for such projects?

POPULAR ART

Т he urge for artistic expression, to embody various aspects of the physical or spiritual world, is as old as mankind. The earliest humans left drawings of animals on the walls of the caves which tell us about life in that far-gone time. Today's artistic expressions are more numerous, varied, and sophisticated, but they still capture in graphic form something about the human environment or spiritual landscape.

Art comes in various shapes, sizes, and locations. One of the oldest and most widely encountered is the tattoo, a form of body alteration, closely allied to more profound body change. Tattoos were very important as expressions of human desires to alter (and improve) the body before clothes became so sophisticated that the wardrobe could accomplish more than tattoos.

But we have always insisted on having art with us in other forms as well. Early on people recognized that all blank space—whether along the roadside, on buildings, on the inside of streetcars and buses, even inside taxis—invites artistic expression. It is as if no space should be allowed to remain silent when it can speak to the esthetic and commercial interests of people. One of the more interesting and powerful statements has been van art, which had early manifestations in such things as fetishes and icons hung from the rearview mirror of vehicles. Van art grew into flashy statements of personal attitudes in the sixties and later and is still with us today.

Other forms of artistic expression include mural painting and trading card art, both of which reflect the variety and energy of ethnic and interest groups in American society and help them to declare themselves socially and politically. The following article discusses another kind of art that has become a prominent element of the American landscape.

Defining Trade Characters and Their Role in American Popular Culture

BARBARA J. PHILLIPS

Trade characters have been used as successful advertising tools in the United States for over one hundred years. American popular culture has quietly become inhabited by all sorts of talking animals and dancing products that are used as a communication system by advertisers. In 1982 a research study found that commercials with advertising-developed characters who became associated with a brand scored above average in their ability to change brand preference. It appears, then, that society is getting the message. However, although popular with advertisers and consumers, trade characters have been largely ignored in the study of advertising and popular culture. Through a review of the relevant literature, this paper will determine what trade characters are, and how they are employed in modern advertising practice to communicate to consumers in society.

Trade Characters: What They Are

Little attention has been given to defining the term "trade character." In a perusal of dozens of advertising textbooks, only a few offer an explicit definition of the term. The rest are silent on the subject or focus exclusively on what a trade character does as opposed to what a trade character is. Of the authors who define "trade character," several offer vague explanations such as "a character created in association with a product." There is little consensus among the remaining definitions; many of the more insightful contradict each other. Therefore, this paper will develop an explicit definition of the term "trade character" that considers four areas of contention: animate versus inanimate characters, nontrademarked versus trademarked characters, fictional versus real characters, and trade versus celebrity characters.

Animate Versus Inanimate Characters

Some of the current definitions of "trade characters" are very broad, identifying a trade character as any visual symbol that is associated with a product. By including all visual symbols, these authors classify inanimate objects such as the Prudential rock as trade characters. On the other hand, several definitions specify that a trade character must be an animate being or an animated object, thereby excluding the Prudential rock (unless it is made to sing or dance).

There are two reasons why trade characters should be restricted to animate beings or animated objects. The first is that the word "character," defined by Webster's Dictionary to mean "person," implies a living personality. This personality is the focal point of the trade character, whether the character is animate by nature, like Betty Crocker, or animated by design, like Mr. Peanut. The second reason for limiting trade characters to animate beings is to eliminate from the category characterless visual symbols, such as corporate logos, and inanimate objects associated with the product through advertising, such as oranges for Tropicana orange juice. Neither of these types of visual symbols functions as a trade character. Thus the first condition used to define a trade character is that it be animate or animated. This includes people, animals, beings (monsters, spacemen, etc.), and animated objects.

Nontrademarked Versus Trademarked Characters

Another contentious issue is the matter of trademarks. Some authors insist that a trade character must necessarily be a legal trademark. Other authors disagree. To resolve this issue, the role of trademarks and trade characters must be briefly addressed.

A trademark is a name, word, or symbol that is protected by law. It is used to identify the sources of the product and to guarantee consistency of quality. When consumers see the trademark "Coca-Cola" on a bottle, they know who makes it and how it tastes. In comparison, most definitions agree that a trade character is used primarily as a device around which to build promotional programs. Trade characters can appear on product packaging, in advertising, in sales promotions, or in other related areas.

Although most trade characters are registered trademarks, limiting the definition only to trademarks would eliminate from the category some characters that have been created for promotional use. This is especially true of characters created for advertising campaigns that do not appear on the product package such as the Marlboro cowboy, the Maytag Repairman, and Raid's cartoon bugs. Because these characters are used in the same way as trademarks such as Tony the Tiger or Poppin' Fresh, the Pillsbury Dough Boy, it is difficult to draw a distinction between them. Therefore another stipulation for the definition of "trade character" is that a trade character does not necessarily have to be a legal trademark. However, it must be used for promotional purposes.

Fictional Versus Real Characters

Another issue that relates to the role played by the trade character is the inclusion of real (i.e., nonfictional) humans in some definitions. By including real people, the definition of trade character could be stretched to cover celebrity spokespeople such as George Burns and even the "common man" found in testimonial advertising. The individuals in these two much-studied genres of advertising are used in a very different way from trade characters. Their value lies in their credibility as realistic spokespeople. On the other hand, the target audience suspends disbelief when entering the fantasy world of a trade character such as a vegetable-growing giant or a dancing raisin. In advertising that uses real people, the target audience must identify with (testimonial advertising) or aspire to (celebrity advertising) the spokesperson. This is not the case when using trade characters. Instead, the target audience relates to a trade character as a symbolic representation of the product. For example, the Marlboro cowboy is a white male, yet he is used successfully to advertise to women and minorities. It appears that these groups do not view the character as a real person speaking for the brand, but as a symbol of the flavor and freedom given by the brand. Therefore, another definition requirement is that trade characters be fictional. Note that although human actors play the parts of such trade characters as the Marlboro cowboy and Mr. Whipple, these characters are still fictional.

Trade Versus Celebrity Characters

Finally, in their work on animation, [Margaret F.] Callcott and [Patricia A.] Alvey draw a distinction between "celebrity" and "noncelebrity" spokes-characters. Celebrity characters are those that originated from a source other than advertising (i.e., cartoons, TV, etc.) for purposes distinct from advertising. Examples of celebrity characters include Mickey Mouse and Snoopy. Advertisers frequently license these characters to cash in on a celebrity's current popularity, such as Bart Simpson's endorsement of the Butterfinger chocolate bar. In fact, these characters function as any other celebrity spokesperson and therefore play a different role than the characters created by the advertising trade, as discussed above. Thus, they should be excluded from the definition of "trade character."

A definition of trade character can be developed by combining the conditions discussed above. A trade character is a fictional, animated being or animated object that has been created for the promotion of a product, service, or idea. A trade character does not have to be a legal trademark.

Trade Characters: How They Communicate

Occasionally, a successful trade character is developed by accident. This was the case in 1904 when the Campbell Kids were added to streetcar advertisements as a visual element that might appeal to women.

Campbell's managers professed themselves to be mystified by the Kids' appeal and subsequent success. It is much more common, however, for advertisers to carefully deliberate over the creation of a trade character and its messages. There are three ways that trade characters are used to communicate with consumers: by creating product identification, by promoting a brand personality, and by providing promotional continuity.

Product Identification

One of the fundamental ways that trade characters communicate with consumers is by creating product identification. A trade character can forge a link between the product, the packaging, and the advertising in the minds of consumers. The uses of trade characters for product identification has its roots in the development of trademarks for branded products.

The explosion of trademarks into use as a general marketing tool took place at the beginning of the twentieth century. "In the course of sixty years, from 1860 to 1920, factory-produced merchandise in packages largely replaced locally produced goods sold from bulk containers," [Hal Morgan says]. The product package became the focus of efforts by manufacturers to differentiate their products from the competition. Trademarks were used to help highlight the differences between brands. Even if actual product differences did not exist, consumers who remembered the trademark or the look of the package could still ask for a specific brand by name. In this way, the trademark helped the consumer to recognize the brand in a purchase situation. Manufacturers encouraged trademark recognition by creating promotions that required consumers to cut trademarks from packages and send them to the manufacturer to receive a prize. As trade characters were developed for advertising use, many assumed the trademark's role of product identifier by appearing on the label. For example, the trade character Mr. Clean is displayed on a bottle as a pictorial representation of the brand name. By viewing the trade characters on the product package, consumers may be able to recognize the product even if the brand name has been removed. Recent research has shown a strong link between trade characters and the products that they identify. Animated noncelebrity (i.e., trade) characters elicited a favorable 71.7 percent correct product recall in respondents.

The use of trade characters for product identification surpasses the trademark's traditional function for identifying the package. The strength of trade characters lies in their ability to form a bond between the product, the packaging, and the advertising. A successful trade character connects the advertising messages to the product so that consumers recall the message when they view the package. The Jolly Green Giant and the Little Green Sprout are examples of trade characters who have achieved a successful product-packaging-advertising link. These characters appear on product labels, in TV and print advertising, and in sales promotions such as coupons and premiums. The two characters tie all of these promotional activities together into a cohesive unit that communicates the message of product quality.

Trade characters do not have to appear on the package to create a strong connection between the advertising message and the brand. When the Marlboro cowboy, who does not appear on the package, was used to advertise cigarettes on television, 95 percent of respondents could identify the sponsor in the first five seconds, as compared to only 16 percent for the average commercial. Currently, in some Marlboro print advertisements, the Marlboro cowboy is shown without mentioning the product name. Because of the strong product-advertising link, the trade character is considered sufficient to identify the brand.

Personality

The trade character's message, however, goes beyond product identification. Trade characters also communicate through their personalities. A trade character's personality can fulfill two functions: it can give meaning to the brand by symbolizing its character, and it can lend emotional appeal to the brand by personifying the product. These two operations, which may be the paramount functions of a trade character, will be discussed below.

Trade characters with distinct personalities were first created during the 1920s. At that time, advertising practitioners uncovered a public desire to be addressed personally by and to receive advice from the media. As traditional sources of information such as the family, the church, and the community became less meaningful to consumers, they turned to advertising to enlighten them regarding their role in society. Thus, advertising took on a cultural role that has continued to the present time.

Advertising "seeks to render otherwise incomprehensible social situations meaningful, so as to make it possible to act purposively within them" [John F. Sherry Jr.].

The new trade characters of the 1920s were developed to fill the informational void. These characters were fictional "people" passed off as real personal advisers and confidantes for everything from etiquette to cooking to personal hygiene. The longest-lived of these characters is Betty Crocker, who was invented in 1921 to sign replies to contest questions at General Mills, and stayed to lend her name to their entire product line.

As fictional "personal adviser" trade characters grew in popularity and became commonplace, the next step became personalization of the product itself. "*Printer's Ink* praised new techniques of bringing the ingredients of products to life by depicting them as 'little characters with names' and . . . called on copywriters to find the 'face' that lay embedded in every product" [Roland Marchand]. Thus, the modern trade character, complete with a distinct personality, was born.

A. Meaning

The first function of the trade character's personality is to give meaning to the brand by symbolizing the brand's character. The trade character does this by transferring its own cultural meaning to what can be an otherwise meaningless product.

Because the manufacturer's process is complex and removed from consumers' daily lives, products have lost the cultural meaning that they once possessed. All advertising, in general, functions to assign meaning to a product by linking the product to a representation of the culturally constituted world. This cultural representation is an image that elicits a cluster of ideas and emotions that are commonly associated with that image. "It is . . . the merchandising of a metaphor which will speak to and be understood by the collective imagination of the culture" [Bruce A. Lohof]. A consumer connects the image with the product, and thereby transfers the meaning of the image to the product. A formerly empty product comes to mean something to a group of consumers. By changing the cultural image that is paired with the product, a product can be made to take on almost any meaning.

The trade character is one cultural image that advertisers use to elicit meaning. Trade characters express meaning through the communication system known as myth. Myth uses visual symbols to send a message that indirectly addresses human concerns. Trade characters are archetypes, actors in the myth that embody those factors that matter to individuals and society.

All trade characters use their personalities as symbols to elicit and transfer meaning to the brand. Mr. Peanut is sophisticated, Poppin' Fresh is lovable, and Betty Crocker is reliable. In this way, trade characters establish a desired product image by visually representing the product attributes or the advertising message. An example of the link between the personality of the character and the personality of the product is illustrated by Chester Cheetah, the trade character used to promote Chee-tos cheese puffs. "Chester Cheetah reflects characteristics of Chee-tos puffs themselves. Chee-tos puffs are orange and 'go fast'; Chester Cheetah is orange and 'goes fast.' Chee-tos puffs are cheesy and lovable; Chester Cheetah is cheesy and lovable too" [William Wells, John Burnett, and Sandra Moriarty]. It is apparent that Chester has been created to embody the attributes of his brand.

However, the creation of a symbolically meaningful trade character is not sufficient to ensure its effectiveness. The consumer must correctly decode the trade character's meaning before it can have an impact. Therefore, advertisers must communicate through a vocabulary of readily understood signs so that consumers can correctly interpret the signs' meaning. Trade characters have to express their meaning quickly and effortlessly if they hope to compete in the cluttered media environment. Thus, "the signifiers that will be used most often will be those that are judged to be at once appealing, communicative, normative, proper, and easily-understood in a particular moment," [Linda Marie Scott says]. The use of these types of signifiers to develop meaningful trade characters will lead to the correct decoding of the trade character's message.

As a result, advertisers frequently use animal trade characters because they are standard mythical symbols of human qualities. For example, "everyone" knows that a bee is industrious, a dove is peaceful, and a fox is cunning. These stereotypical animal symbols are used to express common hopes, aspirations, and ideals. Advertisers link these animals to their products because consumers intuitively know what the animals "mean" and can therefore transfer that cultural meaning to the brand.

It is their unambiguous meaning that makes trade characters popular with consumers. The characters are predictable and constant; they always "mean" the same thing,. As a result, consumers view them as trustworthy and reliable spokespersons in a constantly changing media environment.

B. Emotional Appeal

Note that Chester Cheetah is also described as "fun" and "cool." The second function of a trade character's personality is to give emotional appeal to the brand. A trade character can accomplish this by symbolizing an emotional benefit that is transferred to the product. Also, a trade character lends the warmth of an actual personality to the product and thereby creates an emotional tie between the consumer and the character. This emotional tie is crucial to the persuasive ability of the trade character, especially when the consumer has low involvement with the product category. An advertising executive [John Nieman] asks, "How do you personalize a message that seems miles away, months apart and mostly relevant to wild animals? Make a bear beg. When Smokey says 'Please,' you feel that he means it."

By association, the character can create an emotional tie between the consumer and the brand, and even between the consumer and the manufacturer. This is because the trade character, through its personality, humanizes the product and gives it a conscience that makes the product trustworthy. Consumers may not trust Grand Metropolitan, but they trust Poppin' Fresh. The emotional tie created by the trade character sells the symbolism it represents.

The two functions of the trade character's personality, meaning and emotional appeal, work together to create a successful character. [Harry Wayne] McMahan calls this interplay Visual Image/Personality. It is important that both personality aspects are present, as evidenced by a famous trade character, the Jolly Green Giant. The personality of the Green Giant is full of meaning; he symbolizes nature, healthy product, and the size and strength of his company. However, a giant is necessarily large and remote, and perhaps lacks emotional appeal. This could be one reason why, in the 1970s, he received a sidekick, the Little Green Sprout, who is outgoing and enthusiastic. Both characters work together to fulfill the personality functions. The Giant provides meaning and the Sprout provides emotional appeal.

A second example that highlights the importance of synergy between the two personality roles is the extreme care taken by RCA in naming their new trade character, Chipper. RCA's longtime trade character, Nipper, had all but retired by 1990. In his place, RCA created advertisements that attempted to dazzle consumers with technology. However, these ads were found to be confusing and incomprehensible to the target audience. As a result, Nipper was revived as a symbol of tradition and reliability, and a puppy was chosen as a symbol of growth and change. After careful deliberation, the puppy was named Chipper because the name had four associations:

1. a computer chip (symbolizing technology)
2. a chip off the old block (symbolizing trust)
3. the definition of "chipper" as "happy and upbeat" (suggesting a positive emotional response), and
4. Chipper rhymes with Nipper (promoting a connection between the two characters).

In choosing this name, RCA ensured that their new trade character's personality would give meaning and emotional appeal to their product line.

The linking together of myth and emotion gives an added advantage to the trade character; it is very difficult for consumers to pronounce a trade character or the claims the character makes "false." [Roland] Barthes states that myth is a pure ideographic system, that is, it is a system that suggests an idea without specifically naming it. Because trade characters communicate through myth, they represent ideas and attributes that are never explicitly stated, and therefore are less likely to be rejected. For example, the Jolly Green Giant is a symbol of health and nature, but conveys his message without verbalizing it. His message may therefore be accepted without thought. In contrast, an advertisement that proclaims "Our vegetables are healthy and natural" might be met with skepticism and counterargumentation, since canned vegetables can be far from either. Trade characters make puffery palatable. By entering into the trade character's fantasy world, the consumer gives the character permission to exaggerate.

This puffery effect is enhanced by the emotion elicited by a trade character. As discussed above, a trade character can symbolize an intangible emotional benefit that is transferred to the product. However, a trade character's offer of fun (Kool-Aid Man), friendship (Ronald McDonald), or excitement (Joe Camel) is not easily quantified or measured. Therefore these "soft" benefits are free from regulations, and can successfully persuade without explicitly promising anything. Through the use of myth and emotion, trade characters are free to suggest product attributes and benefits that could not be expressly stated.

Promotional Continuity

The third message that trade characters communicate is promotional continuity. Trade characters can create promotional continuity across advertising campaigns, across brands in a product line, and over time.

A. Advertising Continuity

By appearing in each advertisement, a trade character connects the ads into a meaningful campaign. The trade character, in its role of product identifier, signals to the consumer that the ad is for a specific brand. An example of a trade character used for advertising continuity is Little Caesar's Roman. Whether he is the star of the commercial, or appears at the end as a visual tagline, he unites widely dissimilar promotional campaigns by using his presence and his cry of "Pizza! Pizza!" to identify the sponsor.

B. Product Line Continuity

Trade characters can also provide continuity across brands in a product line. The value of using one trade character for several brands is the resulting cumulative publicity; each product connects to and helps to sell the others. In addition, each product takes on the attributes symbolized by the character. The Keebler Elves are used in this way. Advertisements show the Elves manufacturing everything in the Keebler line from crackers to cookies to chips. The Elves' magic can link these products together in the minds of consumers and affirm that each is made with Keebler quality.

C. Continuity over Time

Also, trade characters can provide continuity over time. Many currently used trade characters have an impressive longevity: RCA's Nipper was created in 1901, Mr. Peanut in 1916, Snap! Crackle! and Pop! in 1932, and Borden's cow, Elsie, in 1936. Live-action characters can also provide continuity: the Maytag Repairman celebrates his twenty-fifth birthday this year. By using these characters for years or even decades, advertisers build invaluable brand equity.

There are several advantages to using these characters over many years. Because consumers have prior experience with the trade character, its role as a product identifier is enhanced. Over time, consumers learn to recognize trade characters and the brands that they represent. At first, consumers attributed Eveready's Energizer Bunny to Duracell. However, the longer the commercials ran, the better the consumers became at identifying the sponsor. Because consumers already know that a character represents a certain brand, they will be able to easily identify the advertiser when viewing a specific ad.

Another advantage to using a character for many years is that advertisers are able to build on an image that already exists in the mind of the consumer. Once consumers understand a trade character's meaning and link it to the brand, future advertising can focus on reinforcing this connection instead of trying to establish a new one. As a result, the advertising message is usually clear and easily understood. When consumers see Tony the Tiger in an ad, they know that Tony's message will be that Frosted Flakes are "grrreat."

There is an added advantage for advertisers who use their trade characters for many years—the characters may become the objects of nostalgia. Nostalgia is a positive feeling toward some part of a person's past life. Because of geographic, occupational, and social mobility, nostalgia for a relatively permanent geographic locale (home) has been replaced by nostalgia for media products rooted in a certain time. This time is usually childhood and adolescence. Therefore many consumers have strong emotional ties to trade characters that were advertised in their youth. If these characters are still in use, the comfortable, positive, loyal feelings that consumers have towards them can be transferred to the brand.

There are several reasons why trade characters can be used and reused over time. One reason is that trade characters are created to symbolize relatively permanent product attributes or consumer benefits. The Maytag Repairman represents reliability, and Snuggle, the fabric softener bear, represents softness. As long as these basic benefits remain valuable to the target audience, these characters can continue to embody them. Also because trade characters are advertising creations, the advertiser has complete control over them. They do not grow old, change their meaning, or demand a raise. The creators of Spot, the 7-Up trade character, state, "Every dollar we invest in Spot over the long term comes right back to the Seven-Up company because he is ours. And Spot is not going to wind up on the front page of *USA Today* for adultery or drug abuse." Finally, trade characters are flexible. They can appear on labels, in advertising, on coupons, on promotions, or "in person." By appearing in different promotional areas, a character's life can be extended. An example is Ronald McDonald, who, in addition to appearing in all of the standard promotional areas, will also be used for a nontraditional promotion. He will appear in a video game aimed at reaching the best fast food customers—adolescents.

D. Limitations of Continuity

There are several limiting factors when using the same trade character for a long time. The character may become dated, may no longer be able to personify the advertising message, or may acquire an undesirable meaning. As styles and fashions change, characters can become dated. They can be kept fresh and effective by modernizing them. Usually, the inner meaning of the character remains the same, but the outward appearance and trappings are changed. For example, Betty Crocker has had her hairstyle and clothing modified many times over the years, and Poppin' Fresh has learned how to rap.

If the advertising message changes, the existing trade character will no longer be able to symbolize its meaning. At that point, the trade character usually has to be retired. Qantas Airways recently abandoned its humorous koala bear trade character for more sophisticated imagery when its focus changed from tourist to business travelers. In another example, advertisers deemed Smokey Bear unsuitable for use in hard-hitting ads that warned the public about jail terms for setting forest fires. The advertisers wanted to keep Smokey's soft, warm, fuzzy image intact for future soft-sell promotions.

As social and political changes take place over time, a benign trade character may acquire an undesirable meaning. This was the case with the Exxon Tiger, who was introduced to convey the concept of smooth, silent power. The character was discontinued in the 1970s because its imagery took on a "wasteful" quality during the austerity of the oil crisis. However, the tiger was reintroduced in the late 1980s once the oil crisis faded and cultural values shifted again.

The biggest cultural meaning shifts that have affected trade characters are those that stereotype humans, especially minorities. It is important to note that a stereotype is not necessarily negative. All trade characters are based on the skillful manipulation of stereotypes; advertisers use a dove to "mean" peace regardless of a dove's actual behavior in the wild. However, stereotypes have a subtle and persuasive influence that gains power through repetition. Once a stereotype of a *group is* imbedded in folklore, it can affect an individual's thoughts and actions. Therefore if an accepted stereotype of a group is essentially negative, this negative view of the group will be perpetuated. Because of the shifting social values, some stereotypical trade characters from the past now convey unacceptable negative meanings to consumers.

Two trade characters who have the dubious distinction of contributing to negative stereotyping of humans are Sambo (and his "brother" Golliwog in the U.K.) and Aunt Jemima. These two characters were popular and accepted for decades, and since many consumers had no personal experience with blacks, they came to stand for the generic black man and black woman. "The chief problem with stereotypes of ethnic . . . groups is that one character . . . is allowed to stand for a whole diverse collection of human beings," [Marilyn Kern-Foxworth has said]. Unfortunately the attributes that these characters presented were largely negative. Blacks were presented as childish, comical, subservient, docile, and servile. Over decades of common use, consumers never consciously considered the ramifications of the myth that they were accepting.

Over time, as cultural values changed, society began to examine these trade characters more closely. [Robert M.] MacGregor found that the social significance of these symbols had gone far beyond their original intent, and they had become images laden with negative stereotypical cultural meaning. Eventually, the Golliwog came to be perceived as a racist symbol by a substantial portion of British society, and the trade character Sambo faded out of use. In 1968, the Quaker Oats Company scrambled to "update" Aunt Jemima into an acceptable image. She "suddenly lost over one hundred pounds, became forty years younger and her red bandanna was replaced by a headband"; in 1990, she was changed even further, into a "black Betty Crocker" [Kern-Foxworth]. These major changes in imagery and meaning were necessary to Aunt Jemima's continuance as an acceptable trade character. Thus, it is apparent that shifting cultural values may limit a character's use and effectiveness over time.

Conclusion

In this paper, a trade character has been defined as a fictional, animate, or inanimate being or animated object that has been created for the promotion of a product, service, or idea. Trade characters have become a common element in American popular culture because of their use as advertising tools. In this role, they can communicate in three ways: by creating product identification, by promoting a brand personality, and by providing promotional continuity. It appears, then, that by effectively fulfilling their advertising functions, trade characters have become an easily understood and accepted communication system between advertisers and consumers. This will ensure that trade characters continue to be an important and enduring part of American popular culture.

From *Journal of Popular Culture* 29, no. 4 (Spring 1996). Reprinted, without bibliographical information, with permission of the author.

SUGGESTIONS FOR FURTHER STUDY

1. How do the trade characters discussed here fit into the picture of elite art? Or any kind of art?
2. This article seems in many ways to be directed toward the advertisers who are going to use trade characters. Should it be viewed with some suspicion?
3. Examine the advertising currently on TV or in other media. Has the line and drive changed much in the last nine years?
4. If you were head of an advertising agency, would you consult this article for ideas?

CELEBRATIONS

Celebrations pepper the landscape of America because the people need to have something to look at and to appreciate, and because celebrations attract both money and attention to a locality. In many ways one could say that a community is known by the celebrations it mounts. Realizing this, communities mount as many as possible, some legitimate and noteworthy, some shamefully faked but effective. Celebrations have a long history and apparently a bright future.

Although America is a young nation, its calendar is filled with commemorations, celebrations, and appreciations of events. Its capital cities are crowded with statues of generals riding horses that often are visited only by pigeons. At times the political objects of celebration get in the way, and for convenience we group them, as in the combined birthdays of George Washington (February 22, 1732–December 14, 1799) and Abraham Lincoln (February 12, 1809–April 15, 1865) into Presidents' Day, which is held on a Monday in February, in order to extend the weekend. One birthday that is vividly commemorated over most of the nation is that of Martin Luther King Jr. (1929–68), winner in 1964 of the Nobel Peace Prize and perhaps the greatest American leader of black citizens in their effort to rise from second-class citizenship to that of full political and social justice. The direction and degree of his accomplishment are sometimes differently interpreted today. Juan Williams, senior correspondent for National Public Radio, political analyst for Fox News Channel, and co-author of *This Far by Faith: Stories from the African American Religious Experience,* chastises the black church of today for not recognizing that King wanted them to continue his message from the pulpits and streets. Most whites take the message as having been obviously sent to blacks but primarily to white Americans, as the following editorial from the *New York Times* recognizes.

The Freedom of Equality

Today marks only the seventeenth time that America has celebrated an official holiday in remembrance of Martin Luther King Jr. Perhaps in a hundred years, this will be just another holiday, a day commemorating a man who changed the world in ways that will be taken for granted. But there is no taking those changes for granted yet, for civil rights are still a patchwork. If many black Americans are living a version of King's dream, they live it with the consciousness that that dream still has sharp boundaries, places, and situations where it does not yet apply. And, as Trent Lott has notably demonstrated, some white Americans still cling to a version of history that denies even the fundamental premise of King's greatest hopes for his people.

The very newness of this holiday should not obscure how old the cause it commemorates really is. Today honors the life of a man who was murdered, still young, in 1968, but it also honors a quest for civil equality, embodied in his life, that began the moment the first black slave landed in the new world. The revolution that we call the Civil War—a revolution against the past—was really a chance to see whether a nation could rebel against its own history, against the pervasively racist assumptions that helped shape that history. It's hardly surprising that that revolution, unlike the original American Revolution, is still incomplete. Throwing off the shackles of another nation is easy compared with throwing off the shackles we forged for ourselves.

Perhaps someday it will seem astonishing that one set of humans suppressed another set of humans because of skin color. Perhaps it will also seem astonishing someday that African-Americans continue to suffer discrimination because of the historic consequences of their skin color, all the systemic effects that arise from having been enslaved and then only partially freed. Of all the holidays in the calendar, perhaps only this one rings with the activism its namesake embodied in his own life. It's an activism that every American can take to heart, for the simple reason that the progress of American freedom will not be complete until every American is equally free.

SUGGESTIONS FOR FURTHER STUDY

1. Read an account of the early struggles of King and argue your point of view.
2. This editorial is brief. Is it convincing in its persuasive power?
3. The struggles of blacks are not yet over, as the editorial points out. What do you think King would be doing today if he were still alive? What should other Americans be doing to carry on his struggle?
4. At Senator Strom Thurmond's one-hundredth birthday party in 2002, Senator Trent Lott said that "all these problems" would have been avoided if Thurmond had been elected president of the United States in 1948 when he ran as a segregationist. Look up articles about the furor Lott's remark caused and comment on whether the Senate, the public, and the president of the United States did right in forcing Lott to step down from his position as majority leader of the U.S. Senate.

Celebrations

Rituals of Popular Veneration

JAMES COMBS

Students of popular culture are drawn to such a vast and difficult subject for a wide variety of reasons, not the least of which is that the culture of the populace offers evidence of unfolding change. In contemporary America, scholars and journalists often point to popular phenomena as evidence of mass changes in attitude and mood. More inclusively, some even use popular culture for bolder historical theses. Such sweeping theses are often so cosmic that popular evidence is not in itself sufficient to diagnose and validate a vast historical shift, but on the other hand ignoring such evidence omits sometimes obvious clues as to what's happening.

For a long time, people have pondered the famous Weberian thesis about the unfolding "disenchantment of the world." Some observers of contemporary times see this in secularization and desacralization, in the delegitimation of institutions, the fragmentation of authority, and the search for alternative meanings and ways of life. We now speak of "postmodernism" almost as a given, sensing that the accumulation of change now is of such force and magnitude as to augur the advent of a world after modernity, and perhaps even after civilization. A glance at the number of "warriors of the wasteland" movies in the tape rental stores offers a clue as to how much the prospect of an imminent world of post-civilizational savagery has become an object of popular play. But if people are disenchanted with the world, if their commitment to institutions and authorities is more fluid, and if they are searching for alternatives that do give their lives new meaning, this suggests that many people will be looking for objects of veneration. They may wish to venerate old and tried things, or new and novel things, but in either case they are seeking something that deserves reverence or awe. And if this thesis is correct, there will emerge in such a fragmented culture a wide variety of popular things that will command the attention, respect, and even worship of groupings of people in search of re-enchanted experience. In other words, we should expect a plurality of celebrations, popular groupings around different things, old and new, familiar and bizarre, sanctioned and condemned, the sacred profaned and the profane made sacred.

Celebrations include a wide variety of human behaviors, involving the recognition and commemoration of something deemed worthy of the acclaim. They can be gay, with jubilant and festive conduct, or they can be solemn, with measured and sober conduct. But in virtually all cases the collective convergence of attention we call a celebration is a ritual of veneration, in that there is a repeatable form of symbolic action directed toward a place, an event, or an object that commands esteem or worship. A ritual of veneration gives shape to a desired collective experience, and a degree of sacred status to what is being venerated. A celebration with at least a modicum of active format and temporal rhythm brings us into the realm of sanctification, and the interplay between, and confusion of, the sacred and the profane.

In the dynamic popular culture of "postmodernity," we observe many examples of popular celebration. We see popular shrines, places of popular veneration; popular festivals, events of popular veneration; and popular groups, gatherings, or affiliations of popular veneration. Some of these are official, others semi-official, and still others unofficial and even counter-official. For example, official places would include the shrines of the state maintained for the purpose of propagating political myth. The Statue of Liberty is a refurbished official shrine recently re-invested with symbolic status in an official festival conducted by a Hamiltonian elite celebrating Jeffersonian mythology, and reopened as newly accessible for popular obeisance to state symbols. A semi-official shrine is an established place of popular veneration with a high degree of social sanction and official approval. A good example is baseball's Hall of Fame in Cooperstown, with its mythic celebration of the athletic giants in the earth and the cultural importance of the national game.

When we come to unofficial shrines, however, we run into conceptual and taxonomic difficulties. The idea of a shrine connotes sanctuary, a hallowed place of respectful veneration; worship, with an attitude of devotion to what the shrine symbolizes; and participation in ritual, which suggests appropriate ceremonial acts. A sacred shrine, such as Lourdes or Mecca, fits our criteria easily enough. But what about popular and "secular" sites that seem to invite such behavior? Here we run into such a rich variety of places with shrine-like qualities that definition and distinction become difficult. An official shrine such as Mt. Rushmore is a designated hallowed sanctuary of Presidential gods, a sort of democratic Olympus, but the visitors are largely tourists on a leisure trip and not a pilgrimage, are hardly worshipful, and perform no ceremonies other than taking pictures. Other official shrines, such as the Lincoln Memorial and Constitution Hall, do seem to invite more respectful behavior and even a degree of devotion to hallowed icons and places, but involve no ritual acts other than a kind of hushed silence. The White House is more of a museum, a palace that once houses Presidential demigods, but the attitude of the millions that stream through the place is one of curiosity and awe, not unlike the many who tour the palaces at Versailles, Leningrad, and even Teheran. The one political shrine that does appear to most adequately meet our sacral criteria is the Vietnam War Memorial, involving for many the sense of a pilgrimage, a worshipful attitude, emotional catharsis, and indeed, ritual acts such as wearing Vietnam military paraphernalia, searching for names, and leaving flowers.

But perhaps we are being too restrictive. Popular celebration does not have to be limited to places of solemnity. Too, in the "postmodern" era we may be dealing with a confusion, and even a collapse of the realms of the sacred and secular. The Weberian "disenchantment of the world" that we associate with secularization simply compels us to seek enchantment in places, events, and objects that hitherto might not have occurred to us. If the world is being emptied of miracle, mystery, and authority, we seek it all the more in experiences that substitute for the institutions—governments, churches, universities—that used to be the agencies of sacral values, but have been eclipsed by their slow but sure delegitimation. In this kind of historical vacuum so reminiscent of the waning of the Middle Ages, several processes seem to be going on at once, centering around the enshrinement of the past, present, or future. Those who would enshrine the past seem to be motivated by the urge to preserve or monumentalize, a celebration of a temporal event or process that cannot be recaptured or undone but needs symbolic remembrance. The Vietnam War Memorial cannot undo that traumatic experience, but it can monumentalize what it meant. Greenfield Village preserves a mythic past by simulating it as it should have been, enshrining Ford's conception of the essential harmony and historical logic of pre-industrial and industrial society, the "machine in the garden." There are plans for a Civil Rights Museum in Memphis. Then there are those who would enshrine a present, either a temporary or an eternal present. Theme parks may well be shrines to socially approved fun, Barnumian sites that ritualize the "sinless carnival" of fun morality. Those who go to the Disneyworlds enter a universe of contrived conviviality, making leisure into a structured ceremonial involving the sacralization of play, the worship of corporate technology and progress, and the celebration of puerility. If this is correct, such shrines suggest entry into an eternal present, what one would do without eternity in a fun heaven. Perhaps Heritage, USA can be explained as a kind of postmodernist evangelical dream of heaven, God's Eternity as a long running PTL show interspersed with ice cream and shopping, the ultimate safe merger of the sacred and the profane. (Jessica Hahn does make a nice Lilith.) Finally, there are those shrines that celebrate the future, however conceived. Perhaps the NASA Museum celebrating space exploration is an example of this, as well as the Museum of Science and Industry and Epcot Center, celebrating the promise of technology.

One conception of contemporary popular shrines has some merit, but doesn't adequately capture the rich and lurid diversity of sacred-secular celebration. The paradigm case of slightly disreputable idolatry is, of course, Graceland. The 1987 celebration of Elvis in Memphis was an astonishing exercise in festive and shrining activity, including tours of his birthplace, a candlelight vigil at his grave, an Elvis memorial service and revival meeting, and an Elvis Presley Memorial Karate Tournament. The endless stream of emotionally moved people who annually flow through Graceland does give us the sense that we are present at an important popular shrine that celebrates a cultural icon of more importance than one might have imagined at his death. Graceland remains to be fully explained, but it does illustrate our notion that we are at a juncture in our history in which the impulse for enshrining itself deserves inquiry. Graceland belies an existential hunger for the sacral in the mundane and even ludicrous, as if we are in a postlapsarian world beyond redemption that can only be memorialized. One may wonder if those who tour Graceland have experienced sacralization or merely pseudo-sacralization, a substitute for a sense of holiness and holy places. Or is the worship or veneration of Elvis simply a new way of sanctification and canonization, a popular method of making a new god? Does the pilgrimage to Graceland offer the pilgrim any more or less genuine religious experience than, say, a visit to Gatlinburg, Tennessee's Christus Gardens, with its "dioramas" of the life of Christ with "life-like wax figures complete with human hair and medically approved eyes," and authentic costumes provided by the creators of wardrobes of *Quo Vadis* and *Ben-Hur?*

Perhaps what we are witnessing is the legitimation of diverse popular experience through enshrinement. From traditional elite institutions to shrines to symbols of faith, patriotism, and knowledge. But popular shrines communicate the legitimacy of popular experience, even if it is lurid, frivolous, or downright kitsch. Elite culture enshrines Presidents at memorials and libraries; intermediate semi-official culture is less marbley but often as pretentious and certainly subject to ridicule (as with Disney's talking mechanical Lincoln and "Hall of Presidents"); popular culture is often more vigorous and openly exploitative (as in the cottage Presidential industries essential to the economies of Dixon, Illinois, and Plains, Georgia) and even more inventive (as with the White House Lodge of Richland Center, Wisconsin, where one "dines at the White House with the forty Presidents" through their portraits, and a view from the translucent acrylic dome and rotunda on top).

For whatever the reason, we are becoming a nation of shrines. Some are venerable institutions, but still characterized by their unofficial but legendary status as a shrine to visit. We have in mind here such shrines as the Corn Palace ("a palace bedecked with corn and other fruits of the land") in South Dakota; Wall Drugs; the Confederama in Chattanooga; Rock City; Old Tucson; the Cowboy Hall of Fame; Christ of the Ozarks, and so on. But recently the extent of enshrining something of popular value has been astonishing. Consider these: the Tupperware Museum of Kissimmee, Florida; the Children's Museum of Holyoke, Massachusetts; the Drainage Hall of Fame, the Accountants Hall of Fame, and the Insurance Hall of Fame; all on the campus of Ohio State University. (Word comes from La Grange, Texas, that local entrepreneurs intend to enshrine "The Chicken Ranch" also known as "The Best Little Whore-house in Texas," by converting it into a museum: "It's going to be taste-ful," said one. "It will be like a national monument. It will be first class, a place to bring the wife and kids.") Perhaps such a shrine would be somewhat in the same spirit as the Barbie Hall of Fame in Palo Alto, California, where the curator argues that "people are seeing that this is no longer a doll but a representation of history." And indeed there are shrines to darker social themes: the Dillinger Jail of La Porte, Indiana, and the Dillinger and Capone shrines in Wisconsin; the Seven Acres Antique Village and Museum, of Union, Illinois, which became a mecca for Hitler buffs with the discovery it had his photo album; and the Tragedy in U.S. History Museum in St. Augustine, Florida, with its wax figurine of Lee Harvey Oswald about to shoot, Kennedy assassina-tion memorabilia such as Oswald's cat, Bonnie and Clyde's death car, as well as Jane Mansfield's, not to mention the ambulance that took the dying Oswald to the hospital and indeed the stretcher he was on.

The latter examples illustrate that shrines can be celebrations not only of life but also of death. Perhaps this helps explain the popularity of the National Atomic Museum near Albuquerque, New Mexico, with its thirty-seven full-scale replicas of nuclear weapons, a defunct B-52, mis-siles, and a poster of Albert Einstein. Just as Graceland celebrates the death of the American Dream, perhaps the Atomic Museum celebrates the political death of a country that enshrines and venerates the tech-nology and instruments of death. Shrines bear mute witness to a wide variety of things, but this may be the only one that is a tribute to annihi-lation. If the Martians were to land at the Atomic Museum after World War III they might well conclude that we had a cult of death that wor-shiped war.

On the other hand, if one wants to engage in cultural psychologizing, other popular shrines would offer Martian Tocqueville's evidence of cults of sex and companionship. There is now the Frederick's of Holly-wood Bra Museum, a shrine to the synthetic history of our post-World War II celebration of women's breasts, and indeed the progressive expo-sure and allurement of the female body through wearing frilly, brief, and often ingenious undergarments. (Feminists may well ponder the state of their movement by reference to the defiant rhetorical question of the Bra Museum's curator: "Where would women be without bras"?) Such a museum obviously symbolizes our obsession with sex and cultural expectations and fantasies about female sensuality. It also suggests the enshrinement of the idea of woman as an object of profane worship, an iconic structure defined by a passive stance of sensual invitation and bodily curvature. In an odd sense, the Bra Museum shares something with the National Atomic Museum: both are shrines to totemic power. The Atomic Museum enshrines male power to rain totemic death through missiles and bombs on those we would dominate by destroying. The Bra Museum enshrines male power to rain totemic submission of women transformed into mannequin-like objects of lust. Perhaps then cults of death and cults of sex are not that different, since both celebrate similar forms of domination and venerate power that is destructive.

But we grow too solemn. As an antidote, let us ponder the meaning of the Dog Museum of America, in Ballwin, Missouri. The Dog Museum is a shrine that celebrates the companionship of the dog, including a collection of dog art, dog memorabilia, and literature on the dog. Like many popular shrines, the Dog Museum was established at precisely the historical moment when the dog has become less popular than the cat. In that case, canine veneration will share the nostalgic impulses often involved with enshrining: that which in passing must be remembered, including the bond between a kid and dog. Shrines that venerate that which has gone or is passing reveal a sentimental streak in us, as well as a sense of loss. In that sense, the Dog Museum emerges from the same impulse as Greenfield Village and the humble birthplace homes of so many prominent Americans, from Elvis (Tupelo, Mississippi) to John Wayne (Winterset, Iowa). In all cases, the thing venerated represents something important to us, and the dog is not the least of these.

There are many more popular shrines we could mention, but the larger question for students of popular culture remains: does contemporary popular enshrinement constitute a movement? If so, why? We have speculated that it has something to do with the decline of the authority of traditional institutions, and the concurrent impulse to re-enchant the world. Perhaps even the celebration of murderers, whores, and bombs is preferable to meaninglessness. If the elite shrines lose meaning, then popular shrines fill the void. If so, then popular shrining resonates from a decay of belief. A shrine gives something sanction; perhaps people are finding new, and more diverse and even bizarre, things to sanction. In that case, we are seeing the glimmerings of postcivil popular religions, with the breakdown of elite hegemony as to what is to be enshrined.

From *Journal of Popular Culture* 22, no. 4 (Spring 1989). Used with permission of the author.

SUGGESTIONS FOR FURTHER STUDY

1. Do you have any kind of museum in your hometown or neighborhood? If so what function is it intended to serve, and how successful is it?
2. Is it possible that museums are driven more by nostalgia than by a desire to commemorate the past, and if so are they successful?
3. As the nation gets older and more diverse, more museums and collections are going to come into existence because people have different interests that they want to "keep alive" and present. What particular aspects of society do you expect to start being housed in museums?
4. There is a growing interest in all kinds of collectibles—some antiques that are very valuable and some items that are valuable only to those people who find them valuable. As you look at the two shows about antiques on television (American and British) and visit all the antique shops lining every street in every community, what is your prediction about the growth of museums housing such items? Are the articles themselves of intrinsic merit?

Sports is one of the most important and powerful drives in societies throughout the world. The ancient Greeks encouraged sports and contests to develop the physical body alongside the spiritual self. Perhaps along with those noble intentions we could observe that sports are needed to take people's minds off the business—and the sameness—of daily life and to channel the physical energy that individuals and societies generate. Sports are individual and societal statements of activity directed toward particular goals through organized drives and specific rules.

The complexity of a culture is revealed in the number and complexity of its sports. Sometimes it seems that sports or a particular sport takes over a culture and wraps the culture around it and to speak for the culture. Cultural historian Jacques Barzun once said that to know America one must understand baseball, the national pastime. American society is more complicated now. One might say that to know America one must understand football. But that means far more than the actual sixty minutes of play. It means the diversion of high school and college from education to developing skill in football; Friday night parties, tailgate parties, sports paraphernalia, weekly talk about the games and ratings of both college and professional games, astonishing amounts of money flowing into gambling; the near-monopoly of space and time by commentators and pundits on the page and on the air; the importance of such supportive activities as cheerleading, which can help develop the careers of both men and women, such as becoming majority leader in the U.S. Senate. One could almost say that if we took away football America would die. But we don't want to take away football. Perhaps change or modify it, as NBC tried to do in the 2000–2001 season by

285

introducing the XFL. But this hyping of the energy and show-off level into half-organized chaos did not succeed because it strayed too far from convention.

So games and interests change slightly to keep up with changing times. Today women are allowed greater roles in sports. Parents, perhaps with too little to do otherwise, are more and more committing themselves to little league activities and to living what they consider unfulfilled lives through the successes of the children. A game new to America became important enough to designate a whole generation of young mothers "soccer moms." We already had the sports fathers, on their feet or as couch potatoes. So sports will never disappear from American society though there are good questions as to what forms they will take in the future. Will soccer—the world's most popular sport—ever become America's major sport, the national pastime?

The following article covers the conventional solid niche in sports with a form of theater which somehow satisfies an ever-growing segment of society. It seems to be important movement in American society. Where does it lead us?

Buckeyes Bask in Glory

OSU's National Title Is for the Ages—Past, Present, and Future

BRUCE HOOLEY

PHOENIX. Ohio State's official celebration of its first national championship since 1968 hasn't yet been planned, perhaps because organizers know they'll have a tough act to follow.

Appropriately commemorating the Buckeye's 31–24 double-overtime conquest of defending national champion Miami is a gargantuan task, because almost anything will pale next to the thrills of Friday night at the Fiesta Bowl.

With perhaps sixty-five thousand OSU devotees down to their last breath in the packed house of 77,502, the Buckeyes emerged with an epic upset already meriting mention among the greatest games in college football history.

"I told all my guys on the sideline when overtime started, 'Boys, this is an instant classic. This is going down in the books as one of the all-time great games,'" Ohio State linebacker Cie Grant said.

"I mean, seriously, name me one game that was better than this. I'm just glad I could be a part of it."

Grant's blitz forced Miami quarterback Ken Dorsey to throw

incomplete on fourth down from the one-yard line on the game's final play, triggering a raucous party by OSU partisans ringing the field.

Players cavorted on the Sun Devil Stadium turf, giddy at following consecutive 7–5 seasons with a 14–0 record unprecedented in Division I-A annals.

"I can't describe it," linebacker Matt Wilhelm said. "You can use whatever joyous word you want—amazing, incredible, fantastic—it's all of those things and more."

Such emotions were still palpable yesterday morning at OSU's headquarters hotel, where fountains spouted majestically into the sunshine as star-struck fans sought autographs from players still pinching themselves.

"I think I got about three hours sleep," offensive guard Adrien Clarke said. "It hasn't sunk in yet that we're national champs."

Coach Jim Tressel, experienced in these matters given four I-AA titles at Youngstown State and now this crown at OSU, isn't sure the Buckeyes can comprehend their achievements quite yet.

"I don't know that they will fully get it until more time passes," Tressel said. "They were starting to get it. I can picture some of them out there saying, 'We're the national champions . . . we did it.' You know, it will be something that will be very, very special the rest of their lives."

Proof of that is the OSU players who still enjoy a measure of celebrity from their performance on the Buckeyes' 1968 national champions—until Friday night, the last Big Ten team to finish consensus number one.

Names like Rex Kern, Jack Tatum, Jim Stillwagon, and Jim Otis still evoke swoons from scarlet-and-gray faithful, which is a heady notion for Wilhelm, who won't be twenty-one until next month.

"That's the exciting thing," he said. "We all had it in the backs of our minds that we had the chance to go out there and gain some respect and be a part of Ohio State history."

Their legacy is now secure as players who, on one majestic night in the desert, secured both OSU's first national championship in 34 seasons and ended Miami's thirty-four-game winning streak.

"We're little kids in the candy store," senior safety Michael Doss said. "It's Christmas for us."

Now the Buckeyes need no longer labor under a lump-of-coal image stemming from losses one game shy of titles in 1969, 1970, 1973–75, 1979, 1996, and 1998.

The ghosts of Randa Vataha, Wally Henry, Tshimanga Biakubu-tuka, and other Buckeye killers of the past finally lay silent, drowned by the sheer delight of OSU's unimpeachable finish atop the polls.

"I was never fortunate enough to win a national championship as a player," two-time Heisman Trophy winner Archie Griffin said. "All I know is this sure feels great to me."

From *Cleveland Plain Dealer*, January 5, 2003. Reprinted with permission.

SUGGESTIONS FOR FURTHER STUDY

1. Although football may not generate as much hysteria as other sports, say soccer, it fires up both players and fans into near madness. Can you explain the emotion?
2. In the middle of the game, players wave to the fans in the seats to get them fired up. Fans are called the Twelfth Player. Do you act as such a player when in the bleachers?
3. Many people—to be sure generally not players—look upon the attention and the costs given to sports as unnecessary and a mis-use of college funds and time. Do you share this sentiment?

POPULAR LITERATURE

A merica has always been a literate society. It is said that in the mid-nineteenth century 98 percent of the population could read. After the Civil War for several reasons the rate of literacy declined but America has always realized that democracy depends on literacy, and has encouraged reading. Two forces have driven the nation's literature. One has been the elite feeling that only "good" literature—that is, the kind they preferred—should be encouraged. The other, increasingly powerful drive has been that literature of all kinds should be allowed or encouraged if that is what the people want. The differences between the two have always been more definitional than real, and in the twentieth century—especially the end of the period—popular literature has become the main reading material of society and the support of the publishing world. Nowadays all publishers try in every way to publish the "block buster" bestseller, and the public rush to read the books highest on the bestseller list. Nowadays you can tell a book by its cover since titles and contents are emblazoned across the cover in ever-growing sized letters and illustrations.

Virtually every subject is covered, sometimes time and again, in current literature. The list ranges wide: horror fiction, romances (in amazing numbers), mysteries of all natures (ethnic, medical, gay and lesbian, true crime, police procedural, regional, religious, historical, seasonal, gothic), comic books, self-help literature, diet literature, science fiction, Western (though not as important now as it used to be), spy (though such literature was essentially a cold war literature and has declined lately with the change in world political temperature), etc.

Especially popular today are thrillers, crime fiction, comic books, and sometimes science fiction. But the widest sellers are conventional types of literature aimed toward a mass market. Often the only differences between the two are style and perhaps complexity of presentation. But we should always remember that most enlightened authors and critics believe that the finest literature is that written simply enough for nearly all to understand.

Dead Men Walking Free

TERRY MCCARTHY

In his art and in his life as a lawyer, Scott Turow takes on the legal nightmare of wrongful executions.

Early in Scott Turow's new novel, *Reversible Errors* (Farrar, Straus & Giroux), defense attorney Arthur Raven realizes his death-row client is almost certainly innocent. Raven, a low-profile corporate lawyer who has been drafted into the case by the federal appellate court, is close to panic. "If something goes wrong here I will feel like somebody sucked the light out of the universe."

Turow, who works as a full partner at a big Chicago law firm while turning out best sellers every three years or so *(Presumed Innocent, Personal Injuries, The Laws of Our Fathers)*, nearly had the life sucked out of his own universe when he handled a similar case in 1991. As if that weren't enough, halfway through writing *Errors*, a book that harks back to that traumatic case, he was appointed to a controversial commission examining all the death-penalty convictions in his state. Following up on that commission's highly critical report, Governor George Ryan last week said the flawed state system could not be trusted and launched a mass hearing of clemency appeals from 142 of the 158 people on Illinois's death row.

Talk about hyping a book. But *Errors* is no crude anti-capital-punishment tract. Moral ambiguity is at the heart of Turow's fictional Kindle County, where the truth is never the whole truth and justice is often merely a point of view. The story of how a wrong man is sentenced to death for a triple murder is told through the eyes of four flawed characters: the middle-aged, despairingly single Raven; Muriel Wynn, the cynical prosecutor; Larry Starczek, a hard-boiled cop; and Gillian Sullivan, a judge known for taking bribes. Turow never promised it was pretty out there.

But the book's central drama of an innocent man facing execution comes just as doubts about the fairness of the capital-punishment system are spreading nationally. "Even [Supreme Court] justice Sandra Day O'Connor has said she is disturbed at the number of innocent people on death row," says Turow, wiping sweat from his forehead after a golf game near his home on Chicago's North Shore. Golf is the only time Turow doesn't work. He writes his novels on the train to his office, works all day on the seventy-seventh floor of the Sears Tower for clients at $450 an hour, then takes the train home for more writing before bed.

The idea for the new novel came from the case of Alejandro Hernandez, who was sentenced to death for the 1985 rape and murder of a young girl. Turow was alerted to the case by a friend. When he read the evidence—which largely rested on a single sentence in English spoken in the midst of a conversation in Spanish—and learned that a convicted child murderer had already confessed to the girl's killing, he says, "I became virtually unhinged. I couldn't believe this was happening in America."

But it was, and it happens more often than anyone wants to admit. Turow eventually won Hernandez's acquittal, making him one of thirteen people on death row in Illinois who have been exonerated since the death penalty was reinstated in 1977. In 2000, Governor Ryan declared an indefinite moratorium on executions and appointed Turow to the death-penalty commission.

Turow is not morally opposed to the death penalty; nor were a majority of the fourteen members of the commission. According to Turow, detailed reviews and cross studies showed "no evidence that killing a killer makes murder less likely." The stronger argument for the death penalty, in the commission's view, was that it provided solace to some of the victim's relatives. "Until the commission," says Turow, "I didn't really understand what it means for some twisted creep to change your life forever." But the mounting evidence of unfair application of the ultimate penalty to minorities, along with sloppy defense counsels, prejudiced juries, and forensic errors, finally persuaded Turow and most of his colleagues that the present system was not fixable.

The light does not go out in Arthur Raven's universe—in the end justice is seen to be done. But if Raven achieves a weary self-enlightenment, nowhere does *Errors* deliver a clear judgment on the death penalty. Instead it conveys a deep sense of unease. A wrongful execution, after all, is one legal error that can never be reversed.

SUGGESTIONS FOR FURTHER STUDY

1. This kind of fiction (called faction), a mixture of fiction based on facts, is popular. Read this novel and see if it is convincing as an argument for reversing the death penalty.
2. Choose another novel of this kind—by Turow or another—and see if the type holds up.
3. Choose a pure fiction crime novel and compare it with one like Turow's. Which is the more satisfying as a good read?

Although the U.S. may have the best judicial and corrections systems in the world, everyone will admit that they are not perfect. It is difficult to establish and maintain the system that metes out justice in the way it should be. The following article demonstrates just how difficult it is to use prison as a means of punishment or of rehabilitation when inmates are allowed to write "literature" that suggests they should have their sentences reduced.

The Killer inside Me

He's a Murderer. And a Model Inmate.
Should Wilbert Rideau Go Free?

SETH MNOOKIN

Lt. Col. Bruce LaFargue is walking a visitor around the interior perime-
ter of Lake Charles, Louisiana's Calcasieu Parish Jail. Most of the pris-
oners are black, most are young, and most are shirtless, showing off
chiseled abs and biceps the size of tennis balls. In one of the barracks-
like rooms sits an older man. He's sixty, with a neatly trimmed mus-
tache. A pile of legal papers is stacked in front of him. He looks up and
holds a visitor's gaze for thirty seconds, then a minute. Finally, he points
back to his work, nods, and looks down.

Back in LaFargue's office, the burly warden says, "That was Wilbert
Rideau. The pods, they hold twenty-four men, but there's only eighteen
in Rideau's. We don't want anyone who wants to be famous and shivs
him, 'cause Wilbert, well, he's more than just a prisoner around here."

That's an understatement. A convicted killer, Rideau has been in
jail longer than any other murderer in Louisiana, yet he's about to be
tried for the fourth time—despite the recommendation of four pardon
boards that he be released. While incarcerated at Angola, Louisiana's
infamous state penitentiary, Rideau won his jailer's trust with his good
behavior and efforts to improve inmates' lives. Yet he seems unable to

muster even the simplest apology for the brutal crime that put him be-hind bars—a move that could help defang some of the passionate oppo-sition to his release. At a time when American prisons are letting less-deserving inmates out early because of overcrowding and budget woes, Rideau's case poses thorny questions about race, rehabilitation, and the power of penitence.

On February 16, 1961, Rideau, a nineteen-year-old high-school dropout, robbed Lake Charles's Gulf National Bank. Armed with a .22 and a cheap blade, he walked in the bank just after closing and walked out with $14,000 cash and three prisoners. He murdered one of his hos-tages, a young teller named Julia Ferguson. He left another lying face down in the woods with her throat slit and a bullet in her spine. The bank's manager escaped with a gunshot wound only because he ran for it before Rideau could take his life.

In the four decades he's spent in jail, Rideau has done everything he can to make himself more than a murderous thug. In 1975 he was named the first black editor of Angola's inmate magazine, the *Angolite*. He led investigations into life on death row. He won a George Polk Award and a Robert F. Kennedy Journalism Award. While at Angola, so great was the level of trust between him and his jailers that Rideau was often let out to tour the state and talk to youth about the dangers of crime. In 1993 *Life* magazine referred to Rideau as "the most rehabili-tated prisoner in America."

While Rideau was refashioning his life, his case was taking a circui-tous route through the American judicial system. Rideau's been con-victed and sentenced to death three separate times in trials redolent of the racist legacy of the American South. The three juries were all white. During the second trial, a member of the white supremacist Citizens' Council openly huddled with the prosecution.

The guilty verdicts handed down by those first two juries were thrown out by higher courts on procedural grounds. And in December 2000, a federal appeals court threw out the third conviction, ruling that Rideau's original 1961 indictment couldn't stand because of racial dis-crimination in the makeup of that long-ago grand jury. Delayed by a series of contentious pretrial motions, Rideau's new trial is expected to begin soon.

The prosecution argues that no amount of good works can erase Rideau's cold-blooded murder. "I don't care if he's black or white or green," says Rick Bryant, the district attorney trying the case. "I'm not in the business of letting out killers." But Rideau's supporters—a group that includes newspaper editors, lawyers, and university professors—say Rideau's paid his debt to society, and that many other convicted murderers have been released. They point out that several pardon boards have recommended Rideau be released.

These are arguments that Rideau is practiced at preaching. "You know, there's still racism in America," he says in measured, careful tones. "Look at me. There's still a judicial mechanism for lynching. I know that, I've had it done to me. I've reached a point where I don't want to be judged by my accomplishments. I just want to be treated fairly."

But Rideau's been steadfast in his refusal to apologize for what he's done. "Rideau seems to be staring across history at a person that seems vaguely familiar but fundamentally different," says Jonathan Turley, a prison-reform expert. "I don't know if he's come to grips with the fact that it is the same person. I have never met a more articulate and engaging prisoner. And he committed some horrible crimes."

When pushed about his feelings about what he did, Rideau stammers, "I'm, I think. I think a lot of bad things happened," Rideau told *Newsweek*. And then he changes the subject.

These days, Rideau spends his days writing and going over legal papers in the Calcasieu Parish Jail. To the prisoner, there are no ambiguities. "I think of a Biblical passage: evil was wished on me, but God wished for good to come from all this," he says. "I'm not angry or bitter about any of it. I recognize it took everything that happened to make me the person I am. I like myself, and that's significant, because there was a time in my life when I didn't."

Don Hickman, the son of the bank manager Rideau held at gunpoint, is less philosophical. "Yeah, I believe in redemption," says Hickman. "Even for murder. But premeditated murder, you shouldn't get out. If you can't do the time, don't do the crime, right? The way I look at it, he's lucky the state didn't execute him."

SUGGESTIONS FOR FURTHER STUDY

1. What does this example tell us about the American legal system? Is it as fair as it can be?

2. If you were on a commission to free Rideau or keep him imprisoned, what would you do?
3. How does this piece throw light on Turow's novel, as discussed in the preceding article?

Throughout literary history, adventure and romance have been particularly appealing to readers. Both represent traveling either physically or emotionally into a world that is different from and superior to the everyday world around us. These adventures—as much of the heart as of the body—have been particularly appealing to women because, although the stories may seem to keep women in subordinate roles, they actually liberate them either covertly or overtly. Today, when women insist that their equality be recognized and guaranteed, the romance must play a role or at least give expression to this recognized or assumed equality. Though always written to a formula, present-day romances are individual expressions to which people are partial and loyal. Called bodice rippers because they always include low-cut blouses and naked breasts (and usually sex), they seem not to be resented by women. It is interesting also that reporters—who are supposedly dedicated to reporting the news—usually condescend to this form of literature, as though they were superior to it. The following review reveals the kind of work and the type of author who writes them.

Rewriting the Romance

Bodice Rippers Are More Popular than Ever, and
Julia Quinn Is Taking Them into
the Postfeminist Future

LEV GROSSMAN

There are two great things about reviewing a romance novel. One is that you don't have to be worried about giving away the ending. Even though Susannah Ballister is stubborn and not conventionally pretty and the Earl of Renminster is stiff and pompous, I will tell you right now; they hook up. Here's the other great thing about reviewing romance novels: people actually read them.

A few statistics: romance novels are read by fifty-one million Americans. They account for more than half of all paperback fiction sold in the U.S. If you thought feminism, postmodernism, and the Internet had done away with the romance novel, think again. The number of romance-novel readers in the U.S. has risen 18 percent since 1998. One reason: romance novels are changing. Julia Quinn, whose *The Further Observations of Lady Whistledown* tells the story of Ballister and Renminster, is one of the people changing them.

Julia Quinn isn't who you think she is. For starters, she isn't really Julia Quinn. That's just a pseudonym she chose so her books would be shelved next to those of the best-selling romance writer Amanda Quick.

What's more, she's not a little old lady with a dozen cats. Julia Quinn is Julie Pottinger, thirty-three, a smart, ambitious Harvard graduate. Quinn spent two years after college fulfilling her pre-med requirements, then went to Yale medical school. But after two months she dropped out to pursue her true purpose in life: writing romance novels.

Quinn's specialty is Regency romances, which are set in the England of the early 1800s—think Jane Austen. There are eight subgenres of romance in all, including paranormal romance (which involves magic and the supernatural) and time-travel romance (love conquers all, including the space-time continuum). This kind of specialization is typical of the genre—romance novels are marketed more like computers or Tupperware than books. They are not works of art. They are highly targeted commodities, engineered to a set of tightly controlled specifications. The formula seems to work: romances novels rang up $1.5 billion in retail sales last year.

But if so many people are buying them, how come nobody wants to admit it? In part because until a few years ago, romance novels deserved their bad reputation. "People who don't read romance novels still have the perception that they are what they were in the 1970s or '80s," Quinn says. "The heroines were doormats, with all these alpha males bossing them around. I can't imagine a romance novel published today where the hero rapes the heroine and she falls in love with him."

Writers like Quinn are reinventing the romance novel for the post-feminist generation. Although she hasn't discarded the conventions of romance, Quinn is more than willing to tweak them. In *Romancing Mister Bridgerton,* her eleventh novel, which spent a month on the *New York Times* paperback best-seller list last summer, the heroine is a plump wallflower. Her hero actually complains, with a sigh, that he isn't "dark and brooding." He is not a sexual predator either. "I can't think of anything in my books that any feminist would find objectionable," Quinn says. "And I consider myself a feminist."

Quinn's latest book, *The Further Observations of Lady Whistledown,* is a set of four novellas by four authors, including Quinn; it's a kind of Julia Quinn production. The stories are all organized around a tart gossip columnist who appears in several of Quinn's novels. Quinn has a smart, funny touch with dialogue that's reminiscent of *Bridget Jones* author Helen Fielding's, and Quinn's characters have a roundness to them that's surprising and appealing. On the grand scale of emotional power, her work delivers about the same punch as a *Friends* episode—which is to say, it isn't Faulkner, but it's nothing one should be embarrassed to read in public.

In her next novel, Quinn plans to explore some darker themes—the hero is a widower whose late wife suffered from clinical depression. It's an interesting direction for a romance writer, one that might bring her perilously close to literary respectability. As she points out, "You always get more respect when you don't have a happy ending." So is she tempted to trade in her soft-focus covers for cultural credibility? To end, just once, with a funeral instead of a wedding? "Oh, no!" Quinn says quickly. "I have a mortgage."

From *Time*, February 3, 2003. © 2003 Time Inc. Reprinted with permission.

SUGGESTIONS FOR FURTHER STUDY

1. It is clear from the tone of the article that the author is somewhat embarrassed to be taking this novel seriously. Do you think he does it justice, is he fair to the author and the public?

2. The author of the article in his own way is trying to justify and to continue the short tradition of "elite" literature that he thinks is represented by William Faulkner. But it is only name-dropping. Not every "serious" literary critic looks upon Faulkner as the top-most author of American literature. Though a small core of authors are considered superior, a growing number are looked upon as more than competent and properly suited for a democratic public. Read a work by Faulkner or some other "elite" author of your choice and agree or disagree with the author of this article.

3. There seems to be a certain sense of guilty self-awareness in the mind of Julia Quinn. Does she sound as if she feels she is "slumming" and will mature into writing something "better" as soon as she has paid off the mortgage?

4. Read one of Quinn's novels or another novel of this type and see if the criticism or praise usually heaped upon the type is justified.

5. If you were teaching a course in modern American literature, would you include a romance, and how would you teach it?

The comic strip began in America on February 16, 1896, with publication of "The Yellow Kid" in William Randolph Hearst's *New York Journal*, but the comic book probably should be dated 1911, when the plates of the newspaper strip were reduced in size and published as a book. As such it was meant to capitalize on the fun aspect of the "funnies," as they were called in the newspapers. We have lived with the newspaper funnies ever since.

But authors of comic books soon found that the stories they were telling and illustrating were capable of far more than mere humor. They then turned to telling stories and illustrating them, or illustrating action and stringing it out on stories. From the first the use of "funnies" in newspapers or comic books has been controversial. They were condemned because their purpose and message were obvious and intentional in their attempt to reach the masses. But comic books were the McDonald's hamburgers of literature. They communicated in a way that all could understand and appreciate, just as McDonald's sells a taste at a price that all like and can afford. Like McDonald's, comic books appeal to millions. They cover all subjects—history, science fiction, social problems, all matters of culture—on two tracks, verbal and visual. As such their impact is twice as appealing, twice as broad, twice as effective. Because they are so porous, comic books soak up all forms of culture and when touched release it easily. They are the world's most popular form of literature and they reflect society and influence it. Because of this breadth of coverage, comic books carry and reveal all aspects of popular culture: mythology, symbolism, formula, stereotype, icons and iconology, myth and symbol, changing historical practices and tastes. Often they are tight expressions of many at the same time. Though long held under some kind of control, they are increasingly recognized as a legitimate form of popular expression, literary or not.

Comic Book Fandom and Cultural Capital

JEFFREY A. BROWN

Mass entertainments have the power to capture our hearts and our dreams. The pleasure we derive from entertainments can sometimes sweep us into what appears consuming and fanatical behavior. But this fanaticism is only evidence of the complexity of our relationship with mass-mediated texts. Rather than blind devotion, fandom is a means of expressing one's sense of self and one's communal relations with others within our complex society. Individual fans and entire fan communities develop intimate attachments to certain forms of mass-produced entertainments that, for whatever reason, satisfy personal needs. These fan communities construct a world as rich and intricate as any traditional perception of *high* or *real* culture. Both the practice of fandom and its object of enthusiasm—TV shows, rock 'n' roll bands, movie stars, romance novels, etc.—are usually perceived with disdain within the dominant value system. As [John] Fiske argues, the culture of fandom is associated with the tastes of the disempowered, of people who are subordinated by the socio-economic system that determines the status of individuals within the general community. The institutionalized image of fans as social misfits devoted to accumulating worthless information about "crass" entertainments has caused fandom to be devalued as one of the basest and most superficial aspects of popular culture. Yet recent cultural studies work, both in America and Great Britain, has opened the door for understanding fandom as a legitimate cultural expression. What I propose here is a consideration of comic book fandom as a complex system with its own rules for determining the worth and stature of popular texts.

Nowhere are the traits of fandom more clear than within the culture of comic book enthusiasts. The well-defined community of comic fans allows a unique insight on "how" and "why" fandom is an important aspect of contemporary culture. Comic fandom, and the practice of comic-book collecting in particular, is evidence of the complex and structured way in which avid participants of popular culture construct a meaningful sense of self. They create a culture that simultaneously resists the tyranny of *high* culture and forms what Fiske calls a "shadow cultural economy" that mimics bourgeois standards. Fiske's term is derived from [Pierre] Bourdieu's metaphor of culture as an economic system divided along the twin poles of cultural and economic capital. Bourdieu's theory provides an apt language for discussing how people attempt to invest in and accumulate qualities that are perceived as valuable within a culture. Like our capitalist economy, the cultural system distributes its resources on a selective basis to create a nonfiscal distinction between the privileged and the deprived. The system ascribes value to certain "tastes" and devalues others. Typically the tastes that are privileged are those associated with the upper class. Dominant tastes are seen as superior by the entire culture (if indeed they are) because the ruling class naturalizes their tastes through the control of institutions such as universities, museums, and art galleries. High culture is socially and institutionally legitimated as the "official" culture, distinguishing between the "haves" and the "have nots." Thus, like economic capital, one can *invest* in an education or *invest* in a good suit to better one's chances of advancing socially and economically up the ladder of official culture.

In his grand opus, *Distinction: A Social Critique of the Judgement of Taste* (1984), Bourdieu crafts an in-depth analysis of social hierarchy in contemporary France. He builds from the basic notion that "good" taste, social status, and economic position are intricately related. "To the socially recognized hierarchy of the arts, and within each of them, of genres, schools or periods, corresponds a social hierarchy of the consumers. This predisposes tastes to function as markers of 'class.'" By considering

both cultural tastes and economic status as measurable capital, Bourdieu constructs a two-dimensional model onto which social and hier-
archical space can be mapped. The chart I have sketched here as Figure
I represents this model of cultural economy at its most basic level. The
north-south axis measures the amount of capital (economic *and* cultural)
one possesses, and the east-west axis measures the type of capital (economic *or* cultural).

Fiske emphasizes two limitations of Bourdieu's model. The first is
Bourdieu's narrow focus on economics and class as the discriminating
features of social position. Other discriminatory features such as sex,
ethnicity, and age need to be included in the model. Fiske's second criticism is that Bourdieu makes the mistake of underestimating the complexity of proletarian culture. The model is primarily concerned with social stratification amongst the "haves" since the "have nots" are assumed
to have no capital with which to negotiate their social position. This view
ignores the power of the subordinated to construct their own semiotic
texts from, and often in opposition to, the original texts provided by the
cultural industries. It is easy to see how people disempowered by sex,

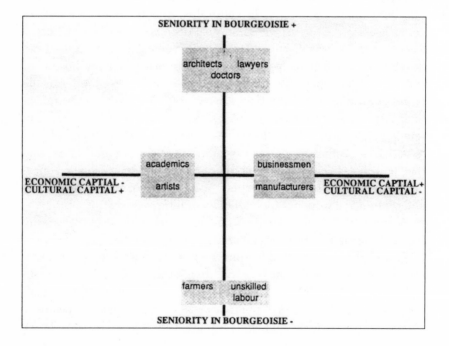

ethnicity, and in the case of most comic fans, age, would fall somewhere in the south hemisphere of Bourdieu's model. But by looking closely at the complex system of meanings that constitutes the culture of comics fandom we can see how the traditionally disempowered act to bolster their social position within the community of fans. Bourdieu's rules for gaining prestige within the general culture are mimicked by popular culture, allowing members of fan communities to accumulate the social status and self-esteem that accompanies cultural capital.

Comic Fandom

A profile of the comic-fan community in North America is a difficult one to sketch. Due to the extremely competitive nature of the comics industry, the major publishers and distributors are reluctant to disclose any detailed information on sales or audience research. The big two publishers, Marvel and DC, are "notoriously tightlipped about the sales figures" [Calvin Reid]. A number of industry publications and fan magazines, or "Fanzines," such as *The Comic Buyers Guide, Wizard: The Guide to Comics,* and *Comics Scene* regularly print lists of the top-ten or top-hundred selling comics of the month and charts showing the market and dollar share of each publisher. By carefully controlling the release of this limited information, the publishers create a sense of a "hot" list that encourages collectors and investors to speculate on which comics they should be purchasing. On the other hand, knowledge of exact sales figures might actually discourage comic book collecting. For example, the sense that the recent *Death of Superman* issue is "hot" encourages investors to purchase at least one if not multiple copies of the issue on the speculation that the monetary value of such a landmark issue will increase dramatically. But if the actual sales figures about that issue are released, a collector might choose to spend his or her comic dollars elsewhere, since the extreme number of *Death of Superman* copies sold indicates that the issue will be far from rare in the next few years and the resale demand of the book will be minimal.

Despite the reluctance of the major publishers to release accurate sales figures, it is possible to estimate the size and nature of the comic-reading community in North America. [Patrick] Parsons draws from several publishing and distribution periodicals to estimate the monthly circulation of comic books to have been over twenty million in 1989. All unofficial accounts indicate that the market has expanded dramatically through the early 1990s. The rise in sales and readership over the past decade is due to the rejuvenation of the industry brought on by the adoption of a direct distribution approach. Direct distribution caters to comic specialty stores, a relatively recent phenomenon in comics culture. Rather than being sold primarily in the magazine section of the corner drugstore, the principal outlet for comics since the late 1970s has been the comic specialty store. These stores deal almost exclusively in comic books and related fan community objects such as role-playing games, "bubble-gum cards," and science-fiction literature. They "operate on a nonreturnable basis with discounts of 50 percent or more and cater to fans and collectors" [Reid]. Maggie Thompson, co-editor of the weekly trade journal *Comic Buyer's Guide*, estimated in 1991 that "there are about five thousand specialty comic shops in the U.S." and that "their annual retail sales rose from $130 million in mid-1986 to $400 million last year [1989]" [Dan Fost]. These stories have provided a focal point for the entire culture of comic fandom. They have taken comics off the bottom rack and placed them front and center where they can be found on a regular basis and in an atmosphere where older readers feel less embarrassed to shop. The comics specialty store mediates between the readers and the publishers and are a place for fans to meet other fans and occasionally artists and writers.

Surveys have indicated that 90 percent of comic fans are male and their age can be broken down into three broad categories. There is the traditional pre-adolescent group aged six to eleven, the growing audience of adolescents between ages eleven and seventeen, and over-seventeen adult market. Since the adult fans have been brought out of the closet by the comic specialty stores, they have become a major marketing focus of the publishers. Their larger disposable income has inspired the comic companies to create mature-theme comics and the most costly graphic novel, or book-shelf quality trade paperback. The older the fan is, from early adolescence up, the more likely he or she is to become a collector rather a casual reader. Studies of comic specialty-store customers from the mid-1980s show the average age range to be between sixteen and twenty-four years old, while Fost reports that "Tom Ballou, the advertising director for DC Comics in New York City, says the average age of a comics collector is twenty-five. Most are college educated, with a household income of $39,000."

In addition to the local comic specialty store, the comic book convention, or "con," is the major focal point of modern fan culture. Cons range in size from the monthly regional ones that attract anywhere from a few hundred to a few thousand fans, to the annual "Super Cons" that last from two to fourteen days and attract tens of thousands of fans from around the world. The bible of comic book collectors, *The Overstreet Price Guide*, describes cons as an event where

> dealers, collectors, fans, whatever they call themselves can be found trading, selling, and buying the adventures of their favorite characters for hours on end. Additionally if at all possible, cons have guests of honor, usually professionals in the field of comic art, either writers, artists or editors. The committees put together panels for the con attendees where the assembled pros talk about certain areas of comics, most of the time fielding questions from the assembled audience. At cons one can usually find displays of various and sundry things, usually original art. There might be radio listening rooms; there is most certainly a daily showing of different movies, usually science fiction or horror type. Of course there is always the chance to get together with friends at cons and just talk about comics; one also has a good opportunity to make new friends who have similar interests and with whom one can correspond after the con.

As Overstreet's description indicates, cons often appeal to a much wider range of fandom than just the comic book enthusiast. What must be kept in mind is that devoted fans tend to participate in several fan communities at the same time. Thus, the cultural negotiation that is conducted within the comic fan community can be somewhat extrapolated to include fans of other media and other genres. The con is seen by many fans as an individual's final point of entry into the social order of comic culture. It is a place for fans to accumulate and demonstrate their cultural knowledge of comics. It is the market place of fandom's cultural economics.

Disempowered Tastes

Despite the swelling ranks of adults within the comic fan community, most people still perceive the medium as childish. They believe comics consist of immature, simple stories and "cartoony" art. This condescending view is, in fact, far from the truth. Modern comics deal with highly complex issues in mature and innovative ways. But the stereotypical perception of comics is a common criticism of all popular fan cultures. The problem is that fan cultures challenge what the bourgeois have institutionalized as natural and universal standards of "good taste." As Bourdieu tells us, the economy of culture is so powerful that any aesthetic tastes not conforming to the established norms of high culture are devalued to the point of being socially unacceptable. Any practices that do not adhere to the dictates of "good taste" are taken as markers of an individual's inferiority. Fans and their subject of enthusiasm are necessarily looked down upon by the greater society because their aesthetic preferences amount to a disruption of, and threat to, dominant cultural hierarchies.

Because pursuing a leisure activity that is in "bad taste" is considered detrimental to one's development, society often adopts a paternalistic attitude of wanting to save fans from the harmful effects of popular mediums. There is a moral backlash that accompanies all new and suspect forms of entertainment, from the early pulp novels and turn-of-the-century movies to modern music videos and role-playing games. In his study of television science fiction fandom, Jenkins points out that "materials viewed as undesirable within a particular aesthetic are often accused of harmful social effects or negative influences upon their consumers. Aesthetic preferences are imposed through legislation and public pressure; for example, in the cause of protecting children from the 'corrupting' influence of undesired cultural materials. Those who enjoy such texts are seen as intellectually debased, psychologically suspect, or emotionally immature." This moral condemnation of undesirable aesthetics and institutionalized regulation of the medium is particularly clear in the history of comics. The criticism of comics under the guise of "protecting children from the 'corrupting' influence" of the medium was almost solely responsible for the drastic decline in sales and the near death of the industry during the 1950s.

At the height of their popularity in the late 1940s and early 1950s, the comics became subject to the moral crusades of the McCarthy era. Critics wanted a scapegoat for the rise in juvenile delinquency and found a susceptible victim in the comics. Several prominent critics accused comic books of being "the opium of the nursery." As a youth-oriented medium, not protected by the aesthetic requirements of "good taste," comic books became the target of middle- and upper-class paranoia.

Columnist Norbert Muhlen expressed the fears of society in his article "Comic Books and Other Horrors" (*Commentary,* 1949): "the newest, widest circulated, least inhibited, and least understood carrier of horror and destruction is the comic book."

The leader of the crusade against the comics was Dr. Frederic Wertham. Wertham, now a legendary symbol of oppression within the fan culture, was a New York psychiatrist who claimed that comic books were a direct, and possibly the only, cause of juvenile delinquency. His initial assaults published in magazines such as *Collier's, Ladies' Home Journal, National Parent Teacher Magazine, The Saturday Review of Literature,* and *Reader's Digest* allowed him to tap directly into concerned middle-class parents. His opinions came to a head with the 1954 publication of his book *Seduction of the Innocent.* Wertham's basic premise was that comic books at worst turned innocent children into vicious delinquents and at best caused an irrevocably distorted view of the world. Wertham summarized the negative effects of comic book reading as:

1. The comic-book format is an invitation to illiteracy.
2. Crime comic books create an atmosphere of cruelty and deceit.
3. They create a readiness for temptation.
4. They stimulate unwholesome fantasies.
5. They suggest criminal or sexually abnormal ideas.
6. They furnish the rationalization for them, which may be ethically even more harmful than the impulse.
7. They suggest the forms a delinquent impulse may take and supply details of technique.
8. They may tip the scales toward maladjustment or delinquency.

The focus of Wertham's inquiry was what he called the "crime comics," a classification that included: cops-and-robbers, superhero, science fiction, western, jungle, horror, and even romance comics. In these, Wertham found examples of every atrocity possible. "If one were to set out to show children how to steal, rob, lie, cheat, assault, and break into houses, no better method could be devised." He claimed that all comics contained glorified images of criminal violence that inspired children to behave in a similar manner. As proof Wertham offered the testimony of several delinquents under his care who claimed, "I got my bad ideas from the comics: stabbing, robbing, stealing guns, and all that stuff." While the grittier urban crime comics were accused of being instruction manuals for delinquents, Wertham accused the most traditional of superhero comics of instigating an even worse criminal activity, homosexuality.

Wertham claimed that superheroes, those handsome muscle-bound men running around in tights, were obviously gay, the most dastardly example being the relationship of Bruce Wayne (Batman) and his young ward "Dick" Grayson (Robin), which he described as "a wish dream of two homosexuals living together." To support his accusations, Wertham related several accounts from young homosexuals he was treating: "At the age of ten or eleven, I found my sexual awakening, my sexual desires, in comic books. I think I put myself in the position of Robin. I did want to have relations with Batman. . . . I remember the first time I came across the page mentioning the 'secret Bat cave.' The thought of Batman and Robin living together and possibly having sex relations came to my mind. You can almost connect yourself with the people. . . . I felt I'd like to be loved by someone like Batman or Superman."

Wertham's methods and logic were far from scientific. Since its original publication in 1954, *Seduction of the Innocent* has been highly criticized as alarmist propaganda. [Sharon] Lowery outlines the faults in Wertham's work, including its inconsistent theory of effect, overgeneralization, lack of evidence, selective illustration without story context, absence of a control group, and complete disregard for the complex nature of juvenile delinquency. But in the early 1950s, the public was not concerned with whether a study was methodologically sound. Wertham played on the fears of parents everywhere and the backlash against comics was devastating. The status quo decided that something must be done about comic books. In *A Cycle of Outrage*, James Gilbert cites the following plea to the American Bar Association's special committee investigating the links between crime and the mass media: "Large metropolitan cities to small hamlets have passed local laws censoring or banning crime comics; state laws are under consideration; groups have been formed, both national and local, to remove crime comics from places of sale and we are currently witnessing in many localities what almost amounts to an hysteria, evidenced by the mass burning of crime comics by parents' and children's groups."

The national hysteria inspired by Wertham lead to the U.S. Senate subcommittee's hearings on Juvenile Delinquency in 1954. Their major goal was to root out the evil influence comics held over the young. Along with the general category of crime comics, the E.C. Comics line of horror titles like *The Crypt of Terror, Tales from the Crypt, The Vault of Horror*, and *The Haunt of Fear* were targeted as being in especially "bad taste," and hence harmful. In the end, the entire horror line at E.C. was canceled and the publishers moved on to create the more successful *Mad* magazine, which was not subject to the same restrictions of content that comic books were forced to adopt. To escape the witch hunts with what little audience they had left, the remaining publishers voluntarily banded together to form the Comics Magazine Association of America, Inc. The CMAA's role was to enforce a highly restrictive code of content by reviewing all comic books before their release. Among other things, the code insisted: a) policemen, judges, government officials, and respected institutions shall not be presented in such a way as to create disrespect for established authority; b) in every instance good shall triumph over evil and the criminal punished for his misdeeds; c) no comics shall explicitly present the unique details and methods of a crime; d) all lurid, unsavory, gruesome illustrations shall be omitted; and e) suggestive and salacious illustration or suggestive posture is unacceptable. The restrictiveness of the code forced some of the major publishers out of business altogether. Fiction House, the publisher of *Sheena, Queen of the Jungle,* and Avon, who had created the very first horror comic, *Eerie,* were two of the more popular companies that disappeared between 1954 and 1956. Through the late 1950s and most of the 1960s, all comics were subject to approval by the CMAA.

It wasn't until the late '60s, with the rise of the counter-culture movement and the cottage industry of underground comics, that books were published and distributed without code approval. The anti-establishment cartoons of Robert Crumb and his followers were often self-published, locally distributed books, but they did achieve an enormous cult following and forced the mainstream publishers to test the boundaries of the code. The 1970s saw Marvel publish an anti-drug story in *Amazing Spiderman* #96 and #97 without code approval. The success of Marvel's story forced the CMAA to reconsider how rigidly their rules should be interpreted. The result was that later in the same year DC was allowed to release their anti-drug story in *Green Lantern* #85 and #86 with code approval. With the adoption of direct-market distribution in the late '70s, CMAA approval was no longer needed to get the comics to the dealers. Most publishers have responded by dropping their participation in the CMAA process altogether, and even Marvel and DC only seek code approval on approximately 55 percent of their titles. This refound freedom of expression allows comics to explore more mature themes with a simple recommendation to the dealer and audience that certain titles are intended for "Mature Readers Only."

Interestingly, although it has taken the industry a long time to recover
from the institutionalized legislation against the "harmful" effects of
comic books, the medium is still occasionally under attack from the
moral right who have closed comic shops in several U.S. cities and in
books such as *Seduction of the Innocent Revisited*, published by the same
people responsible for other great classics of fundamentalist paranoia
such as *Lord! Why Is My Child a Rebel?*, *The Lucifer Connection*, and *Backward Masking Unmasked: Satanic Messages Hidden in Rock Music*.

Comic Collecting and the Shadow Economy

The legacy of the Wertham comics scare is still felt by the fan community, as is the stereotype of comics as childish and the readers as immature "nerds." The problem with comic fandom gaining legitimacy
within contemporary North American society is that it contradicts the
standards of "good taste." Ironically, fandom offends the dominant
class by applying the same standards of appreciation to popular texts
that are supposed to be reserved for the elite texts. As Bourdieu notes,
"The most intolerable thing for those who regard themselves as the possessors of legitimate culture is the sacrilegious reuniting of tastes which
[good] taste dictates shall be separated." The general public regards the
acute attention fans pay to comic books as inappropriate for simple,
mass-produced, disposable texts. The close scrutiny, collecting, analyz-
ing, rereading, and accumulation of knowledge is deemed acceptable
for a serious work of "art" but ridiculous for a mass medium. Yet it is by
mirroring these very practices of "Official" cultural economy that members of the fan community seek to bolster their cultural standing within
their own circle of social contact, their own "milieu."

Comic fandom is rather unique in relation to other popular culture
fan communities because it is almost exclusively centered around a physical, possessable text. For *Star Trek*, *Rocky Horror Picture Show*, or Grateful
Dead fans, it is the experience of viewing the show, hearing the band, or
participating in ritual consumption that is of prime importance. And
while reading the comic is obviously fundamental to comic fans on an
individual basis, it is the possession of the actual comic that acts as the
focal point for the entire community. Other fan cultures can own a New
Kids on the Block album or videotape all the episodes of *Dr. Who*, they
can even purchase all the T-shirts, dolls, and posters they want, but

none of it carries the same ability to substantiate fan authenticity in the way that owning a copy of *Wolverine* #1 does. Knowledge and the ability to use it properly amounts to the symbolic capital of the cultural economy of comic fandom., but it is the comic book itself that represents the physical currency.

Collecting is an important marker of status within official culture. It signifies the ability to distinguish between objects of worth and worthlessness, a knowledge of important canonical features, and a substantiation of "good taste." Elite collecting is based upon the ability to discriminate and thus to acquire the exceptional rather than the common. First editions are far more important than reprints, originals than copies, old rather than new. Fan collecting, on the other hand, is often seen to be "inclusive rather than exclusive: the emphasis is not so much on acquiring a few good (and thus expensive) objects as upon accumulating as many as possible. The individual objects are therefore often cheap, devalued by the official culture, and mass-produced. The distinctiveness lies in the extent of the collection rather than in their uniqueness or authenticity as cultural objects" (Fiske).

This may apply to most media fan communities, but for comic fandom, which is based so intently upon the collection of texts, it is not so much the size of the collection as its uniqueness and its inclusion of canonized comics that counts. In his article "Comicons," [Harold] Schecter describes comic books as icons so powerful that fans marvel at the "special potency—magical, numinosity, call it what you will" of rare originals. But this "magical" awe Schecter describes is understandable when we consider the ability of canonical texts to endow their possessors with cultural status. A fan's comic book collection only reflects well upon the collector if it proves his or her ability to exercise cultural knowledge in making discriminating choices of what is, and what will be, valuable.

To amass cultural capital within the comic community, the fan must build an extensive knowledge of the industry. Fans are what Bourdieu refers to as "autodidactics," individuals who are self-taught in an effort to raise their status in official culture by compensating for their lack of cultural capital and the economic capital that often comes with it. By reading and collecting comics for an amount of time, by participating in cons, and reading various fanzines, fans develop an ability to discriminate between different writers, different versions of a character, and most commonly between different artists. They learn which combinations result in the best comics and which comics will be valuable in the future because they include the first appearance of a writer, artist, or character that will likely become popular. Conversely, many fans can tell at a glance which comics are destined to flop. If a fan is consistently right, then he or she gains status among other fans and his or her collection exists as verification of his or her knowledge about comic culture.

One of the condemnations of popular culture leveled by critics like Allan Bloom and Eric Donald Hirsch is that it is canonless. Elite culture arises from an appreciation of established canons. It professes that certain works of "art" are monumentally significant in the historical development of culture and that the significance of individual works lies in the authoritative presence of a single creator. This is juxtaposed by the belief that popular culture is repetitive formulaic fluff and all works are anonymously produced and uncritically consumed. But the necessarily discriminatory skills of the comic collector disproves this narrow view of media texts. The ability to discriminate between significant and insignificant comic books creates a very specific canon. [Thomas] Inge outlines the "variety of factors that determine which comic books are the most desired by collectors" as a) original issues of popular titles, b) the work of particular creators, c) the titles of a specific publisher, and d) complete runs of favorite characters. These strategies of comic collecting are identical to those of high culture. Like official cultural practices, comic fandom recognizes historically significant events such as the first appearance of Batman in *Detective Comics* #27 or the engagement of Superman to Lois Lane in *Adventures of Superman* #50. And increasingly, the author/artist as creator has become an especially important marker of canonical value. While fans with a moderate understanding of why some comics become valuable can easily discern that a landmark issue like the *Death of Superman* is significant, it takes an experienced eye to tell that a particular artist or writer has what it takes.

In recent years, fan concentration has shifted from devotedly following specific characters to following specific creators. Like official culture texts, comic creators are being recognized as auteurs. Writers such as Alan Moore *(The Watchmen, Miracleman, V for Vendetta)* and Neil Gaiman *(The Sandman, The Books of Magic, Death: The High Cost of Living)*, and artists like Jim Lee *(X-Men, The Punisher, Wild C.A.T.s)*, and John Byrne *(Alpha Flight, She-Hulk, Next Men)* are such fan favorites that having their name attached to a project guarantees good sales. Even characters that have been around for decades are preferred when written/drawn by certain creators; Daredevil is popular but more so when written by Frank

Miller, and likewise, Spiderman when drawn by Todd McFarlane. This shift to a high culturesque preference of individual creators rather than established characters has had a profound effect on the industry and is an indication of the comic book medium's slow rise in status.

Ever since Jerry Siegel and Joe Schuster sold their creative rights over Superman to National Periodicals Publications in 1938 for $150, the relationship between creators and their characters has been contested terrain. The question of comic book characters and copyright law has a long and well-documented history, yet it has dealt almost exclusively with defending the publisher's characters from exploitative piracy rather than the discrepancy between the author's creation of characters and the publisher's owning of all rights to that character. DC, which went on to make hundreds of millions from Superman, has found itself in court many times over the years defending the properties from outsiders like Wonderman, Shazam, and The Greatest American Hero. But the times and comic fandom have changed since the court's decision in 1951 that DC Comics' defense of Superman was not misappropriation or unfair competition because, as the judge claimed, "in the case of these silly pictures nobody cares who is the producer—least of all children who are the chief readers—: the strips sell because they amuse and please, not because of their ownership." Today's reader, adult or child, does care who the creator of a comic book is. With a greater variety of comics on the market and a wider range of content and craftsmanship to choose from, it is only natural that certain creators will be judged better than others.

The recognition of individual authors/artists by the fan community has forced the industry to confront the issue of creator vs. corporate ownership. The canonization of certain texts has resulted in millions of dollars of profit for the publishers, but not necessarily for the creators. The dilemma has sparked numerous convention panels, fanzine articles, and editorials by independent publishers. As comic fandom has established its own shadow cultural economy, it has raised the status of a comic book creator from a nameless hack to an "artist." The industry is now in the process of shifting from a "sweat shop" mentality to a legal and moral recognition of the author/artist as the creative force behind a comic. The auteur ideology that emerged from fan recognition has inspired several of the most popular creators to condemn the old corporate ownership system as inhibiting intellectual and creative freedom. Frank Miller, the acclaimed writer/artist who essentially revamped the entire superhero genre in 1986 when he penned *Batman: The Dark Knight Returns*, has declared:

> You might notice that people's time at these publishers tend to be shorter and shorter. I spent a lot less time at DC than Neal Adams, for example, and certainly less than Gardner Fox did. You can't own your own work, or even a piece of it. You cannot control your work as you produce it. It's a condition intolerable enough to drive me and Alan [Moore] and a number of other people away from those companies and therefore away from these essential folk heroes. So you have to figure what your options are if you want to work with the idea of a superhero. You can't just come up with an imitation Superman—that would be cheap and silly and not as good as the original. So for my part since I can't let go of these heroes, I'm trying to come up with new ones without ripping off the old ones.

In the early 1980s, "Pacific Comics offered creators like Jack Kirby, Dave Stevens, and Mike Cirell the chance to own their own creations, an idea that has become an independent comics standard upheld by First, Eclipse, Kitchen Sink, Dark Horse, Tundra, and many others. Marvel and DC responded with creator-owned imprints (Epic and Piranha Press) and beefed up pay schedule, royalty and benefit programs" [David McDonnell]. By far the largest shift to a creator-owned industry was the development of Image press in 1991. Image consists of some of the hottest creators from Marvel and DC, the last big hold-out companies. They launched an entire line of creator-owned comic books, and each has been selling remarkably well. So well, in fact, that within two short years they have become the second largest comic company, next to Marvel in sales and market share. DC and Marvel have responded to the dwindling pool of creative talent willing to work on a "for hire only" basis by steadily increasing the amount of legal recognition they are willing to grant their staff. The future of comic culture is almost assuredly destined to focus around the talents of individual creators rather than anonymously produced characters.

The cultural economy of comic fandom is based on the ability to acquire canonical texts, as determined by either plot or creator significance. By possessing these comics, the reader substantiates his or her participation in fandom, building a knowledge of creators, characters, and storylines. As previously discussed, comic fandom is unique from the fan cultures that exist around other popular mediums because it is so fundamentally based on the serial, possessable text; it is also unique in that it has taken on a directly economic guise. As the popular press is fond of reporting, rare and significant comic books are worth a lot of money. *Action Comics* #1 with the first appearance of Superman is worth between $100,000 and $120,000, and *Detective Comics* #27 with the first Batman story can fetch $110,000–$125,000. Even contemporary comics like the fourth issue of *A Death in the Family* series, where Robin was killed as the result of a 1-900 phone survey, can skyrocket from a $1.85 cover price to over $100 in a matter of hours. The market value of comics is carefully monitored via weekly, monthly, and annual fanzine price guides. Like any other market, the prices are based on supply and demand.

The fiscal value of a good comic collection allows its cultural value to leak over the boundary into the realm of official culture. While comic fandom is looked down upon, the accumulation of valuable objects is not. Many fans have learned to validate their interest and lend it a degree of status in the eyes of nonfans by citing the economic value of their hobby. They will tell you how much their collection is worth and how much they expect certain issues to increase. In a recent issue of *Wizard*, a popular fanzine, the editors asked a group of young readers what they felt about the stereotype of comic fans as "nerds." The readers agreed they are often perceived as "social misfits" but used the economic value of collecting as an excuse; "sometimes somebody I sorta know will ask me 'Why do I waste money?' I just tell them it's an investment."

The irony of this justification is that the entire comic book market is an unintentional parody of high culture. The real value of the comic is not monetary but cultural. Like the high-culture world of art collecting, value is a relative term. It requires cultural knowledge of the creator, an historical sense of tradition, a knowledge of generic conventions, and a recognition of the avant garde to determine the "hard" value of a work. And as the bourgeoisie scoff at the nouveau riche who can afford to buy fine art but can't really appreciate it, comic fans condemn buyers who are in it just for the money. A fan letter reprinted in the letters-to-the-editor page of the March 1993 issue of *Spawn* #9 sums up the attitude towards nonfan "collectors":

> The day Jason and I purchased *Spawn* #7, we bore witness to the strange phenomenon of brainwashed consumers. It was hard to watch and understand. Three middle-aged professionals walked into the store we frequent and picked the shelves clean like a vulture would a corpse. They bought everything from *Alpha Flight* to *Youngblood*. They were impartial about their purchases, everything was sucked into the ever-growing

stack of comics. Over $70 was spent by each of them and they happily walked away with their prize catches of the week, beaming tidings of joy over their investment—but what is their investment? We could guarantee over 75 percent of the merchandise would not be looked at but merely shoved into polyurethane bags to sit and rot on the chance the market might increase in time.

For a *real* fan the comic can't just be bought. It must be understood and enjoyed. The economic aspects of collecting are false. Simply acquiring the books is the act of a heartless villain: an investor. The fan collects because he or she loves the medium and the stories it tells. As Steve Geppi, the president of Diamond Comics Distributors, wrote in a special issue of *Wizard* celebrating the one hundred most collectible comics, "I found myself automatically listing comic books which have achieved a significant dollar value. Well, I'm not sure if the books I list here will necessarily fall into the category of elite comic investments; but I do know these books are special, and collectible for the best reason of all: they are the stuff which childhood dreams are made of." Thus, to truly understand the logic of fandom, we must realize that all the claims about a comic's monetary value is posturing. The dollar figure attached to each comic in the price guide is an indication of their cultural value, not their monetary value. First and foremost, fans are fans because they share a love of the tales told in comics.

Conclusion

The practice of fandom is a complex intensification of more general aspects of popular culture. Comic book fans do participate in more common traits of popular culture as outlined by Fiske *(Understanding Popular Culture)* and others in the British Cultural Studies tradition. Comic fandom does appropriate for its own uses the materials provided by the cultural industries. A large part of fan culture revolves around the production of amateur fanzines, newsletters, and comic books featuring existing and original characters. The professional comic books and fanzines even encourage these practices by regularly publishing examples of fan art. And in the language of de Certeau, comic fans are "textual poachers" extraordinaire. They borrow characters, images, dialogue, and conventions from the comics and rework them to produce their own narratives.

Comic fandom, like all fandom, is a clear and often exaggerated example of how popular culture functions in contemporary society.

Comic fandom occupies a disempowered position in Bourdieu's model of culture. The fans are disempowered primarily because the comic medium does not fit into the institutionalized standards of "good taste." It is seen by those who have cultural status as a childish medium with subliterate stories and simple art. But fandom constitutes a milieu-specific culture that operates by the same rules as official culture. Fans seek to gain status within their own community to compensate for the status they are denied elsewhere. They do so by accumulating cultural capital that is derived from knowledge of the comic's world. This knowledge is authenticated and demonstrated by the ability to establish a well-chosen comic book collection. The shadow cultural economy of comic fandom observes all the same markers of aesthetic "good taste" that Official culture does. In fact it is this "blurring of the boundaries" that causes fandom to come under the direct attack of the status quo. Official culture seems to feel that by treating mass-mediated popular texts as worthy of artistic evaluation, the fan must be "intellectually debased, psychologically suspect, or emotionally immature" (Jenkins). Still, like Official culture, comic fandom is concerned with recognizing an established canon of extraordinary works based on the merits of individual creators and significant historical events. Comic fandom allows its participants to achieve the social prestige and self-esteem that accompanies cultural capital without surrendering to the hegemonic rules of Official culture.

From *Journal of Popular Culture* 30, no. 4 (Spring 1997). Reprinted, without bibliographical information, with permission of the author.

SUGGESTIONS FOR FURTHER STUDY

1. Judging from the arguments advanced by the author, do you think that elite culture will lose the battle against comic book culture?
2. With the great interest in child culture today, do you think that approval of—or opposition to—comic culture is likely to increase?
3. The author makes valid parallels between comic fandom and other kinds of fans. What do you think is the difference, if any,

between collecting first editions of such writers as Charles Dickens, Mark Twain, and William Shakespeare and collecting special comic books and editions?

4. If education is the goal, what is the difference between a display of, say, first editions of comic books and first editions of Mark Twain? Do they both deserve equal space in a major museum?

5. Is comic culture destroying itself in striving to be as "legitimate" as "high" culture? Should it, like "hip culture," strive to remain outside and rebellious?

6. Does society need outside "threatening cultures" in order to develop?

Mankind's desire to read the future and see his own fate is probably as old as human imagination. But until the nineteenth century mankind lacked the scientific apparatus (real or imagined) to lift him from his own society or the real world into the mechanical world or his imagination. At first people speculated in mythology, fantasy, religion, and other projections into the future based on the real world around them. Science fiction as we know it developed in the nineteenth century in the writings of such authors as Jules Verne with his works *Around the World in Eighty Days, A Voyage to the Center of the Earth, From the Earth to the Moon,* and *Twenty Thousand Leagues under the Sea* (his most successful). H. G. Wells further sophisticated the scientific novel. Since the days of those authors, science fiction novels have played an ever growing part in the popular mind in its effort to understand the physical world, reflecting and widening scientific knowledge and theory. It has also been influential in directing and stimulating the thinking of many scientists. Movies based on science fiction have from the first stimulated the thinking and captured the imagination of "hard scientists," who look to the creative imagination of movie makers who have sound stages, artists, and now computers to carry out their plots. Science fiction and science fiction movies, being based on the world around the authors, will continue to develop on known formulas, myth and symbol, rites and rituals, icons and iconology, on earth-bound human characteristics of love and hate, travel, warfare, set to different and more powerful machinery. They may expand as human beings undergo new experiences, but those experiences are unlikely to change human nature, just mankind's ways of expressing them. Undoubtedly, science fiction films will continue to get more imaginative and influential in the years to come, following the trends discussed in the article below.

Science Fiction Films of the Eighties

Fin de Siècle *before Its Time*

JOHN BEARD

Talking about the future automatically dooms one to failure of one kind or another. Even if a prediction comes true, many will doubt it until the event itself occurs, and the very best predictions often fall short when compared to the actual reality of thirty or forty years later. Perhaps Céline was thinking of this poor track record when he wrote, "Those who talk about the future are scoundrels. It is the present that matters. To evoke one's posterity is to make a speech to maggots."

After all, we human beings operate not only with a historical past as our guide but with possible futures planted somewhat firmly in our minds. This "future" is only a hypothetical construct—an imaginary window through which we see ourselves many, many years from now—but such a "future" can seem almost as comfortably real to us, at times, as the actual facts of the past. Each individual grows accustomed to seeing this "future" in a particular way. Certainly, our versions of the historical past are also constantly edited, resorted, or forgotten; they change with age until the facts of history become somewhat different from the past as *we* wish to remember it. Just so, our hypothetical "futures" undergo progressive renovations and sudden revisions of their own. Futures change.

Quite naturally, science fiction films, which often shoulder the responsibility of presenting possible futures, have traditionally reflected and even helped promote some of these changes. American audiences, especially, have appropriated the future as their own, and Americans seem comfortable there. Evidently, the conquest of the New World, the establishment of a revolutionary new government followed by expansion across a great continent, and the eventual exploration of space have all encouraged a proprietary view toward the future. There is an assumption that the United States *will* be a part of it all. Almost as if it were a democratic birthright, roughly equivalent to free speech and the right to vote, many Americans think they own the future (or at least they used to), and American films have certainly promoted favorite imaginary futures from time to time.

Still, many cinematic glimpses of tomorrow from the 1980s are quite different from those of previous decades. From 1980 to 1990, the imaginary vision of the future that dominated American film turned almost universally dark, broken, and decaying—and audiences *loved* it.

When science fiction films are examined one year at a time, these changes may not appear very dramatic; they become evolutionary—not revolutionary, but if one skips ten years and looks at them, then skips ten again, important shifts appear. For example, consider the futuristic movies of the Fifties. As any science fiction fan sifts through his or her list of "cult" classics, two similarities appear, no matter what the film might be. It could be *Destination Moon* (1950), *The Day the Earth Stood Still* (1951), or *Forbidden Planet* (1956), but the look would be streamlined and the plot would emphasize the very mixed blessings of advanced technology. As critic Marc Mancini points out, smooth, featureless rockets or sleek silver saucers reveal little about the new science that empowers them but a lot about the art directors who designed them for the movies. Such spaceships were conceived by illustrators who had no other means of visualizing tomorrow's machines today except as extensions of that era's own marvels: the jet plane and the atomic generator. Most futuristic visions from the Fifties, according to Mancini, have become legend or joke, not fact, because "movies are, like all artifacts of prophecy, deeply rooted in the soil of their times." A true Space Age was just beginning, but movies about the future already had to project beyond it, and audiences grew comfortable with the look until the "real thing" came along.

Forbidden Planet makes a good example. Many years in the future, mankind has finally perfected faster-than-light travel and journeys to distant planets for colonization and research. The film opens with a shot of a large flying-saucer-type spaceship which is propelled by the harnessed energy of nuclear reaction, and it lands on the "forbidden planet" while buoyed by a beam of light. This science works like a magic charm. However, such sophistication is tarnished when two enormous (and clunky) staircases descend from the craft so these future astronauts can deplane. They have landed in order to rescue the stranded scientist Dr. Morbius and his daughter, as well as the other members of a colony that has been isolated there for years. The good doctor has not been idle; his discovery of the technology left behind by the ancient Krell civilization once native to that planet has enabled him to increase his mental capacities and borrow a few of their lesser marvels: like Robbie the Robot, an obedient jack-of-all-trades. The Krell must have been supreme scientists but, unfortunately, awful psychologists. They developed machinery that would enable them to immediately translate their thoughts into physical reality, but when they unleashed the power of their conscious minds, they unwittingly unleashed their primitive and destructive ids as well, and they were destroyed. In just the same manner, Morbius unknowingly destroys the other members of his colony and almost destroys the visiting astronauts when his secret resentment toward them is manifested in an id-monster that seeks to drive them away from his forbidden planet. Thus, Krell science proves to be too much of a good thing. Mankind must evolve even further, evidently, before such marvels may be controlled.

Movie audiences of the Fifties enjoyed several variations of tomorrow, but the imaginary future in which most felt at home was usually up in the air, or rather up in the skies or in outer space. Smooth rockets and saucers demonstrate the extrapolated development of jet planes and aerospace technology, and cowboy-explorer America is once again conquering a strange new frontier. There were warnings and limits to what this science could or should do, especially about the possibility of nuclear horrors, but few doubted its power. This new science promised an almost magical future, including new angels *and* demons.

The more complicated technology of the Sixties and early Seventies demanded quite a different look. The actual rockets launched by NASA only faintly resembled those streamlined beauties of the Fifties, and flying saucers became jokes. In an age of real satellites and space labs, a time when man finally set foot on the moon, it seemed that our imaginary "future" must contain ever larger and more powerful versions of these present-day marvels. Movie audiences were seeing and touching technology as it developed within the everyday structure of their lives, and a real computer revolution simultaneously expanded and complicated our visual imaginations. Quite simply, a more sophisticated, forward-looking audience demanded a more realistic and detailed future.

By the early Seventies, the future-of-popular-choice was often represented by the huge and detailed starship that dwarfs the old rocket in both size and particulars, slowly filling the screen from top to bottom as it lumbers into our consciousness. One immediately recalls the great warships of *Star Wars* (1977) or the huge greenhouse ships of *Silent Running* (1971), but before these came to be, Stanley Kubrick's *2001: A Space Odyssey* (1968) had to exist. Once on the silver screens of America, *2001* quickly became the model for future films about the future—encouraging realistic detail and extensive use of what appeared to be almost working models of machinery that could outdo even the actual complexity of a real machine revolution. Once again, as in the Fifties, science is presented as a mixed blessing, and the technologically complex but sterile (and somehow threatening) white-on-white environment of the HAL-controlled spaceship in *2001* offers the familiar warning that too much of a good thing can be frightening.

Still, audiences loved the look of this technology. *2001* was the future made real for us, and all the movies that followed had to contend with it. The future had changed. Computers, space science, and astronauts were more familiar to us, and we demanded a certain verisimilitude and exactness from these films. Computers may threaten our control and aliens intervene, but hope still seems to lurk around the corner as the "star-child" embryo fills the screen at the end. Why, then, do the films of the future made during the Eighties want to change these rules? Two particular films help define the nature of this change: John Carpenter's *Escape from New York* (1981) and Ridley Scott's *Blade Runner* (1982). Both present a bleak future where cities and people are decadent and decaying, where hope is a precious commodity best saved for other times or forgotten altogether—nothing good is waiting around the corner.

In *Escape from New York*, New York City of the near future has been turned into a walled maximum security prison where only the most incorrigible criminals and violently insane are exiled to life sentences without parole. No one ever gets out. However, since the President, by chance, has crashed within this prison, the authorities bargain with an incoming prisoner named Snake Plissken (Kurt Russell) to retrieve the

President in return for a full pardon, and Snake flies in under cover of darkness to begin his quest.

Once the action moves inside prison New York, the audience is introduced to a blasted and blighted cityscape that looks as though a war has been fought and lost on every block. Once-great skyscrapers—now gutted and lightless—look over incredibly cluttered streets where fires burn out of control and scattered inhabitants stand ready for instant violence. Snake must literally descend into Hell to retrieve the President from this urban nightmare. He does eventually escape with his prize in tow, but he also destroys the cassette the President carries, an audiotape which is supposed to contain the last hope of avoiding some impending war. The images that remain afterward are ultimately more powerful than the story itself. Viewers feel as if they have seen a bit of the future, and it is a Wasteland.

Blade Runner moves us to the west coast of America and presents a future Los Angeles of about thirty years from now. Unlike Carpenter's prison of New York, Los Angeles is not dead yet, but it is diseased and dying, full of bad growths and strange mixtures of old and new technology. Recently-retired "blade runner" (i.e., android killer) Deckard (Harrison Ford) is forced out of retirement to hunt down four escaped Replicants—artificially created humanoids who are much stronger and potentially smarter than humans, but programmed with only a four-year life span. These four have returned to earth illegally to seek a cure for their mortality. Deckard must sift through gritty street scenes as he trails them across the bowels of this choking future city, successfully executing three before the fourth one unexpectedly saves his life and then dies.

Although reviewers often faulted aspects of the script and the acting, many praised *Blade Runner* for its look. In fact, as Pauline Kael points out, the city itself steals the show: "The congested-megalopolis sets are extraordinary, and they're lovingly, perhaps obsessively, detailed; this is the future as a black market, made up of scrambled sordid aspects of the past—Chinatown, the Casbah, and Times Square, with an enormous and mesmerizing ad for Coca-Cola, and Art Deco neon signs everywhere, in a blur of languages."

A few enormous pyramids containing the rich and powerful rise above the murkiness of ground-level existence, but on the street the future is confusing, dark, and claustrophobic. All white, middle-class residents seem to have moved elsewhere, leaving behind an ethnic miasma of divergent sights and sounds composed of "poor, hustling Asians and

assorted foreigners, who are made to seem not quite degenerate, perhaps, but oddly subhuman. They're all selling, dealing, struggling to get
along; they never look up" (Kael).

Director Ridley Scott has explained that he was seeking some look
that produced a "sense of overload." He wanted to put an audience
into a city of the tangible future, a city "which is in a state of overkill, of
snarled-up energy." Most of the new technology (where it exists) must
be added on or layered over the old, so buildings and machinery mix
old and new to create a strange and somewhat threatening vision of
future techno-junk. For example, instead of renovating old buildings
from the inside out, air, water, and light are pumped from the outside
in through conduits and tubes which snake up the sides of decaying
structures. Imagine a flickering computer console and other electronic
components sitting in a haunted house, water dripping from the ceiling,
and wind whistling at the windows. Syd Mead, one of the conceptual-
ists employed by Scott to develop this look, calls it "retrofitted utilization," where technology cannot replace the old but must be slowly
added on to it instead, the old constantly being refitted with some of the
new. Harlan Kennedy calls it "Scrap-Heap Futurism," while Kael labels it "retro-future," but all refer to this same strange mixture of old
and new.

Escape from New York and *Blade Runner* present a soon-to-be-future
where the sins of the present have come home to roost. These cities of
the future have not escaped the current problems of pollution, violent
crime, and apathy, nor have they tried to meet these issues head on. Instead, these once vibrant and growing cities have slumped into decay
and death, sagging under their own weight, and the average resident
seems to be both victim and cause. The immediate future appears to be
either Wasteland or Junkheap, and survivors must make do with less.

Perhaps the ideal example of this trend toward a junk future is not
an American film at all, but George Miller's *The Road Warrior* (1982), as
well as the later *Mad Max beyond Thunderdome* (1985). These Australian
films did much more than propel Mel Gibson to international promi-
nence; their success in America helped solidify Scrap-Heap Futurism as
the way to view the future. Miller's art director, Graham Walker, produced the now famous images associated with these films. Trapped in
a post-apocalyptic tomorrow, Max (the eternal loner) wanders a real
Wasteland in search of fuel for his retro-fitted auto, encountering many
savages on motorbikes but only scattered remnants of civilization or

functional technology. Everyday objects still exist, but they have been put to radically different uses. Football shoulder pads become armor, kitchen utensils become weapons, and an automobile fender is a watering trough for animals. In broad daylight on a baked desert, Miller dramatically presents the same dead-end future that Scott details so chillingly in the midst and darkness of midnight.

This is not to say that futures weren't threatening before the Eighties. Indeed, ever since the atomic bomb became an accepted reality, all our possible futures have contained an element of danger (mutated ants, alien slime, body snatchers, etc.). However, Robert Sandels points out that future-oriented societies (like ours) must struggle to invent new futures when atomic destruction forces them to consider the end of the future. Most of these earlier warnings were quite harsh, as if to say, "You will either learn from this lesson or perish." For example, in *The Omega Man* (1971), society has been destroyed by plague, but the lone survivor (Charlton Heston) has the immune factor in his blood. Hunted by a fatalistic cult of plague-blighted and dying humanity, Heston is finally killed and his blood spilled for naught—a Christ figure that never redeems.

Again, in *Soylent Green* (1973), future humanity seems doomed, forced to feed upon itself in a constant search for new food sources in an overpopulated world. The impossible overcrowding in the streets is handled by bulldozers and dump trucks, and only the very rich have space enough to live or enough food to eat. Heston, once again, plays hero— a police detective who must move through the various levels of this failed society to eventually discover the fatal cannibalistic secret of "soylent green," a new commercial food source secretly developed from the protein harvested from dead humans. Here, as in several films of the Seventies and earlier (*Silent Running, Rollerball*, etc.) the warning is obvious: mend your evil ways in the present or face retribution in the near future. Such films take an audience to the brink of apocalypse in order to frighten us back to sanity.

In contrast to these futures of dissuasion, however, the imaginative vision of the future in the films of the Eighties was not a warning. They asked to be taken as fact. As one critic puts it, audiences were asked to treat "this grimy, retrograde future as a given—a foregone conclusion, which we're not meant to question. The presumption is that man is now fully realized as a spoiler of the earth" (Kael). Such futures were based on extrapolation of present trends, and our worst fears were often realized in film. Bad news is all the news that's fit to print, and directors did not ask audiences to *prevent* this future from happening. Instead, here *is* the future, like it or not . . . and now for the rest of the story.

Films like *Escape from New York* and *Blade Runner* represent the tip of the proverbial iceberg. Besides James Cameron's *The Terminator* (1984)—which presents a bombed-out future but one where humanity is driven to the edge of destruction by flesh-clothed killing machines— consider this same trend toward a similar future in movie after movie of lesser quality. These films lack the creativity of design or the budget to match the look of a *Blade Runner*, but cheaper versions of apocalyptic futures and junk technology attest to the popularity and commonality of all such futures in the audience's imagination. Films such as *Spacehunter: Adventures in the Forbidden Zone* (1984), *Metalstorm: The Destruction of Jared Syn* (1984), *Def-Con 4* (1986), *Trancers* (1986), and *Cyborg* (1989) all use the same punk wardrobe and realistic-seeming junked science of the more expensive films. Mismatched warrior clothing, retro-fitted weapons, casual violence, and a general aimlessness are associated with characters who are dominated by post-apocalyptic bitterness as they wander about on seemingly hopeless quests through bloated future cities or shattered wastelands. Lacking the polish and flash of a *Road Warrior*, these lesser works must make do with stock formulas of a future which an Eighties audience evidently came to accept and enjoy.

Why this joy? It is unlikely that most Americans suddenly turned fatalistic about the future during the Eighties and masochistically chose to contemplate a private dance with death. No, audiences really enjoyed these films. They *chose*—in the form of repeated ticket sales and popular acclaim—to accept this bleak and grimy tomorrow as their imaginary future home. At least in their imaginations, as play, the audience felt comfortable accepting this as entertainment, a source of enjoyment, but what made it fun?

Of course, there is always the "I-told-you-so" payoff. It may seem a grim satisfaction, although satisfying nevertheless, to see mankind at its worst—even worse than now. As Pauline Kael would have it, a good portion of the audience is more than a little "pleased by this view of a medieval future—satisfied in a slightly vengeful way." It is almost as if we were thinking, "I just knew they would screw it up. Of *course* this is the future, if the future depends on the fools who are now in power. They thought they were so smart, but look at what's happened. *I knew it!*"

Also, the energy of decay displayed in these films can have a certain appeal. After all, something has to first be alive in order to decay and die, and some of the swarming cities of this possible future, choked and poisoned as they are, still twist, stink, and burp like living things. The possibility of rebirth lurks within the death throes of any such future civilization, and audiences evidently preferred this to a casual acceptance of things-as-they-are. Even when residents are down on the very idea of the city and what it may become, they can still enjoy "the punk fantasies about how swollen it is, how blighted and yet horribly alive" (Kael).

Indeed, an odd vein of optimism exists under the guise of seeming nihilism in these films, similar in its appeal to the energy of punk rock at its best; reminding us of the original impetus for the punk movement during the early Eighties. John Lewis explains, in the *Journal of Popular Culture*, that "punk was the celebration of resignation . . . anomie as artistic impulse," and it promoted an unusual brand of "aggressive egalitarianism" where everyone is the same because of the fact that everyone is worthless. According to Lewis, punk surfaced "as one last desperate attempt for white, urban, lower middle-class youths to dramatically express their distaste for a society that had long since expressed its disinterest in them." Mohawk haircuts, pierced noses, cheeks, and breasts, and ripped clothing were outward signs of such internalized rejection. The point was to disgust mainstream culture—to give it something that it couldn't commercialize and consume. By the late Eighties, however, the initial raw edge of this rebellion had long since disappeared, ironically but fatally absorbed into popular fashion and then forgotten, but it left audiences with something of a taste for the ugly side of western culture.

In an imaginary Scrap-Heap future, at least this underside is finally out in the open, and most of the old traditions are discredited or destroyed. *All* rules are broken, so it must be time for new rules. The emphasis is now placed on the individual, not the group, and each individual (whether it is Max in the desert or Snake in New York) must reinvent the world without the overt control provided by the veneer of "civilization." Such rebellion can be hopeful. *The Terminator* promises a future where humans, if they do survive, won't get fooled again into depending on machines to do their thinking or their warring for them. *Escape from New York* gives us Snake Plissken who puts personal survival first, ahead of God and country, but this particular imaginary country and its vengeful God seem particularly deserving of destruction. Many members of the audience would probably trade Plissken for the President and his whole Cabinet. Likewise, *Blade Runner* posits human beings being taught lessons in humanity by androids, but who is Deckard to question the source as long as the lesson is valid? Audiences may have enjoyed this retro-future because of the implied rebellion in it.

Also, in a visual medium like film, never overlook the power of style. The popular "punk" style of clothing and even the watered-down, co-opted, and commercialized "punk" music of the Eighties corresponded to the atmosphere of movies like *Escape from New York* or *Blade Runner*. Movies of apocalypse and urban decline, therefore, became politically correct and stylishly in vogue. Deckard's raincoat and cropped hair, the Terminator's motorcycle jacket and fatal shades, and Snake Plissken's black latex and Army surplus are as much at home in rock videos as in the imaginary future. And how can Tina Turner's songs be divorced from *Thunderdome* or the Vangelis background separated from *Blade Runner*? The musical support further emphasizes an important stylistic connection. World War III may have come and gone, the City may be in its final stages of choking decline, and perhaps machines are going to rule the world, but—damn—don't we *look* good? Right on the cutting edge of cool.

Beyond style and rebellion and irony, however, all of these films also present a future where humans still exist. Science fiction films of the past were occasionally utopian, more likely cautionary, often stopping at the brink of apocalypse—never extending much beyond to see what, if anything, may be on the other side. That is, after all, one aspect of apocalypse—nothing is left. During the Eighties, however, the unthinkable became ever more thinkable, and audiences seemed willing to accept visions of life *after* the fall, more futures after the death of our present future. In some fashion, absolute destruction seemed less absolute. Perhaps the world is not quite as fragile as we once feared. The problems that characters encounter in these artfully constructed cinematic futures are immense, but humanity still exists to contemplate them. True, much of life as we know it has been swept away or buried under loads of decay, but enough of human nature remains with which to identify.

Compared to the very real fear of *no* future at all, a dismal prospect more than hinted by dreams of nuclear nightmare, these films hold out to audiences new futures that contain some humor and occasional glimpses of continuation. Humans die, but they don't die out. It does not seem to frighten audiences as much that big mistakes might be made; they already have been made, but we still endure.

Finally, perhaps the most hopeful idea to come from these films concerns our attitudes towards science itself. Not so very long ago, science fiction films presented science as a marvelous, magical toy. It could and sometimes did perform all kinds of miracles for us, but average individuals never really controlled science. Sometimes scientists were in control of it, but the demon was just as likely to turn on Faust as it was to grant his requests. Like magicians, scientists might hand us mere mortals a lucky talisman (like a cure for polio) or tell us one of their simpler spells (how to use a word processor), but whenever we were given a truly powerful or sophisticated bit of their magic (like nuclear energy), it seemed always beyond our control to know how or when to use it.

In films, science frustrated us. Often it represented a pure power, not evil or benevolent in itself, but capable of doing great good or truly terrible evil in the right hands. Thus, whenever directors attempted to picture the uses of science in the future, they often treated it like unexplainable magic and represented it as an elemental power of the universe—a power often manifested in light: future landscapes used to be bathed in it and machinery often exuded it. These fictional alien machines and devices appeared as models of simplicity worked out in elegant designs that revealed none of their internal complexities. Perhaps such future technology *had* parts—tubes, wires, crystals, something—but these were beside the point. Science fiction films and their characters were not supposed to tamper with these things' innards; they were simply there to be used, like magic lamps. Characters touched them and were delivered a miracle.

Consider the many examples of supposedly advanced science from the future as they appeared in the science fiction films of the Sixties and Seventies. What does it usually look like? For myself, I have difficulty imagining any device more sophisticated than the black obelisks which appear in *2001*, and they have no working parts whatsoever! Likewise, whenever I review old *Star Trek* episodes (from the television series), I can always tell which technology is more advanced because it appears in the form of a magic pyramid, or sphere, or square or some other geometric shape that flickers or beams pure energy which can scatter matter to atoms, or transform atoms into forms—whatever you will—and all at the blink of an eye. These machines may be activated by touch, or sound, or thought, but nothing so mundane as a switch or dial will do, and the simple elegance of their "advanced" design easily puts them out of our reach.

However, in the science fiction films of the future which appeared in the Eighties, technology seems to have a much more practical purpose, and it is usually far from elegant in its design. In fact, exposed circuits pop and spark, conduits drip loose cables and lubricating fluids, and machines often break down or need to be reformed into newer (although junkier) versions. The technology is accessible. In fact, in many of the post-apocalyptic films, technology is subject to greasy hands, patching, mechanical manipulation, and innovation on a daily, if not hourly, basis. Machines are certainly *not* magic. They may be necessary for one's luxury or even crucial to immediate survival, but characters know something about how these machines work and when they will fail. In most cases, the machine, no matter how miraculous it may occasionally appear, cannot replace the human mind that maintains it. Instead, these future machines are like animals that must be bullied or teased into performing for men, but man knows he cannot depend on them.

Truly, the future science portrayed in these films does not seem quite as threatening as one might expect. *We*, in the audience, seem not as threatened by it. It is not so much that we now understand the technology with which we must deal in all aspects of our daily lives (we mostly do not), but people today seem to have a little stronger belief in their own ability to improvise and adapt to it. I do not understand how a word processor works, but I can use one to type this sentence, and if the machinery fails, I can fall back on my old Underwood typewriter—or even a pencil. Good old common sense might just prevail, and today's junk might actually turn out to be a gold mine during some future decades.

In a way, Scrap-Heap Futurism does battle nihilism. Audiences like to see a spirit of improvisation at work, the cat landing on its feet no matter how high it has been thrown for a loop. Perhaps it represents a nostalgia for some lost frontier spunk, or it may just be another sign of rebellion against the conformity promoted by rampant consumerism, but it seems a healthy development. The multi-layered buildings and choking streets of *Blade Runner* and the junkyard city of *Thunderdome* share the same basic appeal. Rats and junkyard dogs may not strike one as very appealing icons, but both represent the grudging respect Americans have traditionally awarded mongrel determination—the bulldog grip that holds on and won't let go.

All this fascination with and enjoyment of a dark and decaying future is not totally negative. Directors and audiences alike have now had the opportunity to vicariously work out several problems in these films. Science as magic is an idea that probably should be discredited, and perhaps the energy of decay needs to be exploited. Many now feel that some radical changes must be embraced in order to give birth to any possible future that can "save" us from ourselves, if, indeed, we do need saving. The violence found in post-apocalyptic movies has also been over-analyzed by critics. The films of the Eighties took such violence as a given—brain candy for this generation of viewers. Once past this fictionalized violence, the real issues appear.

Audiences can now imagine themselves past the Apocalypse, living in a world of change and confusion, but still alive and kicking for years to come. That punk future seems alive with possibilities (if also vaguely threatening) and much to be desired when compared to the imaginative poverty offered, unfortunately, by much of contemporary culture. Perhaps American audiences have already had their brush with *fin-de-siècle* despair and disappointment. We had our end-of-the-century confrontation at the movies during the Eighties. Now the Nineties seem a new beginning, and our dreams about the future will have to change once more. If an apocalyptic future is not quite as likely, then, what will take its place? Are audiences ready to move out of that Wasteland—along with Max—into newer and more hopeful worlds? Ask yourself that question again in thirty years.

From *Journal of Popular Culture* 32, no. 1 (Summer 1998). Reprinted, without bibliographical information, with permission of the author.

SUGGESTIONS FOR FURTHER STUDY

1. Numerous advances have been made in science and technology since this article was published. How have these changes dictated new thinking in fiction and movies?
2. Discuss how sci-fi movies develop and depend upon such modes of development as myth and symbol, rites and rituals, formula, icons and iconology.
3. Revisit one of the movies discussed in this article and see if the reading and understanding of it have changed in the last five years.
4. Think about two recent developments and tell how they may have changed people's attitude toward science, the growth of knowledge, and therefore "equality" in the possibilities in the pursuit of science and scientists. Tell how they may have strengthened skepticism about the good intentions of scientists and science. Do knowledge and equal power darken mankind's viewing of and hope for the future?

MUSIC

No activity is more devoted to self-enjoyment and involves more expense, perhaps, than rock music. You keep up with the latest stars, their lives, and their albums, and you spend millions on their songs. Mainly you concentrate on American stars but when they become tiring or too familiar you look elsewhere for diversion. Since the advent of the Beatles you have always been open to a good band from Britain. The following article predicts an invasion of another group.

The Garage Door Opens

CHRISTOPHER JOHN FARLEY

It's a sunny Thursday afternoon, and Craig David is adding a little garage to the penthouse of midtown Manhattan's hip Hudson Hotel. David, nineteen, is star of U.K. Garage, a dance-music genre that is even more popular in Britain than trading gossipy stories about the Countess of Wessex. The genre is looking for a U.S. break-through. Americans, however, have long had mixed emotions when it comes to British imports: the Beatles were great, of course, but we are understandably concerned right now about foot-and-mouth disease and *Weakest Link* host Anne Robinson. And don't get us started on the Spice Girls.

To combat any stateside skepticism, David's record label, Atlantic, has set up a special showcase at the Hudson to woo U.S. radio programmers and TV bookers. David usually plays arenas in Europe but, dressed in a hip-hoppy Adidas track suit and accompanied only by an acoustic guitarist, he performs in front of this small gaggle of a few dozen people with an endearing, show-bizzy eagerness. He croons tenderly, hits high notes authoritatively, even throws in a few smooth rap interludes. It's a winning mix of the urban and urbane: R. Kelly meets Hugh Grant.

U.K. Garage—sometimes called 2-Step—was born in British clubs in the early '90s when DJs heard the groove-driven sounds of house and drum 'n' bass music echoing out of places like Chicago and New York City. The British softened the beats a bit, added soulful singing and a pinch of Jamaican-style toasting, and came up with U.K. Garage. The name's roots go back to the Paradise Garage, a popular downtown Manhattan nightclub that helped nurture the house-music scene in the '80s. Clubland music sometimes has an Artoo Detoo rhythmic-thud-thud sameness; U.K. Garage, sweetened with vocals, has a suppleness that makes it personable.

Last summer interest in U.K. Garage reached Harry Potterish levels in Britain (David's debut CD alone went six times platinum); this year the biggest stars of the genre are releasing albums in America. David's U.S. debut, *Born to Do It*, is due in July, and the first video from the album is already getting play on MTV, VH1, and BET. Fellow Briton MJ Cole's U.S. debut, *Sincere Train* (Talkin Loud/Island) was just released. A wave of U.K. Garage acts, including Artful Dodger and Zed Bias, are waiting in the wings.

David developed a love of music early on, inspired by Michael Jackson and Terence Trent D'Arby; he became a DJ at age fourteen, won a national songwriting contest at age fifteen, and embarked on a singing career soon after. Last summer's CD—a fluid, flirty collection of R. and B.-kissed ballads—went on to No. 1 on the U.K. charts. David says his DJ training is key to his performing skills. "I understand how a crowd works," says David. "I understand a set needs highs and lows. When I'm in a studio, I understand what grooves people feel."

MJ Cole, twenty-seven, found his groove a little later in life. Born Matthew Coleman, he grew up in London and studied piano, oboe, and music theory at the Royal College of Music. But the nightlife beckoned. "With the clubs, suddenly there was all this rhythm, all this energy and a bit of naughtiness about it as well," says Cole, now concentrating on keyboards while employing others to sing on his songs. "I'd go to raves and clubs, but at the same time, I'd always get in my two hours of piano practice." *Sincere* echoes his background: there is brainy calculation in the song structures; there's also clubland abandon in the rhythms and vocals.

U.K. Garage has already won fans in the U.S. musical underground. In Minneapolis, Minnesota, half a dozen Garage lovers banded together last summer to form Steppers Alliance, a DJ collective that has a website, garageand2step.com, and hosts parties at First Avenue, an area club. In New York City, the nightclub Centro-Fly recently held a 2-Step night featuring Artful Dodger. There were hundreds of twenty-somethings waiting outside the club clamoring to get in. "It's about shut up and dance," says Tom Sisk, co-owner of Centro-Fly. U.K. Garage doesn't quite make up for the Brits' sending us Ginger Spice, but it's two steps in the right direction.

From *Time*, April 30, 2001. © 2001 Time Inc. Reprinted with permission.

SUGGESTIONS FOR FURTHER STUDY

1. How do you rate the U.K. Garage?
2. Do you appreciate why people spend great amounts of time and money on rock music?
3. If you had to choose between rock and TV as your medium of enjoyment, which would you choose? Why?

Alan Jackson,
a Man among Legends

*Singer Says "No way," but Others Say He's One of
Country's All-time Best*

BRIAN MANSFIELD

Backstage after Wednesday's Country Music Association awards, a
journalist asked Alan Jackson about his history-making night. Jackson
had just won five awards, including Entertainer of the Year—a total
matched only by Johnny Cash and Vince Gill.

Noting that most of country's best-known entertainers had never
dominated the awards show to such a degree, the reporter wondered
whether Jackson had realized the full impact of his Hall of Fame–cali-
ber accomplishment.

The lanky forty-four-year-old singer responded with typical humil-
ity. "When I look at George Jones, George Strait, Haggard, there's no
way I could qualify to be in the category of some of those guys," Jackson
said. "And you've just about got to be dead to be in the Hall of Fame, so
I don't know about something like that."

Jackson may have been reluctant to place himself among country's
legends, but other people have started to do that for him.

"Twenty years from now, people will hold him in as high respect as Merle Haggard," says Tim DuBois, who signed Jackson to

Arista Records in the late '80s. "That's the pinnacle of respect as a singer/songwriter."

Country journalist Hazel Smith says, "He's the only songwriter from 1952 until now that I would compare to Hank Williams, because of the types of words he uses to make his point. It's simple, yet it's very profound."

Citing Jackson's CMA achievement, RCS Label Group chairman Joe Galante says: "There are three people who have done this over the course of thirty-six years. Obviously he's at the top of the history books."

Jackson, a native of Newnan, Georgia, first entered the charts in the fall of 1989, a few months after Clint Black and Garth Brooks made their debuts and just as the country format began to experience phenomenal growth. Since then he has had more than fifty records appear on the singles chart. Twenty—including "Chattahoochee," "Don't Rock the Jukebox," and his post–September 11 song, "Where Were You (When the World Stopped Turning?)"—have reached number one.

Other singers have sold more records during that time, and a few may have had more hits. But Jackson, by his quiet dignity and commitment to traditional styles and themes, is the artist of that generation who best represents country music's ideals.

"What he continues to do is take his own story and communicate it to people," says Jackson's producer, Keith Stegall. "If anything that's what the audience connects to. They get to hear and feel a little bit more about Alan Jackson each time he writes a song."

To some extent, Jackson's career will now be defined by "Where Were You (When the World Stopped Turning?)" in the same way that Haggard's was defined by "Okie from Muskogee," another crucial juxtaposition of country and culture.

"In twenty-five years, if you want to understand how the core country audience was feeling in the new millennium, I think you'll be able to listen to Alan's music and get a good picture," says Jay Orr, senior museum editor at the Country Music Foundation. "His songs will paint a better picture of what the nation was thinking than anybody else's."

Jackson's career once appeared to have peaked around 1995, the year he previously won the CMA Entertainer of the Year award and topped the charts with "Gone Country" and "Tall, Tall Trees." But this year's hits—"Where Were You," "Work in Progress," and "Drive (For Daddy Gone)," the latter a song about passing down the pleasures of afternoon drives—have placed his career on an entirely different plane.

"His year, in terms of the songs that he wrote, left an indelible mark," Galante says. "His name will be on the lips of artists and song-writers for years to come."

Jackson possesses qualities that years from now will attract people returning to country's past in search for "roots" and "authenticity." There is a pride and populism to songs such as "Little Man" and "Where I Come From." He sings about country music itself in "Gone Country" and "Don't Rock the Jukebox." He honors the music's history, turning Roger Miller and Tom T. Hill songs into new hits and re-cording an album of country covers, *Under the Influence*.

"Alan has stuck to his guns," DuBois says. "He has not chased trends. He is admirably very bull-headed about his music and creative control on things."

Jackson's manager, Nancy Russell, says: "Alan is going to do his thing, and there is nothing anybody can do to make him change it. He will always listen to what everybody has to say, but he has a keen instinct."

Even country's legends are willing to welcome Jackson as one of their own. Asked whether he believes Jackson deserves mention in the same breath as country's greats, George Jones is emphatic.

"Definitely—I know so. He is not going to fade out. He might drop down a notch or two; everybody does after a while. But he's going to hang in there, and he's going to sell records for years to come."

SUGGESTIONS FOR FURTHER STUDY

1. If you are familiar with Jackson's songs, how do you react to this article's evaluation?
2. If you do not know Jackson, listen to some of the songs discussed here and evaluate his work.
3. What is your feeling about those cultural historians who search for historical evaluations as revealed in country music? Is it "truer" than more "popular" music?

Some forms of music so satisfy and empower a section of society that despite disapproval by the dominant elements it holds on and develops. Such has been the career of hip-hop and rap music. The following essay outlines that career and the purposes the music serves.

The Importance of Hip-Hop and Rap

A Question of Resistive Vernaculars

ROGER CONWAY

Popular media and music industry outlets, especially Web sites, have been rumoring the death knell of hip-hop and rap. Most claim the voice of rap has regressed or yielded to mainstream R&B fusion, soul, or house music. These claims come mostly from rap purists, the same people who lamented the sound texts of rapid yielding to the visual texts (mostly rap videos) of hip-hop. The comparatively rapid rise of hip hop culture from its origins, as a resistive vernacular voice from the rubble of inner city neglect and decay, has attracted negative curiosity from the mainstream of fatuous oracles of propriety and decorum (one thinks here of William Bennett's *Book of Virtues*). And yet, not despite that but rather *because* of that, hip-hop and rap as two texts of this broad and growing phenomenon of popular culture demonstrate the importance of media studies in the academy and in the global community.

The hip-hop culture, of which rap music forms one text, offers an extraordinarily rich matrix of texts for critical analysis and theoretical proofs. Rap music alone offers distinctions in sound, flow, and what some call "rupture" or "beats." This musical phenomenon survives as an integral remnant of the African American oral tradition. In addition to the music, the visual texts of hip-hop culture offer a rewarding mine for discovery and analysis. Very early in the development of hip-hop, graffiti, or "taggin," mushroomed in the abandoned centers of New York and Philadelphia. Also, to the accompaniment of "scratchin" by DJs on dual turntables, young people break-danced in their neighborhoods as well as on Broadway for any spare change that was thrown their way. As hip-hop spread throughout the U.S., the signature couture—the baggy pants, the oversized shirts, the do-rags, and the "floss" (outsized gold and silver jewelry)—became the credential for acceptance into the culture.

But these texts had more importance than merely to make a statement of otherness for the mainstream to target with disdain and exploitation. One needs to review news footage of the ravaged communities of the South Bronx, Compton in L.A., North Philadelphia, and West Baltimore to appreciate how entire communities were decimated, dislocated, and bereft of purpose or hope in the 1970s. And they shared singular noteworthy characteristics—out of control drug trade, lawlessness, and corrupt judicial systems. But African Americans have long experienced threats to their survival, especially after their "emancipation." In addition, they had carried a survival technique with them from Africa, a part of their ethos so deeply embedded in their societies that it came as a natural response to imminent danger, much the same way we all feel our skin crawl or the hair on our necks bristle as we face threats.

This survival technique, a text realized in a variety of mediated formats, provides excellent material for examinations of cultural history brought into the nexus of postmodern experience. Indeed, much of the foremost criticism, including Tricia Rose, Russell Potter, Henry Louis Gates Jr., Nelson George, and Michael Eric Dyson, focuses on the ways rap and hip-hop culture simultaneously express oral traditions engendered deeply in the African and African American traditions yet also articulated in the extraordinary imagery, sound, and discourse of postmodern life. My experience with the students' discussions and research on rap and hip-hop has shown me that they are very comfortable articulating serious investigations into this seemingly mindless and chaotic world view.

My research began with an investigation into the meaning of "signifyin(g)" in the oral tradition of African American culture. Using Henry Louis Gates Jr.'s *The Signifying Monkey* as my resource, I discovered that *signifyin(g)* is an oral challenge meant to get the best of an opponent, especially to bring the opponent down in the eyes (and mind) of community audience. The book *Snaps* explores this with categorical examples. The whole purpose of these "battles" or "snaps" is to avoid physical violence. The process involves tricking the opponent by making him or her get embarrassed or confused by the language. The legends of west Africa feature a character named Esu, a diminutive, dual gendered spirit whose purpose in life is to trick humanity into believing he/she voices the truth of their destiny. Life, then, becomes a serious game the standards of which are set by a trickster and the success of which is based on one's ability to articulate and comprehend the spoken word. The Middle Passage of the slave trade brought this entity to the Western Hemisphere in the characters of the Signifying Monkey and Anansi, a spider, and can be seen as well in Joel Chandler Harris's Br'er Rabbit. Because the language and imagery of this "game" are extremely local, the consequences are a revitalization and reminder of the integrity of the community, as in the chanting of the area code in the climax of the battle scene in *8 Mile*.

This cultural/textual history functions neatly as a key to our investigation of rap and hip-hop. Most American rappers, especially African American and Nuyorican, Hispanic rappers from New York, adopt and "play" various personas. Jay-Z is also Jigga Man and Sean Carter. Puff Daddy is also P-Diddy and Sean Combs. Among the Hispanic rappers, Mellow Man Ace is Ulpiano Sergio Reyes, Kid Frost is Artukro Moliina Jr., Fat Joe is Don Cartegena, and Noreaga is Vincent Santiago. And you might have heard of a white rapper named Eminem, who is also Slim Shady and Marshall Mathers. An essential element of their texts and their performances if that they deliberately challenge their audiences to know whether they are speaking "the truth" or just "playin' witcha." The role they assume depends a great deal on the relationship between the specific lyric and the target audience. For example, Eminem's "White America" is not targeting the hordes of suburban teenagers who identify with him; he is targeting their parents, signifyin(g) on them and, perhaps, even on William Bennett.

Those who attack rap and hip-hop as a harbinger of the death at least of Eurocentric cultural values and perhaps of a total global moral implosion have apparently missed this element in the phenomenon. In fact, serious verbal game playing historically has had as its goal a re-unification of community values. And this is not unique to African or African American culture. An entire school of Chaucer scholarship views *The Canterbury Tales* as a serious verbal game played during the pilgrimage, which simultaneously castigates the shoddiness of most of the titled religious and cultural participants as it exalts the values of the few humble pilgrims. Indeed, one can easily conclude that part of Chaucer's purpose was to alert his audience by holding a mirror up to their values vis-à-vis their behavior. The uniqueness in each culture's tradition, of course, is based on its experience, especially regarding its determination to sustain itself.

Thus we come to the focus of this approach to rap and hip-hop. "Resistive vernaculars" is a rearticulated phrase for a concept that I discovered in Russell Potter's *Spectacular Vernaculars*. Potter's point (and mine) is that rap and hip-hop are postmodern texts of resistance to the dehumanizing experience of contemporary life. As such they express both sympathy and contempt for those who suffer under the moral and physical banalities as well as for those who promulgate them. The contempt manifests itself in various ways not the least of which is a phonetic assault on traditional, accepted standards of spelling. We have become familiar with "Phat Farm," "gangsta," "McLyte," "Bubba Sparxx," and "The Pharcyde" as examples of this challenge to the mainstream texts. I hasten to add here that those among the academics who are taking a serious look at this phenomenon are critically aware of the ways mainstream producers have *commodified* hip-hop and rap so that it cam be exploited for the bottom line. I discovered that my students divided neatly into two camps: the purists, those who seek the various permutations of resistance or, as they would say, the rap that speaks to "the street," and the mainstream apologists, those who seek the appropriate ranking system for who is or is not worthy of platinum awards from mega-sales.

The resistive texts began in the early 1970s, in verbal and aural formats initiated by people like Gil Scot-Heron, and in visual formats by the graffiti writers and break-dancers in Philadelphia and New York City. In each case the motivation was simultaneously twofold: first, to "shout out" or "call out" within the community to remind the people of their commonality; and, second, to confront or "to be in the face" of "the man" or the mainstream institutions which challenged the community's existence. Gil Scot-Heron's legendary "The Revolution Will Not Be Televised" trumpeted this resistance. Ironically, this song or recitation had some brief mainstream popularity, primarily because its contemporary youth audience liked its rebellious social commentary. At the same time, most of the African American listeners realized that it was "double voiced" (to use Gates's term), simultaneously calling out, asking for these micro cultures to stand up or "represent," and shouting out, announcing to "the man" that the Civil Rights movement of the 1960s has morphed into something very different. Todd Boyd's *The New H.N.I.C.* deals with this in some detail. This initial resistive proclamation was followed closely by an audio text established literally on the streets and parks of the Bronx in New York.

On his return from a trip to Africa, Africa Bambatta, a dominant DJ/turntablist, established what he called the Zulu Nation, a prototype of localized hip-hop culture in the housing projects of Bronx River East. These and other Bronx neighborhoods, Kool Herc in west Bronx, DJ Breakout in the north, and Grandmaster Flash in the central, demonstrated the two unique elements that would characterize this culture: its dependence on rapidly developing new technology and its signature of local talent, issues, and imagery. Even today's superstar U.S. rappers, who regularly produce more for the mainstream than for the street, will isolate particular songs as shout-outs and call-outs to their "hoods." Whether it's Jay-Z, P. Diddy, Nas, Lil Kim, Snoop Dogg, Eminem, or 50 Cent—each will reserve some space on the CD for his or her "peeps."

This necessity can create a difficulty for people in the industry. The purists, or "streetists," will hold artists accountable if they drift too far from their origins and become swept into the flood of money that comes from success in the mainstream, making the sound comfortable for the people who don't know and probably don't care about the origins. This has also given rise to the battles over who is and who is not a "wanksta," 50 Cent's pejorative term for a pretender, someone who implicitly claims to be "down with" the street, such as Puff Daddy and Ja Rule who both came from the suburbs, in both style and lyrics. This clash goes back at least as far as Tupac Shakur, who came from a middle class background, and his challenge about the reality, as in "keeping it real," of the thug life, and it includes distinctions among subgroups, for example, lyrics specifying the Hispanic experience among "Nuyorican" rappers like Fat Joe contrasted to lyrics and sounds of West Coast Chicano or Latino groups like Kid Frost, sampling Santana.

The split between the street and the mainstream (sounds and lyrics meant to target the largest consuming public) began in 1979 on a producer's whim to have a group of soul and funk artists called the Sugar Hill Gang create the fourteen-minute single "Rapper's Delight." Judged by today's standards of rapping this sounds like self-parody, but it represented the first time that spoken verse and a dance rhythm or "flow" were joined in the same song. It spurred imitations mainly because it was something that centered on romance and the idealized experiences of youth as well as on dancing. In fact, the flow of the dance rhythm marks perhaps the distinguishing feature between street and mainstream rap. Street rap will usually employ rap's three distinguishing characteristics, flow, layering, and rupture, as explained by Tricia Roise. Layering derives from the utilization of digital technology. Apart from the popularity of "scratchin," the use of dual turntables to create rhythmic sounds from vinyl records using an equalizer, digital technology enabled the minute articulation of audio clips from previous popular songs and show tunes. Rupture is the unique anti-rhythmic practice of establishing a pattern, then breaking it into a new pattern; some of this is done vocally as well as technologically. So in a practical sense, street rap, as an anti-text or resistive vernacular, represents hip-hop culture's anti-establishment role in postmodernism, using the technology against itself, so to speak.

This overview of hip-hop's rich potential for textual analysis demonstrates its potential as an attracting field for media studies within the academy. Students immediately understand the significance of popular culture texts vis-à-vis hip-hop connections with history, visual and aural arts, sociology, psychology, and mass media, to name a few. The students most attracted to this subject were, in fact, new to media studies, and some have decided to change majors as a result. For many of the same reasons, hip-hop has importance to the global community. In fact, a brief look at the different ways various nationalities have adapted it within their cultures explains a great deal about this phenomenon as a resistive vernacular in a postmodern world.

British and Irish rap, generally known as "garage sounds," played first on "pirate" radio, have some close affinities with American rap, but the differences demonstrate the significance of looking at hip-hop's importance in the global community. One of my students did an analysis of British rap's need to discover its own forms for flow, layering, and rupture, having struggled for too long trying to fit the patterns and sounds of British English into the patterns and sounds of American English. Also, as one British rapper has stated, "We often rap about the same things, but the thug stuff isn't so important and we are not so harsh on the women." A characteristic of U.S. rap shared by the British rappers is their expression of micro-cultural distinctions, for example, the difference in emphasis among Anglo-Asian, Anglo-African, and Anglo-Caribbean rappers. Speaking of British rap and matters cross-cultural, the Royal Shakespeare London Company has staged "Da Boyz," a hip-hop adaptation of the Rodgers and Hart musical *The Boys From Syracuse*, which was an adaptation of Shakespeare's *Comedy of Errors*. By studying hip-hop's manifestations globally, students begin to discover all sorts of analogues and distinctions.

Meanwhile, whether MC Solaar, IAM, or Electro Cypher, French rappers focus much more specifically on social protest, or an us-versus-them text. In the case of IAM, the texts become futuristic, the language reminiscent of *A Clockwork Orange*. Electro Cypher, as the name suggests, has a distinctly electro-tech sound which seems more important than the lyrics. Generally, French rap captures more of the uncertainty and fever resulting from the clash between modern and postmodern sensibilities. Even assuming inaccuracies in translation, the following (from IAM) will give you some idea:

> Nourished with the large cases with the clap is necessary that
> Do not strike melodies pouraves, or it is the massacre
> Furtive shades slice the night like shurik' N
> My bokken shines the style of the gull falls down on its prey

Some would say that the language of U.S. rappers (references to cheese, Benjamins, strapped, and Henry) is similarly nonsensical, witness the proliferation of rap dictionaries on the Internet. Nevertheless, the syntax mostly remains familiar.

Two groups currently have dominated the Italian rap phenomenon. Alien Army and Bisca 99 Posse represent that angry social protest feeling shared among the Europeans. It's important to note here that U.S. rappers, especially those true to the street, likewise voice angry protest, but theirs is that special double-voiced protest, simultaneously to and for the community, or as Gates calls it "tropes-a-dope," rearticulating Muhammad Ali's famous "rope-a-dope" strategy in boxing. The Italians bring a singularly strident tone to their raps in both lyric and music. This sample from Bisca 99 Posse illustrates the point:

> The devil is the fascists, the police are demons.
> Saint Anthony come and take them away.
> Light it up!
> Mourning, blood, and bitter tears.
> The prefecture and the government have to be set on fire.

> The police barracks and headquarters have to be set on fire.
> The guards, judges, and the taxman have to be set on fire.
> A flame has to be lit to make the boss man shake.

Even Estonia has joined the chorus. A little known fact about the Estonian resistance movement immediately preceding its displacement of the Soviet rule is that it was called the "singing revolution," because the protestors would take to the streets with nationalistic and modern songs of resistance. Their contemporary versions of the popular music emanating from the U.S. and the U.K. tend to gravitate toward what we call alternative or hard rock and roll. Its lyrics tend to focus on the personal angst and anger of living in an uncertain world. And just so with their rap music. An excerpt of a lyric from Big Art Posse will illustrate the point:

> Stress what a mess
> On tha corners I bless
> I try to get rest and peace
> And I am trying to survive
> Mentally
> but fisicly its crime
> So stress what a mess again I bless
> So what's da use
> day by day gin and juice
> I am trying to chill
> But slowly it kills
> I forgot what I forgot
> But one thing is shure
> Stress what a mess

This strand of unified diversity within the varied texts of global hip-hop and rap communities returns us to the voiced pride of the separate communities or "hoods" in the U.S. Each community's visual and verbal text expresses through its unique "call out" and "shout out" the local pride and distinctiveness of the particular place. Rap music videos and CD's consistently focus on the individual rappers' association with and allegiance to his or her specific locale. These texts are consistent in their adherence to the global common denominator: spectacular resistive vernaculars. Whether in College Park, Atlanta; South East or Queensbridge, Bronx; 8 Mile, Detroit; Marseille, France; West End London; or Tallinn, Finland—rap sustains its multifaceted and multilayered development by serving as a communal voice, expressing universal dissatisfaction, communal identity, and hope in the face of a dominating, Matrix-like adversity. This attitude was expressed in an email I got from a veteran rapper, Parrish Smith (formerly of EPMD, recently as PMD on a new CD "The Awakening") with whom I have recently struck a friendship. He said: "Life always takes the turn its suppose 2. ITS UP 2 us 2 stay out of our own way or ENJOY THE RIDE, im still learning with an open mind (sic)."

"The Revolution Will Not Be Televised" expresses a similar sentiment:

> The revolution will not be right back after a message
> About a white tornado, white lightning, or white people
>
> The revolution will be no re-run brothers;
> The revolution will be live.

As long as this survives, rap and hip-hop will live in their various forms. And we need to embrace the value of these popular texts as manifestations of resistive expressions within mainstream cultural values, such as consumerism, placebo politics, and stultifying personal and group relationships, because that is the role they play in postmodern living.

Original essay. Used with permission of the author.

SUGGESTIONS FOR FURTHER STUDY

1. What part does hip-hop and rap play in your repertoire of popular music?
2. Why does this kind of music tend to tie certain segments of the international community together?
3. If you can, get some non-American rap music and investigate how it parallels American music of similar kind.
4. The author of this essay tries to persuade you about the importance of this kind of music. How well does he succeed?

TELEVISION, RADIO, AND NEWSPAPERS

Americans don't like to waste time or opportunity. Thus we use our ears as well as our eyes constantly for information and entertainment. Historically radios have been the most important electric medium through which we use the airwaves, though now they are supplemented by the cell phone.

Historically it could almost be said that an American was a person with access to a radio. The description is still apt. We own more than five hundred million radios. Some seventy million are purchased annually. Radios are present in 99 percent of American homes, supplemented by those in 95 percent of cars and 84 percent of walk-along players that broadcast on both AM and FM. Though the importance of radios has been challenged by TV it still is important, though its importance began to decline by the 1940s. Still, by the 1990s there were over ten thousand radio stations in the United States. Before the overwhelming advent of TV, radio supplied the home edition of entertainment—not movies—with such perennials as *The Shadow, The Lone Ranger, Dragnet,* and live shows starring Jack Benny and Bob Hope. But radio has been forced to move to other forms and functions. Increasingly they are being used by ethnic minorities and communities such as Latinos and Native Americans, and gays and lesbians, or personal broadcast media to serve particular purposes. Once popular in sports broadcasting, radio's role has been taken over in many fields by TV.

But radio is still powerful among people in special interests—for example, evangelists and especially political talk radio. In both, talkers can inform and appeal to interests that can be ear-oriented.

In the following essay, several important fields of radio are discussed in detail.

357

Number of Religious Broadcasters Continues to Grow

GUSTAV NIEBUHR

To judge by the numbers, these are expansive days for Christian radio. Two decades after evangelical Protestant voters emerged as a force in national politics, conservative Christian broadcasters are continuing to carve out a greater share of the radio market.

Last year, the number of radio stations broadcasting fifteen or more hours of weekly religious programming rose 10 percent to 1,463, said the National Religious Broadcasters, a trade association in Manassas, Virginia. That total was nearly double the number fifteen years ago.

Roughly half those stations are commercial and they find that the economics of religious broadcasting are markedly different from those of their secular counterparts, the purveyors of raucous call-in shows, golden oldies, pop music, and round-the-clock news.

For one thing, religious broadcasters do not accept advertising that offends their moral precepts or those of their audience. For another, they do not attract many large national advertisers, who prefer the demographics of other radio formats. So the religious stations are trying to make a virtue of necessity, by selling their niche audience very heavily to a select group of advertisers.

In interviews this week at the National Religious Broadcasters' convention in Indianapolis, people who work either at or closely with Christian radio stations agreed that to compete in the secular marketplace, the broadcasters needed to promote their special audience.

"Christian radio has the greatest concentration of women of all radio formats," said Gary Crossland, president of Soma Research Inc., a Dallas-based company that does demographic research for religious broadcasters.

Soma, which draws its data from the Simmons Market Research Bureau, reported last year that 60 percent of religious radio listeners were female.

Dick Sickels, the avuncular, bearded general sales manager at WBRI-AM and WXIR-FM, Indianapolis, estimates that 59 percent of his stations' audience is female. The two stations—the former with a religious talk format, the latter oriented to contemporary Christian music—broadcast to eighteen central Indiana counties.

In a remark echoed by other broadcasters, Mr. Sickels said the typical listener is loyal to her Christian station. "When she hears it on the radio, she takes it to the bank: 'That car dealer must be a Christian, because he advertises on my radio station,'" he said.

Mr. Crossland also said that since his company began its work ten years ago, he has seen evidence that the average income level among listeners, and evangelists in general, has gone up. Last year, Soma reported that 55 percent of those listeners had annual household incomes of $30,000 or more, 59 percent were married, and 63 percent owned a home.

But Soma's data show that many other formats have audiences with higher incomes. The Salem Communications Corporation said that its thirty-five stations nationwide, including WMCA and WWDJ in the New York area, reach a weekly audience of 5.5 million people. Stations broadcast teaching and preaching programs to encourage "traditional family values," Stuart W. Epperson, the company's chairman, said.

Given that goal, certain potential advertisers have been ruled out: "Any type of tobacco product," Mr. Epperson said. "Certainly, R-rated movies, certain types of books that are considered risqué, alcoholic beverages, lottery ads, gambling advertisements." A medical service that provided abortions would also be out of bounds.

"A large chunk of potential advertising dollars is eliminated right up front," Mr. Epperson added. "So we have to make up for it in very aggressive spot sales to local advertisers and national advertisers."

He offered a brief list of likely advertisers: clothing stores, department stores, car dealerships, and food companies.

"The issue is not only what works, but is it offensive to our basic audience?" he said. "We want to build as large an audience as possible."

Advertising rates generally reflect both the size of a radio audience and its demographics. Salem sells time on its KKLA-FM, Los Angeles, station for $130 to $150 for a sixty-second spot, compared with $1,200 to $2,000 for a minute's advertising on Howard Stern's top-rated morning show in New York, broadcasters estimated.

Mr. Sickels in Indianapolis said he tried to take a "positive approach," aiming for companies whose products or services would fit the needs of a socially conservative audience, "instead of blacklisting businesses." "We go to them," he said. "They don't come to us. Because they don't know what we have to offer."

The two stations have about 120 advertisers, including car dealerships, real estate brokers, household-service companies, banks, and churches.

Indeed, advertisers who approach Christian radio stations tend to be self-selecting, said Joe D. Davis, Salem Communications' vice president and also general manager of WMCA in New York. "They're as sensitive about us as we are about them."

The station he oversees broadcasts to a heavily urban audience divided fairly equally among blacks, whites, and Hispanics, Mr. Davis said. Advertisers include businesses that sell health and nutritional products, legal services, insurance agencies, mental health care providers, Christian bookstores, and charities like the Salvation Army.

Mr. Davis spends a certain amount of time visiting the stations' natural constituency—New York's churches. So far, he said, he has visited 154 congregations, turning up on Sundays to meet and talk with members.

"We do it for two reasons," Mr. Davis said. "One, we're seeking listeners. But two, we're genuinely interested. This is more than a format to us; we care about the people."

SUGGESTIONS FOR FURTHER STUDY

1. Listen to a Christian station and a regular commercial station and compare the formats and contents.
2. How do you account for the fact that more females than males listen to Christian radio?
3. Listen to a Catholic radio broadcast and compare its format and contents with that of an evangelical counterpart.
4. How do you account for the popularity of radio now with other more sophisticated electronic means of communication so prevalent?

Newspapers generally have been considered culturally and political "liberal." Many reporters are likewise "liberal," and the newspapers reflect their opinions. Students' opinions are considered "liberal," in being both antiestablishment and in favor of those who, like themselves, are not part of the establishment. The subject of the following article by a student is very much a part of the intense political, religious, and cultural conflict over the rights of gays in our society.

Protect Religious Freedom

KEITH J. POWELL

The philosopher Voltaire once said, "I may not agree with what you have to say, but I will defend to the death your right to say it." Voltaire obviously never met the Reverend Fred Phelps or heard of his Westboro Baptist Church in Topeka, Kansas. However, if he had I think even Voltaire would have thought twice before rushing to defend the Reverend's right to free speech.

The Reverend Phelps first attracted national attention when he appeared at the funeral of Matthew Shepherd brandishing signs reading "God Hates Fags." As if that wasn't enough of an insult to the young man who was brutally tortured and beaten to death for no reason other than that he was gay, this supposed man of God has now decided to take the matter one step further.

Phelps recently announced plans to build a monument in Casper, Wyoming, Shepherd's hometown. The monument will carry a picture of Matthew and an inscription that reads "Matthew Shepherd, Entered Hell October 12, 1998, in Defiance of God's Warning: Thou shalt not lie with mankind as with womankind; it is abomination. Leviticus 18:22."

At this point you might be saying to yourself, "There is no way the City Council will allow him to get away with something like that." Well, you'd be wrong. The City Council is in fact legally obligated to allow him to get away with it, and they have no one to blame but themselves. According to the Tenth Circuit Court of Appeals, any city that houses a "Ten Commandments monument on public property must allow monuments espousing the views of other religions or political groups on that same property." It was the City Council who allowed the Fraternal Order of Eagles in 1964 to erect a Ten Commandments monument, and it is the City Council who has subsequently refused attempts to have the monument removed. In their refusal to remove a blatantly religious monument from public property, which is in and of itself already a direct violation of the separation of church and state, the Council has left itself open to exactly the kind of obscenity Phelps hopes to install in the City Park.

As of now, the City Council is frantically trying to find a way to thwart the Reverend's monument without actually bothering to remove the Ten Commandments monument itself, and try as I might, I just can't bring myself to blame them. After all, they are just the City Council of Casper, Wyoming, a town with a population of 47,100 with which to contend. Maybe it's just me, but I just don't see what is so challenging about the notion of separation of church and state. It seems like a fairly straightforward concept, as well as a fairly essential one to any true democracy. The government should not be able to influence or endorse one set of religious beliefs one way or another. Most people would agree with that, except when it comes to the matter of displaying the Ten Commandments on public property, for whatever reason people want to view this as the exception.

Here are the hard facts: the fathers of this country were not Christian, nor did they subscribe to a Judeo-Christian doctrine. Rather they were Deists, which according to Webster's Dictionary means they "denied the interference of the Creator with the laws of the universe." If the framers of the Constitution were alive to see this debacle today, they would find the entire matter ridiculous, as I'm sure they viewed the matter conclusively settled some two hundred years ago.

Just as it is unacceptable to argue the Ten Commandments are the foundation for law in this country, it is likewise unacceptable to hold them as an example of the earliest form of law. If you want to erect a monument to commemorate the earliest known set of laws, the Code of

Hammurabi predates the Ten Commandments. Why not erect a monument for Hammurabi?

What it boils down to is simple: people who want to blur the line between separation of church and state run the risk of lending support to bigotry such as that professed by the Reverend Phelps. The Ten Commandments come from a series of teachings that have been used time and time again as the basis for discrimination against Jews, foreigners, women, gays, and provided the moral justification for slavery and segregation.

In the end the undeniable truth is that Phelps's comments regarding Matthew Shepherd come from the same doctrine as the Ten Commandments themselves, and as such neither has any business on public land. This isn't a matter of free speech: this is a matter of a basic freedom—the freedom from religious oppression.

From *Bowling Green State University News*, October 8, 2003. Reprinted with permission.

SUGGESTIONS FOR FURTHER STUDY

1. Verify the author's facts so that you can test his arguments.
2. If his facts are correct are his generalizations too sweeping?
3. How do you react to his arguments? If you disagreed, has he convinced you?
4. What is the value of having students' comments published in the school paper?

No medium of mass communication to date has saturated and impacted society like television. It incorporates in a dramatic way all the effective aspects of social and outside communication. It presents heroes and heroines and icons through gossip, voyeurism, and intimacy. In fact, TV is life on the screen before us in beautiful color and high definition. It brings the world inside our private living quarters so that we can enjoy it in whatever mood we like. It intensifies every individual's life and shapes and changes it. If one person owned all TV channels, as some entrepreneurs seem to be trying to do, that person could rule the world. TV crackles in the air one breathes, what one witnesses, nearly all one's life. The majority of people obviously approve of TV and what is broadcast, though we still have those critics who see mostly evil on the airwaves and a few who for one reason or another will not have a TV set in the house.

TV provides access to virtually everything—shopping, documentaries of all sorts, travel, nature shows, pornography. The following article is about women, on the screen and in the audience.

Strong, Funny . . . and Female

Prime-time TV Has Focused on Women

ELAINE LINER

In the beginning, there was Lucy. Then along came Mary (Tyler Moore). And Roseanne. Now there's Felicity, Buffy, Moesha, the *Gilmore Girls*, Sabrina, Dharma, Grace, and Joan (Cusack, not Rivers). There are no hotter characters on cable than *Sex & the City's* hilarious all-girl foursome on HBO.

TV is full of strong, funny women these days. Strong serious ones, too. Like Max the *Dark Angel*, *X-Files's* Agent Scully, Marg Helgenberger's no-nonsense investigator on *C.S.I.*, Carmela Soprano and Dr. Melfi of *The Sopranos*, the DAs on *Law & Order* and *The Practice*, social crusader *Kate Brasher*, and a judge named Amy.

While it's still rare to find feature film hits centered on any female character who isn't young, sexy, and played by a bankable star—*Erin Brockovich* and *Bridget Jones's Diary* being recent examples—TV, a friendlier medium for female producers, writers, and performers, is finding success with shows starring women characters of varying ages, types, and professions.

This season, half a dozen new comedies, including the modest hits *Three Sisters* on NBC and *What about Joan* on ABC, focus on women and

367

are written by staffs dominated by women. This was the best year for TV comedies by and about women since the 1980s, when prime time was dominated by *The Golden Girls, Murphy Brown,* and *Designing Women.*

"Diversifying portrayals of women—creating roles which better reflect the diversity of the population—is not unrelated to the increasing presence of women in the industry," former Federal Communications Commission chairman William Kennard said recently. "The TV shows where women get a better shake tend to be the ones produced by women."

All the new girl-centric comedies owe a flip of the hat to the old *Mary Tyler Moore Show,* the now-classic comedy that was one of the first half-hour series to present a woman in her thirties who was single by choice and on a big-city career track.

Producer James L. Brooks created the ABC sitcom *What about Joan* for Oscar-nominated comic actress Joan Cusack with the idea of updating the type of lovably wacky, single Midwestern woman he wrote for Mary Tyler Moore on her show in the '70s.

"There's a thread between the two characters," says Brooks. "Mary is brilliant, with very specific talents. It's interesting that Mary was a Midwestern girl, too."

The biggest difference between the two shows, said Brooks, is the presence of more women in the writing room. "With *Joan* we talk so much about women's issues as we're writing. [The topic] is much more alive because there's a lot of women on the writing staff, more so than in the Mary Tyler Moore days. It's a very lively debate," said Brooks.

Cusack accepts comparisons to Moore, but said she relates more directly with the kind of physical humor Lucille Ball employed on *I Love Lucy.* But with a modern spin.

"Lucy put herself in such embarrassing situations that were so painful. I think a more modern take on that is there are a lot of embarrassing, painful situations in life. On our show, it's more about how you figure them out, how you deal with them, how you live your life if you're a person with feelings," Cusack said.

Networks have turned their focus to women for the same reason TV does anything: money. In prime time this season, 6.5 million more women than men tuned in to TV nightly. That's a number advertisers play close attention to.

"Advertisers have long realized that women are the key target audience," said TV historian Tim Brooks, who also is vice-president of research for women-oriented Lifetime Television (and is not related to

James L.). "As a result, they've told the programmers they want large female audiences."

Brooks sees the broadcasters and cable programmers moving away from shows that feature women merely mimicking traditional male roles (*Xena: Warrior Princess,* for example) and toward shows about smart, "relatable" women.

"A show like *Judging Amy* wouldn't have run ten years ago," said Brooks. "Not only is the lead character a judge, but her chief protagonist is her mother. It's very female-centric in many dimensions."

Lifetime, available on most basic cable lineups, has been ahead of this trend for several years. Nicknamed the "channel for women," Lifetime is watched by an average 1.6 million cable homes nightly, more than any other cable network including USA and TBS. Lifetime is the most-watched cable network among women on Saturday and Sunday afternoons, when it features back-to-back reruns of its original, made-for-cable movies. The channel's Sunday night original dramas featuring lead women characters—*Any Day Now, Strong Medicine,* and *The Division*— benefit from the huge tune-in earlier in the day and have been renewed for more new episodes. Name stars like Whoopi Goldberg, Sissy Spacek, Ellen Burstyn, Brooke Shields, and Laura Dern are lining up to bring projects to Lifetime.

This summer the Lifetime franchise adds a third network called Lifetime Real Women. (Lifetime also has the Lifetime Movie Network on cable.) Real Women will feature all reality shows "told from a woman's perspective," according to Lifetime president Carole Black.

Added Tim Brooks, "It's a short step from dramatic shows about women to shows about real women. Women have come to know that Lifetime is a channel that, whatever's on, they'll probably like it."

Two of the most popular young female characters in prime time are Felicity Porter of the WB's drama *Felicity* and Max, the darkly witty, muscular heroine of Fox's *Dark Angel.*

Felicity, now wrapping up its third season on the WB, has let its title character grow up this year, evolving from a confused, flighty teenager who chased her dream date to college, into a confident, self-possessed young adult.

"When we first met her, she was someone who hadn't found her voice and tested her strength," said *Felicity* creator J. J. Abrams. "She was full of dreams and no experience. The last three years have been full of trials for her."

Young viewers, especially women, relate to Felicity Porter (played by Keri Russell) because "she's had failures and successes. She's become stronger and stronger at every turn," Abrams said.

The show's "flowery, soft title" belies the character's toughness, said Abrams. Some viewers have perceived the series as mushy simply because of Russell's angelic looks. "But the character is surprisingly strong and confident," Abrams said. "And she's increasingly risk-taking, learning through her experiences."

While waiting to find out if the WB will renew *Felicity* for its fourth season (long enough to let the character graduate from college), Abrams currently is producing the ninety-minute pilot for another series about a strong, determined young woman. *Alias,* commissioned by ABC, is about a spy (Jennifer Garner) learning the ways of espionage from her male mentors (Victor Garber, Ron Rifkin, Carl Lumbley).

The polar opposite of a character like Felicity might be Max, the futuristic, keister-kicking heroine of *Dark Angel.* Played by Jessica Alba, Max is a direct descendant of similar characters in the movies *Terminator* and *Aliens,* both directed by *Dark Angel* creator James Cameron.

"I think women respond to characters who appear strong and capable," Cameron told TV critics recently. "But you balance that with vulnerability so that they're real."

Men aren't necessarily turned off by such formidable women on film or TV, Cameron said, a notion that studio execs sometimes find hard to grasp. "When I started doing these types of characters with *Terminator* and *Aliens,* there was a sense among the powers-that-be at the studios that this was going to push away the typical eighteen-year-old male audience. Well, that's not true. They want to see girls kick butt, too."

From *Toledo Blade,* May 13, 2001. Reprinted with permission.

SUGGESTIONS FOR FURTHER STUDY

1. What are your reactions to the new image of strong women on TV?
2. How does TV stereotype women and how does it portray them as heroines?
3. Choose one of the shows discussed in the article and evaluate it for its several goals—successful TV, commercial viability, realistic presentation of women.
4. Do the shows inspire the women readers of this article to "kick butt" or do the readers look upon the shows merely as more published and academic theorizing about the everyday world?

WORLD OF MOVIES

T he movie industry since its beginning has created heroes and heroines and myths and rituals. It does so by enabling us to see a projection of ourselves as we think we are or as we wish we were. To satisfy the demands of audiences, producers search all the media for ideas and then develop them for the screen. Each production demands an evaluation in the form of a "review." Each continuation in a series cries out for comparison with the preceding production and with perhaps the one to come in the next chapter. The following review exemplifies this practice.

Mild about "Harry"

DAVID ANSEN

Chamber of Secrets is finally here: Our precocious Hogwarts are bursting with confidence, but the new film has more monsters and mayhem than magic.

Chris Columbus's *Harry Potter and the Sorcerer's Stone* may have made many hundreds of millions of dollars but only kids seemed to be genuinely enthusiastic about it. (*A lot of kids*, to be sure.) Grownups, who were equally bewitched by J. K. Rowling's books, felt let down by the movie: it followed the letter of the tale but missed the spirit, mistaking special effects for magic. Would the filmmakers learn from their mistakes in the second installment? Wanting to give the movie the benefit of the doubt, I avoided reading *Harry Potter and the Chamber of Secrets* before I saw Columbus's follow-up. This time the twists and turns of Harry's adventures at Hogwarts—where he encounters even greater perils—could take me by surprise.

The real surprise, alas, is that *Chamber of Secrets* has been turned into a kiddie monster movie. It *is* aimed at an older audience this time—*tween and teenage* boys. Now the walls of Hogwarts are defaced with dire warnings written in blood. Harry and Ron are terrorized by an army of giant spiders that scuttle about like stragglers from *Starship Troopers*. Our hero, no longer the diffident, uncertain wizard, wields a sword in mini-Schwarzenegger style as he faces down a gargantuan snake that is sure to traumatize the under-six set, and just as likely to produce yawns from elders who have sat through one too many creature-filled Hollywood action extravaganzas. Somehow I don't think this is what Rowling had in mind. The monsters are all straight out of the book, but they are vanquished briskly on the page. Rowling never belabors the violence; Columbus can't think of anything else to do. For him, the action set pieces are the movie's raison d'être, and they contribute mightily to the bloated two-hour, forty-five-minute running time.

Before it degenerates into *Indiana Potter and the Chamber of Doom*, the movie holds promise. Cinematographer Roger Pratt has replaced John Seale, and the images are crisper and less murky. The three young stars—Daniel Radcliffe, Rupert Grint, and Emma Watson—radiate a newfound confidence. Kenneth Branagh adds a nice flourish of comic relief as Gilderoy Lockhart, the celebrity Defense Against the Dark Ages professor, whose towering self-regard is matched only by his magical incompetence. Further chuckles are supplied by the computer-generated Dobby the House Elf (voice of Toby Jones), a mischief-making masochist whose servility disguises his true intentions. Alan Rickman, the highlight of *Sorcerer's Stone*, takes a back seat here; villainy honors go to Jason Isaacs's Lucius Malfoy (blond father of blond Draco). Isaacs, memorable as the bad Brit in *The Patriot*, oozes freeze-dried evil. Sadly, the recent death of Richard Harris adds a special poignance to his final turn as the great wizard Dumbledore. His sweet, whispery line readings sound as if they're etched on delicate, aged parchment.

Columbus has boasted that *Chamber* is faster paced than the original, because it's not bogged down with exposition. He doesn't seem to realize that the exposition—also known as character development—is what gives the tale charm. Someone coming to this movie without having seen the first would have no sense of what makes brainy, supercilious Hermione special. Steve Kloves's script is so busy keeping the action coming that the quirks of Rowling's characters get lost. Yes, *Chamber of Secrets* moves with a brisk stride, but speed isn't necessarily an improvement if it flattens out the emotional landscape. *Chamber of Secrets* seems even more an impersonal studio project than the first—a trend that perhaps Alfonso Cuaron *(A Little Princess, Y Tu Mama Tambien)*, the next installment's gifted director, can buck, if Warner Bros. lets him.

Columbus's movie ends (I'm not giving anything away) with a stand-ing ovation in the Hogwarts' dining hall that's meant to be a rousing emotional moment. But oddly, the object of the celebration hasn't done anything in the course of the movie to warrant the outburst—he's been on the sidelines of the action. The scene, which isn't in the book, is just a generic feel-good climax arbitrarily pasted on, and the film-makers obviously think nobody will notice. But it hints at why the Harry Potter movies aren't half as wonderful as they should be, why they feel created from the outside in. Magic isn't made by compromise.

SUGGESTIONS FOR FURTHER STUDY

1. Do you think the critic has given the movie a chance at success?
2. If you have the opportunity, see the movie and write your own review.
3. As mentioned above, it is hard to make a sequel to a movie that pleases everyone. People expect too much, a rising plane of ac-complishment. Choose your own movie and its sequel and eval-uate the accomplishments of the sequel.

SURVEY OF YEAR'S POPULAR ENTERTAINMENT

Movies follow the trends in society. If nostalgia is the magic word, then movies try to find subjects that treat nostalgia. If daily family life is the approved theme, movies try to find subjects that picture daily life. If adventure—which is usually a dominant theme—then high adventure energizes us in the theater.

During any year the world of popular entertainment undergoes great changes. Old stars fade away and new ones are born, often with great promise that may not be realized later. It is therefore useful to pause at the end of a year and see where the world of popular entertainment has come and gone. The author mistakenly refers to popular entertainment as "culture." But other than that the survey is comprehensive and analytic.

The Big Fat Year in Culture

JAMES PONIEWOZIK

So much for the post-9/11 warm-and-fuzzies. In 2002 the popular world got weird again.

In a year's books, TV, movies, music, and theater, it's possible to see deeply and clearly into the hearts and minds, the secret dreams and fears of a nation. Until you try explaining *The Ketchup Song (Hey Hah)*. Page 251 of the pop-culture-sociopsychologist's handbook tells us that we must have used this novelty tune as an escape from relentless bad news amid war and recession. O.K., so what did that make *Macarena* in 1996? If America's fortunes have changed since 1999, why hasn't Harry Potter's popularity? And can any blather about America's longing for superheroes change the fact that a competent adaptation of *Spider-Man* with Kirsten Dunst in a wet blouse would have been gold in any year you threw a dart at?

It's better to think of America's pop-culture choices not as a monolithic State of the Union address but rather as a mix CD we make every year. The tempo and tone don't always mesh. Some of the songs have a direct message; some have emotional meaning; and some, in gimlet-eyed retrospect, make you wonder why you ever picked them in the first place (this means you, Anna Nicole). But then you play that CD back on the stereo, a few older, fatter years later. Your toe taps. A memory comes back. And you realize that in that nonsensical mess of cotton-candy lyrics and throwaway choruses, you somehow managed to write down your life.

A Date That Lived in Infamy, Again

One of the recurring strains of this year's mix (to finally kill the metaphor) was a gloomy tune from 2001, remixed several ways. This time last year, we were still asking if and how 9/11 would change pop culture. In 2002 we got some answers. Defying warnings of tragedy fatigue, books about 9/11 *(Bush at War, Let's Roll, The Cell)* dominated the best-seller lists. CBS drew some thirty-nine million viewers for *9/11*, a tear-jerking documentary shot inside the World Trade Center on the day of the attacks. All broadcast and many cable networks tossed out their normal programming schedules (and their advertising) on the anniversary, as if super-saturating the airwaves—turning September 11 into a virtual national holiday—could magically confine the terrible events to history, never to be repeated. There was mawkishness, anger, finger pointing, navel gazing, bathos, pathos—every possible response except forgetting.

But of all the cultural predictions after 9/11, the first proved to be the wrongest: that grief and war would moderate our culture and elide our differences. Movies would stop blowing up buildings; reality shows would stop humiliating people; comedians would stop being idiotic. *Atlantic Monthly* editor Michael Kelly envisioned a day when American men and women would again be able to wear fedora hats without smirking. It was a fleeting moment for cultural critics who, like *The Great Gatsby*'s Nick Carraway, longed to see the world "in uniform and at a sort of moral attention forever."

In 2002 we got the moral attention but not the uniform. 2001 couldn't last. It was the temporary, shocked pulling together of a feuding family after a sudden death. 2001 gave us the music community performing *A Tribute to Heroes*. 2002 gave us Eminem electrocuting Dick Cheney (in the video for "Without Me") and country singer Toby Keith, in his controversial song "Courtesy of the Red, White, and Blue," promising the nation's enemies, "We'll put a boot in your ass / It's the American way." The culture wars returned, with books from political playground scrappers like Michael Moore and Sean Hannity. Online, the explosion of self-publishing weblogs revealed a community as divided and outspoken as in the angry-white-male '90s. Architects last summer released their first proposals for rebuilding the World Trade Center site—and the designs were quickly smacked down by the public as too blah and timid: a more adventurous set of plans, replete with soaring towers and sky gardens, was unveiled in December. During its second season, the terrorism drama *24* planted a nuclear bomb in Los Angeles. *The Sopranos* showed how quickly tragedy can become a banal, catchall excuse, as mobster Tony Soprano phonily blamed his behavior on 9/11 during a therapy session. Oh, and that business about movies not blowing up buildings? *The Sum of All Fears* blew up Baltimore, Maryland.

You could say that pop culture was the one American institution that whipped terrorism. Osama bin Laden would have liked little better than to subdue America's entertainment-media machine. That thong-wearing, freedom-flaunting international corrupter of values inflames his followers as painfully as any military base in Saudi Arabia, and there is no irony in Osama's Islam. But pop culture, as it turns out, is the Western equivalent of al-Qaeda: it's hard to kill because it is borderless, amorphous, and stateless, and because it throws back at you the weapons you use against it.

If 9/11 changed culture in 2002, it was to make it more of what it already was. Niche culture continued to erode mainstream culture. Except for a few united events—the 9/11 anniversary, the opening weekend of *Attack of the Clones*—the mass market continued to fragment, with a digital cable channel and a bootleg Internet remix for every consumer, while the online version of real-life-simulation game *The Sims* promised players a chance to be virtually together, alone. The mainstream became more mainstream (that is, more reverent and safe); the niches got nichier (more outré and provocative), *E pluribus, pluribus.*

Who's the Boss

Nobody embodied the mainstream niche better than Bruce Springsteen and Eminem. (They also showed that mainstream and niche are about sensibility, not sales. Eminem's CD actually moved 5.5 million more copies than Springsteen's, according to SoundScan.) The typical victim in the Twin Towers was a man under fifty, from New Jersey or New

York, blue collar or not many generations removed from it—in other words, Springsteen's born subject matter. With 2002's tribute album *The Rising* Springsteen became the mainstream's Maya Angelou of 9/11: the event's unofficial poet laureate, the articulator of the most heartfelt—and publicly acceptable—forms of response, with something for the grandfolks and something for the kids.

Springsteen has made provocative albums before, channeling the grievances and yearnings of Vietnam vets and drifters. But with *The Rising*, released near the September 11 anniversary, he stuck to what we could all agree on: a feeling of sadness and a yearning for hope. Maybe because of the latter, *The Rising*'s music can be oddly cheery—"Empty Sky" and "Lonesome Day" are awfully toe tapping for songs of mourning—as Springsteen keeps circling back to one central image: the clear blue sky over the Eastern seaboard on the morning of September 11, 2001. *The Rising* is poignant, even wrenching ("Without you I'm . . . an ice-cream truck on a deserted street"). But if it has any political doctrine, it is on-one-hand-on-the-other-handism. Several tracks look at the East-West clash, but Springsteen's only prescription is one unobjectionable song title: "Let's Be Friends."

It is not clear that Eminem has ever wanted to be friends with any-body, even his fans. But he sure wants to talk. While *The Rising* was hailed as pop's first major response to 9/11, that title really should go to *The Eminem Show*, released in May. It was as polarizing as *The Rising* was unifying. When Eminem declared, "We need a little controversy . . . it feels so empty without me," it was, like many of his lyrics, arrogant, self-aggrandizing—and true. Beyond the self-serving message—those other messages are boring, so buy mine—the lyric was also a pointed rejection of the get-alongism that prevailed after 9/11. (As if his words weren't enough, he dressed up as Osama bin Laden in the video.) On the album's opening cut, "White America," the rapper whose lyrics pre-occupied moralists in Congress in the summer of 2000—when they had more time on their hands—declared war on the Bush Administration and slammed his critics as racial hypocrites who discovered rap only when white teens started listening to it: "Hip-hop was never a problem in Harlem, only in Boston." It's Eminem's most political song, even if it is rooted in his bottomless sense of personal grievance, which seems to grow in direct proportion to his bank account. On "Square Dance," he anticipated that Iraq would be next on America's target list long before it dominated the headlines: "When I say Hussein, you say Shady," he taunts, alluding to his nom de rap, Slim Shady. "F—in' assassins hijackin', Amtraks crashin' / All this terror America demands action."

Outside the studio, Eminem continued to act like someone who listens to too many Eminem CDs. At the MTV Video Music Awards, he threatened to deck Moby, the pencil-necked vegan techno musician who criticized him for his homophobic lyrics. And yet this fall Eminem managed to win over even pc middle-aged white critics with his semi-autobiographical movie *8 Mile*, playing a rapper from Detroit who defends gay men and pulls himself up by his vocal cords to escape wage-slave trailerdom. The movie's implicit premise is one that our public figures rarely acknowledge: that a poor white kid has more in common with poor black kids than with more-well-off white kids, that is, that class still matters in America. His obnoxiousness aside, Eminem is the first music superstar to make class in America a major subject since, well, Bruce Springsteen. Meet the new Boss.

Prime-Time Crime and the Fear Factor

As the country waited for the other shoe to drop (somewhere, that is, besides Kenya, Moscow, and Bali), it had to do something with all that surplus anxiety. The news and entertainment media were happy to oblige. Stories of random shootings and disappeared and murdered girls were everywhere, from the increasingly graphic, grisly prime-time franchises of *CSI* and *Law & Order* to the orange DANGER!—DANGER!—DANGER! graphics of *Connie Chung Tonight* and the rest of the cable-news cohorts. (Curiously, from the news media's perspective, little girls miraculously stopped being abducted as soon as the Washington sniper drew his first bead.) Some dozen-and-a-half cop shows dominated prime-time series TV, not counting the numerous cable crime series and a steady stream of increasingly popular reality shows like *Forensic Files*. The result was a feedback loop of fear in a society that was not experiencing any crime wave except this virtual one: crime news begat crime curiosity, which begat crime dramas, which begat more crime curiosity, which begat more crime news.

It's not much of a stretch to see all these investigations and authority figures as a kind of shadow of 9/11. (Who is stern-talking Oprah protégé Dr. Phil, after all, but a more down-home John Ashcroft?) Hollywood's crime stories were neither uniformly authoritarian nor bleeding heart.

FX's cop drama *The Shield* introduced Vic Mackey (Michael Chiklis), a crooked, brutal—and extremely effective—L.A. cop, and left it up to us to decide whether his results justified his means. HBO's *The Wire* used the story of a single Baltimore drug investigation as a parable for the crisis of confidence in American institutions. Its conflicted, bureaucracy-ridden cops could just as well have been wearing priests' collars or Enron workers' pinstripes. And in *Minority Report,* we learned that a futuristic, omniscient crime-fighting system involving government-enslaved psychics and near total surveillance is actually kinda neat—at least until it targets Tom Cruise.

The dead-girl motif surfaced most poetically in publishing surprise sensation of the year, Alice Sebold's *The Lovely Bones.* In its bravura opening, the narrator, Susie Salmon, lucidly describes her brutal rape-murder at age fourteen, then goes on (telling the story from heaven) to show us the slow journey of her family and friends to recover from her loss. (This is not only a 2002 phenomenon, of course. *The Sixth Sense* and *Crossing Over with John Edward* both indulged our need to believe that our lost ones are still aware and, more important, still aware of us.) Women's nonmortal distress also got its share of attention— *The Nanny Diaries* and *I Don't Know How She Does It*—that comically examined mothering anxiety (at least among affluent, educated white women), even as Sylvia Ann Hewlett was warning young women, in *Creating a Life: Professional Women and the Quest for Children,* that they had better get married pronto if they ever wanted to have children. With bad men on one side and indifferent men on the other, biological and career clocks hammering in both ears—and with Oprah no longer serving up female-positive fiction to her book club—what was the stressed-out career woman to do?

She Watched *The Bachelor:*
The Past Ain't What It Used to Be

We heard a lot about nostalgia this year: the vogue for vintage blue jeans (or mock-vintage blue jeans at premium prices); the continuing popularity of retro design elements (like '30s club chairs and surfaces "distressed" to look antique); punk and garage-rock revivalists like the White Stripes, the Hives, the Strokes, and the Vines. *The Bachelor,* with its retro-style dating theme, was just one among many nostalgia-oriented television shows. There were reunions of *The Cosby Show*, *The Mary Tyler Moore Show*, *M*A*S*H*, and numerous others (for God's sake, even Alf made a comeback, if only in commercials). But if *The Bachelor* was retro—even Paleolithic—in its harem-style courtship setup, that's not the same as saying it was nostalgic. Rather, it was an example of the ambivalence underlying most of today's so-called nostalgia: the past is a nice place to visit, but we don't really want to live there.

Instead, the typical reality-TV hit of 2002 took a retro format and gave it a good nose piercing. *The Osbournes* was a good '50s nuclear-family sitcom with dog poop, drug rehab, and F words. *American Idol*, with its aspiring teen stars and vicious-insult wars, was Ted Mack's *Original Amateur Hour* as reconceived by Jerry Springer. And *The Bachelor* wed—literally—'50s gender relations with twenty-first century sex. The show's secret (clear to its viewers but not to the paleofeminists and moralists who decried it) is that while *The Bachelor* pretended to celebrate a primitive dating ritual, its audience was meant to laugh at it. That's why its viewers, mostly young women, watched: they didn't aspire to be one of the twenty-five dewy-eyed bimbos seeking their M.R.S. degree any more than your average young male *Fear Factor* viewers want to eat earthworms.

In music the White Stripes, the Vines (who wowed critics but didn't come close to selling a million records), et al. were not nearly so successful as real relics such as James Taylor, Santana, Springsteen, and even Elvis Presley, whose remixed "A Little Less Conversation" shook its pelvis up the singles charts twenty-five years after the King's death. This phenomenon was as much a matter of technology as psychology: with the spread of CD burning and online music piracy among kids, middle-aged folks are essentially the only people who buy music anymore.

Theater, meanwhile, tried to keep from likewise aging itself out of business by expanding into youth-targeted productions like *Def Poetry Jam* and a *La Boheme* from *Moulin Rouge* director Baz Luhrmann. But it also repeatedly reached back to baby-boomer-and-beyond icons (nostalgic, perhaps, for a time when you could get people to see an original Broadway show). It revived *Oklahoma!* and *Into the Woods* and *Flower Drum Song*. It adapted movies: *Hairspray* (John Waters's movie about early-'60s Baltimore), *The Graduate*, *Marty*, *What Ever Happened to Baby Jane?* It even got choreographer Twyla Tharp, for *Movin' Out*, to become the first person to hold the phrases *Billy Joel* and *dance number* in her head simultaneously since whatever poor sap directed the video for "Uptown

Girl." In all, the best way to get onstage was by having been a movie or a pop song. Being theatrical helped, but being theater didn't.

Used Celebrities for Sale—Cheap

There are years of national crisis in which America worships its celebrities more lovingly than ever, hoisting them atop pedestals so that their glamour might light the way through our darkness. 2002 was not one of those years. True, it is still not entirely bad to be famous. Jennifer Lopez continued her hip-swinging march to world domination. Denzel Washington and Halle Berry enjoyed a night as Oscar royalty the evening the Academy finally recognized two actors of color. But if America took any comfort from the famous, it was mainly this: celebrities had things far, far worse than we did. Martha Stewart got pan-roasted for her suspicious stock dealings. Robert Blake and Winona Ryder had run-ins with the law. Britney Spears and Michael Jackson fell off the tabloids. And none of them had the good sense to sell their indignities as cable reality series.

On TV, the prestige of celebrity was dropping like shares of World-Com, while the has-been market was booming. It started innocuously with Ozzy Osbourne taking out the trash, doddering around his mansion, and becoming America's new favorite dad—Homer Simpson without the articulousness. Of course, there has always been PR value in celebrities' pretending to be jus' folks; that's why every time J. Lo has another hit movie or picks up a zillion-carat engagement ring, she releases a single that reminds us that she's still "real," that she's just "Jenny from the block." But once Ozzy came down to the audience's level, it was a short trip from there to laughing at Anna Nicole Smith (and Liza Minelli, whose show didn't even make it on the air), watching the celebrity edition of *Fear Factor,* and seeing Tonya Harding knock the last scrap of dignity out of Paula Jones on *Celebrity Boxing.* If you're wondering, "What's next—pimping out has-been celebrities on blind dates?"— then you haven't got around to watching *Star Dates,* now playing on the E! network.

Still, at least TV's has-beens had the chance to be stars once. The biggest movies of 2002 were not necessarily even about actors: *Ice Age* starred endearing digital animations; *The Two Towers* featured a soulfully CG Gollum; and as for *Attack of the Clones,* no one has acted in a

George Lucas film since Leia told Hans she would just as soon kiss a Wookie. Who was the big *human* movie star of 2002? We would say Vin Diesel, but not until he lets us check the back of his neck for rivets. Instead, we must nominate Nia Vardalos.

My Big Fat Greek Wedding inspired the question of the year among film critics, namely: "What the *hell?*" The little indie romantic comedy snowballed into a $200 million-plus smash on the strength of ninety-five minutes of affable, *chuzzburger-chuzzburger* multiculturalism that boldly grabbed the torch of swarthy ethnic stereotype from the Jews and the Italians. Yet for the Mediterranean men talking with their hands and women serving steaming trays of lamb and mother wit, there was something touchingly real about it—or, really, about its Rubenesque writer-star, Vardalos—in a Hollywood whose usual idea of an ugly duckling is Sandra Bullock. It was an anti-celebrity film for an anti-celebrity year, and maybe that was enough to persuade moviegoers to overlook the gobbets of flaming cheese. That, plus a crowd-pleasing love-conquers-culture-clash, which ends with the father of the bride noting that her name and the Wasp groom's came from the Greek words for *apple* and *orange*. "We're all different," Dad pronounces, "but in the end, we' all fruit." Except for celebrities, who continued to prove, to our endless satisfaction, that they're mostly nuts.

The Year in Television

Best Social Criticism

The Wire. Ostensibly about cops and drug dealers, this series was really about how institutions use up and spit out their workers. Sadly, if you were laid off this year, you probably couldn't afford the HBO fee to watch it.

Best Performance by a Former Daddio

Michael Chiklis, who played doughty nice guys on *Daddio* and *The Commish,* ignited FX's *The Shield* as a dirty cop who does his job disturbingly well.

Best Reason Not to Become a Sitcom Writer

MTV's *The Osbournes*. Ozzy, upon seeing his stage set: "Bubbles?! I'm the Prince of f—ing Darkness!" A roomful of *Harvard Lampoon* alums couldn't write a line that memorable. Nor could Ozzy remember it.

Best Reason for Even Tivo Users to Watch a Commercial

Nike's Move. A beautifully synchronized ninety-second celebration of sport and motion, it was better than the Olympic ceremony that it interrupted.

Most Overblown Controversy

Nightline's near axing. If ABC has a moral obligation to give us a late-night news show, why isn't anyone complaining that CBS and NBC never aired one?

Best Year in Theater

Best Musical

Movin' Out. Twyla Tharp took Billy Joel's music, added a corps of amazing dancers, and gave a jolt of life to the rock musical.

Most Underrated Play

The General from America. Richard Nelson's drama about Benedict Arnold (produced at Houston's Alley Theater and off-Broadway) was politically savvy, morally complex, and theatrically cunning. The critics, alas, dismissed it.

Most Overhyped Broadway Event

La Bohème. Baz Luhrmann gave the opera younger singers, prettier sets, and an updated libretto—and called it a revolution.

Best Cause for Liberal Actors

The Exonerated. Stars like Richard Dreyfuss and Marlo Thomas rotate in and out of this off-Broadway play drawn from transcripts of interviews with real death-row inmates later released. Righteous and harrowing.

Worst Play by a Once Good Playwright

Boston Marriage. David Mamet switched from Chicago lowlifes to upper-crust nineteenth lesbian lovers in an insufferably arch stunt.

The Year in Music

Worst Song

"A Moment like This." This Kodak commercial disguised as a coming-of-age ballad from *American Idol* winner Kelly Clarkson will be a fixture on the wedding and bar mitzvah circuit for years—as will its singer.

Biggest Faux Trend

Garage Rock. The reemergence of the Hives, the White Stripes, and the Strokes would have been a welcome trend had they actually emerged. None came close to going platinum, and all three combined were outsold in 2002 by their grandparents, the Rolling Stones.

Best Album by No One

The Best Bootlegs in the World Ever. . . . Mash-ups, the combination of a vocal track from one song with the instrumental from another, violate every copyright law known to man, so this mash-ups compilation is highly illegal. Still, Freelance Hellraiser's blending of the Strokes and Christina Aguilera is worth breaking the law for.

Best Incomprehensible Artist

Shakira. She learned her English at the Charo School of Distorted Vowels, but Shakira sang (and wiggled) strenuously enough through schlocky hits like "Whenever, Wherever" and "Underneath Your Clothes" to make the world forget about J. Lo, if only for a moment.

Best Song

"Love Yourself." Eschewing profanity (almost), Eminem tells the story of his serial adolescent loserdom and subsequent rise to success in six of the most intensely focused musical minutes since "Smells like Teen Spirit." A rap song even Trent Lott can love.

The Year in Books

Best First Line

The Lovely Bones. "My name was Salmon, like the fish; first name Susie. I was fourteen when I was murdered on December 6, 1973." O.K. that's really two lines, but we defy you to put down first-time novelist Alice Sebold's surprise best-seller after reading them.

Worst Title of a Great Read

The Crimson Petal and the White. Every part of Michel Faber's sprawling epic, about a bad girl who makes good, crackles with tension and wit, except that forgettable title.

Best Book about September 11

Heart of a Soldier. Most books about the attacks felt as if they were written in ten minutes. James Stewart's effort, about a soldier of fortune who lost his life at the World Trade Center, reads like the product of ten years of careful research and meditation: it's calm, carefully composed, and consoling.

First Book to Be Read by a Roaring Fire

Ninety Degrees North. In Fergus Fleming's riveting history of attempts, most unsuccessful, to reach the North Pole, one of his hypothermic heroes, Robert Peary, finishes his career with only two toes—the pinkies. Read the book, and you'll see that he got off easy.

Best Final Twist

Atonement. The novel is by no means a mere mystery, but its subtle, stunning surprise ending makes author Ian McEwan the thinking person's answer to Agatha Christie.

SUGGESTIONS FOR FURTHER STUDY

1. The author of this article is pretty hard on those people who are interested only in entertainment, and on the producers of "mere" entertainment. Do you think he is too harsh in his criticism? How and where do you differ with him?
2. The author differs with the evaluations of other authors in this book. Which do you agree with and why?
3. Choose one of the subjects that the author discusses, examine it carefully, and prepare an answer to Poniewozik.
4. Draw up your own list of successful and failing items in the media for the year. Then justify your choices, comparing your list with Poniewozik's.

ADVERTISING: THE SOFT AND THE HARD SELL

Perhaps it is appropriate to end this study of popular culture on a subject that is with us constantly, advertising. From the first examples of individualism and competition one of the truisms—in American life at least—has been that it pays to advertise—anything you have, any superiority you feel over another or the world. The only trouble is that every medium of communication or advertising soon saturates the market. Billboards almost blot out the sun, the telephone rings constantly with telemarketers hawking some bargain or gift. E-mail is overwhelmed with spam consisting of millions of messages from people selling everything from pornography to religious relics.

The new extension of advertising seems to be designed for captive audiences; we find it on buses, in taxis, wherever the individual can be contacted at eye level. It catches the subject in possibly embarrassing localities and situations. Perhaps advertisers are only seeking new space, or market research has discovered some hidden truth that we have ignored.

There's No Escape from Ads, Even in the Backseat

LENORE SKENAZY

In bathroom stalls, elevators, and now even the backseats of taxis, they just can't stop doing it. How disgusting! Have they no shame?

I'm speaking, of course, about advertisers. They're sticking ads everywhere, even in hitherto virgin territory.

"We've done urinal mat advertising," says Marcie Brogan, managing partner of Brogan & Partners in Detroit. Her competition, Flush Media of the Bronx, places ads discretely above the urinals—as well as in bathroom stalls and smack-dab in health club shower rooms. What exactly do they advertise there: Soap? Shampoo? Liposuction?

"It has reached way past the point of silliness," says Scott Donaton, editor in chief of *Advertising Age,* musing on the ubiquity of marketing messages. "The question these days is, where isn't there advertising?"

His magazine has reported on the European fad of planting ad slogans on live cows—presumably, not for Big Macs. And then there's the Amsterdam ad agency offering free pre-printed strollers to parents who don't mind pushing Precious in a billboard on wheels. Advertisers are placing ads on movie ticket stubs, shopping carts, and—how could they resist—ATM screens. As long as you're waiting for your money, they might as well tell you how to spend it.

Commercials blare, too, from the checkout counters and computer screens. They're playing in movie theater lobbies and again before the film. There's even a Florida company that has started placing ads inside golf holes. For what? Root repair? In case you get (ahem) a hole in one?

But personally, Donaton most resents the ad invasion of his office building's elevator, where a nonstop TV broadcasts news, commercials, and trivia. "I work on the second floor. God forbid I have five seconds to myself to have an independent thought," he mutters.

My most recent and vexing ad assault came Christmas Day, when my family was taking a taxi to a friend's apartment. "Welcome to our world of toys!" sang the TV—yes, TV!—embedded in the backseat. We couldn't turn it off, which meant the kids sat glued to a smarmy toy soldier pitching the magic of the season—i.e., overpriced presents—even as the winter wonderland of a real live white Christmas passed by their windows, unnoticed.

Thank goodness, taxi TVs might not be here to stay. Right now, they're in just about 120 of the city's 12,187 cabs, says Taxi & Limousine Commission spokesman Allan Fromberg. Seven companies have placed them there as part of a year-long pilot project.

Some of the TVs are interactive, providing listings of restaurants and museum exhibits. But some, like the one I saw, are simply a mind-numbing loop of ads mixed with so-called public service announcements advising us to do things like buckle our seat belts. It's enough to make you—and the agonized driver—pine for Elmo. Our cabbie said he gets $100 a month to endure the pain, and it's not worth it.

The public is invited to register its enthusiasm or gigantic lack thereof at nyc.gov/taxi. "If it's good and useful and the public likes it," says Fromberg, the TVs will stay, incorporating the features that consumers enjoy most.

But the feature I enjoy most is called my sanity. With ads blaring from every nook, its meter is running out.

From *New York Daily News,* January 1, 2003. © New York Daily News, L.P. Reprinted with permission.

SUGGESTIONS FOR FURTHER STUDY

1. What is your feeling about the continuing invasion of your space by advertising?

2. Nobody has ever even intimated that the latest manipulation of space by advertising will be the last. The principle seems to be that if it can be done it will be done. Which leads us automatically to the question of invasion of the private home by means other than telephone, computer, radio, TV, newspapers, magazine, "junk mail," telemarketers, and others. Is the inevitable final goal the rec room and bedroom?

3. If you had the power—which in fact you do possess—how would you combat the invasion of this micro or mini advertising? Do you feel your liberty is wounded by it?

4. Is the complaint by adults about the invasion of micro-advertising evidence that the adults are more susceptible to advertising than they will admit and find it irresistible? Do they claim they want to protect children when in fact they are trying to protect themselves?

General Look at
Popular Culture Studies
Backward and Forward

RAY B. BROWNE

This general investigation of the profiles of popular culture has looked only at the mountain ranges and the valleys between them. If the graphic pictured in the introduction of this work is to be believed there are many other kinds of popular culture which affect our lives in one way or another and to one degree or another. As someone has said, we are what we eat and we are what we wear, even more we are the culture we create and in which we live. If we are to know ourselves, and even perhaps be protected from ourselves, we must know the culture of our lives. Some of the elements of the culture are obvious. Others, perhaps, must wait for the paleontologist to locate and read. But the wise society does not wait for the future to decipher the present; the society reads its own tea leaves.

On the basis of the examples given in this book you should be able and encouraged to examine the world around you and understand it. You are invited to augment the educational process by using the materials presented here to spur yourself to think and reason about the life about you. Education is not learning facts so much as it is the stimulation of reasoning. Give America a thinking public and we will have an educated society. America, society in general, and you yourself deserve no less.

SUGGESTIONS FOR FURTHER STUDY

1. Most of the essays in this book treat popular culture as broad-based, general, and all inclusive, not regional, personal, or by type or motif. Choose some cultural phenomenon that you consider less than general and discuss it as a part of popular culture.

2. Choose the essay in this collection which in your eyes best encompasses and summarizes the various components of popular culture—formula, heroes, myth, repetition, etc.—and discuss the development of those parts in the essay.

3. Does greater knowledge of popular culture, as developed by studying the examples in this collection, strengthen or weaken your respect of the everyday phenomena?

4. There are no essays in this collection treating folklore as such and how it is an antecedent of popular culture, in other words the popular culture of the "folk," whoever they are. Choose some aspect of folklore that you are familiar with—say, music—and discuss it as a forerunner—or a contemporary—of popular culture.

5. Except for those artifacts that are copyrighted or otherwise identifiable, many items in popular culture have developed as need and opportunity arose. Choose such an item from the many you know and discuss it as one that has grown from opportunity and need.

6. If your instructor assigns independent research in some area, what will you choose?

A RAY AND PAT BROWNE BOOK

Murder on the Reservation: American Indian Crime Fiction
Ray B. Browne

Profiles of Popular Culture: A Reader
Edited by Ray B. Browne

Goddesses and Monsters: Women, Myth, Power, and Popular Culture
Jane Caputi

Mystery, Violence, and Popular Culture
John G. Cawelti

Baseball and Country Music
Don Cusic

Popular Witchcraft: Straight from the Witch's Mouth, 2nd edition
Jack Fritscher

The Essential Guide to Werewolf Literature
Brian J. Frost

Popular Culture Theory and Methodology: A Basic Introduction
Edited by Harold E. Hinds, Jr., Marilyn F. Motz and Angela M. S. Nelson

Rituals and Patterns in Children's Lives
Edited by Kathy Merlock Jackson

Images of the Corpse: From the Renaissance to Cyberspace
Edited by Elizabeth Klaver

Walking Shadows: Orson Welles, William Randolph Hearst, and Citizen Kane
John Evangelist Walsh

Spectral America: Phantoms and the National Imagination
Edited by Jeffrey Andrew Weinstock

King of the Cowboys, Queen of the West: Roy Rogers and Dale Evans
Raymond E. White